METERS TO YARDS

1 meter	=	1 yar
5 meters	=	5 1/2
10 meters	=	11 ya
20 meters	=	22 ya.
30 meters	=	33 yards
40 meters	=	44 yards
50 meters	=	55 yards
60 meters	=	66 yards
70 meters	=	77 yards
80 meters	=	87 yards
90 meters	=	100 yards
100 meters	=	110 yards
500 meters	=	550 yards
1,000 meters	=	1,100 yards
2,000 meters	=	2,200 yards
3,000 meters	=	3,280 yards

MW00811373

1,000 feet	=	305 meters
2,000 feet	=	610 meters
3,000 feet	=	915 meters
4,000 feet	=	1,220 meters
5,000 feet	=	1,525 meters
10,000 feet	=	3,000 meters

FORMULAS

1 meter = 1.09 yards/3.2808 feet/39.37 inches
1 yard/3 feet/36 inches = 0.9144 meters

KILOMETERS TO MILES

1 kilometer	=	2/3 miles
2 kilometers	=	1 1/4 miles
3 kilometers	=	1 7/8 miles
4 kilometers	=	2 1/2 miles
5 kilometers	=	3 1/8 miles
6 kilometers	=	3 3/4 miles
7 kilometers	=	4 1/3 miles
8 kilometers	=	5 miles
9 kilometers	=	5 1/2 miles
10 kilometers	=	6 1/4 miles
20 kilometers	=	12 1/2 miles
30 kilometers	=	18 1/2 miles
40 kilometers	=	25 miles
50 kilometers	=	31 miles
100 kilometers	=	62 miles
500 kilometers	=	310 miles
1,000 kilometers	=	620 miles

MILES TO KILOMETERS

1 mile	=	1.6 kilometers
2 miles	=	3.2 kilometers
3 miles	=	4.8 kilometers
4 miles	=	6.3 kilometers
5 miles	=	8 kilometers
10 miles	=	16 kilometers
20 miles	=	32 kilometers
25 miles	=	40 kilometers
50 miles	=	80 kilometers
100 miles	=	160 kilometers

FORMULAS

1 kilometer = 0.621 miles
1 mile = 1.6093 kilometers

mm/cm

0

5

10

15

NATURE IN TOKYO

A little pond surrounded by trees—typical of Tokyo's small but rich habitats.

Amadokoro Solomon's seal lilies

Mayutate-akane red skimmer dragonfly

Kaki-tsubata iris

Haguro tonbo damselfly

Murasaki shikibu berries

Yamakagashi keelback

Tokyo daruma pond frog and water lily

WINTER WATER BIRDS

Widgeon

Tufted duck

Green-winged teal

Pintail

Mallard duck

Pochard

Mandarin duck

Coot

Spot-billed duck

Great cormorant

Shoveler

Great Egret

Higurashi cicada

Small copper

Kogane-gumo orb web spider

Shōryō-batta grasshopper

Paper wasp queen

Hime-janome brown

WILDFLOWERS

Kawara-nadeshiko pink

Common speedwell

Yama-yuri forest lily

Mamushi-gusa jack-in-the-pulpit

Hirugao bindweed

Day flower

THE YEAR IN FLOWERS

Spring—rape and cherry blossoms

Summer—lotus flowers

Autumn—red spider lilies

Winter—winter peonies

NATURE IN TOKYO

Kevin Short

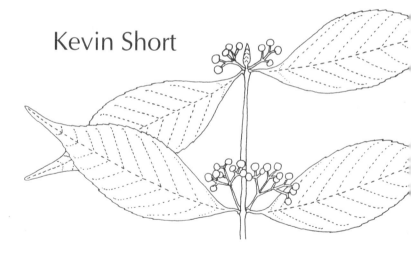

KODANSHA INTERNATIONAL
Tokyo • New York • London

NOTE TO THE READER

Since distances, heights, and lengths are given in the metric system on Japanese signs and in park literature, the metric system has been used throughout this volume. Detailed CONVERSION CHARTS with often-used figures can be found in the end papers at the front of the book.

A chart of HISTORICAL PERIODS appears in the history section and a MAP OF JAPAN can be found in the end papers at the back of the book.

JAPANESE NAMES appear in the traditional Japanese manner, family name followed by given name.

PHOTO CREDITS
Ben Simmons, pages 1, 2–3 (large).
Remaining color and black and white photos by the author.

Published by Kodansha International Ltd., 17–14 Otowa 1-chome, Bunkyo-ku, Tokyo 112–8652, and Kodansha America, Inc.

Distributed in the United States by Kodansha America, Inc., 575 Lexington Avenue, New York, New York 10022, and in the United Kingdom and continental Europe by Kodansha Europe Ltd., 95 Aldwych, London WC2B 4JF.

First edition, 2000
1 2 3 4 5 6 7 8 9   04 03 02 01 00
ISBN 4–7700–2535–1

CONTENTS

Introduction   13

Hints for Enjoying Your Excursions   15
The Lay of the Land   20
The Human Touch—A Capsule History of the Land   26
Tokyo Habitats   32

PART I   ANIMALS

Mammals   39
Birds   47
Reptiles   76
Amphibians   85
Insects   93
Tidal Flat Wildlife   131

PART II   PLANTS

Broadleaved Evergreens   147
Deciduous Trees   155
Conifers   167
Street and Park Trees   182
Spring Wildflowers   196

Summer Wildflowers   218
Autumn Wildflowers   237

PART III   NATURE SITES

The Yamanote Uplands   249
The Musashino Uplands   284
The Shitamachi Lowlands   308
Around the Waterfront   321

Glossary   336
List of Species Names   343
List of Nature Sites   356

Acknowledgments   358

INTRODUCTION

Many of my friends stopped and scratched their heads when I told them I was writing a book about nature in Tokyo. Could there be, they wondered, enough nature in Japan's crowded capital to fill the pages of a book? Tokyo is not especially known as a nature or garden city. The name Tokyo typically conjures up images of endless stretches of gray steel and concrete shimmering in the summer heat.

Indeed, there are some sections of the central city that do fit this image. These neighborhoods are not very inviting, especially during the "Dutch oven" days of high summer, when the steel and concrete reflect and store the stifling heat. On the other hand, the city is actually brimming with small parks and gardens, often hidden in the midst of the most overbuilt neighborhoods. In fact, Tokyo is by far and away the greenest of Japan's big cities. Furthermore, the city is surrounded by countryside and coastal habitats bursting with wildlife.

For those of you willing to take time and look, Tokyo offers a surprising variety of plants and animals to study and enjoy. This book is designed to guide you through the city's various nature sites, and introduce you to the fascinating local flora and fauna. With just this book and a little spirit of adventure, you can watch shorebirds and collect clams on a mud flat, examine native wildflowers in a municipal cemetery, spend a day chasing frogs through the rice-paddy countryside, or learn to identify half a dozen species of cicada by their song alone!

Observing nature is great fun and you don't have to be a trained botanist or biologist to enjoy yourself. In fact, Parts One and Two of this book contain all you need to get started. Here are found most of the common plants and animals that live in the Tokyo area. The descriptions, photographs, and sketches will help you recognize the different species, and the background information will help you to understand their behavior and ecology. Even an absolute beginner will soon be calling his local street trees by name, pointing out birds in the parks and gardens, and stopping to admire tiny wildflowers growing right out of cracks in the downtown sidewalk.

Stuck on where to go to see wildlife? Part Three offers a wealth of suggestions— from inner-city parks where businesspeople can learn to distinguish the native turtledove from the common domestic pigeon on a lunch-hour stroll, to wild salt marshes that will take a day to study and explore. Want to know where to see giant toads fighting in a great free for all, or to enjoy a diving show put on by graceful dragonflies? Want to sketch plants that look like pit vipers, or make herbal teas from common roadside weeds? Just follow the directions.

A little bit of nature watching can go a long way towards restoring our sense of wonder. Just spend ten minutes of your lunch hour carefully observing a sheet-web spider in the hedges outside your home or office, and the rest of your day will seem carefree.

Looking for something that you and your children can really enjoy together? Try catching cicadas and grasshoppers in a nearby park. Teach your child how to tell a grasshopper from a katydid, then let him or her show you the three ruby eyes on the top of a cicada's head. Tired of expensive drinks and dinner in Roppongi? Then take your date for a Saturday afternoon of birding along the bay, or a more intimate evening of owlsong in a western park.

In no time at all exotic-sounding names and ecological facts will be rolling off the tip of your tongue: *shirakashi* live oak, brown-eared bulbul, ginkgo tree; Japanese tree frog, spot-billed duck, reed-bed crab; the uplands, *yato* valleys, the Shibuya River watershed.

Once your eyes are open, you'll see that Tokyo is bursting with plants and animals just waiting to be discovered and enjoyed, and you'll know exactly why the answer to my friends' questions was always a resounding *yes*!

HINTS FOR ENJOYING YOUR EXCURSIONS

USING THIS BOOK

This book consists of three main parts. The first two introduce the common animals and plants found in the Tokyo area. All the animals are grouped in Part One, while the trees and herbaceous wildflowers are discussed in Part Two. The third part provides basic information on places where wildlife can be enjoyed.

The animals are organized by taxonomic group, starting with mammals, then moving on to birds, reptiles, amphibians, and insects. The last chapter, however, is based on the coastal wetland habitat, and includes animals from various groups.

The trees are split into three major chapters—trees with wide, flat leaves that stay green all year around (broadleaved evergreen), trees with wide leaves that are bare in winter (broadleaved deciduous), and trees with needle-shaped leaves (conifers). A fourth chapter is set aside for trees that are commonly planted along streets and in parks. The wildflowers are presented by the season in which they bloom.

The opening chapters discuss the local geology, topography, history, and major habitats, information basic to understanding all the subsequent discussions. From there, the reader can pick and choose among favorite topics, such as wildflowers, mammals, coastal wildlife, birds, insects, reptiles, or amphibians.

IDENTIFYING PLANTS AND ANIMALS

Often the sheer diversity of the natural world overwhelms beginning naturalists. One despairs of ever learning the names of local plants and animals. The key here is to stay calm and to work slowly, savoring even small advances. Parts One and Two of this book are designed to be used as a basic reference and field guide to help in identifying local animals and plants. With the photographs, sketches, and descriptions in these parts, and the definitions and sketches in the glossary, even a first-timer can soon learn to identify many of the common local species.

There is, however, no short-cut to becoming familiar with the natural world, and simply no substitute for repeated observation and field work. In fact, becoming a naturalist is far more a matter of persistence and perseverance than ability or education. Every time you stop and examine a plant or animal you become a little bit more familiar with it.

WITH TREES, for example, it is important to spend a few minutes in careful observation of the leaves. Note the shape of the leaf, and feel the edge to see if there are teeth. Also note the pattern of the veins, the length of the stalk, and whether the right and left leaves are attached directly opposite one another or at staggered intervals. Compare your notes with the sketches and descriptions in this book.

WITH FLOWERS, be ready to poke your nose inside. Use the glossary to help identify the various parts. Count everything in sight, not only the petals and sepals but stamens and pistils as well. Note the patterns on the petals, and also closely examine the leaves and stalks. Compare your notes with the photographs and sketches in the book.

INSECTS are very hard to identify on the wing. You can catch them, place them in a small clear plastic box, observe them carefully, then release them when finished. Remember, the number of insect species in any given area is staggering, and you may not be able to identify your specimen down to the species level (see Taxonomy in the Glossary). Many of the most common species, however, can be easily recognized. Look carefully at the fine points: the length of the antennae; the shape of the jaws; the color patterns on the chest, wings, and abdomen. First try to decide what group of insects your specimen belongs in, then worry about determining the species.

FROGS AND CRABS can also be captured for study and later released. Snakes, birds, and mammals, however, must usually be observed at a distance. Still, the same basic principle applies: *Note the details*! When looking at a bird, for example, note not only color patterns, but the length of the tail, posture, and flight pattern (straight line or undulating).

The plants and animals presented in this book cover only the most common species in the Tokyo area, so don't be discouraged if you come across specimens that you can't identify. Even if you don't know a plant or animal's name you can still enjoy observing it, and you can still make a record of your observations.

EXPANDING YOUR UNDERSTANDING
Identifying the species is only the first step in enjoying wildlife. Next comes the real fun part—adding information about ecology, behavior, and relationships. The descriptions in these chapters provide some background data, but there is much more to discover on your own. For example, when you find an attractive flower, first sit down and examine it closely. Try to see it not from the eye of a human, but from the viewpoint of a visiting insect. Looking at the structure of the flower and the position of the stamens and pistil, try and imagine how the flower attracts insects and uses them to carry its pollen. Then, if you have the time, wait

quietly until an insect arrives, then test your hypothesis through field observation.

When you have an insect in hand, look closely at its jaws. Try to imagine what and how the insect eats by the shape of the jaws. Also look at the relative size of the legs and wings. Do they indicate an insect that is primarily a flyer, or a ground runner? Bird bills work the same way. Try to match characteristics of a plant or animal with aspects of its lifestyle, such as where it lives or what it eats.

Always make a record of where and when you observed a particular plant or animal. This will help you understand what sort of habitat each species prefers, and what time of day or year they are active. Think of the plants and animals that you meet as new friends: first you want to know their name, then you want to find out as much as possible about their lifestyle.

HELPFUL TOOLS

This book contains everything you need to get started as a Tokyo naturalist. There are, however, a few other items that will greatly enhance your enjoyment. The first of these is a magnifying glass, which is essential for studying the details of flowers and insects. In *Alice in Wonderland*, Alice was able to shrink herself by eating pieces of a magic mushroom. You can achieve the same effect with a simple magnifying lens. A plastic glass of 3.5 times magnification can be bought for a few hundred yen at any well-stocked stationery store. Ask the clerk for a *mushi-megane*. More powerful glasses are often sold at eyeglass counters, and sometimes in camera stores.

Binoculars are useful for watching birds, mammals, and snakes. I recommend beginners start off with a pair with a magnification of seven or eight. More powerful pairs are actually harder to use, because their limited field of vision makes it difficult to locate and follow the animal you want to observe. In choosing a pair of binoculars you have to make a trade off in terms of brightness and weight. The wider the diameter of the lens, the brighter the image you see, but at the same time, the heavier and bulkier the binoculars. I recommend a solid pair made by one of the large and well-known optical manufacturers, usually costing between 10,000 and 20,000 yen. The discount camera stores all have a wide selection of binoculars to try out. When comparing models, take your time. First heft the different pairs and feel the weight. Think about carrying them in your bag and hanging them around your neck. Next, try focusing them on different spots in the store. Conduct your own little eyeglass exam. Pick a spot with small writing as far away as possible, then compare the ease with which you can read the writing using different pairs. To compare brightness, pick a poorly-lit spot in the shadows rather than a brightly lit counter. Remember that differences in performance will show up best under difficult conditions.

Another invaluable aid is a field note set—notebook, pen, and box of colored pencils. Recording your observations, and making even simple sketches, will go a long way towards learning more about nature.

If you can read Japanese, there are dozens of field guides available to support your observations. English-only readers can make use of the following books:

> *Wildflowers of Japan* by Ran Levy
> *A Field Guide to the Birds of Japan* by the Wild Bird Society of Japan
> *A Birdwatcher's Guide to Japan* by Mark Brazil

PLANNING AN OUTING

Part Three contains only a sample of the many places where nature can be enjoyed. The central city parks and gardens are fine for anyone who happens to be in the area, or for readers with a special interest in horticulture and garden design. When planning a longer field trip, especially with children, the larger parks in the Musashino, or the tideland parks along Tokyo Bay provide a wider area and greater diversity. Once familiar with the lay of the land, many readers will begin discovering their own favorite nature-watching spots.

Beginners should first visit spots which provide plentiful background information on the local ecology. These include the Institute for Nature Study at Meguro, The National Science Museum at Ueno, Koishikawa Botanical Gardens, Jindai Botanical Park, Mizumoto Park, and Rinshi no Mori Park. In addition, the city of Tokyo operates a series of "Green Centers" (*Midori no sōdanjo*) in municipal parks. These centers feature small reference rooms, maps, and displays, and the latest information on local trees and flowers in bloom. The centers are usually open from 10:00 to 16:30, and have no admission charge. Look for municipal Green Centers in Hibiya Park, Ueno Park, Mizumoto Park, Toyama Park, and Jindai Botanical Park.

To get started watching birds along the bay, visit one of the parks that are equipped with spotting scopes and staffed by docents. These include Tokyo Port Wild Bird Park, Kasai Seaside Park, Gyōtoku Sanctuary, and Yatsu Tidelands.

When planning an outing along the bay, be sure to check the tide charts. Annual charts are often available free at fishing tackle stores. Tokyo Bay tides run from about fifty centimeters to two meters. Remember that tidelands are most interesting when the tide is out. Check the time for low tide, and try to arrive a few hours earlier. That way you can follow the tide out, exploring new areas as you go. Keep a close watch on the moon. The tides will generally be biggest (and thus expose the most tidelands) around the new and full moon, and smallest around the half moon. A bucket and shovel are useful for digging up crabs and clams.

Remember that marine crabs cannot live in fresh water, so release them after studying and sketching them.

SAFETY PRECAUTIONS

The Tokyo area is relatively safe. There are no large animals that will attack you, and only a few poisonous species of snakes and spiders. Poison ivy and poison oak are quite uncommon compared to most areas of the United States. Still, a few basic precautions will go a long way towards ensuring your safety.

- Never walk barefoot when exploring marshes or tidal flats. There are often pieces of sharp metal and glass; also sting-rays, with poisonous spikes on their tails, might be hiding in the sand. A pair of old sneakers is the ideal footwear. Bring them along and change before beginning your fieldwork.

- When exploring marshes and tidal flats, always head back toward shore well before the tide turns. The flooding tide sometimes comes in fast through channels in the flat, and you can be cut off from shore if you are not careful.

- Remember, there are two species of very poisonous snakes in our area. Never touch or pick up a snake unless you are confident in identifying it as harmless. Never walk barefoot or bare-legged in high grass or wet meadows and marshlands. If bitten, remain calm and seek immediate medical help.

- Never poke sticks or throw objects at hornet or paper wasp nests. These insects will defend their nest viciously, with dire consequences to an intruder. If stung, seek medical attention.

- Memorize the three-leaf pattern of the poisonous sumac vine (page 172), and avoid direct contact.

- Be aware of the few species of caterpillar (page 121) and spider (page 139) that are potentially dangerous.

- The small mud crabs can be handled with impunity, but the large swimming crabs and reedbed crabs can deliver a painful pinch with their powerful claws.

- Do not touch any jellyfish with red stripes. Remember, a jellyfish's poison-tipped stinging cells are designed to trigger automatically when touched, and remain dangerous even after the jellyfish is long dead. Even dried and crushed specimens can sting.

THE LAY OF THE LAND

The city of Tokyo sits at the northern head of Tokyo Bay, and at the southern terminus of the Kantō Plain, a flat, low-lying region built up by the Tone and Ara river systems. These rivers have their sources deep in the mountains that surround the plain on the west and north.

The microtopography of the Tokyo area is often complicated and difficult to decipher under layers of concrete and steel, but the general lay of the land can be easily understood in terms of four basic geological structures (figure 1):

1. THE ALLUVIAL PLAIN—A flat, low-lying plain formed by the combined deltas of the Ara and Edo rivers. The term "alluvial" is used to describe sediments that have been carried and deposited by a river. The southernmost portion of this plain, near the deltas and adjacent to the historic city center, is commonly called the Shitamachi, or "Low City." Most of the Shitamachi is only a meter or so above sea level. Some areas are actually lower than Tokyo Bay, and like the coastal lowlands of Holland, have to be protected by dikes.

2. THE UPLANDS—Several areas of relatively level, plateaulike rises, called *daichi* in Japanese. These uplands border the alluvial plain on the west (the Musashino Uplands), east (the Shimōsa Uplands), and northeast (the Ōmiya Uplands). The western part of the central city, commonly called the Yamanote, or "side of the hills," forms the easternmost edge of the Musashino Uplands.

3. THE HILLS—Several sets of low hills, called *kyūryō* in Japanese, that border the Musashino Uplands on the west and southwest. These hills range in height from 80 to 200 meters.

4. THE MOUNTAINS—True bedrock mountains, called *yama* or *sanchi* in Japanese, that loom to the northwest of the Musashino Uplands. Many visitors, and even some Japanese, are surprised to learn that within the administrative district of Tokyo are mountains between 1,500 and 2,000 meters high.

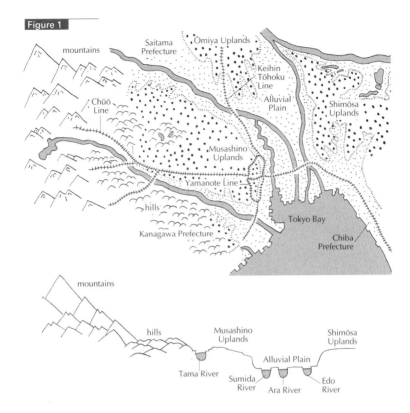

Figure 1

YAMANOTE AND SHITAMACHI

In central Tokyo only the first two topographic levels can be found. In fact, the city is essentially divided in half by the boundary between the alluvial plain and the Musashino Uplands. This boundary can be clearly seen by riding the JR Yamanote or Keihin Tōhoku line north from Tokyo Station, and is a trip well worth taking. (For details and map see the Yamanote chapter in Part Three.)

Tokyo Station and the three stops to the north (Kanda, Akihabara, and Okachimachi) are all located well out on the alluvial plain. However, from the fourth station onward (Ueno), the tracks begin to run right underneath the cliffs that mark the edge of the uplands. In fact, Ueno Station itself is built right smack up against and over this cliff. If you come out either the lower central exit (*chūō-guchi*) or the Shinobazu exit you are still standing on the alluvial plain, but if you take the park exit (*kōen-guchi*) you emerge on top of the uplands.

As the train travels north from Ueno, the upland cliffs are clearly visible on the left side of the train, rising about twenty meters or so above the alluvial plain. Immediately after Tabata Station, the Yamanote Line makes a sharp left turn to the west and heads into a trench cut into the uplands, but the Keihin Tōhoku Line continues northward along the edge of the cliff. To the right of the tracks the alluvial plain stretches eastward, across the Sumida, Ara, and Edo rivers and on into Chiba Prefecture, where it finally butts into the Shimōsa Uplands.

These cliffs form the basic boundary between the Shitamachi and Yamanote sections of Tokyo. As is often the case, topographic differences are carried over into cultural distinctions. The Yamanote high ground has traditionally been considered the enclave of the upper classes—first the samurai, then the nobility, and now the wealthy and chic—while the Shitamachi lowlands have always been thought of as home to the common city folk, such as artisans, laborers, and small merchants and traders.

GEOLOGY OF THE UPLANDS

Unfortunately, the cliff edges in Tokyo are either smothered in concrete or covered with vegetation, so their geological strata are hidden from view. From open cuts in the surrounding countryside, however, a general picture of the strata and geological history can be readily reconstructed. At the base of the slope is silt that originally collected on the bottom of a warm shallow sea, called Paleo-Tokyo Bay (figure 2), which covered the southern Kantō about 110,000 years ago. During this time the earth was considerably warmer than today, and much of the ice around the north and south poles had melted, causing the oceans to rise.

This warm sea was inhabited by all sorts of marine creatures, including whales, an enormous shark related to the great white only much larger and heavier, and a strange mammal that may have been a sort of marine hippopotamus. We know these creatures by the fossils they left behind. The sea was also home to a great number and variety of shellfish and other bottom-dwelling marine invertebrates. In some areas the shells of millions of dead clams, snails, and sand dollars accumulated on the sea bottom and were covered with mud, forming extensive fossil beds (figure 3) that are found throughout the sands at the base of the uplands.

On top of the marine strata are several layers of volcanic ash, mostly from the Hakone mountains and Mount Fuji but also from as far away as Kyūshū. The volcanic ash, called the Kantō Loam, was carried here on the prevailing winds from the west, and the loam layers thus tend to get thicker as one moves from east to west, toward the mountains. Finally, on top of the loam is the modern organic soil, built up over the past 12,000 years from decaying wood and leaf litter.

Figure 2

Paleo-Tokyo Bay coastline about 110,000 years ago

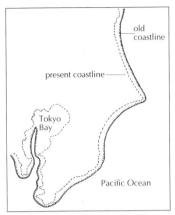

Tokyo/Kantō coastline about 20,000 years ago, during the last glaciation

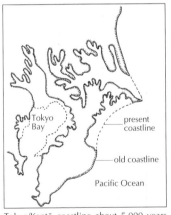

Tokyo/Kantō coastline about 5,000 years ago, during the Jōmon Transgression

Figure 3

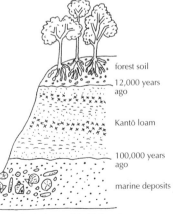

Geologic Strata of the Tokyo Area

THE *YATO* VALLEYS

Walking across Tokyo's alluvial plain is easy. The only slopes encountered are those at the approach to bridges. In the Yamanote area, however, one's legs seem to be constantly yelling "hill!" Yamanote place names also bespeak a complicated topography: *ya* as in Yotsuya, Shibuya, and Ichigaya means "valley"; while *saka* or *zaka* as in Akasaka, Kagurazaka, or Dōgenzaka means "slope." The *yama* in Aoyama means "mountain," and *kawa* or *gawa* as in Udagawa or Koishikawa means "river."

The top of the plateaulike Musashino Uplands in the Yamanote area may be relatively flat, but the entire structure is laced with an amazingly complicated network of narrow branching valleys, called *yato* in the local Tokyo and Kanagawa dialects (*yatsu* in the Chiba and Ibaraki dialects). With a pattern resembling the twigs of an elm tree or the antlers of a stag, these *yato* valleys are the product of river erosion and sea level changes over thousands of years.

About 80,000 years ago the earth began to cool off, entering a glacial period. As the amount of ice around the poles increased, the levels of the oceans dropped. By about 20,000 years ago it was much colder than today, and the sea level a hundred meters or so lower (see figure 2). At this time the coastline of the Kantō thrust outward, and most of Tokyo Bay, a shallow body of water, was dry land. A huge plateau, heavily forested with hemlock and spruce, covered the Tokyo area. Several big rivers and their numerous tributaries cut deep into the plateau.

The last glacial period ended about 12,000 years ago, after which the climate gradually warmed and the sea levels rose. Around 5,000 years ago (see figure 2), the climate had warmed to a point 2° or 3° Centigrade (4° or 5° Fahrenheit) hotter than today, and the ever-fickle sea level had risen several meters higher than it is now. The sea pushed inland, turning the alluvial plains and *yato* valleys into shallow sea inlets.

The extent of this marine invasion can be accurately traced by the distribution of large heaps of discarded shells, called shell middens (*kaizuka* in Japanese). These middens were left by groups of prehistoric people during the Jōmon period. The Jōmon peoples lived at the edges of the uplands overlooking the shallow inlets, and gathered the local shellfish for food, piling the empty shells up in great middens behind and alongside their villages. The distribution of these Jōmon middens thus marks the limits of the inland invasion of the sea waters, which in their honor is usually called the Jōmon Transgression.

As the climate cooled and the seas retreated, the inlets turned into the *yato* valleys we see today. A typical *yato* valley has a flat bottom with a small stream flowing through the center, and steep sides leading up to the surrounding uplands. The streams have their sources in natural seeps and springs at the base of the slopes and especially at the headwaters of the narrow side valleys. When the techniques for wet-rice agriculture were brought to Japan from China and Korea, the marshes

Yato valleys (lighter color) photographed from a plane approaching Narita Airport. The Tokyo area would have looked exactly like this four hundred years ago.

along the bottom of the *yato* valleys were easily converted into rice paddies. Water from the natural seeps was first collected in small holding ponds, called *tame-ike*, then sent down through the paddies in a network of irrigation canals and ditches.

Today, in the central city, many of the rivers that originally ran through these valleys have been filled in or diverted underground, and only the slopes remain to remind us of their existence. A typical Yamanote slope, such as Dōgenzaka behind Shibuya Station, or along Omotesandō Dōri in Harajuku, is a short but steep climb, gaining about twenty meters in altitude over the course of a hundred meters or so.

HILLS AND MOUNTAINS

The Musashino Uplands stretch westward from Tokyo until they run into the third level in the local topography, a series of low hills composed of marine and river gravels and sands overlaid by the wind-carried volcanic loam. The hills are broken into several groups. The Sayama Hills form almost an isolated island in the midst of the uplands, while the Kaji, Kusabana, and Takayama hills have pushed up along the middle reaches of the Tama River. The Tama Hills, which form the most extensive hill lands in the southern Kantō region, stretch along the southern and eastern shores of the Tama River, with the Tsurumi River forming the watershed on the Kanagawa Prefecture side.

Geologists consider the Tokyo area hills to be a sort of transitional zone between the uplands and the true mountains, which form the fourth and final geological level. The mountains are composed of solid rock, and range from the 600-meters-high Mt. Takao to the 2,000-meter-peak of Mt. Kumotori, the highest point in the Tokyo administrative district.

THE HUMAN TOUCH
A Capsule History Of The Land

True pristine wilderness is virtually nonexistent in the Tokyo area. With the exception of some of the highest mountain slopes, some human influence is always visible on the landscape. Still, many of the traditional agricultural landscapes, as well as waterways and city gardens, were actually very rich habitats, supporting a great variety of wild plants and animals. In fact, over thousands of years many species have adapted their life cycles to the rhythms of Japan's traditional land management practices.

THE PRE-POTTERY PERIOD

Archeologists cannot seem to agree as to when humans first set foot in Japan. Some recent discoveries suggest that Homo erectus hominids, contemporaries of the famous Peking Man, may have been here as far back as half a million years ago. We know for sure, however, that Homo sapiens was living on the Kantō Plain by at least 20,000 or 30,000 years ago, during the last glaciation. These people were true big-game hunters, chasing a variety of animals, including elephants and giant elk, across the open grasslands that dominated the cold, dry landscape. These glacial-period peoples did not make pottery, and Japanese historians usually refer to this epoch as the Sendoki, or Pre-pottery, period.

THE JŌMON PERIOD

About 12,000 years ago, as the climate warmed, the open grasslands were gradually replaced by dense forests and marshes. A new lifestyle developed, based on fishing, hunting of smaller animals, and intensive gathering of a great variety of wild fruits, nuts, seeds, and tubers. Later, when the climate warmed even more, the sea rose and pushed inland, making enormous clam beds easily available to people living along the edge of the uplands.

About this same time the early inhabitants of Japan began to make a distinctive style of pottery, with unique markings made by laying or rolling twisted cords over the surface of the pots. The name Jōmon, or "cord marked," is thus applied to stone-age cultures stretching from about 10,000 B.C. to the rise of wet-rice agriculture, around the beginning of the Yayoi period.

The sort of intensive hunting-gathering lifestyle practiced by the Jōmon people was very stable, and by the later part of the period the villages were already supplementing their economy with dry-field agriculture and the management of woodlands and nut orchards. The Jōmon people were thus able to live in large, settled communities, producing beautiful pottery, adornments, and ceremonial artifacts.

THE YAYOI AND KOFUN PERIODS

About 300 B.C. the techniques for irrigated paddy agriculture were brought to Japan, most likely from Korea and China, initiating the Yayoi period. Analysis of fossil pollen at archeological sites indicates that irrigated rice production in the Kantō area started first in the narrow *yato* valleys, which offered a natural supply of water that could be easily dammed up and utilized.

As the surplus from the rice crop grew, so did the complexity of the local communities. By the end of the Yayoi period (300 A.D.) and the beginning of the subsequent Kofun period, local chieftains were controlling larger and larger sections of countryside. In the fifth and sixth centuries these chieftains began building immense *kofun* burial tombs, with the outside lined with such funerary accessories as ceramic figures (called *haniwa*), bronze mirrors, and other imported or luxury items of status.

THE CLASSICAL PERIODS

In the sixth and seventh centuries, powerful leaders began to unite the local chiefdoms into a single kingdom, known as Yamato. In 710 a great capital city, designed on Chinese models, was built in Nara. In 794 the capital was moved to Kyoto, and the nation was ruled by an Imperial Court headed by the emperor. Poetry and art flourished, and these centuries are usually thought of as Japan's classical period.

Throughout the classical period, however, the center of Japanese culture and politics was always in the western area of Japan, and the Kantō was considered to be a boring cultural backwater, inhabited by crude barbarians and ruled by rustic warlords.

THE EARLY FEUDAL PERIODS

Eventually, the Imperial Court began to collapse in on itself, and power was wrested from the aristocracy and placed in the hands of the growing samurai or warrior caste. Two powerful families, the Heike and Genji, fought for dominance. In 1192 the Genji emerged victorious, and their head, Minamoto no Yoritomo, was proclaimed shogun.

Yoritomo set up his capital at Kamakura, in Kanagawa Prefecture, hundreds of miles east of Kyoto and Nara, and only a short distance from Tokyo. Japan's present day capital, however, remained a sleepy little fishing village at the edge of the Musashino Uplands, where the great Sumida River emptied into Tokyo Bay. At this time, the whole area around the river mouth was one immense stretch of tidal flats and salt marshes. In fact, Edo, the original name for Tokyo that was applied to both the village and the clan that governed the area, means the door or entrance to a sea inlet.

The Edo clan ruled from a small fort which they built at the edge of one of the finger-shaped protrusions of the uplands that pushed into the marshlands. In 1457 a samurai named Ōta Dōkan, a vassal of the powerful Uesugi clan, took over the fort and constructed a sizable castle. The little village of Edo soon developed into a small castle town, with a thriving port. Dōkan, however, was assassinated in 1496, and the town lost much of its vitality.

Throughout most of the sixteenth century, Japan was embroiled in a series of terrible civil wars, with samurai clans from all over the nation fighting one another over control of territory. Gradually, however, several strong leaders, first Oda Nobunaga and then Toyotomi Hideyoshi, began to gain ascendancy, and step-by-step the nation was unified.

THE EDO PERIOD

Tokugawa Ieyasu was a warlord originally from the Shizuoka area, and an important vassal of Hideyoshi. In return for his service, Ieyasu was awarded the entire Kantō area as a fief. Actually, many historians believe that Hideyoshi secretly feared Ieyasu, and tried to neutralize him by banishing him as far away from Kyoto as possible, where the seat of power had relocated in 1392.

Most people assumed that Ieyasu would establish his capital at the historic centers of Kamakura or Odawara, and were quite surprised when in 1590 he took over Edo Castle instead. Hideyoshi died in 1598, leaving doubt as to who should succeed him. Ieyasu defeated Hideyoshi's descendants at the Battle of Sekigahara, initiating the Edo, or Tokugawa, period, which lasted more than 250 years, until the overthrow of the feudal system in the Meiji Restoration of 1867. During this entire time span Japan was ruled by the Tokugawa shoguns, the descendents of Ieyasu.

The first Tokugawa shoguns were not only great military strategists, but also visionary planners and extraordinary civil engineers. The new city of Edo was planned and laid out with the castle at its center. Construction of Edo Castle began in 1604. Only a few earthenworks were left over from Dōkan's time, so the city was essentially designed and built from scratch.

Moats were dug to protect the castle, and some of the marshlands were filled in to make new land. A fabulous network of canals allowed goods of all descriptions to be unloaded and delivered from ships calling at Edo Port, the harbor that developed at the mouth of the Sumida River. The shogun's relatives and allies built huge manors atop the Musashino Uplands. These manors, called *daimyō yashiki*, often included elaborate formal gardens for entertaining and relaxation. Numerous temples and shrines, surrounded by protective groves of trees, were constructed throughout the city.

Edo must have been a truly beautiful city, full of waterways and verdant gardens. On the very outskirts of the city began the Musashino countryside, a rich mosaic of oak coppices, upland fields filled with vegetables, and rice paddies that functioned like seasonal marshes. In addition, the shores of Tokyo Bay were rimmed with tidals flats and salt marshes. The abundant resources of the bay not only provided the growing city with a steady supply of animal protein, but supported immense flocks of migratory waterbirds—shorebirds in spring and autumn and ducks, geese, and cranes during the winter.

Even today, much of Tokyo's greenery can be traced back to the Edo period. The lands of the *daimyō yashiki*, for example, have survived, and now form the nucleus of the central city's parks and gardens. The moats and canals also provide vital open space and wildlife habitat.

THE MEIJI PERIOD

The Tokugawa shogunate was overthrown in 1867. The city's name was changed to Tokyo, and a new civilian government was formed. The Emperor Meiji and his Imperial Court were moved from their traditional residence at Kyoto to Edo Castle, which became the new Imperial Palace. Historians call this time span, from 1867 until the death of the Meiji emperor in 1912, the Meiji period.

During the Meiji period the city expanded and grew more crowded. The *daimyō yashiki* manors were taken over by the army or the newly emerging industrial and commercial elites. Still, the city, as well as the surrounding baylands and countryside, remained essentially green.

THE MODERN PERIOD

Tokyo grew steadily throughout the twentieth century, but in a very unplanned and haphazard fashion. The legacies of the Edo period—abundant greenery and open space, and easy access to waterways—began to disappear as factories and residential areas grew.

The city was leveled twice, first by the great Kantō Earthquake of 1923, then again in the fire-bombing during World War II. Both these disasters presented opportunities to change the direction of growth. Unfortunately, the urban planners at this time were not as farsighted as the Tokugawa rulers had been. Rather than re-design the decimated areas of the city from scratch, with abundant greenery and open space, Tokyo was simply allowed to rebuild and expand in an unchecked and unregulated fashion.

With little zoning restriction or planning for open public spaces, many neighborhoods were left with nothing more than a hodgepodge of urban clutter. The once-beautiful countryside was also developed with no concepts of planned growth, resulting in the endless stretches of densely packed residential areas that now surround the city. At the same time, almost all of the bay's rich coastal wetlands were filled in to make new land for port and industrial facilities, while air and water pollution, also unchecked, threatened to destroy much of the remaining natural resources. Gruesomely mutated and deformed fish, called *obake-haze*, or "monster gobies," appeared in the now stinking bay waters.

NATURE TODAY

The peak of pollution and uncontrolled growth in the Tokyo area occurred in the late 1960s and early 1970s. Fortunately, by then the citizens of Japan had had enough and forced the government to pass basic antipollution laws and enact improvements in air and water quality.

Since then the Tokyo environment has improved somewhat. Water quality has recovered, and fish from Tokyo Bay are now considered safe to eat again. Over the past decade or so, there have been concerted efforts to restore the city's tree groves and water habitats. Once forgotten canals have been turned into parks, street trees have been increased, and park managers have come to realize the importance of biodiversity. As a result, central Tokyo is becoming greener by the year.

Unfortunately, the agricultural countryside is not faring quite as well. Suburban sprawl and golf course development continues to impinge on the fields and paddies, and although some parks now include traditional countryside features such as coppice forests and *tame-ike* irrigation ponds, the government has yet to identify a practical strategy for conserving and restoring the working countryside landscape. Interest in traditional land management practices, however, is increasing, and citizen groups are joining forces with farmers in ingenious and inventive schemes for restoring and maintaining the beautiful and biologically rich landscape.

Until very recently the Tokyo Bay coastal wetlands had also been faring poorly. Japan has no laws for the conservation of wetlands, and environmental impact assessments are usually perfunctory, making landfill permits very easy to obtain. In 1999, however, the government finally relinquished a long-standing plan to fill in the Sanbanze, one of the bay's few remaining wetlands. As a result, there now seems at least some hope for preservation and hopefully restoration of tidal flats and salt marshes.

Notwithstanding the ceaseless development, there is still a lot of nature to be enjoyed in the Tokyo area. A wide variety of habitats, from city parks to rice paddies, can be found in and around the city. These habitats support rich flora and fauna and are conveniently located for lunchtime and weekend naturalists.

JAPANESE HISTORICAL PERIODS

PREHISTORIC
Jōmon ca. 10,000 B.C.–ca. B.C. 300
Yayoi ca. 300 B.C.–ca. A.D. 300
Kofun ca. 300–710

CLASSICAL
Nara 710–94
Heian 794–1185

MIDDLE AGES (MEDIEVAL)
Kamakura 1185–1333
Northern and Southern courts 1333–92
Muromachi 1392–1573
    Warring States 1482–1573

PREMODERN
Momoyama 1573–1600
Edo (Tokugawa) 1600–1867

EARLY MODERN/MODERN
Meiji 1867–1912
Taishō 1912–26
Shōwa 1926–89
Heisei 1989 to present

TOKYO HABITATS

FOREST HABITATS

Japan is one of the most heavily forested countries in the world. Botanists generally divide the nation's native old-growth forests into three basic types:

1 Broadleaved evergreen forests of chinkapin, laurel, and live oak, characteristic of the subtropical and warm temperate zones
2 Broadleaved deciduous forests of beech and oak, typical of the cool temperate zone
3 Coniferous forests of spruce and fir, found mostly in the subarctic regions of central and eastern Hokkaidō, and at high elevations in northern and central Honshū.

Tokyo is situated very near the northern limits of the warm temperate zone, and the true local natural climax, or old-growth, forest is a dense, dark grove of chinkapins, evergreen oaks, and other tall broadleaved evergreens. These trees are slow growing, but long lived. Once fully established they form a dense crown of thick, leathery leaves that block the sun and keep the forest dark and damp throughout the year. Smaller shade-tolerant trees—such as camellias and aucuba—form a sparse understory.

Beech trees and other denizens of the mature deciduous forests do not grow in the uplands and hills adjacent to the city, but can be found in the mountains surrounding the Kantō Plain. The closest examples are along the upper ridges

Distribution of Japan's three types of native old growth forests. In addition to latitude, the distribution is also influenced by elevation. Black areas represent subarctic coniferous forests; hatched areas, cool-temperate deciduous forests; and unmarked white areas, warm-temperate broadleaved evergreen forests.

Inside a coppice forest. Note the cleared undergrowth and coppiced trunks.

of Mt. Takao to the west, and around the summit of Mt. Tsukuba in southern Ibaraki Prefecture. Secondary deciduous woodlands, however, can be enjoyed anywhere in the countryside, and even in many inner city parks.

Secondary woodlands form within the forests's natural cycle. When a fire or windstorm topples the climax forest, or one of the old giants dies of age or disease and crashes to earth, a light, airy stretch, called a gap, is formed. This gap is first invaded by opportunistic wildlfowers, followed by taller weeds such as the *susuki* plume grasses. Birds and wind, however, soon carry in seeds of oaks, hornbeams, dogwoods, and other light-loving deciduous trees. In a few years these fast growers take over the gap, forming a young secondary woodland. Japan has one of the fastest rates of secondary reforestation in the world. The secondary woodland is an open, airy habitat, leafless from late fall to early spring. Even in summer the thin leaves let in some light and wind.

Even as the secondary woodland flourishes, however, the broadleaved evergreen saplings return and begin to grow. Slowly but surely they overtake the shorter-lived oaks and hornbeams and reestablish the original mature forest. Botanists estimate that this natural forest cycle takes between 150 and 250 years.

Coppices or coppice forests, often called *zōki-bayashi* or *shintan-rin* in Japanese, form a special type of managed or semi-managed secondary woodland. In a coppice forest the trees are cut down regularly, and the forest floor is annually cleared of saplings and bamboo grass.

Japanese villagers traditionally maintained coppice forests on the outskirts of their village. The cut wood was used for firewood and charcoal manufacture, and the fallen leaves were collected and made into organic compost. A coppice forest is a very productive resource. The coppiced trees are cut down at their base, but new shoots grow directly from the stump. Regrowth is rapid, and in the Tokyo area the oaks could be coppiced every twenty or thirty years. The villagers kept the woodlands in a secondary condition by regularly cutting the undergrowth, which prevented the evergreen saplings from gaining a foothold.

Coppice forests, although semi-managed and thus not true natural forests, are very rich in wildlife. Small wildflowers benefit from the annual clearing of the bamboo grass, which chokes the forest floor if allowed to grow unchecked. Many insects, including huge rhinoceros and stag beetles, thrive on the oak trunks, and the various species of trees, shrubs, and vines provide an autumn bounty of berries and nuts for birds and small mammals.

Typical coppiced oak tree, with multiple trunks

The Tokyo countryside is also home to commercial bamboo groves, which are often interspersed among the coppice forests, adding further to the local diversity. The two most common species are *mōsō-chiku* and *ma-dake*. The new shoots of both species are eaten as *takenoko*. *Ma-dake* is also used in fencing and various handicrafts, while *mōsō-chiku* makes superb charcoal. The two species can be told apart by looking closely at the joints. A smaller species of bamboo grass, *azuma-nezasa*,

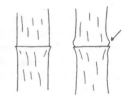

Joints of *ma-dake* (right) and *mōsō-chiku*

grows wild as forest undergrowth and sometimes forms dense, impenetrable thickets. Several other varieties of bamboo grass, all low-growing evergreen shrubs with wide leaves, are planted as undergrowth in Tokyo parks and gardens.

Unfortunately, over the past several decades many farmers have abandoned their coppices and bamboo groves because charcoal and firewood have been replaced by fossil fuels, leaf compost by chemical fertilizers, and bamboo by plastic. Abandoned coppices are taken over by bamboo grass, or revert to the original cycle, eventually turning into mature broadleaved evergreen forests.

Old growth forests and secondary natural woodlands are also becoming rarer and rarer, and the type of forest most frequently seen today is a tightly packed grove of conifers, usually cryptomeria (*sugi*) or cypress (*hinoki*). In the postwar years, national forestry policy encouraged villagers to cut down the native broadleaved trees and replace them with these dense conifer plantations. Neat rows of perfectly matched conifers may look pretty, but are poor in wildflowers, insects, and other wildlife.

Typical conifer plantation. Trees have pointed tips and are tightly planted in neat rows.

Still, there is a lot of secondary woodland left to be enjoyed in the Tokyo area. Mature broadleaved evergreen forests also survive in small stands around Shinto shrines, where the trees are considered sacred and have traditionally been left untouched. The Meiji Jingū shrine is an excellent example. Some functioning coppice forests are left in western Tokyo and the Sayama Hills of Saitama Prefecture (a fine example can be seen in Sengenyama Park). There is also a resurgence of interest in charcoal, natural compost, and bamboo products, and a small but steadily growing movement to restore and maintain the vital natural and traditionally managed habitats.

AQUATIC HABITATS

The Tokyo area is blessed with abundant rainfall (about 150 centimeters a year), and one is never far from a lake, marsh, or river. In addition, there are various manmade aquatic habitats, mostly associated with the traditional system of wet-paddy rice agriculture, that are surpisingly rich in wildlife.

Unfortunately, many of Tokyo's rivers have been converted to ugly concrete channels that support very little wildlife. Some have even been filled in or moved underground. In recent years, however, the Ministry of Construction, which controls big river environments, and the local municipalities, which control those of smaller streams, are gradually changing their priorities. The Tamagawa Aqueduct, for example, has been restored over most of its length, and sections along the Edo, Ara, and Tama rivers are being allowed to return to a natural state. The presence of extensive reed beds along the river's edge is a good indication that there should be plenty of aquatic insects, fish, and birds to watch.

Irrigation ponds, called *tame-ike* in Japanese, were originally part of the rice-culture infrastructure. They were constructed by damming up a small section at the head of a narrow valley, where water naturally sprang out of the slopes. These ponds were usually ringed with reeds, cattails, and other aquatic grasses, and with a constant supply of clean water supported many species of aquatic insects and wildflowers.

Today, most of the rice paddies served by these ponds have been filled in for residential development, and even in areas with working paddies the water is now pumped up from rivers or wells. *Tame-ike* have thus lost their original function. Still, many of these ponds remain, and have been preserved in excellent shape within parks like Inokashira, Zenpukuji, and Shakujii. They are superb habitats for botanizing, birdwatching, and catching dragonflies.

COASTAL HABITATS

The salt marshes and tidal flats that once ringed the bay have been reduced to a minimum, but those that do remain are very rich in wildlife. Ironically, with so little habitat left to utilize, the bay's shorebirds tend to be concentrated in small preserves where they are easy to locate and observe. The Tokyo Port Wild Bird Park, Kasai Seaside Park, Gyōtoku Sanctuary, and Yatsu Tidelands all have observation centers equipped with telescopes and served by volunteer and professional interpreters.

For those who like to get muddy there are small sections of salt marsh along the Tama and Edo River Drainage Canal, and tidal flats that you can safely walk on are found at Kasai Seaside Park and Funabashi Seaside Park. These tidelands are great not only for birding, but also for hands-on study of clams, bristleworms, crabs, and other coastal invertebrates.

URBAN HABITATS

For those stuck in the central city, all it takes is an hour or so to explore many of Tokyo's parks. These range from tiny "pocket parks" with a few trees to huge blocks of woodlands. Most of the formal gardens also have a sizable section with dense stands of native trees, while temples and shrines, usually surrounded by solid groves of mature broadleaved evergreen trees, are worth visiting if you happen to be in the neighborhood.

Even those with impossibly busy schedules can enjoy nature while walking from one appointment to the next. Tokyo is blessed with abundant street trees, which will often be filled with birds and even cicadas in summer. In addition, large hedges are often overgrown with bindweed and other interesting native vines. If you have a few minutes to spare, take a detour through the smaller streets behind the wide avenues. Even in the central city there will be small one-family houses surrounded by gardens with trees that flower and fruit, attracting insects and birds.

PART
I

ANIMALS

MAMMALS

Mammals are not a very conspicuous element in the Tokyo area fauna. The central city appears virtually bereft of them, and even on a hike in the hills or countryside one rarely encounters a mammal. This comes as quite a surprise to Americans who are used to seeing rabbits and squirrels at every turn, and to running over skunks and raccoons on a regular basis.

To begin with, the habitats around Tokyo are simply not broad enough to support large mammals. Thus the boar, black bear, deer, and serow are not encountered until one gets fairly deep into the mountains. Macaques are also rare, although in 1999 one wandered into central Tokyo and spent several days cleverly avoiding capture, creating a media frenzy.

Even most medium-size mammals are restricted to the hills and mountains. Foxes and badgers, for example, do not inhabit the nearby countryside. Japanese squirrels (*Nihon risu*) are found in the countryside, but never in large numbers. They apparently were far more common until several decades ago, when a disease, thought to have been spread by a longhorn beetle, wiped out most of the red pine groves, thereby eliminating one of their major food sources, pine cone seeds. Escaped populations of the Taiwan squirrel inhabit parts of Kamakura and Enoshima, and a program to reintroduce Japanese squirrels is being implemented at Inokashira Park.

Two medium-size mammals are still quite common in the Tokyo area. One of these is the Japanese hare (*no-usagi*); the other is a strange critter called the *tanuki,* or raccoon dog. Both of these mammals, however, are almost entirely nocturnal, and thus are rarely met on countryside hikes.

Another highly secretive local species is the masked palm civet (*hakubishin*), found mainly on the Miura Peninsula. This short-legged, long-tailed animal is brown with distinctive white face markings. It is the only member of the mongoose family found in Japan (the mongoose itself has been introduced on some islands to help control snake populations), and its spotty distribution has lead some researchers to believe it may have been artificially introduced a long time ago. The masked palm civet, a nocturnal omnivore, is maligned in some districts for raiding persimmon and other fruit crops.

Ear tufts of the Japanese squirrel are long and pointed in winter

Walking in the rice-paddy countryside, one occasionally catches a glimpse of a reddish brown blur disappearing into the weeds alongside an irrigation canal. This is the Japanese weasel (*itachi*), which hunts mice, frogs, and snakes, but is also known to eat insects and even berries. Higher up in the mountains, there is also a slight chance of encountering a marten (*ten*). Martens are much larger than the weasels and practice a more arboreal lifestyle.

Pine cones that have been stripped by a Japanese squirrel

Smaller mammals are also quite common, but generally hidden from view. The large Japanese field mouse (*aka nezumi*), for example, inhabits the forest floor and is always quick to hide in the leaf litter, while the cute little harvest mouse (*kaya nezumi*) lives and nests in dense fields of reeds or plume grass.

The mounds of the small Japanese mole (*azuma mogura*) can be seen in parks and sometimes even on the dikes between rice paddies. Moles are expert diggers and live in long, complicated tunnels well beneath the surface. The mounds are dirt that has been excavated as they dig these tunnels. There is also a shrew-mole (*himizu*) that digs tunnels closer to the surface, and a shrew (*togari nezumi*) that lives and hunts inside the forest leaf litter.

Several species of bat are found in the Tokyo area. By far and away the most common of these, especially in more densely populated areas, is the *abura kōmori*, which roosts and nests in the attics or under the eaves of farmhouses and other wooden buildings. A commonly used nickname for this bat is *ie kōmori*, or "house bat." The house bat hibernates during the winter, but emerges on clear evenings from spring to summer, catching moths and other flying insects on the wing.

Tokyo-area mammals rarely show themselves to the casual observer. To find them, one has to search carefully for signs or get in the habit of going for countryside strolls at night.

JAPANESE HARE

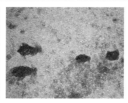

Tracks of Japanese hare in upland field. The large tracks in front (to the left) are the rear legs. The hare is moving from right to left.

Fans of Japanese fairy tales should be immediately suspicious of any story that mentions a "rabbit." The only rabbit native to Japan is the **Amami black rabbit**, a primitive species endemic to the island of Amami Ōshima, south of Kagoshima. The long-eared creature known simply as *usagi* or *no-usagi*, which hops around Japanese forests and farmlands, appears in folktales and legends, and is even seen on the moon, is not a rabbit at all, but a hare.

Some people might think this is splitting hairs. Rabbits and hares are both lagomorphs (members of the order Lagomorpha), animals with powerful rear legs and a unique style of running. They start off with a great push from the strong rear legs, then fly through the air, landing first on their front legs. Before the next leap, however, the rear legs actually cross over and position themselves before the forelegs.

This style of leaping can be read in the tracks that lagomorphs leave behind: two long prints side by side, followed by two smaller prints that are usually staggered or offset. The long prints in front are made by the rear legs during push-off, while the smaller ones in back are made by the front legs during landing.

Lagomorphs also share a distinctive set of dentition. Like rodents, they have a pair of sharp, continuously growing incisors in the front of their upper and lower jaw, with flat cheek teeth set further back and separated from the front teeth by a gap called the diastema. The front incisors are used for gnawing, clipping, or chiseling food, while the cheek teeth are for chewing. The incisors are made of soft dentine, but are covered on the front surface with hard enamel. Although the teeth continue to grow, as the animal cuts tough plant material, the soft dentine is worn back at an angle, forming a sharp, chisel-like edge on the front of the tooth.

Lagomorphs differ from rodents in that they have an extra set of incisors in the upper jaw, hidden right behind the front pair. This second set of incisors, however, are small and seemingly functionless. The evolutionary relationship between rodents and lagomorphs has yet to be clarified. Some paleontologists believe that both groups originally sprang from a common ancestral lineage.

All lagomorphs are herbivores. Their dentition is specialized for clipping and chewing grasses, herbs, and even young tree saplings and tree bark. A reliable field sign showing lagomorphs at work is plant stems that have been cut off neatly at an angle, as if some miniature samurai had been practicing during the night with his sword.

Lagomorphs also employ a unique digestive system ideally adapted to efficient processing of large amounts of rough plant matter. After chewing, the plant material is sent through the gut, where the rough material, poor in nutrients after partial digestion, is filtered out and excreted in neat little round scat balls. The softer, more nutritious, and only partially digested material is also excreted, but is immediately reswallowed, and sent right back to the digestive tract for further processing. In this manner, lagomorphs are able to extract the maximum amount of nutrition from their diet.

Both rabbits and hares have long ears, exceptionally long rear legs, and short tails. Rabbits (genus *Sylvilagus*) usually live and nest in dens, sometimes large communal affairs called warrens. Their young are born naked, blind, and essentially helpless. Hares and jackrabbits (genus *Lepus*), on the other hand, don't usually dig dens. Their nest is a simple depression in the grass, called a scrape, and their young are born fully haired, with their eyes open.

The **Japanese hare** (*no-usagi*) is common in the countryside around Tokyo, especially in areas where vegetables are grown on dry upland fields. These animals are primarily nocturnal, so you will rarely see one. Instead, you will usually have to settle for observing their abundant tracks, scats, and feeding remains.

For a hare, the Japanese variety has comparatively short legs and ears. The hares in the Tokyo area and throughout most of southern and western Japan stay brown all year around. Those in the heavy snow country of Tōhoku and the central mountains molt into a pure white coat in winter.

Scats of Japanese hare

In mountainous regions, the hare's greatest natural enemies are golden eagles, owls, foxes, and traditional hunters. In the Tokyo area, their chief worry is farm and feral dogs (very few cats would be willing to take on an adult hare, which can deliver powerful bites and kicks). Like most hares, the Japanese *no-usagi* is an extremely alert animal. Without a den to retreat to or hide in, the hares rely first on their excellent hearing to warn them of the approach of an enemy. They then put on a burst of incredible speed to escape, easily leaving most attackers, including dogs, in the dust.

Young hares, however, are more vulnerable. Mother hares only suckle their young for a few weeks, and even then only a few times each day. The rest of the time the young are left to their own devices and must quickly learn how to find food and escape predators. They grow fast, feeding indiscriminately on almost all locally available plants (including the farmers' precious vegetables) and are ready to begin mating before they are a year old. They would probably be insulted to know that in some translations of fairy tales they are called rabbits!

Tanuki

The ***tanuki***, or "raccoon dog" as it is sometimes called in English, is by far and away the most prolific star of Japanese fairy tales. This small member of the dog family is portrayed as a master of metamorphosis, able at will to turn itself into a beautiful woman, fearsome monster, or devout priest. The *tanuki* is also a classic trickster, loving nothing more than playing jokes and setting traps, especially if some food can be gained in the bargain. Many fairy tales tell of battles of wits between *tanuki* and farmer, with the human usually emerging victorious.

One reason that the *tanuki* plays such a prominent role in folklore is that these animals tend to live on the very outskirts of towns and villages. Their preferred habitat is deciduous woodlands and semimanaged coppice forests. Yet, local fields and farmyards are often part of their foraging grounds. People and *tanuki* have thus been in intimate contact in Japan for thousands of years. On the one hand, the Japanese see the *tanuki* as a bringer of luck and fortune. Statues frequently seen outside stores and houses readily attest to this. On the other hand, farmers suffer considerably from the *tanuki*'s raids on their vegetable fields and poultry cages.

Several years ago a chicken farmer in the Chiba countryside asked me to come and get a *tanuki* he had recently trapped. This *tanuki* had been appearing nightly at his coops, biting the heads off chickens that stuck their necks out of their cages. If this were a typical fairy tale, the *tanuki* would have been in for some horrendous punishment, like the antagonist that got a knot of burning firewood strapped to his back in the famous story "*Kachi-kachi yama.*" I simply released the poor critter in an isolated park area just south of Tega Marsh. I haven't heard from the chicken farmer since, so I suppose that *tanuki* is still limping around the park.

Tanuki are considered to be the most primitive living member of the dog family. Paleontologists believe that they first evolved in North America, then crossed over to Eurasia via the Bering Strait. Yet the name raccoon dog in English is somewhat misleading, as the raccoon is not a member of the dog family and the resemblance between these two animals is purely superficial.

Most members of the dog family are gifted with great speed and endurance, which they use to run down prey in open habitats. The *tanuki*, however, is squat and short-legged and, like most Japanese mammals, is adapted to a forest habitat. Rather than actively chase down swift prey like hares, the *tanuki* employs a more leisurely style of foraging for a wide variety of food. A typical *tanuki* menu includes birds and their eggs; small mammals such as rodents and insectivores; a variety of worms, grubs, insects, spiders, and centipedes; stream crabs and crayfish; as well as acorns, nuts, berries, and fruit.

Animals that are very set in their ways often have trouble adapting to different or changing environments. *Tanuki* naturally take advantage of almost any food source locally available and, as such, are very adaptable. In the suburbs, they have learned to forage around garbage disposal areas and to steal food set out for domestic dogs and cats. Unfortunately, these scavenger *tanuki* are susceptible to distemper, mange, and other communicable diseases caught from dogs.

The plight of hard-pressed suburban *tanuki* is vividly and humorously portrayed in the animated movie *Heisei tanuki gassen ponpoko* (Studio Jiburi, 1994). The setting is Tama Hills, in western Tokyo, where the *tanuki*'s favorite habitat, the rich agricultural countryside, is being replaced by an immense bedroom community housing complex. The local band of *tanuki* try to use their magic to win back their homeland. Eventually, like the foxes before them, they are forced to metamorphose into human form to survive.

Tanuki

BADGER

Japanese badger

Sometimes one finds an English translation of a Japanese fairy tale that talks about "badgers." There are certainly badgers in Japan. In fact, the **Japanese badger**, called *ana-guma* (literally, "hole bear"), is considered to be a subspecies of the common badger found from Great Britain clear across the Eurasian continent. In fact, the animal depicted in the story is usually not a badger at all but a *tanuki*.

I guess the translators can be forgiven for their mistake. The two animals do resemble each other superficially. Both are about as big as a medium-size dog and both have a long snout with masklike patterns around the eyes. A closer look reveals that the badger has shorter legs and a thicker, wider, more powerfully built body. In addition, badgers walk with a distinctive gait: the front legs turn inward slightly, making the animal appear a little bowlegged.

Close scrutiny also shows that the shape of the nose and markings on the two animals' faces are actually quite different. The badger's nose is even longer and pointier, and its "mask" forms two vertical stripes, while the *tanuki*'s mask spreads out more to the sides in classic Zorro style. The badger's short, round ears also serve as a reliable field mark.

Even without a close look a quick check of the paw prints will easily identify the animals. Badgers, being members of the weasel family, leave five-toe prints, while *tanuki*, belonging to the dog family, leave an impression of only four.

Both badgers and *tanuki* are omnivores. The badger tends to rely a little more on animal food than the *tanuki*. Worms, in particular, are often an important part of the badger's diet. Badgers are superb diggers, using their long front claws to uncover not only worms and grubs but moles, shrews, edible roots, and tubers. In some parts of the countryside, the resident badgers have developed a special passion for digging up peanuts, yams, and sweet potatoes, much to the chagrin of local farmers.

Tracks of Japanese badger (left) and *tanuki*

The powerful front claws of the badger are also used to excavate the dens they live in. In southern Great Britain, badgers dig immense communal dens, known as sets, but Japanese badgers are more solitary. Males tend to stick to themselves, while females usually forage with their cubs. Nevertheless, a dozen or so badgers may collect and feed peacefully together in places where food is abundant.

Badgers have an especially keen sense of smell, which helps them to locate food buried underground or hidden in leaf litter. Their hearing is also excellent, but their eyesight is poor. For this reason badgers are usually portrayed as near-sighted in English children's stories.

Badgers tend to shy away from people more than *tanuki* do. They prefer to dig their dens on heavily forested slopes, well away from human habitation and activities. Thus, badgers are not as successful as *tanuki* in adapting to urban sprawl. In the Tokyo area, for example, the *tanuki* is found throughout the sub-urbs, almost right up to the inner city, while the badger is limited to the more isolated hills and low mountains.

In Japan, the badger is distributed on the main islands of Honshū, Shikoku, and Kyūshū, but is not found on Hokkaidō. This distribution suggests that these animals entered Japan from the west, crossing over from the Korean Peninsula during a glacial period, when the rising sea levels almost connected Kyūshū and western Honshū with the continent. From there the badgers spread eastwards and northwards, but were blocked from entering Hokkaidō by the Tsugaru Strait, which is deep and wide enough to have formed a substantial water barrier even during the glacial periods. Many other Japanese mammals, such as the black bear, serow, wild boar, and Japanese hare, arrived here via this same route, and are likewise not found on Hokkaidō.

Like the fox and *tanuki*, the badger is associated with magical powers and frequently shows up in local legends, especially in mountainous areas, where these animals were traditionally hunted for their fur and meat, which is deemed excellent. *Tanuki-nabe*, a local meat stew popular in some regions, is more likely to contain badger than *tanuki*.

Traditional techniques for capturing badgers included digging or smoking them out of their dens. A special tool, like a pair of giant tongs, was also used to pull them out, and dogs were trained to enter the den and drag the badgers out. Today, badgers are rarely hunted, although they are not considered an endan-gered species.

As urban sprawl takes over the countryside, the first mammals to disappear are usually wild boars and foxes, followed by badgers. The *tanuki* and Japanese hare can hang on longer. Eventually, even they lose their tenuous foothold.

● ●

BIRDS

The Tokyo area, with its varied habitats, is a friendly place for birds and bird-watchers. Waterfowl, for example, find the numerous lakes, ponds, and rivers much to their liking, while long-legged long-necked wading birds are perfectly at home in the rice-paddy countryside. Bush warblers, bamboo partridges, and other secretive forest birds hide in the deciduous woodlands, whereas urban avians such as jungle crows and brown-eared bulbuls stalk through the city's streets and parks like mayorial candidates. The coastal wetlands of Tokyo Bay are home to their own unique shorebird avifauna.

Some of these birds, called residents, spend the entire year right here. Spot-billed ducks, great cormorants, and little egrets are a few typical residents. Other birds, such as barn swallows, little terns, and reed warblers, are in Tokyo only for the summer breeding season. These summer breeders arrive in spring, raise their chicks, then depart in autumn for more southerly climes. Still other birds are winter visitors that nest further north. They come here in autumn, spend the winter, then fly north again in spring. Most of Tokyo's ducks and seagulls are winter visitors. A final group of birds neither reside, breed, nor winter here. They simply pass through twice a year: once in spring on their journey north, then again in autumn on their way south. Many of the sandpipers seen on Tokyo Bay mudflats are transients of this sort.

Birdwatching is a great hobby! All you need to get started is a pair of sturdy binoculars with a magnification power of seven or eight plus the Wild Bird Society of Japan's *Field Guide to the Birds of Japan*, which illustrates all of the nation's birds in full color. There is also plenty of support available for the beginning birder or visiting hobbyist. Many nature centers have installed powerful spotting scopes along windows overlooking tidal flats or lakes, and interpretive rangers are on hand to help identify and study the local birds. The Gyōtoku Sanctuary, Tokyo Port Wild Bird Park, and Yatsu Tidelands all boast well-equipped birding facilities.

Winter, with many tree branches bare of leaves, is a surprisingly good season for birdwatching. Food is scarce during the cold months, and birds that normally stay hidden in deep brush often come out to forage in more open areas. A tree with ripe berries or winter flowers can quickly become a gathering spot for local birds. In addition, lakes and ponds during winter will be full of various species of ducks and other waterfowl.

URBAN BIRDS

Pigeon

Steel and concrete, plus heavy human traffic, make cities undesirable habitats for most birds. Some species, however, have learned to take advantage of the unique opportunities—such as free handouts and all the garbage you can pick through—presented by the urban landscape. The classic example, of course, is the **pigeon** (*do-bato*). Originally a native of northern Africa and the Mediterranean, this bird has established colonies in almost all the world's large cities.

Sparrows (*suzume*) are also typical city slickers. On the streets of central Tokyo, common European sparrows can often be seen competing with the pigeons for bread crumbs or potato chips. These sparrows also get a great kick out of the city's abundant cherry blossoms. Brown-eared bulbuls and Japanese white-eyes use their long bills to lick nectar out of the cherry flowers. Short-billed sparrows are unable to perform this delicate feat. Instead, they get their fair share by simply clipping a flower off at its base, licking the nectar out from the rear, then dropping the flower. From the standpoint of the cherry trees, these sparrows are

Sparrow

nothing but thieves, getting a free meal without pollinating the flowers.

If the sparrows and pigeons in Tokyo seem a bit nervous, they have very good reason to be. Enormous black **jungle crows** prowl the streets and parks, causing any unwary sparrows or pigeons to quickly end up as a statistic in the urban food chain. In fact, some researchers believe that predation by crows is gradually

Jungle crow

turning the city's pigeons black. Black pigeons stick out less than lighter-colored birds and are thus more likely to escape notice.

Jungle crows themselves (they look more like ravens than crows) are a true marvel of urban adaptation. Their original native habitat is mountain forests and coasts, where they feed heavily on carrion. Their huge, thick bills, which give them their Japanese name *hashibuto-garasu* (literally, "thick-billed crow"), are ideal for opening up a carcass. These same bills also allow them to rip into heavy plastic garbage bags.

Jungle crows are active only during the day, arriving at choice garbage spots at dawn. The backstreets of the Ginza area, where high-class restaurants throw out plenty of uneaten Kobe beef, lobster, and tuna *sashimi*, are among these birds' favorite traditional haunts. In no time at all, the hungry crows turn the street into a garbage-strewn mess. The cleanup is such an ordeal that some urban communities have hired private sector sanitation companies to come get their garbage in the middle of the night, while the crows are still asleep.

From autumn through winter, jungle crows spend the night in large communal roosts. They prefer parks and gardens that are closed to the public at night. The Institute for Nature Study in Meguro is one favorite roost. Meiji Jingū Shrine is another. From dawn to dusk, the crows fan out over the city, hunting and scavenging. In late afternoon, they begin gathering, forming larger and larger groupings as they work their way back toward the roost.

In early spring, the roosts break up into nesting pairs. Nests are built in large trees as well as on telephone and utility poles. Nest material consists mainly of thin sticks. The crows have also developed a special fondness for colorful wire clothes hangers. Many Japanese housewives prefer to dry their wash on the verandah rather than use a drying machine, thus supplying the crows with a wide choice of the latest colors and styles in wire nesting material.

During the spring and early summer nesting period, jungle crows become very aggressive. They not only chase away other birds, but dive-bomb cats and even people that stray too close to the nest. The late nesting period, when the chicks are growing active, is especially dangerous. In midsummer, the fledglings—as large as their parents but still virtually helpless—wander into crowded shopping and entertainment districts, usually causing a minor panic.

Gray starling

As one might expect, jungle crows are not greatly appreciated by many Tokyoites. In a contest for the least popular bird, they would probably run neck and neck with the **gray starlings**. These medium-size birds, called *muku-dori* in Japanese, are ubiquitous on park lawns and any stretch of open ground. During the summer months, when they are busy feeding their young, they don't cause much trouble. But from autumn through winter, they form huge roosts that make crow gatherings seem like kindergarten parties. In addition, while the crows roost in parks and gardens, starlings are quite happy with plane trees and other street trees in commercial and residential districts. In early evening, the incessant chattering of hundreds or even thousands of these birds startles unwary strollers that pass under the trees. Home owners, too, complain vehemently about the noise, smell, and droppings. A huge starling roost is an unwelcome development in any neighborhood.

Starlings are primarily ground feeders. Their body is grayish overall, with a white streak around the eye. The bill is yellow, with a dark tip in adult birds. In flight, a round patch of white shows on the upper side between the tail and the wings, making identification easy.

In stark contrast to the crows and starlings are the city's unobtrusive **rufous turtledoves** (*kiji-bato*). Many park strollers don't even realize that turtledoves are different from pigeons, but a close look will show the distinctive black-and-gray stripes on the side of the neck.

Turtledove

Unlike their domestic cousins, Tokyo's turtledoves rarely appear in large flocks. They are often seen in pairs or, from late winter through spring, in small groups, with one or two males busily displaying to their favorite female. Turtledoves sometimes become so engrossed in these endeavors that they will allow people to approach very closely.

Turtledoves nest in street trees, parks, and yards. They usually forage on the ground. Their diet is almost exclusively vegetarian, including a variety of seeds and berries that have become caught among blades of grass on park lawns. Like all members of the pigeon family, turtledoves rarely take insects even during the breeding season, raising their squabs instead on "pigeon milk," a protein-rich substance that both males and females are able to produce. This liquid food contains more protein and fat than human or cow milk. An enticing cooing, described in Japanese as *dede-poppo*, is a sure sign that turtle- doves are nearby.

The dusky thrush often hops several times, stops, then hops again, but can also run fairly fast when pressed

The starling and turtledove are year-round resi- dents in the Tokyo area. Another similar-size bird, the **dusky thrush** (*tsugumi*), is but a winter visitor from Siberia. These robinlike birds are dark brown on top and whitish below, with a clearly visible white streak just above the eye and dark blotches on the chest. Like the turtledove and starling, the dusky thrush spends much of its time foraging on park lawns, but also feeds on fruits and berries in the trees.

Dusky thrushes arrive here from their Siberian breeding ground in mid- autumn. For several months, however, they remain in dense cover. Only in full winter, when they come out to forage on park lawns and other open spaces, does their presence really become obvious. Dusky thrushes can be seen in the Tokyo area until late April. In the past, they were heavily netted along their migration route for utilization as food and in medicine.

One of our most conspicuous urban and suburban birds is the medium-size **brown-eared bulbul**. Loud and boisterous, bulbuls usually announce their arrival with a shrill *pii-piii piyo-piyo* call. The Japanese name *hiyo-dori* is derived from this call. In contrast with starlings, turtledoves, and thrushes, bulbuls are highly arboreal and rarely descend to the ground.

Loud and aggressive birds often tend to be clumsy, but the bulbul is a superb acrobat. Perched on a tree limb, these birds twist their necks to probe delicately into flowers for nectar or pollen. Their balancing act can be seen in camellias, plums, and cherries.

Berries are among the bulbul's favorite food items. Throughout the winter months, bright red berries of aucuba, firethorn, and holly, all planted widely in parks and yards, attract the noisy bulbuls. As these birds are large enough to swallow most berries whole, rather than simply picking away the soft outer part, they play a major role in dispersing seeds. Wooded areas are often full of seedlings that have sprouted from seeds regurgi- tated or defecated by bulbuls.

Brown-eared bulbul. The chestnut-brown scar be- hind the eye is a good field mark.

Interestingly, the bulbul is a relatively recent convert to urban lifestyle. Originally a summer breeder in the countryside and low hills, the bulbul made the transition to urban residency in the 1960s and 70s, taking advantage of the increasing greenery in the city's parks, gardens, and backyards, which are often full of berry-bearing trees and shrubs.

Azure-winged magpie. Note extra long tail in flight silhouette.

The bulbul has silver, frosty streaks on its head and chest, and a reddish-brown patch, shaped somewhat like a crescent moon, behind the eye. In flight, the short, round wings contrast with the long tail. Bulbuls fly in a wavy, undulating pattern, rather than in a straight line, a field mark which allows one to quickly distinguish them in flight from the similarly sized starling, turtledove, or thrush.

The azure-winged **magpie** is another berry lover that frequents gardens and backyard trees. The Japanese name *onaga* means "long tail," and indeed this bird's tail is as long as its body. The magpie's call is more hoarse and guttural than the bulbul, and its gray body, light blue wings and tail, and black cap are unmistakable field marks.

Barn swallows (*tsubame*) are summer breeders that over long centuries have adapted very well to human habitation. Their favorite nesting sites are buildings. In the inner city, they nest under the eaves of temples, stores, and private homes. In the countryside, they prefer farmhouse vestibules and storage sheds. In fact, many farmers appreciate the swallow's capacity for consuming great quantities of pesky insects, and even make special holes in their doors so that the birds can enter and leave at will. In storage sheds, however, the swallow nests are sometimes victimized by large *ao-daishō* rat snakes (see the next chapter).

Barn swallow. The long, forked tail is a good field mark.

Swallow nests are made of mud. All day long, the swallows work hard catching mosquitoes and other insects on the wing. Even city residents recognize the value of these birds in controlling gnats and mosqui-

Nest of barn swallow

toes and welcome their arrival in early spring.

The joys of Tokyo urban bird life appear to be attracting new species on a regular basis. **Common kingfishers** (*kawasemi*), for example, were formerly rare in the city, but are now seen regularly in several of the city's central parks, including the ponds at Meiji Jingū Shrine. Kingfishers are only about the size of sparrows, but their huge bill and stunning plumage—iridescent blue markings on the head and back, and bright orange color on the chest—make them appear much bigger. They either perch motionless on tree branches overhanging the water or hover in place. Then, prey in sight, they plummet straight down into the water to snare fish or small frogs. In urban parks, they often perch on the immense leaves and flower stalks of lotus plants.

Body of the common kingfisher is only about the size of a sparrow, but its long bill makes the bird appear larger

White wagtails (*haku-sekirei*), once birds of the coast and countryside, have also moved into the inner city over the last decade or so. Wagtails are long, thin birds, usually seen flying low or running across the ground. When standing still, they move their tail up and down in a distinctive style. Their diet consists mostly of flying insects, which the birds leap into the air to catch. In winter, they can be seen foraging right smack in the midst of some of the city's heaviest traffic, dodging trucks and taxicabs. Out in the country, one also runs into the similar-looking **Japanese wagtail** (*seguro sekirei*).

White wagtail (right) and Japanese wagtail. White wagtails are far more numerous.

Great tits (*shijū-kara*) and **Japanese white-eyes** (*mejiro*) are regular players in the central city parks and gardens, especially those with a solid block of woodland. In more natural parks, such as those in western Musashino, a determined birder will also find such specimens as the **varied tit** (*yama-gara*), **hawfinch** (*shime*), **Oriental greenfinch** (*kawara-hiwa*), **Siberian meadow bunting** (*hōjiro*), **rustic bunting** (*kashira-daka*), **long-tailed tit** (*enaga*), **jay** (*kakesu*), and **Daurian redstart** (*jōbitaki*). In some parts of the western

Great tit (left) and varied tit. Great tits are more common.

wards, large, stunning green **rose-ringed parakeets** (*wakake-honsei-inko*) have escaped from pet owners and are now naturalized and breeding.

Japanese white-eye

COR-MORANTS

Great cormorant drying its wings at Shinobazu Pond

Tokyo visitors and residents frequently spot big, heavy-set black birds roosting in trees, resting on wharfs and pilings, fishing in the rivers and moats, or just flying back and forth high over the city streets. These are **cormorants**.

Out of the water, cormorants appear ungainly. Their short legs, webbed feet, and heavy bodies make walking about on land a difficult task. Takeoff and landing techniques are awkward and, even in flight, their continuous deep wingbeats give the impression of sheer power rather than grace.

Underwater, however, is where cormorants really show off their stuff. The thickly webbed feet, so unwieldy on land, turn into wide flippers for fast and powerful swimming strokes. Ornithologists describe the cormorant's feeding method as underwater-pursuit diving. They dive from the surface and are fast and agile enough swimmers to actively chase down fish and squid. The cormorant's long, thin, hooked beak is also ideally adapted to snatching fleeing fish, and their eyes can adjust to compensate for the distance distortion experienced underwater.

Cormorants are often seen perched with their wings spread out. The outer portion of their wing feathers are designed to absorb some water, thereby reducing buoyancy and allowing the bird to swim fast and maneuver tightly underwater. From time to time, they find it necessary to take a break and dry these feathers in the air and sun.

The cormorant seen around Tokyo is the **great cormorant**. When perched, its wings and body appear mostly dark, with a sheen of iridescent bluish black on the chest and a bronze tint on the wings. There is some yellow skin at the base of the bill, and the cheek area is white. The eyes are an amazing green! In flight, the neck and head protrude straight forward. The tail also sticks out further backwards than it does in ducks.

A separate species of cormorant, **Temminck's** or **Japanese cormorant**, winters on Jōgashima Island off the tip of the Miura Peninsula. In Japanese, the great cormorant is called *kawa-u* ("river cormorant") and Temminck's cormorant, *umi-u* ("ocean cormorant"). The Temminck's cormorant prefers open oceans and rocky coasts, while the great cormorant sticks to shallow estuaries, rivers, and inland lakes and marshes. It is the Temminck's, rather than the great cormorant, that is used in

Great cormorant resting on the Imperial Palace Moat

traditional cormorant fishing on the Nagara River. This fishing is performed at night, using huge torches. Specially trained cormorants, tethered at the neck by a strong line, are released from the boats. The cormorants dive into the river and catch fish. When they return to the surface they are hauled in by the tether line and the fish is taken away before they have a chance to swallow it. Temminck's cormorants, adapted to the rough ocean waters, are said to be better suited to the swift flowing river than the great cormorants, which normally fish in quiet waters.

During the breeding season, the great cormorant's head feathers push up into a small crown, and the sides of the neck are streaked with white feathers called filoplumes. There is no easy way to separate males and females by sight alone, save for during the nesting season, when males can be identified as those that carry the nesting material. Younger birds are a dull brown with lighter underparts.

The great cormorant is found throughout the temperate regions of Europe, Asia, and Africa. Though it was once abundant over most of Japan, by the middle of the twentieth century overhunting and the deterioration of its breeding and feeding habitats had reduced the entire Japanese population of the species to only several thousand birds.

Great cormorants nest and breed in large colonies. Their traditional nesting habitat was in densely wooded areas along the shores of lakes and rivers, habitats that have been eliminated by Japan's ubiquitous and ill-conceived river impoundment projects, which usually replace the original riparian vegetation with baseball fields and golf courses. As a result, cormorants have had to move their nesting grounds to protected parks.

Tokyo's best-known cormorant colony is at Shinobazu Pond, in Ueno Zoo.

This colony was founded in the early 1960s, when cormorants raised at the zoo were released and began breeding on a small island in the pond. These birds were later joined by birds from other colonies. Eventually, the city constructed artificial trees as additional nesting platforms.

Since the 1970s, water quality and fish resources have recovered somewhat, resulting in the steady increase of the great cormorant population. Unfortunately, not all people are happy to see these birds making a comeback. Fishermen, for example, generally despise cormorants, seeing them as all too efficient competitors for scarce resources.

Local residents as well as park and garden managers also dislike the birds, as a large colony can create quite a visual and olfactory nuisance. In the past, farmers would place bundles of straw on the ground under the cormorants nests. Over the course of a season, the straw would become soaked with bird dung and could then be chopped up to make a potent fertilizer. These days, however, chemical fertilizers are readily available, and the cormorant dung merely continues to build up until it destroys the trees and becomes a sanitation hazard.

Nobody seems to want the Tokyo cormorants these days. Landowners and park managers actively discourage colonies by knocking down nests and scaring the birds with brightly colored cloth. The Shinobazu colony is welcome, but the limited area, frequently interrupted by dredging work, currently supports only about two hundred birds.

A colony in the Hamarikyū Garden, on the other hand, that grew rapidly over the past decade eventually contained roosts for as many as eight thousand cormorants. Park managers in this quiet garden were at their wits' end in trying to deal with all these birds. Fortunately, the birds recently moved en masse to more hospitable environments.

Today, the main Tokyo cormorant colony, containing about three to four thousand birds, is on a small, uninhabited island in the port district. This island is one of the Battery Islands, which were constructed in the nineteenth century to protect the city from seaborne invasion. The island is located almost underneath the famous Rainbow Bridge (see the section on Odaiba Seaside Park in Part 3). Another colony of equal size has moved into the Gyōtoku Sanctuary, just across the Edo River in Chiba Prefecture.

SEAGULLS

Black-headed gull in winter plumage

Over the course of millions of years of evolution, many plants and animals have become specialized, their anatomy and behavior gradually adapting to take advantage of one or two specific habitats or feeding methods. Shorebirds, for example, have long bills ideally shaped for catching crabs and worms on sandy beaches and tidal flats, while cormorants have wide, webbed feet for chasing fish underwater. **Seagulls**, however, have remained generalists. They are strong and agile flyers, can float on the water for hours at a time, and are totally at home walking on land.

The gulls' versatile skills allow them to take advantage of a wide range of locally available food sources. One might call gulls "jacks of all trades, masters of none." As they do not normally deep dive, they catch their fish by waiting until the fish swim up near the surface; on a beach or tidal flat they can snare slower-moving crabs and shellfish (although compared with plovers and sandpipers, they are rank amateurs at these endeavors). In addition, gulls are not that fussy and will work the strand line, turning over fronds of seaweed and driftwood to scavenge dead fish and other goodies pushed up by the waves.

Gulls are also very adaptable, always ready to take advantage of new food sources. Thus they follow trawlers, purse seiners, and other commercial fishing boats, in search of fish that drop out of the nets or "trash fish," species with no commercial value that are dumped overboard after the catch is sorted. Gulls also frequent port areas and garbage dumps, and soon learn to accept handouts at public parks and ponds.

Another trick in the varied gull repertoire is kleptoparasitism: waiting until some other bird catches a morsel, then stealing it. Gulls are big and strong enough to bully most other birds into dropping their prize. Plovers and sandpipers are typical victims of thieving gulls.

Gulls belong to the family Laridae, which includes terns and noddies as well. About forty-five species of gull, all in the genus *Larus*, are found worldwide. Several species winter in the Tokyo area and can be observed at park ponds, lakes, rivers, garbage dumps, harbors, and tidal flats.

One of Tokyo's most common gulls is the small **black-headed gull** (*yuri* *kamome*). This gull is the official bird of the Tokyo municipality. During the breeding season, the entire head is solid black (actually a very deep chocolate brown), which gives this gull its common English name. In its winter plumage, only a few dark smudges remain on the side of the head. The bill, short and thin compared with that of larger gulls, is orange with a black tip. The feet are also orange. The bird's wings are light gray with black at the tip, and the tail is pure white. Immature birds have lighter, more yellowish bills and feet and show a thin black band at the edge of their tail.

Black-headed gulls are common in parks, and there is always a sizable flock fighting with the ducks for handouts at Shinobazu Pond in Ueno. They can also be observed on tidal flats at Yatsu Tidelands; Funabashi Seaside Park; and Gyōtoku Sanctuary, where they often bully curlews and dunlins into giving up their hard-earned crabs and worms.

Another common winter gull is the **black-tailed gull**, a medium-size gull with dark gray wings and a distinct horizontal black band on its tail. The Japanese name, *umi-neko*, means "sea cat," and refers to the bird's kittenlike meowing cry. The feet are light yellow. The bill is yellow with a distinctive black-and-red tip.

The black-tailed gull has a limited distribution, which centers around Japan and includes the eastern edge of the Eurasian continent, from Taiwan north to Sakhalin and the Kurile Islands. For this reason, it is also sometimes called the **Japanese gull**. Several large breeding colonies are found along the coasts of northern Honshū and Hokkaidō. In spring, most of Tokyo's black-tailed gulls migrate northwards to these breeding sites. A small number, immature and still too young to breed, remain over the summer months.

Herring gulls (*seguro kamome*) are familiar coastal birds throughout the northern hemisphere. They are slightly larger than black-tailed gulls, with pink

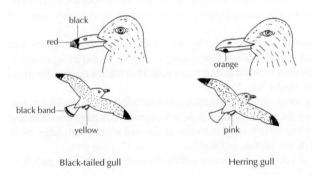

Black-tailed gull   Herring gull

feet and a yellow bill. A bright orange spot decorates the lower bill. This spot is thought to serve as a target for nestling chicks. When the chicks see the spot, they instinctively peck at it, prompting the parent to regurgitate food into the waiting chick's mouth.

Gulls take from two to five years to reach sexual maturity. They make up for this slow maturation with a long life expectancy that allows them to breed many times. Immature gulls—as big as the adults—are difficult to identify. They are almost all mottled brown and do not show the distinguishing colors and patterns of the adults. Young black-headed and herring gulls can be told apart by relative size, the latter being a bit larger.

In spring, most of the gulls disappear from the Tokyo area, heading north for their breeding zones. The **little tern** (*ko ajisashi*), sometimes mistaken for a gull, arrives to take their place. Terns winter south of Japan, then fly here in spring to breed along the shores of Tokyo Bay.

Terns, although related to gulls, are slighter in build, with longer bills and wings and deeply forked tails. While gulls usually nest on seaside cliffs, terns are primarily level-ground nesters. In Japan, the terns' traditional nesting grounds have been along river gravels. They lay their eggs in a simple scrape of sand and pebbles, relying on camouflage—the eggs look exactly like stones—to protect them from predators. Large colonies can also mount a unified defense in chasing away crows, hawks, and other natural enemies.

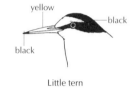

yellow

black

black

Little tern

Little tern chicks at an abandoned construction site along Tokyo Bay

Too bad for the terns! Over the past few decades, Japan has pursued a policy of straightening curves in rivers and replacing gravel and natural banks with concrete channels. Good nesting ground has thus become extremely rare. To make matters worse, the few areas remaining are often overrun with four-wheel drive vehicles during the summer breeding season.

The little tern is currently listed as an endangered species. Only a few thousand are left throughout the world, and just about all of these breed in Japan. Surprisingly, Tokyo Bay and Osaka Bay host several of the major colonies. In the postwar years, thousands of acres of landfill were created along the shores of these urban baylands. Due to the "ongoing economic downturn" many of these landfill sites have yet to be developed. The terns have thus found nesting grounds on empty construction sites, gravel parking lots, and garbage dumps.

Eventually, even these areas will be built up on, and the terns will lose their last breeding grounds. As a result, local ornithologists and environmentalists are currently experimenting with artificial roof-top breeding areas on top of warehouses and other big buildings, a technique which has worked well for similarly endangered least terns in Florida, in the south of the United States.

In addition to their breeding habitats, the terns are also experiencing problems with their feeding habitats. In contrast with their jack-of-all-trades cousins, the gulls, terns feed almost exclusively by a technique that ornithologists call plunge diving. They hover high over the water, searching with their keen eyes for fish swimming near the surface. When they spot a likely target, they fold their wings back and plummet straight down into water. Their dive is very shallow and, unlike cormorants and grebes, they don't chase after fish underwater. If they do not get their fish on the plunge, they retreat skyward and try again.

Plunge diving works well where schools of small fish swim near the surface. Along the coast, terns thus feed frequently on shallow shoals and, especially, on tidal flats, when schools of gobies and other fish come in with the flood tide. Unfortunately, almost all of Tokyo Bay's shoals and flats have been landfilled, leaving the terns few prime fishing grounds.

Look for terns fishing around the bay, along rivers, and on inland ponds and marshes, from spring through autumn. These birds also frequent the Sakurada Moat on the west side of the Imperial Palace Grounds.

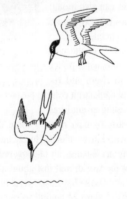

Plunge diving

WATER-FOWL

Pintail couple

In the Tokyo area, one is never very far from a marsh, lake, river, or canal. These watery habitats are prime spots for watching birds throughout the year. From spring through summer, several species of waterfowl build their nests and raise their chicks in the reed beds along the water's edge, while from autumn through winter, large flocks of ducks and swans can be seen resting on the open water.

Ducks are typical waterfowl. Male ducks are colorful, and even a beginner can soon learn to identify the different species. The females are harder to tell apart, but ducks begin pairing up in winter, so the females are often swimming together with the males.

Ornithologists divide ducks into various tribes. Most of the ducks commonly observed in the Tokyo area belong to either the dabbling duck or the diving duck tribe.

Dabbling ducks, also called **marsh ducks** or **puddle ducks**, are seen mostly on inland bodies of water, but also spend some time in coastal wetlands such as salt marshes and tidal flats. They rarely dive or swim underwater, preferring to feed at the surface or stick their neck and head down into the water, with their tails sticking straight up into the air.

A half dozen or more species of dabbling duck winter on park ponds and city canals. These include **mallards** (*ma-gamo*), **shovelers** (*hashihiro-gamo*), **teals** (*ko-gamo*), **widgeons** (*hidori-gamo*), **spot-billed ducks** (*karu-gamo*), **mandarin ducks** (*oshidori*), and **pintails** (*onaga-gamo*). In the surrounding countryside, these familiar species are joined by **gadwalls** (*okayoshi-gamo*), **falcated ducks** (*yoshi-gamo*), and even **Baikal teals** (*tomoe-gamo*).

Shovelers are the absolute masters of surface feeding. Their wide bill is equipped with comblike attachments that can be used to strain algae and plankton from the water, a feeding style much like that of the huge baleen whales. Shovelers can usually be seen swimming in tight circles with their necks forward and bills in the water. These ducks thrive on the waters of the Imperial Palace's Inner Moat, which is loaded with algae and plankton.

Pintails can easily be told apart by their long, pointed tails. Even the females' tails are longer than those of other ducks. Pintails are often the most common bird on winter ponds, especially if free handouts are available. Teals are Tokyo's smallest species—small enough to be identified in silhouette by size alone. Widgeons are comfortable in both fresh and salt water, and feed heavily on floating marine algae. They also munch on *nori* (laver), a marine algae which is farmed in the bay, making them unpopular with the local fisherman.

Dabblers take off from the surface of the pond in a single powerful burst, often rising at a steep angle. Once settled into level flight, they beat their long, pointed wings at a relatively slow pace. These ducks often come up on land to feed or rest. They "duck walk" competently, but with a comical waddle. Many species readily adjust to artificial feeding, taking bread right from people's hands. Watching these interactions at a local pond, one sees how wild ducks must have first been domesticated. In fact, the mallard, thought to be the progenitor of our common barnyard duck, still occasionally mates with pet ducks that have been discarded at lakes and ponds. Their mixed offspring, called *ai-gamo* in Japanese, show irregular mottled patterns of white and color. The spot-billed duck also occasionally interbreeds with domesticated ducks, and with mallards as well.

Diving ducks are more completely adapted to an aquatic lifestyle. They tend to be a bit smaller than the dabblers (except for the tiny teals). They have thicker, heavier bodies, and ride lower in the water. Their wings are shorter, and they fly with faster wingbeats. When taking off, they must first run across the water for a distance, gaining speed and momentum before lifting off at a low angle, much like a heavily loaded cargo plane on a long runway.

Dabbling ducks are better flyers than the divers and are far more at home on dry land. The diver tribe, however, wins out easily in any swimming contest. Their legs are short and positioned well back towards the tail, awkward for walking but ideal for propulsion in the water. Wide feet serve as perfect paddles.

Divers may occasionally feed at the surface, but get the bulk of their food by diving underwater. These ducks feed mostly at night, feeling their way along the bottom while searching for shoots of aquatic plants, as well as clams, crabs, worms, or other small animals.

In the Tokyo area, the **tufted duck** (*kinku hajiro*) and the **pochard** (*hoshi hajiro*) are frequently seen during the day on ponds, lakes, canals, and even the Imperial Palace Moat. They compete bravely with the dabblers for free handouts, but are often bullied by the much larger pintails and spot-billed ducks. **Greater scaups** (*suzu-gamo*) are also common divers, although they spend most of their time out on the Tokyo Bay shallows, where they feed on short-necked clams (*asari*) and other shellfish. The Japanese name *suzu-gamo* means "bell duck," and refers to their soft, sweet, tinkling cry. During the day, greater scaups can be seen resting in great rafts of thousands or even tens of thousands.

The male pochard can be easily identified by its reddish-brown head and neck, black breast, and light gray body. Male tufted ducks stand out with their black back, white belly, yellow eyes, and long crest, which hangs down the back of the neck. Greater scaups can be distinguished from the tufted ducks by the lack of a crown, a greenish sheen on their head and neck, and a grayish rather than black back.

Female spot-billed duck with brood crossing path at Shinobazu Pond

Both dabbling and diving ducks can be seen in almost any park or garden with a fair-size lake. Almost all of the species arrive in autumn and stay until April or May, when they leave to breed on lakes and tundra marshlands from Hokkaidō north through Siberia. The spot-billed duck and the mandarin duck are the only resident duck species that can be seen regularly throughout the year, although some injured mallards and pintails may be unable to fly north to their breeding grounds. A mother spot-billed duck leading her brood of up to ten or eleven ducklings is a familiar sight around ponds that are fringed with reed beds. Every June, television news programs feature duck families that have captured the hearts of local residents.

Spot-billed ducks nest in reed beds, while mandarin ducks are unique in that they nest in holes in old trees. Suitable nesting sites are now hard to find in the Tokyo area. Most of the mandarins that winter here thus migrate further northwards in spring. Inokashira Park provides artificial nesting boxes and is attempting to restore local breeding populations.

The **coot** and **gallinule** (or **moorhen**) are often seen swimming with ducks, but belong in the rail family. They are common throughout the year in reeds around the edge of a pond. The coot is black with a white forehead, while the gallinule is smaller and brownish, with some red on its bill and forehead. Coots

Coot

Comparison of coot and gallinule: coot (top) is black with white bill and forehead. Gallinule has red on forehead and base of bill and yellow on tip of bill.

often swim out into the open water. Gallinules tend to stay in the reeds and frequently come up on shore.

Little grebe

Another very familiar local waterbird is the **little grebe**, a year-round resident on lakes, ponds, and the Imperial Palace Moats. This smallest of the grebes is a proficient diver, chasing after small fish in the same manner as the cormorants. They build floating nests in the reeds and, in late spring and early summer, the female can be seen with one or two tiny chicks riding on her back.

Swans, with their long, graceful necks and magnificent white plumage, are as fascinating to poets, artists, and musicians as they are to ornithologists and bird-watching enthusiasts. These big birds glide effortlessly through the water, almost as if propelled by some magical force.

Japan is a winter home to two species of swan: the **whooper swan** (*ō hakuchō*), with wingspan well over two meters, and the slightly smaller **whistling swan** (*ko hakuchō*). A third species, the **mute swan** (*kobu hakuchō*), is an introduced species found throughout the year on the inner moat and many park lakes.

Whistling swans breed in the tundra regions along the northern edge of the Eurasian continent. They then migrate south in small groups, arriving at Lake Kutcharo and Lake Utonaito, in Hokkaidō, in early autumn. As winter approaches, they gradually work their way southward, stopping at lakes and river mouths in the Tōhoku region. Young swans stay with their parents during the first winter.

Whooper swans breed over a much larger area of northern China, Mongolia, and Siberia. Both whooper and whistling swans have yellow-and-black bills. In the whooper, the yellow part extends forward to a point beyond the nostril, while in the whistling swan, the yellow part ends further back, behind the nostril. The patterns of yellow seen on the whistling swan's bill show a great deal of individual variation. Local observers use these patterns to distinguish individual birds.

Mute swan

Swans appear to be the ultimate waterfowl when, in fact, their feathers must be constantly preened with oil to remain waterproof. The big birds can be seen regularly lifting their wings slightly and poking their bills into the rump feathers at the base of the tail. A special "preen gland" is located here. The bill is used to spread oil secreted from this gland onto the feathers. The oil is thought to keep the feathers flexible and waterproof, and also to prevent growth of harmful bacteria and fungi.

Takeoff for a bird as large and heavy as a swan is no easy matter. The birds usually run across the surface of the water, heading into the wind, until enough speed is gained to allow lift-off. They also usually land into the wind, using wind resistance as a means of braking and adjusting speed.

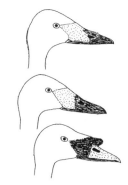

Comparison of swan beaks: on whooper swan (top), yellow patch behind bill extends a little past nostril, while on whistling swan (center) it stops before nostril. Mute swan (bottom) has black at base of bill and orange towards tip.

Because of their difficulties with takeoff and low-level flight, swans tend to stay settled in a favorable pond or lake. Here they feed by dunking their long neck down to reach soft buds and roots of water grasses. In slightly deeper water, they may stick their tail straight up in the air, stretching their neck down as far as possible. However, they never dive underwater in pursuit of food and are thus usually found in relatively shallow ponds or along the edges of deeper lakes and marshes.

Swans are often accompanied by widgeons, pintails, gallinules, and other smaller nondiving waterfowl. These birds stay close to the swans and take advantage of its feeding habits. As the swan pulls roots and stems from the bottom, pieces of plant matter are uprooted and float to the surface, providing a free meal for the smaller birds.

The number of swans wintering in Japan has been increasing steadily over the past decade. Current estimates place the number at about twenty to thirty thousand for each species. One reason for this increase is that local farmers and bird enthusiasts often provide the swans with leftover grain and other food. The swan wintering range also appears to be gradually extending southward. Both species can now be seen in the countryside, on the very outskirts of Tokyo. In addition, both species can be observed and compared closely at the Aquatic Zoo at Inokashira Park, where injured birds are cared for.

Silhouettes of common winter
shorebirds: black-bellied
plover (left), curlew (center),
Kentish plover (top right) and
dunlin (bottom right)

Shorebirds are long-legged birds that forage for small animals in shallow wetland habitats. Although some visit rice paddies and riversides, most of the Tokyo-area birds can be seen on tidal flats around the bay. Two families, the **plovers** (*chidori*) and **sandpipers** (*shigi*), account for the majority of species. Deciding whether a shorebird is a sandpiper or plover is the first step in identification. Fortunately, observation of the body shape and feeding behaviors is usually sufficient to tell them apart.

Plovers are small- to medium-size birds with big heads; short necks; short, thick bills; and large eyes. They hunt primarily by sight and can often be seen scurrying across a tidal flat, stopping regularly to scan for prey. When an unwary crab or lugworm is sighted, the plover strikes down with a lightning lunge, attempting to snare the prey before it has a chance to flee down its burrow hole.

Sandpipers are more varied than plovers, ranging in size from tiny stints to huge curlews. The diversity of their bill shapes is one of the wonders of evolution. Some species have almost ridiculously long bills, that may be either perfectly straight, turned slightly up at the tip, or bowed into a graceful downward curve.

In contrast to plovers, sandpipers tend to hunt more by feel than sight. They poke their bills into the mud to feel for worms or directly into the holes of burrowing crabs and shrimp. Special tactile cells near the tip of the bill allow them to feel their prey without seeing it, and the flexible bills are able to open even when shoved deep into the mud.

Sandpiper probing for mud crab

Curlew

During winter, the species are few and easy to separate. **Curlews** (*daishaku shigi*; see also Tidal Flats, Crabs) and **dunlins** (*hama shigi*) are common winter sandpipers on Tokyo Bay. The curlews walk deliberately across the flat, poking their long, down-curved bill into the holes of the larger mud crabs. The dunlins, on the other hand, are busy feeders, rapidly driving their bills in and out of the mud like miniature sewing machines. In fact, ornithologists call this kind of feeding "stitching."

Dunlins feed in large flocks. When disturbed, the entire flock takes flight as one, twisting and turning together on a dime, and alternately showing their brown backs and "flashing" their white stomachs. A flock flying like this seems to be a single well-tuned organism and makes you wonder if the birds are capable of telegraphing their moves in some unique way. According to scientists, the birds are simply reacting at super-fast speeds. One bird begins the turn, and then the others follow the cue. This happens so fast, however, that to the naked eye it appears simultaneous.

Black-bellied plovers (*daizen*) and **Kentish plovers** (*shiro chidori*), also called **snowy plovers**, can also be sighted on winter tidal flats. A really lucky birder might catch sight of a rare **oystercatcher** (*miyako-dori*). These impressive black-and-white shorebirds—which are neither plovers nor sandpipers, but constitute a family of their own—have a thick orange bill. They feed heavily on oysters and clams.

Black-bellied plover in winter plumage

Black-bellied plover in summer plumage

In spring the numbers of species picks up dramatically. Spring migrants begin arriving in April, and by early May the local shorebird fans are in birdwatcher heaven. In a few hours, even a beginner can expect to see at least a half-dozen species of sandpiper. In addition to the winter visitors, a typical list of sightings might include the **terek sandpiper** (*sorihashi shigi*), **ruddy turnstone** (*kyōjo shigi*), **gray-tailed tattler** (*kiashi shigi*), **greenshank** (*aoashi shigi*), **black-tailed godwit** (*oguro shigi*), **bar-tailed godwit** (*ō-sorihashi shigi*), **whimbrel** (*chūshaku shigi*), and **rufous-necked stint** (*tōnen*). These transients are eager to get to their breeding grounds and thus only stay for a few weeks. Most stop by again in the fall, usually beginning around late August. The autumn transients are on a more leisurely schedule. Some stay around almost to early winter.

Summer is a slow season for tidal-flat birders. The sandpipers disappear and only a few species of small plover remain to breed. Kentish plovers are joined by **little ringed plovers** (*ko chidori*) and **Mongolian plovers** (*medai chidori*). These plovers utilize the same type of on-the-ground breeding habitat as the little terns. A typical Tokyo Bay colony may have terns and several species of plover breeding together. Needless to say, plovers currently face the same housing shortage problem as terns.

Summer plumage of three small plovers: Mongolian plover (left), Kentish plover (center), little ringed plover (right)

Little ringed plover in May rice paddy

Egg clutch of little ringed plover on unused construction site along Tokyo Bay

The rice paddies in late April and early May are also good places to spot shorebirds. When the farmers fill the paddies with water, usually during the Golden Week holiday in early May, a shallow wetland full of snails, frogs, insects, and small fish springs up overnight. The **golden plover** (*munaguro*), whimbrel, ruddy turnstone and little ringed plover seem to have access to a planting schedule. They usually time their migration so as to arrive just in time to enjoy the rice-paddy feast. The **common snipe** (*ta shigi*), a humorous sandpiper with a short neck and relatively short legs but a long straight

May rice paddy shorebirds: ruddy turnstone (upper left), common snipe (center left), whimbrel (upper right), little ringed plover (center right), and golden plover (bottom). With the exception of the snipe, all these species are common on the tidal flats as well.

bill, can also be seen hunting around the edge of the paddies. **Lapwings** (*ta geri*), large plovers with iridescent plumage and a long, upturned crest, are seen in the paddies throughout the winter months.

Visitors to Gyōtoko Santuary and Yatsu Tidelands can enjoy **black-winged stilts** (*seitaka shigi*) all year round. These tall, skinny black-and-white shore-birds, with medium-length straight black bills and incredibly long pink legs, nest in the reed marshes. Every so often, an **avocet** (*sorihashi seitaka shigi*) wanders into Yatsu Tidelands, and photographers flock in from all over the country. Advocets look a lit-tle like the stilts, but have sharply upcurved rather than straight bills.

Black-winged stilt

WADERS

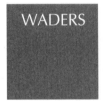

Little egret

L ong-legged, long-necked wading birds are fixtures in the Japanese rice paddy countryside. The paddies and irrigation ditches are chock full of the delica-cies that these birds favor: frogs, crabs, insects, snails, and small fish. The most common waders are white egrets, called *shira-sagi* in Japanese. Although many people lump all these birds together, there are actually several distinct species.

The **little egret** (*ko sagi*) is the most common species and is a year-round resident in the Tokyo area. This wader frequents rice paddies and irrigation canals. In flight, it can be easily identified by its black legs and bright yellow feet. During the breeding sea-son, several long plumes droop from behind its head.

Another common resident white wader is the **great egret** (*dai sagi*), which is noticeably larger than the little egret, with a longer, more gracefully curved neck. The great egret does not usually hunt in paddies or

Great egret patiently wait-ing to nab a fish

canals, preferring to try for fish in slightly deeper water around the edge of ponds, lakes, and marshes. These birds can also be seen on tidal flats, fishing for gobies, mullet, and other prey that come in on the rising tide.

The little egret often dances through the water, stirring the mud with its feet and flushing small crabs and frogs out into the open, while the great egret is a more patient hunter, usually standing stock-still in the water, with its neck extended and head turned slightly to one side. When an unwary fish passes too close, the neck snaps out with amazing speed, scissoring or sometimes even spearing the fish with the long bill. The egret then maneuvers the catch around and swallows it whole, always head first so that the sharp fin spines do not catch in the throat. The great egret's bill is yellow in winter and black in summer.

As if little and great egrets are not enough to confuse beginner birders, there is also an **intermediate egret** (*chū sagi*). Most of these are summer breeders. The bill is similar in color but noticeably shorter than that of the great.

A final local white egret is the **cattle egret** (*ama sagi*). These are summer breeders that arrive here in late April, just as the rice paddies are being transplanted. They follow the tractors across the field, snapping up insects and other delicacies turned up by the machine's blades. When they first arrive, the cattle egrets are still in winter plumage, pure white with only a hint of orange-brown on their heads. In only a few weeks, they develop their breeding plumage, a magnificent mane of orange feathers on their head and neck.

Gray heron

In addition to the whites, there are several dark-colored herons and bitterns. The **Chinese little bittern** (*yoshi-goi*) and the **green-backed heron** (*sasa-goi*) are shy summer breeders that stay hidden in dense reeds. The immense **gray heron** (*ao sagi*), on the other hand, is a year-round resident frequently seen around the edge of lakes and marshes, especially in late afternoon. In fact, at some ponds and marshes, it almost seems as if the great egret and gray heron are working the midday and late afternoon shifts of the same job! As big as or bigger than the great egret, this huge grayish bird, with yellow bill and black crest feathers, is unmistakable.

The **black-crowned night heron** (*goi sagi*) is a nocturnal hunter. Mature birds are gray with a

Black-crowned night heron

dark grayish-blue head and back, long white plumes on the head in summer, and almost scary red eyes. Immature birds are a mottled brown, with yellow eyes.

The night heron lacks the long neck of the other waders and has a shorter, thicker bill. These birds are powerful hunters and will eat not only fish and frogs but small mammals and snakes as well. They have a special fondness for huge bullfrogs and can be counted on to visit holding ponds (*tame-ike*) from late evening onward. Their cry is a mysterious caw, which has earned them their nickname *yo-garasu* (literally, "night crow").

There is a man that hangs out at Shinobazu Pond who has trained some of the night herons. Every afternoon around four-thirty or so he brings pieces of bread, which he feeds to the fish. The herons have learned to perch alongside the man, snapping up the fish that come to get his bread. In some parts of Japan, herons have been observed using pieces of feather or paper as "lures" to attract fish within snapping distance.

The big egrets and herons are a great joy to watch. They fly with slow but deep, powerful wing beats, their necks pulled back in a graceful S curve. Takeoff is accomplished by crouching and jumping to gain a little height, then flapping away, picking up speed gradually rather than rocketing off like a duck. Landing in a strong wind is a superb performance: beating their wings against the wind until reaching a midair standstill, then dropping to the ground.

Unfortunately, long-legged waders are declining in the Tokyo area and throughout Japan as well. The consolidation of small rice paddies into larger ones, and the concreting over of dirt irrigation canals has robbed the birds of their traditional countryside feeding habitats, while the filling in of tidal flats and salt marshes has taken away their coastal grounds. In addition, as with the cormorants, the egrets and herons are currently experiencing a severe housing pinch.

Egrets and herons build their nests in trees and usually nest together in large colonies called *sagi-yama,* or "egret mountains." Often several species will be mixed together, with hundreds of nests in a grove of tall trees. From late spring through summer, these colonial nesting sites are noisy and smelly, and local residents often complain to the town office, which then drives the birds away. Good nesting sites are becoming rarer and rarer, and one fears that all these egrets and herons will soon go the way of the **Japanese crested ibis** and **Oriental White Stork**, other waders that depended heavily on the countryside landscape, and have declined to the very brink of extinction.

COUNTRY BIRDS

Grasshopper hung out on barbed wire by shrike

...ith numerous woodland and aquatic habitats, is home to a ...bird species. To introduce them all here would be impossi-...deserve special notice.

The **Ural owl** (*fukurō*), a large bird without ear tufts, was once a common resident in the Tokyo area but is becoming rarer and rarer. One problem the owl faces is loss of prey. Another is the shortage of suitable nesting holes. These owls like to nest in holes in huge old trees, yet such trees are now quite scarce. In the rice paddy countryside, the owls can usually find nesting sites only in protected groves behind temples, shrines, and farmhouses. Nocturnal hunters, the owls feed mainly on mice and other small mammals. Their

Ural owl

hoot, which sounds like *goroske-hoh-hoh* to the Japanese ear, is heard in winter and early spring. The flight silhouette, with rounded head, wide body, and relatively short, thick wings, is unmistakable.

The **brown hawk-owl** (*aoba-zuku*), a much smaller species with a chocolate head and stunning yellow eyes, is a summer breeder here. This owl is famous for feeding on large rhinoceros, stag, and longhorn beetles. The owls deftly pluck the soft abdomen out of the beetle's hard armor, leaving the remaining carcasses scattered on the ground as evidence of their handiwork (crows also seem to feed in this fashion).

The **Japanese pygmy woodpecker** (*ko-gera*), just the size of a sparrow, is the only woodpecker common in the rice paddy countryside. Like the Ural owl, these birds are most frequently seen around Shinto shrines and old farmsteads. They peck out their nest hole in partially rotted branches. The female has a rounded head, while the male's head is more pointed, with a very tiny reddish dot near the tip. The **great spotted woodpecker** (*aka-gera*)

Japanese pygmy woodpecker, often seen running vertically up trunk of tree and **Japanese green woodpecker** (*ao-gera*), both nearly twice as large as the pygmy, are occasionally encountered in the hills and low mountains to the west of the city.

The **skylark** (*hibari*) thrives in open countryside, such as dry upland vegetable fields and rice paddies in wide, flat areas. Recently, they can also be seen in great number on large empty lots near residential developments. Skylarks nest on the ground. From early spring through summer, the males engage in spectacular display flights, flying higher and higher while singing their unique song, which Japanese

Skylark superbly camouflaged when sitting still in brownish fields

observers describe as *pichuloo-pichuloo-bilibili*. A sharp crest on the back of the head and white bands on the outside edge of the tail are good field marks.

The **gray-faced buzzard-eagle** (*sashiba*) is the most common bird of prey that nests in the Tokyo area. This medium-size raptor, a little smaller than a jungle crow, arrives here in early spring and builds its nest in tall conifers, usually overlooking a narrow valley filled with rice paddies. Its diet includes a lot of frogs, snakes, and other typical rice-paddy delicacies. Two or three crows mobbing a buzzard-eagle is a common sight in the spring countryside. These birds nest in similar habitats, and the crows presumably don't want the raptors getting too close. **Goshawks** (*ō-taka*) also nest in the Tokyo area, but are far rarer. In

Gray-faced buzzard eagle

fact, goshawks are listed as an endangered species, and a nesting pair is usually enough to stop or change small development projects. Goshawks feed primarily on small birds. The **marsh harrier** (*chūhi*), **peregrine falcon** (*hayabusa*), and **kestrel** (*chōgenbō*) are common during the winter months. Harriers are often seen hunting around reed beds and along the coast. They glide low, with their wings held up in a V shape. Kestrels also hunt in marshes, tending to search for prey by hovering rather than gliding.

The medium-size **bull-headed shrike** (*mozu*), a little smaller than the brown-eared bulbul, is actually a fierce bird of prey. Although seasonal movements are poorly known, it appears that the shrikes breed in Tokyo in early spring, then leave for the mountains during the hot summer months, returning in early autumn. From autumn through winter, each bird maintains its own feeding territory, often at the edge of a woodland or coppice that overlooks a rice paddy.

The shrike loudly scolds all intruders, including people. In autumn, it also engages in a unique practice, which the Japanese call *hayanie*, of impaling small animals on thorns or barbed wire. These include frogs, lizards, fish, small birds, and various insects. Grasshoppers seem to be a special favorite. One theory is that the shrike is storing away the catch as winter food, while another holds that the impaled animals serve basically as territorial markers. Japanese folk wisdom relates that the severity of the coming

Bull-headed shrike

winter can be foretold by the height of the shrike's victims: the higher the *hayanie*, the deeper the snow will be. Look for shrikes perched on poles among open rice paddies, and staked victims on barbwire fences and along the edge of thickets.

Common pheasant male with detail (left) and female

The large **common pheasant** is unmistakable, especially the male with his long, trailing tail, iridescent neck and chest, and huge, bright-red flaps of bare skin, called wattles, which cover the side of his face. The male's loud, resonant two-note call is heard from late winter through spring. During these months, each male establishes and aggressively defends a breeding territory, fighting off any other male that tries to intrude. Once the mating is finished, the male leaves the job of raising the chicks entirely to his mate.

The female is all drab, with a shorter tail. Late-summer strollers in the countryside often see females hurrying across a narrow farm road, leading her brood of up to six or seven chicks.

Pheasants are omnivorous, gleaning the forest floor for fallen seeds and fruits as well as insects and other small animals. Farmers consistently report seeing the pheasants eating young snakes, too. These birds have a sometimes unsettling habit of remaining stock-still until a person approaches within a few yards, then rising suddenly with loud booming wingbeats.

Pheasants are the chief target for hunters in the Tokyo area, and local groups release artificially bred birds. The season usually runs from November 15 to February 15. Look for pheasants throughout the countryside, and in your wallet as well. The male (standing at left) and female (nesting at right) decorate the reverse side of the ten-thousand-yen note.

Unlike the citified jungle crow discussed in detail in the section on urban birds, the **carrion crow** (*hashiboso-garasu*) is more of a country boy, feeding on a wide variety of natural food available in the paddies and woodlands, including berries, nuts, insects and frogs, and other small animals. Few people realize that there are actually two separate species of crow native to the Tokyo area. The Japanese name for the carrion means "thin-billed crow," and indeed the shape of the bill is the best field mark for separating the two species. Currently, as urban sprawl invades the countryside, the carrion crow is steadily losing ground to the jungle crow. Ecologists consider the presence of large numbers of carrion crows an indication that the countryside ecosytem is still in good shape.

Young carrion crow

Carrion crow (right) and jungle crow

In a land where squirrels are rare, it is the **jay** (*kakesu*) that is primarily responsible for regenerating the local oak woodlands. These medium-size birds have a great fondness for acorns, carrying several at a time in their cheeks and burying them all over the place as winter food. Uneaten acorns germinate the following spring. A brown bird with a whitish crown and distinctive blue markings on the wings, the jays of Japan are not nearly as noisy and aggressive as their American cousins. Look for them wherever there are substantial oak groves.

Jay

REPTILES

Reptiles, having evolved from the first primitive amphibians that emerged from the water, proceeded to colonize the dry land. Like amphibians, reptiles are ectotherms, which means that they rely on external sources of energy to heat their bodies.

Early reptiles evolved a new system of reproduction and embryo development that allowed them to overcome their amphibian ancestors' reliance on watery habitats. This not only enabled the reptiles to spread out over the land, but also set the stage for later evolution of dinosaurs, birds, and mammals.

The reptile innovations included the ability to fertilize their eggs internally, inside the body of the female. (Amphibian eggs are usually fertilized externally and thus must emerge soft enough to allow the sperm to penetrate. As these soft eggs are susceptible to desiccation, they must be laid in water.) By contrast, the early reptiles' internally fertilized eggs were fitted with a tough, leathery covering before being released. These protected eggs could be laid on dry land, away from the water, without worrying about drying out. In addition, the reptile embryos, which fed on the large yolk, were able to pass through their aquatic stage inside the egg and emerge as fully formed air-breathing, land-living creatures.

Modern-day reptiles are divided into three main orders: Squamata, which contains the lizards and snakes; Chelonia, or turtles and tortoises; and Crocodilia. In Japan, Crocodilia are found only in zoos, whereas snakes, lizards and turtles are common natives. Tokyo is home to a half-dozen or so species of snake, three kinds of lizard, several native turtle, and at least two species of turtle that were originally kept as pets but have now escaped (or been turned loose by irresponsible owners) and naturalized.

HARMLESS SNAKES

Ao-daishō rat snake

Scientists believe that snakes originally developed from a group of primitive lizards that took to a burrowing lifestyle, eventually giving up their legs, external eardrums, and movable eyelids. The skin of both lizards and snakes is covered with scales, and the outermost layer is shed periodically as the animal grows.

Rat snakes are large and formidable-looking creatures, but are harmless and will not attack people without provocation. Three species are found in the Tokyo area. The largest of these, the ***ao-daishō*** (literally, "green master" or "green general") can grow up to two meters in length. *Ao-daishō* feed primarily on mice and other small mammals, and as such have traditionally been welcomed by farmers, who call them *o-nushi*, or "master." They are excellent climbers and are known to steal eggs and chicks from bird nests. The *ao-daishō* is common around farmhouses in the countryside and is the only snake found in most central city parks and gardens.

Ao-daishō that have just shed their skins are a beautiful greenish blue, but after a while their color turns brownish, with indistinct black stripes. A related species, the ***shima-hebi*** (literally, "striped snake") rat snake, has a more pointed snout, red rather than brown eyes, and four very distinct black stripes running down its back. The *shima-hebi* prefers to dine on frogs rather than mice and birds, and is usually found in and around ponds and rice paddies. Both these rat snakes are superb swimmers.

Shima-hebi rat snake

Shima-hebi in rice paddy

A third species of rat snake, the ***jimuguri***, is only rarely encountered in the countryside. The Japanese name means "digger" and refers to this snake's habit of burrowing into the forest litter to hunt for voles and shrews. The *jimuguri* is a beautiful snake, with copper-brown mottled markings on top and irregular yellow and copper-brown tile markings underneath.

Side view of *jimuguri* rat snake's head

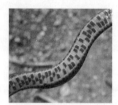

Underside of *jimuguri*

Another harmless local snake, the **hibakari**, has a distinctive slanted stripe on its cheek. The *hibakari* feeds on small tree frogs, tadpoles, and minnows in the rice paddies, but also takes earthworms and other forest-floor delicacies.

Tokyo's most secretive snake is the **shiro-madara**. These beautiful black-and-white striped snakes are nocturnal, and extremely shy. They feed almost exclusively on other reptiles, including lizards and smaller snakes. They capture their prey by constriction, wrapping their coils around the victim and slowly strangling it, just like huge pythons and boa constrictors do. Their length is up to a meter or so.

Head markings of *hibakari*

Hibakari

Shiro-madara

All of these snakes are nonpoisonous but will bite if handled in a rough or careless fashion. From frequent experience, I can assure you that the bite of a two-meter-long *ao-daishō* is nothing to laugh about.

POISON-OUS SNAKES

Mamushi pit viper

There are two species of poisonous snake in the Tokyo area, a pit viper and a back-fanged keelback, that are not only dangerous but potentially deadly. The pit viper, called ***mamushi*** in Japanese, is the most feared snake on the island of Honshū. A very close relative of the American copperhead, the *mamushi* is small, thick, and sluggish, and prefers heavily vegetated moist habitats. It is common in marshes and rice paddies. As this species is mostly nocturnal as well as shy and retiring, it is seldom seen. Biting incidents occur mainly from careless handling or when someone accidently steps on or touches a viper in hiding.

Like all pit vipers (a subfamily that also includes rattlesnakes), the *mamushi* is equipped with a heavy load of potent poison and an incredibly advanced system for delivering it. Two hollow fangs, located in the front part of the upper jaw, are connected directly to the poison sacs in the cheeks. When the mouth is closed, these fangs fold down to the rear, but when the mouth opens they stand up automatically and tilt forward. Rather than actually bite their victims, pit vipers simply stab them with these two fangs. The poison travels right through the hollow fangs and is injected directly into the prey from holes at the tip, like a medical syringe. Pit vipers are also equipped with special heat sensors that allow them to find warm-blooded prey, such as birds and mammals, in the dark. Two "pits," located between the nostrils and eyes, lead to these sensors.

Mamushi feed on frogs, and small mammals and birds. In turn, these snakes are sought by raptors, owls, and powerful night herons.

The tail of young *mamushi* is a bright yellow, a color that fades away as the snake grows. Herpetologists speculate that the young snake uses its tail as a lure to attract frogs, which mistake it for a worm. Even tiny baby *mamushi* are deadly poisonous and should not be picked up or handled.

Young *mamushi* pit viper, with pale yellow tail tip

Mamushi never attack people and will flee if given a chance. They bite only to defend themselves. Several years ago a man in Yokohama was fatally bitten while trying to force a live *mamushi* into a bottle of *shōchū* (a distilled Japanese liquor). Home concoctions such as this are popularly used to cure colds and as a general restorative or aphrodisiac.

The **yama-kagashi** keelback is a beautiful snake with striking red, black, and yellow markings. It feeds heavily on frogs and is thus found most often around water. Adults can grow to well over a meter in length. In many older guidebooks, the *yama-kagashi* is mistakenly listed as harmless, but it actually has a poison which is as lethal as the pit viper's.

Young *yama-kagashi* keelback, with broad yellow band behind the head marking the position of poison ducts

The *yama-kagashi*, however, does not have an efficient delivery system for its poison. The poison sacs open onto short fangs at the very back of the mouth. The poison cannot be injected directly under the victim's skin and instead drips down into the wound made by the fangs. A *yama-kagashi* thus has to bite deeply and hold on tenaciously for its poison to take effect.

When threatened, the *yama-kagashi* first tries desperately to escape. If cornered, it quickly switches to intimidation tactics, spreading its head out almost like a cobra. The yellow band just behind the head sticks out prominently in this pose. In fact, the yellow

Older keelback with faded yellow band

marks the spot where the snake is able to eject a separate poison from pores in the skin. This mechanism works in a fashion similar to that of the toad, whose poisonous liquid is designed to be squirted into the mouth of an attacking cat or weasel.

There is little danger of being bitten by a *yama-kagashi* while walking. Almost all of the snakebites reported to date have been the result of people handling the snake in a careless fashion. Remember, a snake in the open is never dangerous. All you have to do is give it a wide berth. Care should be taken never to walk barefooted or bare-legged through marshlands or around rice paddies. If bitten by a *mamushi* or *yama-kagashi*, stay calm and seek immediate medical attention.

Comparison of poison delivery systems of *mamushi* (left) and *yama-kagashi*

LIZARDS

Skink

Common Tokyo-area lizards include a gecko, skink, and a lightning-quick grass lizard. Geckoes are comical looking critters with short, stocky bodies and splayed fingers and toes. Numerous tiny bristles on the underside of the fingers and toes grip irregularities in the surface of a wall or tree trunk, allowing the gecko to walk on or cling tightly to vertical surfaces and even walk upside down across ceilings.

Japanese gecko

Japanese geckoes are found around farmhouses, shrines, temples, and other wooden structures. They especially like the mud wattle-and-daub walls of old farm outbuildings, which are full of neat little hiding places and rich in the insects that they prey on. Geckoes are primarily nocturnal, hiding away during the day and emerging at dusk to hunt. The Japanese name, *yamori*, means "protector of the home," and may refer to the gecko's beneficial habit of gobbling up cockroaches and other unwanted guests.

Geckoes, like many lizards, are capable of autonomy, or the spontaneous discarding of their tail when seized by a predator. The tail breaks off at one of several fracture planes, where special muscles can be used to pull apart the vertebrae and close the blood vessels to minimize blood loss. The discarded tail continues to wriggle, keeping the predator interested while the lizard scurries away.

Skinks are small lizards with shiny, wet-looking scales and thick bodies that make the legs appear short and inadequate. The **Japanese five-lined skink** (*Nihon tokage*) is dark brown. During the mating season, in April and May, the throats and chests of the males turn orange. The males also have wider heads and more powerful jaws than the females. They engage in fierce biting matches during the mating season, but these battles usually end before either of the combatants is seriously injured.

The female skink lays her eggs in a protected spot and guards them until the young hatch out. Many young skinks have a bright blue tail, which is thought to serve as a distraction to predators. The predators grasp the skink by the colorful tail, which is quickly discarded.

The **Japanese grass lizard** (*Nihon kana-hebi*) is a lighter brown than the skink, with a thinner body and a longer, whiplike tail. These little lizards are common on lawns and in abandoned fields, where they hunt for spiders, worms, and insects. They are exceptionally quick and a challenge to catch by hand. For their size, they also bite ferociously, though fortunately not very painfully.

Grass lizard, with long whiplike tail

Life is hazardous for small lizards such as the gecko, skink, and grass lizard. Hawks, owls, crows, pheasants, and other birds find the lizards delectable prey. In autumn, one often encounters lizards impaled on thorns by shrikes (see Country Birds). *Tanuki*, weasels, and many species of snake also include lizards on their varied menus.

TURTLES

Kusa-game

A **turtle**'s most distinctive characteristic is its shell, which is an amazing protective device consisting of two layers: an inner core of bony plates that are fused together and an outer layer, of interlocked shields, or scutes, created from a hornlike substance called keratin. A turtle's shell grows along with the animal and, unlike a snake or lizard's skin, it does not have to be shed periodically.

Turtles lack teeth but are able to grasp and tear food with their horny jaws, which are fitted with sharp, almost knifelike cutting edges. Turtle food preferences run from complete herbivore to devoted carnivore. Many species are omnivorous, eating whatever is available, be it animal or vegetable. Predatory turtle species often lie motionless, hoping to ambush unwary prey. When the crucial moment comes, they snap out with a surprising burst of speed.

Turtles sunning themselves on banks and logs are a common sight at Japanese parks, shrines, temples, and gardens, most of which include a small pond or lake. The most numerous turtle is an exotic species native to America, the **Mississippi red-eared slider**, called *akamimi-game* ("red-eared turtle") in Japanese. Baby sliders are cheap and popular pets, but soon grow too large to keep in little plastic boxes. The irresponsible owners then just take the turtles to the nearest park and release them in the pond. Over the years, this species has bred well in Japan and, unfortunately, has replaced the two

Kusa-game

once-common native species, the ***kusa-game*** and ***ishi-game***, in many areas.

The *kusa-game* can be identified in the field by yellowish green scribbling markings on the side of its face. These medium-size turtles, up to twenty centimeters or so in length, are frequently seen sunning themselves on rocks and logs. In inner-city parks they are often lined up alongside the sliders and are easy to distinguish.

The *ishi-game* prefers slightly faster-flowing streams than the *kusa-game*, but their range often overlaps. The last row of scutes on the rear of the *kusa-game* are smooth, while those on the *ishi-game* form a wavy pattern. Seen from above, the head of the *ishi-game* is completely smooth, while that of the *kusa-game* is covered halfway with rough scales.

At some park ponds, there are warning signs reading "Beware of the Turtles." The turtles in question here are soft-shelled turtles, called ***suppon*** in Japanese. Soft-shelled turtles lack keratin shields. Their carapace is instead covered with a layer of leathery skin. Perhaps because they lack the typical turtle's passive defense system, they are highly aggressive and can deliver a nasty snap with the sharp edges of their jaws. Their long, pointed snout makes an easily recognizable field mark.

Suppon live in lakes, ponds, and slow-flowing streams and rivers, where they spend most of the time buried in the mud, occasionally sticking up their long necks and snorkel-like nose to the surface for a breath of air. They are entirely carnivorous, lying in wait to ambush small fish, crayfish, and aquatic insects.

The meat of the *suppon* is served in many regional dishes and is also considered to be a general restorative and aphrodisiac. Traditional pharmacies sell dried and powdered *suppon*, often mixed with powdered *mamushi*. This market is so large that the *suppon* are now raised on specialty farms throughout the country.

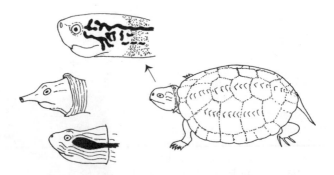

Kusa-game with extended head (top) showing distinctive markings. *Ishi-game* facial markings (not shown) are not as distinct. Soft-shelled turtle (center left) and red-eared slider (bottom left).

In the past decade or so, another species of exotic turtle appears to have escaped and begun breeding. This is the **American snapping turtle** (*kamitsuki-game*). These huge carnivores are sold as pets, but soon grow too large to keep even in the bathtub. One specimen found in the northern Chiba marshlands weighed more than ten kilograms. The big snappers feed on bullfrogs and crayfish, also imports from the American countryside.

Snapping turtle

AMPHIBIANS

Amphibians are the most ancient class of terrestrial vertebrates. Their distant ancestors, an offshoot of ocean fish, colonized the land more than three hundred million years ago and eventually diversified into dinosaurs, reptiles, birds, and mammals.

Amphibians still thrive today, but retain their ancient reliance on water for breeding. Their soft eggs lack a shell and are usually fertilized outside the female's body. Their larvae, such as the familiar frog larvae we call tadpoles, emerge from the egg as water-breathers equipped with gills, then later metamorphose into air-breathing adults with lungs. This life cycle ties them to waterside habitats.

Japan's rice paddy countryside, with abundant watery habitats, is a perfect home for amphibians. Frogs are especially numerous, with ten or so species found in the Tokyo area. In the rice paddies of late April and May, three or four species may be singing away at once, producing a marvelous symphony which the Japanese call *kaeru no gasshōdan*, or "frog chorus."

The Tokyo countryside is also home to a beautiful red-bellied newt and a small black salamander.

TREE FROGS

Japanese tree frog. Dark markings surrounding eye are distinctive.

The most common local amphibian, the **Japanese tree frog**, is also the smallest and loudest. Wide pads at the tips of their fingers and toes enable these frogs to climb up and cling to even vertical surfaces. They are often seen crouched patiently on stems and leaves, well camouflaged and waiting in ambush for an unwary spider or insect to wander by.

Japanese tree frogs are called *ama-gaeru* ("rain frogs," in Japanese) because of their tendency to call on overcast days or before rain (*kaeru* or *gaeru* means "frog"). Their song, a stubborn *gwah-gwah* sound, is heard throughout the countryside from April well into autumn. Similar-looking tree frogs of the same genus (*Hyla*) can be found in most parts of the world.

Feet of tree frog, with padded toes and minimal webbing

Tree frogs breed mainly in rice paddies, but will take advantage of almost any substantial body of standing water, including large puddles. These tiny hunters are true ninja, able to change skin color and pattern to match their background. They accomplish this with multiple layers of special pigment cells that can be contracted or expanded at will. The skin color of the Japanese species ranges from pure green to mottled gray and from dark brown to nearly black.

Tree frogs of the genus *Rhacophorus* (called *ao-gaeru*, or "green frogs," in Japanese) are sometimes mistaken for the *ama-gaeru*, but are usually a little larger. **Schlegel's green tree frog** (*Shurēgeru ao-gaeru*) is common in the rice paddy countryside. These frogs scoop out a shallow depression in the wall of the rice-paddy dikes, then lay their eggs in a white foam mass about the size of a baseball. When the eggs hatch, the tadpoles drop down into the paddy below. Schlegel's tree frogs have a pure, hard, high-pitched stac-

Schlegel's green tree frog. Head and body are solid green without markings.

cato song, usually described as *li-li-li-li-li-li-li*, with a fast beat that sounds like a flamenco dancer rapidly clapping away on hardwood castanets. Along with the *ama-gaeru* and pond frogs (see Bullfrogs and Pond Frogs), they begin breeding in early May, right after the paddies are filled with water for transplanting the rice seedlings. Only male frogs sing, and this to advertise their presence and attract mates.

Schlegel's green tree frog has a longer, more pointed nose than the *ama-gaeru*, but the best way to tell these two frogs apart is to look closely at the side of the face. The *ama-gaeru* will show an irregular line of dark markings in front of and behind the eye, while the Schlegel's has no markings at all.

Another species of green tree frog, the ***mori ao-gaeru***, is found higher up in the hills and mountains. This species is slightly larger than the Schlegel's, with orange rather than gold eyes. It lays its eggs in a foam mass on tree branches that overhang a pond, marsh, or lake. These frogs are sometimes solid green, like the Schlegel's, but may also show a black-and-gold spotted pattern.

The Japanese tree frog lays its eggs directly in the paddy, where the floating eggs often collect around the young rice seedlings. Schlegel's green tree frog lays its eggs in a depression in the side of the rice-paddy dike. These two species breed at the same time, but are able to avoid direct competition by choosing slightly different spawning habitats.

Japanese brown frog. These frogs require both paddy and coppice forest habitats, and are considered by ecologists to be an indicator of the ecological health of a countryside ecosystem.

Brown frogs are small- to medium-size amphibians with brown or reddish-brown backs and legs. Their underside is often a deep reddish color, earning them the name *aka-gaeru*, or "red frog," in Japanese. Ten or so species are found in various regions and habitats throughout Japan, but only two are common in the Tokyo hills and rice paddy countryside.

The most familiar species is the **Japanese brown frog** (*Nihon aka-gaeru*). These frogs are early-bird breeders, usually beginning in late February. Their eggs are laid in round, gelatinous masses, preferable in paddy fields but also in ponds and stagnant ditches. Their call is soft and the breeding season is short, so few people actually hear them.

In late spring, brown frogs leave the paddies and spend much of their time hunting on the floor of the nearby coppice forests. They are exceptionally quick and, when surprised, flee away with a series of long, rapid jumps. In the past, these frogs were captured and eaten by villagers: in times when food was scarce, such as the hard years during and immediately after the war, they were a vital source of protein in the local diet.

The **Montane brown frog** (*yama aka-gaeru*) prefers steeper and more heavily forested terrain. When viewed from above, the lowland Japanese brown frog will show two straight ridge lines running down its back, while the Montane will show ridge lines that angle first inward then outward again.

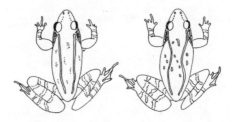

Japanese brown frog (left) and Montane brown frog

BULL-FROGS AND POND FROGS

Bullfrog

Bullfrogs (*ushi-gaeru*) are not native to Japan, but were brought here from the United States in the 1920s. The original idea was for financially strapped farmers to earn extra income by raising the bullfrogs for the export frog-legs market. This scheme actually worked for a few decades, but the bullfrogs, being great jumpers and runners, occasionally escaped from their tanks. Today they are naturalized in the countryside and even in many city parks, where their deep soulful mourn, such beautiful music to the ears of an American country boy, is often dismissed by local residents as "noise pollution"!

Legs of American bull-frog showing powerful muscles and wide webbed feet

Bullfrogs prefer substantial ponds over rivers or irrigation ditches. They are superb swimmers and rarely venture more than a long jump from the water. Voracious predators, bullfrogs will eat not only insects but fish, smaller frogs, and even chicks of grebes and other waterfowl. Their favorite prey is the American crayfish, which was brought here as food for the captive frogs. (Like the latter, the crayfish also managed to escape!) On the other side of the food chain, a big, juicy bullfrog well over ten centimeters from nose to tail, and weighing more than half a kilogram, makes a sumptuous meal for a hungry weasel, and one is sure to find black-crowned night herons hunting around the edge of a bullfrog pond.

The **Tokyo daruma pond frog** (*Tōkyō daruma-gaeru*) is a beautiful species found chiefly in irrigation canals and ditches. In deeper ponds, these smaller frogs have often been displaced by the immense bullfrog. They never venture far from the water and, when disturbed, will plunge in and hide among the aquatic vegetation. Color ranges from brownish to green, with darker splotches and one to three yellowish green stripes on their back. Pond frogs are prominent members of the May "frog chorus." Their song is softer than that of Schlegel's tree frogs, almost reminding one of Woody Woodpecker's hysterical laugh.

Tokyo daruma pond frog. These frogs are dependent on irrigation-canal habitats and are wiped out when the traditional dirt canals are turned into concrete channels.

JAPANESE TOAD

Japanese toad

Toads are the buffoons of the animal world: fat, slow, and clumsy, with sad eyes and great warts all over their massive backs. The **Japanese toad** (*azuma hiki-gaeru*) grows as big as the bullfrog, and can be found throughout the countryside and even in most central city parks, including Hibiya Park.

Toads awake from their winter hibernation in late March and head straight for the nearest pond, rice paddy, or irrigation canal. Their loud and boisterous mating behavior is called "scramble competition," by zoologists, and *kaeru-gassen* ("frog free-for-all") by the Japanese villagers. A male grasps a female and hangs on for dear life, while rivals attempt to displace him with a repertoire of pushes, kicks, and throws that would be the envy of a professional wrestler.

Hundreds of toads gather at prime mating spots, and individual bouts go on for days at a time before a powerful male eventually wins out. The males are equipped with special "nuptial pads," patches of tough black calluses on the surface of their fingers, which help them hang on to their chosen mate. The eggs are laid in a long string of clear jelly, which protects them from desiccation. A single string may be several meters long when stretched out and contain thousands of eggs.

Japanese toads mating

Once the mating festival is over, the toads mellow out and move away from the water, spending most of their time lazily foraging on the forest floor, or around farmhouses and shrines. They eat spiders, worms, pillbugs, and other small terrestrial critters. Unlike most frogs, which spring on their prey, the toads have adopted a laid-back approach. The toad sits still in ambush, waiting for a promising customer to wander by. When the prey is still ten centimeters away, the toad zaps it with a long, sticky tongue. This move is so fast, it appears as a blur. In a fraction of a second,

Egg mass of Japanese toad. Many species of frog breed in the rice paddies, but minimize competition by spawning at different times, sort of like a nature time-sharing policy. Brown frogs breed in late February, toads in late March, and tree frogs in late April to May.

the victim has disappeared inside the toad's ample mouth. On summer evenings, toads can be found underneath street lamps, gleefully zapping fallen moths and beetles.

The slow and clumsy toads seem like easy targets for predators. Their protective coloration, however, helps them to hide on the forest floor. When pressed to the limit, they fall back on a truly nasty secret weapon. Behind the toad's eyes run high ridges pocked with little holes. These holes are actually special glands that can excrete a milky liquid poison, called a batrachotoxin. This poison, squirted into the mouth of a predator, has been reported to paralyze and even kill small animals such as weasels, cats, and dogs. On the other hand, a medicinal salve, called *gama no abura*, is made from the toad's skin excretions. This salve was traditionally used to treat sword cuts and various everyday ailments and is still made and sold at the foot of Mount Tsukuba in Ibaraki Prefecture.

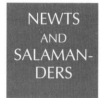

NEWTS
AND
SALAMAN-
DERS

Newt

Newts and **salamanders** are often mistaken for small, slow-moving lizards. Lizards are reptiles, while newts and salamanders are amphibians with tails. The adults may be discovered hunting insects and worms on the forest floor, but the eggs and larvae are always found in water.

The **Japanese fire-bellied newt**, a popular pet throughout the world, is native to the hills and mountains surrounding Tokyo. This amphibian was also once a fixture in the lowland rice paddy countryside as well, but has been driven to near extinction by loss of habitat. Today, it survives in isolated pockets, mostly around old holding ponds that have been protected as shrines to the local water gods.

Newts are called *imori* or *aka-hara* ("red belly") in Japanese. Their bright belly, which shows individual variation ranging from deep red to yellowish orange, is actually a warning signal to predators. Like the toad, the newt is able to excrete noxious and foul-tasting chemicals through the skin. Birds, snakes, frogs, and weasels soon learn to leave the newts alone.

Male newts have shorter, broader tails than the females. During the midspring mating season, the male's tail takes on its nuptial colors, a soft purple haze laid over the dark brown. The newts practice a truly bizarre mating ritual. First a male swims in front of his potential mate, blocking her forward progress. Next he flexes his tail back and forth, showing off his beautiful purple color and at the same time releasing mating pheromones. The male then swims away from the female who, if properly impressed, follows after him. When all goes well, the male deposits his sperm in a small bag on the bottom of the stream or pond. The female then picks up the bag with her egg-laying organ, and uses the sperm to fertilize her eggs.

A dozen or more species of **salamander** in the genus *Hynobius* are found throughout Japan. These species live in different regions and habitats but are very difficult to tell apart. In Tokyo and the surrounding countryside, only one species, the ***Tōkyō sanshō-uo*** is commonly encountered. Outside the breeding season, the adults live a solitary and mostly secretive life hunting for worms, spiders, and pillbugs on the forest floor. Nocturnal animals, they spend the days hiding away in burrows or deep in the moist leaf litter and are thus rarely encountered.

In late February, *Tōkyō sanshō-uo* assemble in rice paddies and shallow ponds for mating. Usually several males surround a female and compete to spread their sperm over her eggs as they emerge. The eggs emerge together with a special chemical substance. Once the eggs have been fertilized, this substance expands and solidifies into a jellylike mass that protects the eggs. Whereas frog tadpoles feed heavily on algae, the young of newts and salamanders are predators right from the start, feeding on water fleas and other tiny aquatic animals.

Salamander

Salamander eggs attached to a fallen leaf on stream bottom

INSECTS

Living in or visiting Japan is a great opportunity to become acquainted with the insect world. The city parks and countryside are home to various bugs, dragonflies, butterflies, grasshoppers, hornets, paper wasps, plus a half-dozen species of cicada, and enormous stag and rhinoceros beetles.

The Japanese rank among the world's greatest insect fans. Poets celebrate the songs of crickets and katydids, and bookstores and libraries are packed with excellent books on local insect ecology. Most of these books are aimed at children, but many contain superbly illustrated texts describing how insects walk, fly, feed, and mate. The insect stories of the great nineteenth-century French entomologist J. Henri Fabre are perhaps even more popular in Japan than in his homeland.

The Japanese even have a special word, *konchū shōnen* (literally, "insect boy"), to describe children who love insects. The late Osamu Tezuka (1928–89), Japan's premier comic book and animation artist, was in his youth a typical *konchū shōnen* and readily attributed much of his superb imagination and creativity to the magic of beetles and other insects. Many other leading Japanese artists and photographers have derived their inspiration from local insects.

Insects are usually classified in the class Insecta, within the phylum Arthropoda. This phylum also includes crustaceans, such as crabs and shrimp; arachnids, such as spiders and mites; and scorpions, centipedes, and millipedes.

In terms of sheer number of species, the insects are, far and away, the most successful group of living creatures in the world today. In fact, well over one-half of the 1.5 million or so species of plants and animals currently known to science are insects. In most parts of the world, the number of species in just one order of insects, the Coeloptera or beetles, outnumbers all the local plant species put together!

The basic insect biodesign is a body divided into three sections: head, thorax, and abdomen, with three pairs of jointed legs attached to the underside of the thorax. The head contains the mouth and jaws, and the sensory apparatus, which includes palps for tasting, joined antennae for touching, and well-developed eyes. Most species have two large compound eyes that produce clear, multiple images of what they see, and a number of small simple eyes, which do not form a clear image but are sensitive to light, shadow, and movement. The abdomen contains the directive and reproductive systems.

Basic body plan of an insect, viewed from above with its wings folded over on its back. This is a ground beetle, the favorite of cartoonist Osamu Tezuka. His pen name "Osamu" comes from *osa mushi*, the Japanese name for ground beetles.

Most insects also have at least one (but usually two) pair of wings attached to the upper side of the thorax. The outside of the insect body consists of a hard exoskeleton, which surrounds and protects the soft, inner parts. Their muscles, surprisingly powerful for such small creatures, are attached to the inside surface of the exoskeleton.

The exoskeleton is secreted by special glands in the skin. Once dried, it is not able to expand. As the insect outgrows its exoskeleton, the old shell is periodically shed and a new one secreted. This process is known as molting. Most insects molt about five or six times, passing through a different larval stage with each molt. The final molt, during which they reach the sexually mature adult stage, is called a metamorphosis. Once an insect metamorphoses, it stops molting and growing.

Entomologists divide insects into two major groups: those with incomplete metamorphosis and those with complete. In the first group—which includes bugs, cicadas, dragonflies, grasshoppers, katydids, crickets, and mantises—each successive larval stage looks more and more like the adult. In the second group—which includes beetles, flies, ants, bees, wasps, butterflies, and moths—the larva do not look anything at all like the adult (think of a caterpillar and a butterfly). The final-stage larva usually makes some kind of a cocoon in which to perform the last molt, emerging as a fully formed adult.

To properly appreciate insects, you need two basic tools, a net and a loupe. Fortunately, both of these can be bought just about anywhere. From spring through autumn, simple nets with bamboo handles are available for a nominal price at supermarkets, toy shops, and even many convenience stores throughout Japan. A three-and-a-half power loupe can be found at any stationery store for as little as three or four hundred yen.

To study all, or even most, of the insects in an area would be a formidable task. The best approach is to become familiar with the different orders (the taxonomic category one level above family) and to learn to identify a few of the most common or interesting local species in each group.

 BUGS

Akasuji-kin kame-mushi,
one of the most colorful
shield bugs

The term "bug" is often used to describe all insects, or any small creepy crawler, especially when the reference is derogatory. Entomologically speaking, **bug** refers specifically to insects in the order Hemiptera. Their chief characteristic is a long, piercing mouthpiece that can be thrust into a plant or animal. The mouthpiece is hollow and is used to suck out the fluids in a strawlike fashion. Fossilized insects clearly identifiable as bugs have been found in strata dating to the Carboniferous period, nearly three hundred million years ago.

Bugs come in a wide variety of forms, from tiny aphids to huge predatory toe-biters. One of our most common local species, and a real beauty at that, is the **shield bug** (*akasuji-kin kame-mushi*), with magnificent gold, red, and green markings. The name in Japanese means literally "red-lined gold bug" (*kame-mushi* is the generic term for "bug").

Shield bugs are so named because of the protective armor plates that cover the top of their thorax and upper abdomen, giving them a broad-shouldered, pentagonal look when viewed directly from above. They are also called **stink bugs** for their masterly chemical defense systems. Two tear-shaped scent glands are located on the underside of the thorax, between the second and third pair of legs. A fine mist sprayed from these glands produces a truly awful smell. The shield bug uses this mist as a defense against predators, and the outrageous colors are meant as a warning to stay away . . . or else.

Bugs do very well in aquatic environments. Many aquatic bugs sport front legs that have evolved into spiked claws, ideal for grasping and holding prey while sucking out the bodily fluids. Our most common aquatic predator is the aptly-named **water scorpion** (*taiko-uchi*), found in ponds, rice paddies, and irrigation canals. The tip of the abdomen in this species has been modified into two long, thin structures that when fitted together form a tube. Using this as a snorkel, the bug is thus able to breathe while remaining submerged, lying in ambush for unwary prey. Another similar species of water scorpion, the **_mizu kamakiri_** has a longer and thinner body and is less common. Water scorpions feed on other insects, tadpoles, and even small fish and frogs.

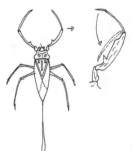

Taiko-uchi water scorpion. The long appendage at the rear of the abdomen is a snorkel-like device for breathing underwater. The front-leg pincers are used in snaring prey.

The **pond skaters** (_amenbo_) that glide over the water surface at tremendous speeds are also bugs. They feed on helpless insects that fall into the pond, using the minute ripples caused by the splash as a means of finding their prey. Just drop a piece of grass or soil into the water and watch them swarm to the spot.

Pond skater on surface of water. Millions of tiny hairs on the legs help keep the insect afloat. Note that the two antennae also rest on the surface of the water. This helps the insect to pick up vibrations from mosquitoes and other small insects that fall in.

CICADAS

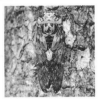

Niinii-zemi. Note superb camouflage effect.

*K*anakanakana minminimiiin jinjinjiii nininiii tsuktsuk*. From mid-summer through autumn, Tokyo parks and the surrounding countryside are filled with the sharp, often ear-splitting cries of **cicadas**.

Cicadas are closely related to bugs. They have the same sort of piercing, strawlike mouth-parts, which they use to thrust into tree trunks and suck out the sap. Japan is a paradise for cicadas, with twenty-odd species throughout the country. About six of these can be easily observed in the Tokyo area, even on street trees in heavily developed urban neighborhoods.

Front view of cicada head showing long mouth-part used for piercing and sucking

Only the male cicadas sing. They do this to announce their presence to potential mates and rivals. Inside the male's abdomen is a set of drumlike membranes, called timbals, that are alternately compressed and released by powerful muscles, producing the tinny sound vibrations. The sound is then amplified in empty air sacs, and finally modulated by a pair of flaps that can be opened and closed like the reeds on a musical instrument. These flaps can be seen on the underside, just behind the rear pair of legs, and are a sure way of determining if a cicada is a male or female.

Male cicada (left) with skirtlike flaps just below rear legs, and female with knifelike ovipositor. Both viewed from below.

Each species of cicada has a unique song, which can be easily identified. The ***niinii-zemi*** is one of the first species to begin singing in early summer. This is Tokyo's tiniest cicada, with mottled wings that make for superb camouflage on the trunks of the zelkovas and cherry trees that it prefers. The song is a simple and insistent *niii-niii-niii*.

The ***higurashi*** is a medium-size cicada that prefers dark, damp forests of cypress and cryptomeria. The song, a high-pitched *kana-kana-kana* repeated several times at a steady tempo then slowing and breaking up towards the end, can be heard only in early morning and late afternoon.

The **tsukutsuku-bōshi**, about the same size as the *higurashi*, is green and brown, with transparent wings. It has the most complicated song of all of the local species. The song has three parts, starting off with an *ui-tsuck* note repeated several times at an increasingly faster tempo, followed by an *uuui-usss* note repeated three times, then completed by a long string of tinny *giii* notes. The first two parts of the song are underlain by an incessant chattering! The *tsuku-tsuku-bōshi* sings from late summer well into autumn.

The **minmin-zemi** is a large cicada with a beautiful green-and-black head and transparent wings. The first part of the Japanese name comes from this species' song, which consists of a series of five or more similar notes, increasing in tempo as the phrase progresses, then ending with the final note stretched way out, sort of like *min-min-min-min-miii-iiin* (*semi* or *zemi* is but a generic term for "cicada").

Minmin-zemi with complex pattern on upper body

Abura-zemi is about the same size as *minmin* but with mottled wings and black head. Often the most common cicada on urban and suburban street trees.

The **abura-zemi**, about the same size as the *minmin-zemi*, is perhaps the most common local species. The head is black and the wings are mottled brown. The song is a tinny *jin-jin* or *jii-jii*, sometimes sounding like a broken or poorly oiled machine. This species is very numerous on urban zelkovas and cherries, and along with the *niinii-zemi* fills the skies over countryside pear orchards.

The **kuma-zemi**, Japan's largest species (the name means "bear cicada"), is primarily an inhabitant of western Japan and is only occasionally encountered in the Tokyo area. Anyone on a summer business trip to Osaka will soon become intimately acquainted with its incessant call of *sha-sha-sha-shen-shen-shen*. The head is black like the *abura-zemi*, but the wings are transparent rather than mottled.

Adult cicadas live for only a week or so. They sip tree sap to keep up their energy levels and are always alert for potential predators, such as birds, mantises, and, of course, children. In addition to their two large compound eyes, cicadas have three well-developed simple eyes, called ocelli, arranged in a triangular pattern on the center of their head. These ocelli do not form clear images, but are very sensitive to shadows and movement, making the cicadas extremely difficult to sneak up on.

Head of *minmin-zemi* cicada showing position of ocelli

The real purpose of the adult cicadas, however, is not feeding but mating. After copulation, the female uses the hard, sharp, knifelike ovipositor (egg-laying organ) at the tip of her abdomen to make a slit in a twig. She then deposits her eggs in the slit. The eggs hatch out—either that autumn or the following spring, depending on the species—and drop to the ground. Those that are not immediately consumed by ants burrow into the soil, where they live for several years, sucking sap out of plant roots.

Abura-zemi mating

The amount of time required to reach the adult stage varies by species. Japanese cicadas require from two or three years for the smaller species and up to six or seven for the larger. (Some American cicadas are cyclic. The entire population breeds in the same year, then disappears underground for thirteen or seventeen years before emerging again to breed! The Japanese cicadas, however, do not reproduce on a fixed cycle. This mean that every species can be seen each year.)

When ready, the final-stage larva crawls out of the ground and up a tree, where it hooks onto a trunk, branch, or leaf and metamorphoses into an adult. This metamorphosis usually takes place at night, when most birds are asleep, but ants sometimes follow the larva up the tree and attack when the newly emerging adult is still soft and helpless.

Discarded larval skin. Note huge hook on front leg, used to anchor shell when metamorphosing.

A good cicada tree can be quickly identified by the numerous perfectly round holes in the ground under the branches, showing where the larva crawled out. The discarded larval skins can also be easily found and collected as specimens. If the skin is very small, rounded, and covered with mud it is the *niinii*. If it is clean of mud, somewhat thin and fragile, and only about two centimeters or so in length, it is either the *tsuku-tsuku-bōshi* or *higurashi* (very difficult to tell apart). If it is fairly tough and strong, and about three centimeters long, it is the *abura* or *minmin* (also very difficult to tell apart). If it is close to four centimeters long, it is probably the *kuma*.

Weakened cicadas often fall from the trees and litter the ground, after which there is no sense in trying to save or revive them. Following years of life underground, their life is drawing to a close. Cicadas will neither bite nor sting, so one best just consider the fallen specimens as windfalls for close study and observation.

Japanese poets appreciate cicada song, calling it *semi-shigure*, or "cicada serenade." This term has a sort of nostalgic image, symbolizing a fragile and temporary beauty, as well as the last days of summer. To children, however, the cicada song is an invitation to spend an afternoon racing through the park or woods with a long-handled insect net.

SUMMER DRAGON- FLIES

Female *shiokara tonbo*

Blessed with abundant rainfall and packed with rice paddies, ponds, and marshes, Japan is an ideal home for **dragonflies**. In fact, an ancient poetic name for the country is Akitsushima, or "Dragonfly Island." According to legend, one of the earliest emperors was bitten by a horsefly, which in turn was caught and consumed by a dragonfly. The grateful emperor bestowed the poetic name on his domains.

Dragonflies and their close cousins the damselflies belong to the ancient order Odonata, among the oldest insects and perhaps the first of earth's creatures to fully adapt to life on the wing. Fossilized dragonflies, some of them as huge as modern-day eagles, have been recovered from rocks dating back to more than three hundred million years ago. The dragonflies we see today, although much smaller, have changed little in form from these early ancestors.

Dragonflies are unable to fold their stiff wings, and are thus considered primitive insects. This sort of primitiveness is sometimes seen as an indication of inferiority. An alternative interpretation is that the design features of the Odonata are so good that there has simply been no need to change or improve them. These design features include large compound eyes, strong wings stiffened with tough veins, and biting mouth-parts for capturing and tearing up prey. The dragonfly's short legs are useful for perching, and for seizing and holding prey, but not for walking.

Almost 5000 species of Odonata are recognized worldwide, and Japan is home to about 180. A typical countryside ecosystem on the outskirts of the city, with rice paddies, irrigation ditches, and holding ponds, may harbor up to 30 or 40 species. Even urban parks, which invariably feature small ponds and pools, usually support a dozen or more species.

Local Odonata range from tiny, fragile damselflies up to huge darners as big as sparrows. One of the best-known species is a medium-size skimmer called the **shiokara tonbo**. The Japanese name literally means "salty dragonfly," and refers to the bluish gray coloring of the adult male.

The *shiokara* is highly adaptive. From late April until October, it can be found throughout the countryside and even in most urban parks. The males establish and defend a territory along a ditch, stream, or pond's edge. They like to perch on the tip of a prominent reed or stick, but are almost constantly engaged in vigorous competition, chasing away rival males that try to wedge in on their territory. The males sometimes even initiate exciting acrobatic chases with dragonflies of other species.

Shiokara females are a beautiful golden brown color. The Japanese even call them by a separate name, ***mugiwara tonbo*** (literally, "wheat-straw dragonflies"). The males, when they first metamorphose, are actually the same straw color but turn salty blue within a week or so, as they mature.

Like all dragonflies, *shiokara* mate near the water. Males are quick to approach any female that ventures into their territory. The ensuing mating rituals are often executed entirely in mid air, treating the spectator to a truly exceptional performance.

At first, the male grasps the back of the female's head with special claspers at the tip of his tail. The mated pair then fly in tandem, with the male leading. The female twists her body around in a circle, pressing her ovipositor against a tuft of hair on the underside of the male's abdomen, where his sperm capsules are stored. These are then transferred to the female. (Checking for the tuft of hair is a sure way to determine if a dragonfly is male or female.)

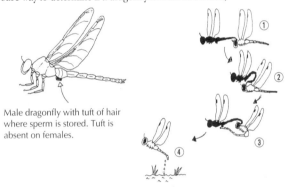

Male dragonfly with tuft of hair where sperm is stored. Tuft is absent on females.

Typical dragonfly mating sequence: 1) Male (dark) clasps female's head. 2) Male bends body, transferring sperm from reproductive organ near tip of tail to tuft of hair at base of abdomen. 3) Female bends body, pressing ovipositor against tuft of hair to receive sperm. 4) Female drops fertilized eggs into water. In some species, the pair remains coupled while the female lays her eggs.

After mating, the pair separates and the female begins dropping her fertilized eggs directly into the water. She usually hovers just above the surface, depositing the eggs one at a time in shallow, heavily-vegetated areas near the water's edge. The eggs soon hatch into aquatic larva, called naiads, which live in the water until the following spring, when they emerge and metamorphose into adults.

Out in the countryside, one occasionally encounters a related species, the **ō-shiokara tonbo**. As the Japanese name suggests (the *ō* prefix means "large" or "great"), this species is slightly larger and heavier, with a much deeper blue color, and black rather than green eyes. The female is a brighter yellow.

Another common summer dragonfly is the **koshiaki tonbo**. These medium-size dragonflies have black heads and bodies, with an easily recognized white or yellow ring on their abdomen. The male has a much wider and brighter ring than the female, as well as distinctive yellow coloring on his face.

The *koshiaki* prefers well-shaded ponds rather than flowing rivers or canals. Basically a subtropical and warm temperate species, it can be found from Taiwan and southern

Koshiaki tonbo. The black-and-white pattern is easily recognized.

China as far north as the Tōhoku and Chūbu regions of Japan. In the Kantō area, it is common from the alluvial plain up into the hills. The *koshiaki*'s favorite habitat is irrigation ponds in the rice paddy countryside, though it also thrives in big city parks.

As with the *shiokara*, the *koshiaki* males establish and defend territories along the pond's edge. Males can sometimes be seen hovering in place above an attractive perch, facing each other in what appears to be more a duel of nerves than an actual aerial combat. After a while, the two adversaries rise high into the air. Somehow, a winner emerges who then returns to the perch. Females lay their eggs directly into the water, choosing spots among the reeds and cattails growing at the edge of the pond.

The most impressive dragonfly imaginable is the **oni-yanma**, an immense darner that grows to nearly ten centimeters in length and which can easily be mistaken for a small bird. The nymphal skins, sometimes found on stalks of plants around the flowing streams that this species prefers, are as long and thick as a man's pinky. The thorax and abdomen are decorated with yellow and black stripes, and the eyes are a stunning green.

Oni-yanma: Japan's largest dragonfly

Big darners prefer small streams and irrigation canals with a steady flow and constant supply of fresh water from natural springs. They are one of the favorites of the *konchū shōnen* "insect boys." In the past, country boys used to pride themselves on their ability to catch a female by hand. They would then tie a long string around her waist and use her as a lure to catch a male.

Oni-yanma head on. Note tiny antennae and immense compound eyes.

AUTUMN DRAGONFLIES

Noshime tonbo is slightly larger than the other red skimmers. Brown wing tips are a good field mark.

A long with *susuki* plume grasses, bright red skimmer dragonflies are a well-recognized symbol of autumn in the Japanese countryside. Most people simply call these dragonflies *aka tonbo* (literally, "red dragonflies"). A quick perusal through an insect field guide, however, shows that there is no species listed under this name. *Aka tonbo* is actually a common term applied indiscriminately to many different species of red skimmers in the genus *Sympetrum*. The genus includes about twenty species in Japan, some of which are found only in limited areas. In the countryside just outside Tokyo one can enjoy at least seven or eight species. Three or four of these can be seen in urban parks as well.

As the *aka tonbo*'s color is yellow when they metamorphose each year in early summer, few people even notice them. The deep red associated with these insects is their nuptial color, which does not appear until the onset of the autumn mating season. Even then, the truly spectacular pure reds are reserved for the males, with the females showing a duller brownish red or yellowish red.

Learning to distinguish among the various *aka tonbo* species is a fun exercise in observation and comparison. Start by checking the color patterns on the wings. Most species have transparent wings with no dark markings at all (other than the strutlike veins and a rectangular block, also part of the structure, on the leading edge), but others have a dark, brownish tip. The most common *aka tonbo* with brown wingtips is the ***noshime tonbo***, which is a large, highly adaptable species found even in big city parks and gardens. The ***miyama akane***, which has a dark brownish band that stops short of the tip, is found only in the hills and mountains.

To distinguish further, one has to net the dragonflies and carefully inspect the markings on the face and the sides of the thorax. In most areas, if the wings have no brown tips or bands and there are clear, easily seen black lines on the thorax, the *aka tonbo* is either the ***aki akane*** or ***natsu akane***. In the *aki akane*, the thickest black line in the center of the thorax tapers to a sharp point, while in the *natsu akane* it ends in a clean, straight, slightly angled razor edge.

A few species have easily recognizable features that help in identification. The male ***maiko akane***, for example, sports a bluish white coloring on the face that

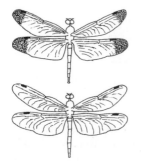

The three most common *aka tonbo*. *Noshime tonbo* (top) has brown wing tips. *Natsu akane* and *aki akane* have the same clear wings and can be told apart by the patterns on the side of their thorax.

Thorax patterns: *aki akane* (top) has a sharply pointed black line in the center of the thorax, while *natsu akane* has a line that is truncated at an angle.

reminds people of the makeup powder used by *maiko* (young geisha). The male **mayutate akane** has a tail that points sharply upwards, accounting for its somewhat lewd scientific name, *Sympetrum eroticum*.

Most *aka tonbo* species prefer to breed in rice paddies. Some drop their eggs into the water from the air like miniature bombs, while others slap the tip of their abdomen into the water. The eggs remain in the paddies over winter and hatch out early in the following spring. The aquatic naiads (*yago*, in Japanese), are great predators in their own right, seizing prey with an extendable, spike-tipped lower lip that can be snapped out with lightning speed. They then suck the body fluids out of their prey with a sharp, piercing mouth-part. Naiads grow and molt several times and by early summer are ready to metamorphose. The final-stage naiad crawls up a rice stalk and finds a steady spot on a leaf or stem. The skin then splits lengthwise, allowing the adult dragon-fly to emerge. The adults do not grow or molt anymore. They breed that autumn, then die with the onset of cold winter weather.

Red skimmer eating leaf hopper

DAMSEL-FLIES

Ajia-ito tonbo

Damselflies, called *ito tonbo* ("stringy dragonflies") in Japanese, are close cousins to the true dragonflies, but can be easily distinguished from the latter by the positioning of their eyes and the shape of their rear wing. In dragonflies, the huge complex eyes push up against each other at the center, while in damselflies there is a noticeable gap between the eyes. The rear wing of a damselfly is shaped essentially the same as the front, while the base of a dragonfly's rear wing is usually much wider than that of the front.

The manner of holding the wings at rest also differs between these two groups. The stiff-winged Odonata are unable to fold their wings down on their back. Dragonflies can only hold their wings out to the sides, whereas damselflies can fold them together and point them upwards as well.

The *ajia-ito tonbo*, with a tiny, incredibly thin green body, is a locally common damselfly that is seen around ponds and irrigation canals. Several other closely related species, very difficult to distinguish from one another, are also encountered. A slightly larger species, the *haguro tonbo* prefers habitats with better water quality. The male of this species has dark wings and a long, thin body of stunning iridescent green.

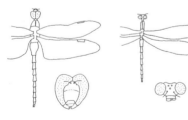

Comparison of typical damselfly (right) and dragonfly

Haguro tonbo

GRASS-HOPPERS

Shōryō batta showing mixed green-and-brown markings. A strikingly beautiful hopper.

"**P**akistani army mobilized to fight invading hordes crossing the border from southern India." This fast-breaking news report of several years ago may have sent chills down the spines of listeners and readers. The hordes referred to here were not Indian army troops but great swarms of **grasshoppers**.

Very few insects rate military intervention, yet some species of grasshopper have a way of making their presence felt in a big way. Flying across the countryside in a swarm so thick that the sky is blotted out for miles around, these insects can strip entire regions of all edible greenery.

Not all grasshoppers are so devastating. Most are solitary critters that never stray far from their place of birth. Grasshoppers, or "hoppers," are classified in the order Orthoptera, which also includes crickets and katydids. They are mostly peaceful herbivores, with solid jaws for cutting up leaves and stems, and extremely long and powerful rear legs.

Grasshopper antennae are short, and their eyes are well developed, indicating a strong reliance on visual clues in locating food, mates, and enemies. As a result, hoppers are mostly active during the day. They are often found in open habitats, such as lawns, grassfields, riverbeds, and the dikes that separate rice paddies. They can be easily caught but are most difficult to hold, constantly kicking out with their powerful rear legs and also spitting out a foul brown liquid that smells and stains the skin and clothes.

Late summer and autumn are the best times for studying grasshoppers. Hoppers are actually around from early spring but are too small to be noticed. Once they metamorphose into adults they become very obvious. As a first step in learning local species, divide hoppers into those with pointy heads and those with squared-off heads.

The *shōryō batta* is the largest of the pointy heads. Females, which in grasshoppers are usually considerably larger than the males, reach lengths of close to ten centimeters. Often found around grasses, this hopper comes in various shades, from pure light brown, to pure deep green, to beautiful combinations of these colors. Hoppers can not change their color at will, as can tree frogs. A general rule is that individuals that metamorphose in dry surroundings come out brown, while those that metamorphose in wet surroundings are green. A closely related species, the **shōryō batta-modoki** is smaller, with a straighter body that sometimes sports pink or purple lines.

Another well-known pointy-headed variety is the smaller **onbu batta**. Usually one finds these hoppers in pairs, with a small individual riding piggyback on top of a much larger one. The Japanese term *onbu* means "to carry someone on your back" (*batta* is a generic term for grasshopper). The hopper getting a free ride on the female's back is not her baby, however, but her marriage partner! When a male finds a suitable partner he just rides around on her back until she is ready to mate.

Shōryō batta-modoki

Out in the countryside, the most common squarehead is **kobane inago**. This medium-size hopper has a passion for the leaves of the rice plants. In September, when the rice is harvested, hoppers that have been hiding peacefully in the paddies suddenly find themselves in the open, where they are the target of unwanted attention from shrikes, crows, egrets, and small hawks. Carrion crows and cattle egret often walk right behind the combine, snapping up the hoppers before they have time to know what hit them. Sometimes the farmer or his wife will fill a cloth sack with the hoppers, which they boil and season with sugar and soy sauce to make a delightful *tsukudani* snack called *inago*.

Onbu batta pair mating. The small hopper on top is the male.

Kobane inago. The wings are much shorter than the abdomen.

The king of all Japanese hoppers is the huge square-headed **migratory locust**. In fact, the Japanese name, *tonosama batta*, means "lord [or king] grasshopper." Females grow close to seven centimeters in length. Japanese boys traditionally catch the male with a small rectangular block of wood tied to a string. The male mistakes the block for a female and hangs on tightly trying to mate.

Migratory locust

Like most hoppers, locusts are marginal fliers. When alarmed, they use their powerful rear legs as the springboard for a short, usually erratic flight. Under some conditions, however, locusts metamorphose into a special version, whose longer, more powerful wings and shorter, more streamlined body is capable of flying over great distances. These long-range fliers emerge when the larvae grow under severely crowded conditions, for example, a sudden increase in the population due to an unusually good season.

Under the normal workings of population dynamics, such a bumper generation would soon consume all the locally available food supplies, causing their numbers to come crashing down as starvation takes its toll. The special generation of long-range fliers, however, is able to leave the stripped homeland behind and take off for greener pastures. Thus are born the great locust swarms that have plagued mankind since biblical times, if not before.

The migratory locust found in Japan is the very same species of locust responsible for the great swarms of south Asia and northern Africa. Several similar-looking species can be easily confused with it. The best way to make sure that you have a locust is to hold the hopper between your fingers and spread out the rear wings. If the wing is clear, it is the locust; if there is a black crescent-shaped mark, it is most likely the very common **kuruma batta-modoki**. Wrestling with a big powerful hopper will leave your fingers scraped and stained, but there is no permanent damage and it brings a reward: the rear wings unfold like beautiful Japanese fans.

Male hoppers stridulate to attract their mates. They produce their song in a fiddlelike movement, rubbing pegs on the inside of the rear leg against hardened veins on the outer surface of their front wing. A hopper's ears are located on the side of the body, hidden by the wings. The females usually lay their eggs by thrusting their ovipositor, the egg laying organ located at the tip of their abdomen, into soft ground. Their abdomen is incredibly flexible, capable of stretching out to several times its normal length. Checking the tip of the abdomen is the best way to determine if a hopper is a male or female.

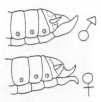

Tip of abdomen on male and female grasshoppers

Grasshopper ears on sides of the body, hidden beneath the wings

Female katydid with sickle-shaped ovipositor at tip of abdomen

Katydids (called "bush crickets" in Great Britain) look a lot like grasshoppers, but can be easily distinguished by their long, whip-like antennae which, when swept back, usually protrude well beyond the tip of the abdomen. On the other hand, most katydids have small beady eyes. As one might surmise from this combination, katydids are primarily nocturnal. They prefer dense vegetation to open habitats and rely more on tactile clues (feeling with their antennae) than visual ones.

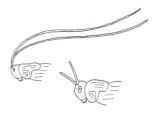

Typical katydid (left), with long, whiplike antennae, and grasshopper with short, stiff antennae

Male katydids also stridulate, but produce their song in a fashion quite different from that of grasshoppers. They raise their front wings over their backs and rub a notched file on the outer surface of the left wing against a hard scraper on the inner surface of the right. The wings move so fast that they appear only as a blur.

Most katydids mate during late summer and early autumn, singing away after the sun goes down.

Small oval on second segment of front legs is an eardrum

Their songs are greatly appreciated as symbolic of the changing seasons and provide vivid images for haiku poets. Katydid ears are located in the strangest place, on the second segment of the front legs!

Female katydids can be easily told from their mates. Their ovipositor, located at the tip of the abdomen, is a long, sharp instrument, shaped like a sword or sickle, depending on the species. It is thrust into the ground or into the stem of plants when laying the eggs.

One of the most common local katydids is *kubikiri-gisu*, a long thin species (up to six centimeters for females) with a very sharply pointed head. The underside of the head, around the jaws, is often a bright red. Like many katydids, this species is predatory and sports powerful jaws which, when firmly attached, hold on like a bulldog. If pulled strongly, the katydid's neck will sometimes rip off before the jaws relinquish their hold. *Kubikiri*, in Japanese, means "chopping off at the head."

A bite from this katydid is painful and can draw blood. For this reason, or perhaps because of the blood-red color around the

Kubikiri-gisu

jaws, children call this insect "***chisui batta***," or "blood-sucking grasshopper." This species is rare in that the adults do not die off during the winter. They survive, hidden deep in dense vegetation, through early spring, when they begin their love songs, a continuous high-pitched almost electrical *jiiiiii* buzzing.

Another representative katydid is the huge ***kutsuwa-mushi***, which produces a very loud gushing *gasha-gasha* song in late summer. The head is small and squared off, and the wings are considerably broader than other species.

Crickets are closely related to katydids, but have flattened bodies. They are also mostly nocturnal, with long antennae. They sing in the same manner as katydids, except that the position of the scrapers and file is reversed.

Several large brown crickets (the generic Japanese term is *kōrogi*) are found in the Tokyo area but are very difficult to tell apart. A smaller brown species, called ***suzumushi***, has a beautiful song and is a popular children's pet. The song is a sweet tinkling *liiin-liiin*, like a soft bell (the Japanese name means "bell-insect"). Come midsummer, these *suzu-mushi* can be purchased cheaply at almost any pet or department store.

Suzu-mushi or "bell cricket"

In the inner city and in densely packed suburban residential areas, the most common cricket is a green arboreal species called ***ao-matsu-mushi***. Its song is a loud high-pitched *lii-lii*. This cricket is not a native, but an escaped species originally from central China.

Ao-matsu-mushi

MANTIS

Ō kamakiri female and smaller male (on top). Note that the male is missing his head!

When I was a small boy growing up in the United States, people always warned me never to kill or injure a praying mantis. The local farmers and gardeners all harbored great respect for these insects, which feed on grasshoppers and other agricultural pests.

Mantis are clearly related to hoppers, but are usually placed in a separate order called the Mantodea. The name derives from the Greek word for "prophet," and relates to these insects' habit of standing very still with their front legs raised and folded as if in prayer. The Mantodea are not a diverse order, with only about two thousand or so species worldwide.

Three or four species of mantis can be regularly observed in Tokyo parks and gardens. All of these show a one-year life cycle: the eggs, laid in autumn, hatch out the following spring, and the mantis grows and molts over the summer months. By early autumn they have grown large and are easily spotted.

Mantis are great predators. Their front legs are armed with wicked spikes, which are used to trap prey in an inescapable grasp. An especially long spike near the tip of the leg is used like a grappling hook to initially spear the prey and drag it within grasping range. Once the mantis securely subdues its prey with its front legs, it proceeds to tear the victim apart with sharp, powerful mandibles.

Although fierce in action, mantis appear low-keyed most of the time. They do not attempt to chase after or run down potential prey, but instead rely on ambushing techniques. Mantis are cryptically colored and blend in well with their background. They wait motionlessly, sometimes for hours at a time, with their front legs poised and ready to strike out should a victim wander within striking range. They frequently stake out promising ambush points on leaves and stems, and are often found waiting just underneath a flower that is sure to attract some insect prey.

Mantis locate their prey by eyesight. They have large compound eyes and are able to turn and twist their neck with a wide range of motion. They appear to use movement as a visual clue for recognizing potential victims, and are known to completely miss well-camouflaged prey that remain perfectly still.

The mantis female is usually considerably larger than the male. Females have even been observed decapitating and consuming the male during or after mating.

Some entomologists believe that this behavior is the exception rather than the rule. Mate cannibalism is now thought to occur mostly when the male makes a mistake in his set routine or the mating process is somehow interrupted or disturbed. A male who is able to perform his task smoothly and competently lives to mate again with another partner.

Once the female finishes mating, she lays her eggs inside a protective sac called an ootheca. The sac is composed of tough foam secreted by special glands in the female's abdomen. As the foam emerges, the female skillfully employs several long, flexible appendages to spread it out and work it into a shape distinctive to her species, almost like a determined plasterer might use a spatula. Later, the foam hardens into a tough, fiberlike nest that protects the eggs until the following spring.

Ō kamkakiri female in the process of laying her eggs

The most common mantis in the Tokyo area is the immense **ō kamakiri**, the females of which may be close to ten centimeters long. The **chōsen kamakiri**, a similar but slightly smaller species, can be distinguished by a bright orange marking on the thorax, between the two front legs; while the **harabiro kamakiri** is smaller still, with a much thicker abdomen. Tokyo's smallest mantis, the **ko kamakiri**, has distinctive cream-and-black markings on the inside surface of the forelegs.

Ootheca of *ō kamakiri*

Ootheca of *ko kamakiri*

Comparison of some local mantis: *ō kamakiri* at left, showing black markings on rear wings; *chōsen kamakiri* at center, with bright orange "bowtie"; at right is *ko kamakiri* with distinctive markings on inside of foreleg.

Ko kamakiri. Note distinctive markings on inside second segment of front leg.

HORNETS

Kiiro suzume-bachi nest in late summer, with a thousand or more workers

Wasps and **bees** are members of the insect order Hymenoptera, which also includes ants. These three groups share a body architecture that features a thin "waist" separating the thorax from the abdomen. The Hymenoptera are also famed for their advanced systems of communal living, division of labor, and caring for young, although only a small percentage of the total number of species are true social insects.

Bees, because of their economic value as honey producers and flower pollinators, usually receive the most attention. It is the predatory wasps, however, that truly fascinate a naturalist.

Wasps do visit flowers to sip honey but are not nearly as adept at this task as bees are. A bee's mouth is designed for sucking up liquids, while a wasp has a set of powerful pincerlike jaws for ripping and tearing prey. Wasps thus supplement their honey gathering with taking of prey. In particular, many species raise their larva on a primarily meat diet.

Some wasps are solitary hunters, preying on spiders and caterpillars, which are paralyzed but not killed and then sealed inside the nest along with the wasp's eggs. When the eggs hatch, the larvae feed on the paralyzed prey. Other wasp species, however, build communal nests and form great colonies.

The king of the social wasps are **hornets**, of the genus *Vespa*. The generic Japanese name, *suzume-bachi*, literally means "sparrow bee" (*hachi* or *bachi* is the generic term for a bee or wasp), and indeed some of the hornet species are truly enormous insects (though comparing their size to that of sparrows is a slight exaggeration).

Hornet nests are made of tough paper. The insects use their powerful jaws to scrape fibers from the bark of a tree or the side of a wooden building. They then chew the fibers into a pulp, mix it with saliva, and spread it out in a thin sheet, a process and use of materials similar to paper-making techniques. In fact, some historians believe that the Japanese discovered how to make what was to become traditional handmade paper (*washi*) by watching hornets at work.

A hornet nest consists of hexagonal interior compartments arranged in several tiers and completely surrounded by a tough marbled covering, called an envelope, that protects them from the elements. As the insects use variously

Close up of workers on nest, with beautiful patterns of nest envelope

Nest with envelope removed. The compartments are organized in six tiers.

Close up showing fat yellow larva and sealed cocoons

shaded sources of woods for their construction work, the outside surface of the nest is often a magnificent piece of abstract art.

By late autumn, hornet nests can reach the size of a large beachball. All these huge nests are built in a single year, starting from scratch in early spring. They are abandoned with the onset of winter.

A hornet nest always starts with a single queen, who chooses the spot and constructs a small first-generation nest with twenty or so compartments. A single egg is laid in each compartment. After the eggs hatch out, the queen must work hard to feed the hungry grublike larva. When ready, the grub spins a silk cover over the entrance to its cell and then performs its final metamorphosis while hidden inside. The new adults chew their way out of the cocoon and become the first generation of workers.

From this point onward, the workers, all females, take over the tasks of gathering food and enlarging the nest, while the queen devotes all her time and energy to egg-laying. Throughout the summer and early autumn, the nest grows and grows, the rate of growth increasing rapidly as more and more workers appear. By mid-autumn several thousand workers may be on hand.

It is about this time that the queen begins laying special eggs, which are fed and treated differently, as they will become the males and new queens. When the males hatch out, they leave their natal nest, flying around until they find another nest of the same species. There they hang out for a while, waiting for the new queens to emerge.

Each nest produces several new queens, who fly out and quickly mate with the waiting males. With the sperm from this mating stored in a special pouch, the new queens begin looking for a warm place to spend the winter, often under the bark of a dying tree or inside a partially rotted log. As the temperature drops, the males, the old queen, and all the thousands of workers die off, and the nest is abandoned. The new queens wake up the following spring, when each will use her stored sperm to begin a new nest of her own.

Hornets drink flower nectar and collect sweet tree sap and will chew into a fruit to get at the delicious juices inside. Some species are known to eat mushrooms. Still, they raise their larvae primarily on meat.

Hornet prey includes caterpillars, grasshoppers, and other agricultural pests. Japanese farmers have long been aware of this behavior and treat the hornets as beneficial insects. Hornets often build their nests under the eaves of farmhouses. Most farmers will leave them be. In winter, when the nests are abandoned, the farmers carefully cut them down, paint on a preservative shellac, then mount them in the vestibule. These nests are thought to protect the home and family.

Ō suzume-bachi worker collecting sweet sap on the trunk of a kunugi oak

Like bees, hornets are equipped with a wicked stinger at the tip of their abdomen. This superior weapon is hollow and connected at the rear to a sac containing powerful poison. When the stinger is inserted in the victim, the poison is squeezed through the hollow tube and injected into the prey from a hole at the tip, much like the working of a hypodermic syringe. The stinger has evolved from the ovipositor (egg-laying organ) and is thus present only in females.

Most true bees sting only to protect their nest, and their stinger is fitted with tiny barbs that embed themselves solidly in the enemy's flesh. As the bee pulls away, its abdomen is ripped apart and the bee dies. Bees can thus sting only once. Hornets, on the other hand, use their stingers for hunting prey and thus must be able to sting over and over again. As might be expected, their stingers are smooth, lacking the bee's barbs.

The most common hornet in the Tokyo area is the ***kiiro suzume-bachi***, a medium-size species with a yellow fuzz (*kiiro* means "yellow"). This hornet builds immense nests, usually under the eaves of buildings. In recent years these nests have been increasing in urban and suburban areas, causing problems with local residents. Another common species, the ***kogata suzume-bachi***, is slightly smaller and usually builds its nest in the branches of evergreen shrubs. A single lookout is always posted at the entrance hole.

The absolute and undisputed king of the hornets is the ***ō suzume-bachi***. Workers are four centimeters long and queens, even bigger. This species builds its nest underground, on a sunny bank or in the bosom of a rotted tree trunk. In late autumn, as food becomes scarce and the nest grows large, patrols set out to attack the nests of honey bees and even smaller hornets. A dozen or so

First generation nest of *kogata suzume-bachi*, a familiar sight under temple roof eaves in the countryside

of these monsters can wipe out an entire colony of several thousand European honey bees in no time flat. The native Japanese species of honey bee, however, has evolved a strategy for fighting the hornets. Rather than trying to sting the attackers to death, hundreds of honey bees simply mob each hornet, killing her by raising her body temperature above the critical level.

Ō suzume-bachi shown in actual size

PAPER WASPS

Paper wasp queen on new nest in early spring

Paper wasps (*ashinaga-bachi*, or "long-legged wasps" in Japanese) are of the genus *Polistes*. Their life cycles, and ecological and social behavior, are basically similar to those of hornets. They are not nearly as large and heavy, however, and their nests are far smaller and simpler.

Paper wasps build their nests of pulp also but do not cover it with a protective envelope. The compartments, which are open to the air, are built on a solid base that is attached, usually in a down-pointing position, to a tree branch. In midsummer you can see workers busily fanning their wings

Paper wasp nest in mid summer

on the surface of the nest, a behavior which is thought to help cool the developing eggs and larvae. Five or six species are found locally, with the *futamon ashi-naga-bachi* being the most common.

Both paper wasps and hornets defend their nests with tremendous ferocity. Anyone who deliberately or accidentally disturbs the nest is in for an awful time.

Often one individual in a group is singled out for a concentrated attack. This is because the insects spray chemical markers, called pheromones, as they sting. These pheromones mark the stung person as an enemy of the nest and function as a target identifier for all the rest of the attackers. Anyone stung by either paper wasps or hornets should seek immediate medical attention.

BUTTER-FLIES

Common cabbage white sipping nectar

Colorful and graceful **butterflies** are among the most widely appreciated insects, while their close relatives the **moths** fare poorly in popularity contests. Caterpillars, which are the larvae of both groups, are frequently despised.

Butterflies and moths are of the order Lepidoptera. The defining characteristic of the order is tiny scales that cover the wing membranes. Insect wings are generally made of clear membranes supported by a framework of stiff, hollow veins. In the Lepidoptera, the membranes are covered by an outer layer of flat scales, almost like overlapping roof tiles. These scales contain the pigments that give these insects their magnificent colors. Some scales even have ridges that refract and scatter light, producing amazing iridescent tones that seem to change color as the wings move.

The Lepidoptera are also equipped with a unique system for extracting flower nectar. Their mouth parts have evolved into a long, flexible hoselike device called a proboscis. When not in use, the proboscis is kept rolled under the head like a garden hose; when extended, it allows the insect to reach nectar

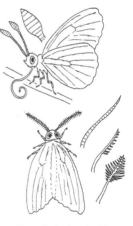

Typical butterfly (top) with club-shaped antennae, and moth (bottom). Moth antennae can be straight or comblike. Note that butterfly perches with wings held upright, while moth folds wings over its body.

hidden deep inside the flower without having to crawl inside. Some flowers, such as lilies, have their anthers and stigma at the end of long stalks, ideally placed to brush the head of feeding butterflies or moths.

In general, moths are nocturnal, have comblike antennae, and fold their wings neatly over their back while at rest; butterlies are active during the day, have club-shaped antennae, and hold their wings open or folded together in a vertical position while resting. There are, however, numerous exceptions to these rules.

Butterflies may win out handily in popularity but, in terms of evolutionary success, it is the moths that come out squarely on top. In most regions the number of moth species is ten or more times that of the butterfly. Japan boasts about two hundred species of butterfly, while the number of moth species is at least five thousand, and probably much more.

Tokyo's abundant flowers attract large numbers of butterflies. The most common species is the **cabbage white** (*monshiro-chō*), a butterfly that enjoys a cosmopolitan distribution and is a familiar sight in parks all over the world. In Tokyo, it can be seen throughout most of the year, from early spring well into the following winter. The male is all white with dark trimmings and spots on the inner wing surfaces, while the female has a stronger yellowish tint and larger markings. Adults frequent flowers in the mustard and sunflower families, though the eggs are laid almost exclusively on the former, which includes, unfortunately, many valuable commercial crops such as cabbage and daikon radishes.

The **black-veined white** (*sujiguro monshiro-chō*), with black vein markings, is found throughout Asia. Interestingly, this species is thought to have originally inhabited shaded mountain valleys and to have later adapted to big cities by sticking to the shady habitats created by buildings and park trees.

Yellows are not quite as common as whites, especially in urban parks, but several species in the genus *Eurema* (such as *ki-chō*) are occasionally seen. The **orange sulfur** (*monki-chō*) can be told from the yellows by a dark spot on the forewing.

Browns are among the least spectacular butterflies when seen from a distance. The drab wings seldom attract peoples' attention. Up close,

Orange sulphur on red clover

the wings turn out to be decorated with fascinating patterns of circular markings, which lepidopterists call "eyespots." These spots may work to confuse predators, especially birds. The predator strikes at the eyespots, and comes away with a piece of wing, while the butterfly flutters off to live another day. Butterfly wings may appear fragile but are actually among the strongest in the insect kingdom. In some cases, the eyespots may also be used to surprise and frighten smaller predators. Several browns are common in the Tokyo area, and can be identified only by a close inspection of their eyespots.

Gliders are easily distinguished at a glance by their unique black-and-white pattern. There are several local species, including the **common glider** (*ko misuji*), which is distributed throughout Eurasia and North Africa. This species is sometimes seen drinking water or feeding on animal dung. Not all species of butterfly engage in this behavior, and even among those that do, it is only the males that seem thirsty. Lepidopterists speculate that the males require the water or dung to replace vital minerals lost in producing sperm.

Tokyo-area butterfly spotters can enjoy a wide variety of beautiful species, including the cosmopolitan **small copper** (*beni shijimi*), **admirals** (*aka tateha*), **painted ladies** (*hime aka-tateha*), and several species of tiny **blues** (*shijimi-chō*). **Commas**, such as the *ki tateha*, have superb orange-and-black patterns on the inner-wing surfaces, yet when the wings are folded closed and only the outer surfaces show, it looks just like a fallen leaf.

Tokyo's most spectacular butterflies are the large and colorful **swallowtails** (*ki ageha*). As their name suggests, these butterflies have trailing extensions at the rear of their wings, much like the long, forked tails of swallows.

The swallowtail itself is one of the most common butterflies in the world, distributed from Europe clear across the Eurasian and North American continents. The dark band on the hind wings is powdered with a delicate blue and contains a reddish eyespot. The adults fly in sunny areas, visiting thistles, lilies,

Typical brown, probably *hime janome*. Note eye spots on wing.

Common glider with distinctive black and white markings

Small copper on white clover

Yamato shijimi. One of several tiny blues (the upper surface of the wings are blue or light purple).

and spider lilies, but the eggs are laid on plants in the carrot family, including carrots and other commercial crops. The *ageha-chō* is a similar-looking yellow-and-black swallowtail. These two species can be distinguished by looking at the base of the forewings. The *ki ageha* shows a uniform dark brown coloration here, while the *ageha-chō* has a clearly defined lined pattern. The *ageha-chō* lays its eggs on plants in the rue (citrus) family such as the *sanshō*, a shrub used to make the green herbal seasoning that is commonly sprinkled on broiled eel.

Comma on thistle

Tokyo is home to several large blackish swallowtails. You have to look closely to tell them apart. The **monki ageha** has small whitish or yellowish markings on the rear wings, while the **kuro ageha** shows red half-moon markings in the same area and a distinct red eyespot. The **karasu ageha** can be told from these two by a magnificent green iridescent sheen that covers the wings.

Common swallowtail

The **blue triangle** (*aosuji ageha*) is also blackish, but can be easily distinguished by its beautiful pastel-blue wing markings. This butterfly usually lays its eggs on trees in the laurel family, such as the camphor tree.

Ageha chō. Note that lined markings at base of wings stand out clearly.

Caterpillars, as every child knows, are the larvae of butterflies and moths, who usually lay their eggs directly on a particular host plant. The eggs hatch out into tiny caterpillars with voracious appetites and powerful jaws for biting off pieces of leaf. The caterpillars eat, grow, and molt, passing through several larval stages, until finally retiring into a cocoon to metamorphose.

Plump, soft-bodied, slow-moving, and often exposed on the leaf, caterpillars seem like easy pickings for any hungry predator that happens along. Caterpillar defense systems, however, are among the most varied and diabolical in the animal kingdom.

Some caterpillars protect themselves with simple camouflage or mimicry, while nature has provided others with more aggressive armor, covering their bodies with wicked, often poison-tipped spines. Surprisingly, many species seem to be deliberately advertising their presence with bright color combinations. Most of these have noxious or toxic chemicals in their body tissues, sometimes obtained from the plants they feed on. Their bright colors are therefore designed as warnings to potential predators. The unspoken message is: "Here I am. Go ahead and try me if you want, but you'll be sorry if you do!" Indeed, any bird that swallows one of these morsels spits it right out, and soon learns to recognize and avoid that particular color combination.

The **gypsy moth** (*maimai-ga*) caterpillar is a small crawling fortress, armed with long, poison-tipped spines. Brightly colored circles, blue near the head and red toward the tail, decorate the back. These caterpillars are not at all fussy about their food, feeding on the leaves of most local tree species. The *iraga* is a green caterpillar with especially powerful poison on the tips of its spines. Both of these species can inflict extremely painful stings, and should never be handled.

Gypsy moth caterpillar is a walking fortress. Dotlike markings on half the body are blue, but on the other half are red. DANGEROUS.

The *ki ageha* swallowtail caterpillar, resplendent in green with black stripes and orange dots, is a typical employer of chemical weapons. In addition to distasteful chemicals in its flesh, this caterpillar has a secret weapon, a forked gland, called an osmeterium, which is normally kept hidden in a pouch just behind the head but can be inverted when the caterpillar is disturbed. This gland emits a foul odor that deters predators.

Iraga caterpillar is even more heavily armed than the gypsy moth. DANGEROUS.

Familiar "**inchworms**" are also the larvae of various moth species. The name comes from the distinctive style of crawling, which looks like a carpenter estimating a length by walking his hand along a board. The Japanese name, *shakutori-mushi*, is similarly derived. *Shaku* is an old unit of length, and *tori* is "to take" (a measurement).

Caterpillars are easy to study and observe. Most local species can be handled safely, or gently moved with a pair of chopsticks to a more convenient spot. Being genuine insects, caterpillars have only three

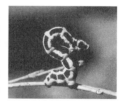

Tonbo-edajaku, a typical "inchworm" moth caterpillar

pairs of true legs. In addition, they have rows of special suction-cup–like claspers (usually five pair) that help them to cling and crawl. The eyes are reduced to tiny ocelli (simple eyespots), which probably enable the caterpillars to only vaguely distinguish light and the direction from which it comes. They rely on their antennae for tactile clues and on special attachments to the jaw, called palpi, for tasting potential meals.

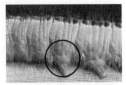

A close look at the side of the abdomen shows a small elliptical gland on each segment. These are the spiracles, or respiratory organs. Having no lungs, insects move air in and out directly through these spiracles.

A close-up shows the suction-cup claspers and oval spiracles, or breathing holes, one per side on each segment of the abdomen

BEETLES

Male rhinoceros beetle, the prize catch of all young insect collectors. Females are almost the same size but lack the horn like projections.

Come summer vacation, the Japanese countryside takes on an air of great secrecy. Grammar school boys can be seen whispering in small groups or sneaking into oak woodlands at daybreak, only to emerge a little later carrying a sackful of something that, to them at least, is obviously precious cargo.

Inside the woodland, the boys will usually be found at the base of a wide *konara* or *kunugi* oak tree (see the Deciduous Trees chapter), desperately fending off hornets while trying to capture immense rhinoceros and stag beetles. The **beetles**, as well as the hornets and various butterflies, are attracted to the sweet sap that oozes from cuts in the tree bark.

Country boys love to catch and play with the big beetles. They scour the local woodlands, searching for good beetle trees, and treat their discoveries like buried treasure, sharing the location of their secret trees only with their closest friends.

The best beetle trees produce copious amounts of sap and serve as gathering spots for various insects with a sweet tooth. Many species of beetle are equipped with brushlike mouth-parts that are designed specifically for mopping up this sweet tree sap. The most spectacular of these, and the most sought after by Japanese boys, is a great **rhinoceros beetle** (*kabuto-mushi*). The males have one huge horn projecting from their head (*kabuto* is a traditional samurai's fighting helmet) and another from their thorax. They use these horns to bulldoze competitors off of the choicest feeding spots. Boys keep their beetles in little plastic cases and stage wrestling matches in which the beetles fight to push one another off of a branch or log.

Running a close second to the rhinoceros beetles, in both power and popularity, are several species of **stag beetle**. The most common is the *nokogiri kuwagata*. The formidable jaws of these insects are shaped like the antlers of a stag and can deliver a painful squeeze. Like the horns of the rhinoceros beetle, the stag beetle's jaws are not employed directly in gathering food. They are social organs used for sexual display and feeding competition. An opponent is seized in the

Male stag beetle

great jaws and flung right off into space. Both rhinoceros and stag beetles can be purchased at many pet shops and department stores and can even be bought through mail-order houses.

Longhorn beetles, named for their magnificent antennae, have a unique lifestyle. The adults feed on tree sap. Come mating time, the female chews a hole in the tree and deposits her eggs inside. The growing larvae chew their way right through the tree, digesting the raw wood. The larvae molt and grow inside the tree, then excavate a small chamber in which they metamorphose into adults. The adults then chew their own way out. In large species this process takes up to three years, and you can stick your pinky into the hole they leave after chewing their way out. This hole then becomes an outlet for sap, starting the cycle anew.

Three locally common longhorns are the solid brown *miyama kamikiri*; the *shirosuji kamikiri*, a dull black specimen with irregular yellow-white splotches; and *gomadara kamikiri*, a jet black beetle with white markings. The generic Japanese name for longhorn beetles is *kamikiri*, or "paper cutter," referring to their sharp jaws. These jaws can deliver a painful nip, so take care when handling big longhorn beetles.

Shirosuji kamikiri longhorn beetle

It is easy to understand the magic that small boys see in these huge beetles:

the insects are built like miniature walking fortresses. They are slow and ponderous, but heavy and seemingly impervious to attack—endearing qualities they share with two other perennial children's favorites: fighting robots and movie monsters.

The same characteristics that account for the beetles' popularity also make them the most successful group of animals alive today. The order Coleoptera, in which all beetles are classified, currently contains about 350,000 species, or about one-fourth of all known species of plants and animals. As mentioned earlier, in most areas of the world, the number of beetle species easily outnumbers that of all plants combined!

The secret of the beetles' evolutionary success lies in a conservative protection strategy. The head and thorax are covered with heavy chitinous armor, while the front wings have evolved into stiff, hard structures called elytra. These front wings are useless for flying but can be folded over the soft rear wings and abdomen when the insect is at rest.

Other local beetles include **fireflies** (*hotaru*), which appear in summer. The most common species in the uplands and alluvial plain is the ***heike-botaru***, which thrives in slow-flowing irrigation canals. The ***genji-botaru*** is found in the swifter waters of the hills and mountains. Fireflies lay their eggs on aquatic plants. When the larvae hatch out, they drop into the water and crawl inside the shell of a snail, which they feed on.

The familiar **ladybug** (*tentō-mushi*) is also a beetle, as are many of the aquatic insects found in ponds and streams. The rear legs of these water beetles are flattered into paddles and covered with long hair to aid in swimming. Water beetles are the original scuba divers. They trap a bubble of air between their wings and body before diving, and can thus stay under for a long time.

Hime-gengorō, locally
common water beetle

ANT LION

Ant lion larva removed from the bottom of a trap

In *The Return of the Jedi*, the third installment of *Star Wars*, by George Lucas, the vile gangster Jabba the Hutt attempts to throw the heroes into a great sandy pit. At the bottom of the pit is a fearsome monster with a set of powerful jaws, waiting to crush anyone who comes sliding down the steep slopes. This creature may seem a bit far-fetched, a horror brought to life to fulfill our worst nightmares. But the creators of *Star Wars* were actually good entomologists, and the inspiration for this monster comes not from some demented imagination, but from the amazing world of insect ecology: a creature that actually inhabits the environs of local shrines and temples. Fortunately for us, this creature is only a centimeter or so in length, and its victims are not intergalactic heroes, but ants, crickets, pillbugs, and other tiny crawlers.

The inspiration for the *Star Wars* monster is an **ant lion**. Its English name, as well as the Japanese *ari-jigoku* (literally, "ant hell"), reflects this insect's unique style of capturing prey.

The first indication that ant lions live in the vicinity is a series of curious conical pits, about two centimeters or so deep, in the soft sand. The ant lion itself lies totally concealed in the sand at the apex of the cone. When a victim stumbles into the pit, the vibrations and shifting sand are sensed by the ant lion, which then swings into action, throwing up sand so that the victim has an even harder time struggling up the steep, unstable sides of the pit. Eventually, the victim falls within range and the ant lion reaches out to grasp it with great, sickle-shaped jaws armed with wicked, inward-pointing spikes.

Ant lion sand traps. Each trap is about the size of a golf ball. Look for them in soft sand that is protected from the rain.

Ant lions use digestive juices to dissolve the soft, fleshy parts of their victims. They then hurl the remaining inedible hard parts out of the pit. One thus finds a tiny garbage heap of empty pillbug shells, cricket wings, small beetle armor, and other debris surrounding the pit.

Ant lions are actually the larvae of a **lacewing insect** (*usuba kagerō*). When ready, the ant lion makes a cocoon of mud and silk and emerges as an adult that looks like a delicate damselfly but is totally unrelated. These adults live only a short time and seem to hardly feed at all. Their main purpose is to mate, then lay the eggs that will hatch into the next generation of ant lions.

Lacewings are a peaceful flying insect, almost the exact opposite of their larva

In order to dig their pits, ant lions require soft sand that is well protected from the rain. This sort of habitat is readily found under the deep eaves of shrines, temples, and farm buildings. You can dig the ant lion out or just do a survey around the pit to see what it has been eating. Children (and impatient adults!) usually choose to drop a pillbug or small insect into the pit and force some action.

SPIDERS

Orb web spider

Spiders, along with ticks, mites, and scorpions, constitute the class Arachnida, also within the phylum Arthropod. This name comes from the maiden Arachne, in Greek mythology, who was skilled in weaving. Fatally confident in her skills, she challenged the goddess Athena to a contest. When both were finished, Athena admitted defeat but, in her rage, destroyed Arachne's tapestry. Brokenhearted, the maiden hung herself. Athena took pity on the girl and loosened the rope around her neck. The rope then changed into a spider's web and Arachne, into a spider.

Like insects, spiders are arthropods with a hard exoskeleton that must be shed as the animal grows. In contrast to their insect cousins, spiders lack wings and have eight rather than six legs. Also, their head and thorax are fused into a single structure called the cephalothorax. All spiders are carnivores, equipped with a pair of pincerlike fangs, called chelicerae, which function like hollowed-out syringes to inject poison into their prey.

Spider silk and webs are among the great wonders of the natural world. The spiders make the silk, which is a type of protein, in special glands located at the tip of their abdomen. The protein is squeezed out through narrow tubes, called spinnerets, and hardens as it emerges. A single strand of silk may be only several millionths of a centimeter thick but is as strong as a steel cable of the same diameter!

Spiders are able to manufacture several different kinds of silk. The structural parts of the web, such as the bridge line, which provides the vital top anchor, as well as the main supports and spokes, are usually made of nonsticky thread, while the fill-in mesh is made of a sticky variety. The spider avoids the sticky threads and moves about by grasping the dry framework with special claws and notched hairs at the tip of its legs.

When a victim strikes the web, the spider immediately senses and locates it by the vibrations produced. Usually the prey is injected with poison, then wrapped or bound to the web with strong threads. Spiders do not have jaws for chewing up their victims. They inject special digestive enzymes into the prey that dissolve the soft innards, then suck out the juices using stomach muscles that function like a pump.

The queen of Japanese arachnids is a great yellow **orb web spider**. Around midautumn, strollers in the countryside or urban parks are often surprised to find their path blocked by a thick golden spider web. Just above the center of the web sits an immense spider, shining yellow-gold and gray. Despite its appearance, the species is harmless and provides a superb chance to study spiders and their webs up close.

Orb web spider

The webs of these orb spiders are true masterpieces of civil engineering. The bridge line can be several meters long. I have seen bridge lines stretched between lampposts across a two-lane road. The web is further anchored and supported by heavy frame lines along the edge. Often, two thinner, sparser webs are constructed parallel to the main web, turning the structure into a three-dimensional trap capable of stopping even the heaviest dragonflies. In tropical Asia, there are even larger species in this genus that are known to trap small birds, and the aboriginal peoples of New Guinea and northern Australia are reported to use orb webs as fishing nets!

The spider itself will usually be resting motionless a little above the center of the web. The huge yellow-and-gray abdomen and yellow-and-black striped legs are unmistakable. Seen from the opposite side, a bright red patch near the tip of the abdomen is another good field mark. The Japanese name for this beautiful, colorful spider is *jorō-gumo*. *Kumo* or *gumo* is the generic name for "spider," and *jorō* has the nuance of a *femme fatale*.

A careful search along the edges of the web usually reveals one or two other spiders, only a third or a fourth as long as the big one. These are actually males, waiting for a chance to mate with the female. Spider females are usually larger than the males, and in many species the male must perform an elaborate courtship to convince his mate that he is not just another victim to be eaten. In orb web spiders, the males are so small that the females do not even recognize them as potential prey. They can thus move in, mate, and move out in relative safety.

A mating pair of orb web spiders. The small one is the male.

The female lays her eggs on the trunk of a tree, the side of a building, or even the underside of a leaf. If she lays them on a leaf, she conscientiously sews the leaf stalk solidly onto the branch. The eggs are fastened to the surface with special thread and remain dormant throughout the winter, hatching out the following May. The adults all die off with the onset of winter.

Two other related yellow-and-black spiders are found throughout the countryside. One of these, the **kogane-gumo**, has a fat, round abdomen, and matures around midsummer. The **naga kogane-gumo** has a longer, thinner abdomen, with a denser pattern of yellow-and-black stripes. It matures from late summer through early autumn.

Kogane-gumo, the only large yellow-and-black spider seen in midsummer, with partially completed X-shaped stabilamentum

Both these species adorn the center of their web with a structure that entomologists call a stabilamentum (*kakure obi*). These are reinforced sections made of thick, very shiny silk. The *kogane-gumo* stabilamentum shows an X-shaped pattern, and the *naga kogane-gumo* an I shape. Scientists disagree as to the function of this structure. As the spider usually waits motionlessly within the pattern created by the thick silk, one theory focuses on camouflage. Another interpretation is that the shiny silk reflects ultraviolet light much like a flower does, thus attracting insect prey. A third is that the shiny silk

Naga kogane-gumo. Matures from late summer into autumn.

is designed to warn birds of the presence of the web. Spider thread is made from protein, which is always in limited supply. Spiders will usually consume broken threads and thus recycle the protein, but if the threads are carried away by a bird (or person) they may not have enough reserves left over to rebuild the web.

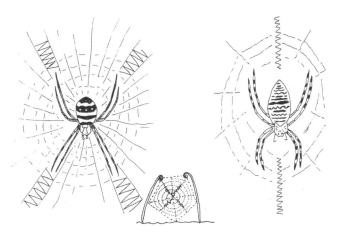

Kogane-gumo showing full
X-shaped stabilamentum

Naga kogane-gumo showing
full I-shaped stabilamentum

For central Tokyo businesspeople and residents, the most accessible arachnids are the little **sheet-web spiders** (*kusa-gumo*) that build their horizontal webs in the hedges and borders along streets, in parks, and around buildings. The spider itself, about the size of a one-yen coin, will usually be hidden in a funnel-shaped retreat woven at the rear of the web. A close inspection of the web will yield the dried out husks of victims, mostly flies and mosquitoes, and perhaps a discarded exoskeleton left over from the spider's last molt.

Not all spiders build webs. **Hunting spiders**, also called **wolf spiders** or **fishing spiders** (generically called *hashiri-gumo*, or "running spiders" in Japanese), ambush or chase down their prey on the ground. Tokyo's most common species, the ***iō-iro hashiri-gumo***, prefers slightly moist hunting grounds. During summer, the female is often seen carrying a huge brown ball of silk. These are her eggs. She carries them around with her until they are ready to hatch, then weaves a simple web for the young spiders to climb on. The protective mother guards her offspring until they are ready to disperse and start life on their own. Young spiders disperse by simply crawling around and also by "ballooning," floating on the wind with a length of silken thread.

Iō-iro hashiri-gumo carrying sac of eggs in midsummer

All spiders will bite if handled roughly. Some spiders have venom capable of causing serious harm to humans, but only one of our local species, the **kabaki komachi-gumo** is considered dangerous. This small, nocturnal hunting spider lives in dense vegetation, often along the edges of an irrigation canal. The female constructs a neat apartment by bending and binding the leaves of

Nest of *kabaki komachi-gumo*, Tokyo's only dangerous species

tall grasses, such as *susuki*, in which she lays her eggs. She guards her eggs courageously and, after they hatch, performs the ultimate sacrifice, offering up her own body as the first meal for her hungry offspring!

Spiders seem invulnerable but actually have many enemies, including birds, toads, frogs, and salamanders. Certain species of hunting wasp even specialize in spiders. The wasps first sting the spiders, paralyzing them, then haul them back to their nest alive. Back at the nest, an egg is laid next to the spider. Once hatched, the growing larvae will feed on the fresh meat of the spider.

TIDAL FLAT WILDLIFE

Coastal wetlands are among the most misunderstood and underestimated natural habitats on earth. Often appearing as nothing more than empty expanses of mud or reeds, these habitats have for decades been polluted or filled in to make new land for residential or industrial development. For example, most of the industrial, port and entertainment areas in the Tokyo area, including all of the chemical and steel plants that fueled the "economic miracle," as well as Haneda Airport, Disneyland, Makuhari Convention Center, and the various chic spots in the thriving waterfront districts, are built on former coastal wetlands. Almost all of these were filled in during the postwar decades, under a prevailing philosophy known as *mu kara yū*, "making something out of nothing."

Coastal wetlands are actually extremely vital habitats. To begin with, they support dense populations of small animals, such as clams, crabs, and bristleworms, that in turn provide food for fish and birds. They also serve as spawning grounds and nurseries for many species of ocean fish, including valuable commercial species. Coastal wetlands thus play an important role in maintaining biodiversity and fishery resources.

Wetlands also act as a sort of buffer zone, protecting the land from high waves and storm tides. In addition, the wetlands' billions of crabs, clams, and worms filter excess plankton and organic debris out of the seawater, thus functioning as a natural water purification tank.

Finally, coastal wetlands are prime destinations for local naturalists. Birders congregate along the shores, focusing their binoculars and high-powered field scopes on great flocks of sandpipers and plovers. Those willing to get a little wet and dirty can also spend long hours studying crabs and other small animals that live on or in the tidal flat mud.

When approaching the study of tidal wetlands, it helps to analyze the habitat in terms of challenges and opportunities, especially in the intertidal zone, the area between the high- and low-tide lines. For a small plant or animal living here, one obvious challenge is how to avoid desiccation from exposure to the sun and wind while the tide is out. A related challenge is where to hide from predators, especially birds, which are intelligent, lightning-quick, sharp-eyed hunters.

Most small tidal flat animals have met these challenges by learning to dig themselves into the mud. Crabs, for example, excavate deep burrows, while clams have wide, extendable feet that allow them to quickly pull themselves down into the substrate. On the other hand, sandpipers and plovers have evolved into tidal-flat specialists, skilled at catching these small animals unaware, or even using their long bills to pull them right out of their burrows. In this manner, the small tidal-flat animals and the shorebirds have been evolving together, in a sort of one-upmanship pattern played out over millions of years.

For those species that have adapted to its challenges, a tidal flat offers one of the most productive food-chains on earth. The rivers that build up the flats bring immense loads of nitrogen, phosphorous, and other nutrients from the land. As a result, phytoplankton, tiny microscopic single-celled plants that float in the seawater, reproduce at phenomenal rates. Zooplankton, tiny animals that feed on the phytoplankton, also flourish in the seawater. When the tide is out, another type of algae grows on the surface of the flat. In addition, decomposing dead plants and animals brought down by the river are broken down by scavengers and decomposers, producing tiny pieces of organic matter called detritus.

This algae, plankton, and detritus form the bottom levels of the tidal-flat food pyramid. Given the tremendous richness of these base levels, the clams, crabs, and worms that form the next step in this pyramid are often found in incredible numbers. One study conducted on a Tokyo Bay tidal flat found more than ten thousand worms living in a single square meter plot. Crabs scurry over the flat in huge herds, and clam beds, packed solid with short-necked clams and other edible species, have supplied people in the region with food for upwards of five thousand years.

Fish feed voraciously on the worms, and birds such as egrets, terns, and cormorants dine on the fish. Shorebirds eat the crabs and worms, while diving ducks and oyster catchers prefer clams. The great flocks of shorebirds and waterfowl attract falcons, kestrels, harriers, and other birds of prey, which, along with human beings, form the absolute tip of the tidal-flat food pyramid.

CLAMS

Razor clam showing a long, flexible foot at left and siphons at right

Clams and their relatives are among the most familiar of marine animals and are the most important tidal-flat residents in terms of human food resources. Almost any child can recognize a clam shell washed up on a beach, and most of us have at least tasted clam chowder or some other clam dish. Some of us may even have spent a day or two clamming on a tidal flat or sandy beach. Still, very few people stop to think about what kind of animal the clam is.

Clams belong to the phylum Mollusca, commonly called mollusks, an amazing group of animals that also includes spiral-shelled forms such as conches and tritons, as well as squid, octopus, and even the famous chambered nautilus. The common snails and slugs that we see in our gardens are also mollusks.

Clams and their relatives form one major subgroup, called **bivalves**, within the mollusks. Their most obvious feature is the two shell halves, or "valves," which protect the animal's internal organs, muscles, and other soft body parts. These two valves are connected at the base by a series of interlocking hinges and can be opened and closed by powerful muscles and ligaments.

Most bivalves favor habitats with soft bottom sediment, such as sand or mud, into which they can burrow. Burrowing is accomplished with a wide, flexible foot that is one of evolution's masterpieces. This foot can not only be extended and retracted but also widened or thickened at any point by shifting the fluids contained within. To burrow, the bivalve first makes its foot long and thin, thrusting it deep into the sand or mud. It then shifts fluids to the tip of the foot, which widens into a sort of anchor. Finally, the bivalve contracts the foot, pulling its shell down into the sand. This may sound like a tiresome process, but some bivalves can disappear into the sand or mud in no time at

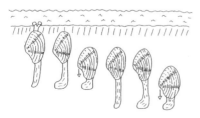

A diagram showing how a clam uses its miraculous foot to dig itself into the sand. Two cycles are shown. Each cycle consists of extending the foot, inflating the tip of the foot to serve as an anchor, then pulling the shell downward by contracting the foot.

Some common bivalves of Tokyo Bay. At left is a razor clam (*mate-gai*; top) and Japanese Dosinia (*kagami-gai*; bottom). In the center is an oyster (*kaki*; top) and Asian trough shell (*baka-gai*; bottom). At right is a short-necked clam (*asari*; top), a smaller trough shell (*shio-fuki*; center), and a ribbed cockle (*sarubō*; bottom). A ten-yen coin is shown at upper right for size comparison. All specimens collected at Kasai Seaside Park in Tokyo.

Almost all bivalves feed by filter feeding, a method accomplished with two siphons, the length of which varies according to species. The incurrent siphon is used to suck in a steady stream of seawater. This water is then passed through the clam's gills, which act like a fine-meshed sieve to filter out food particles such as algae, plankton, and detritus. Once the food particles have been removed, the water is returned to the sea through the excurrent siphon.

Tidal-flat bivalves spend most of their time dug into the sand or mud on the bottom, with only their two siphons sticking out into the water. Species that live deep in the sediment have long siphons, while those that live near the surface have shorter ones. Bivalves that live within the intertidal zone feed only when the tide is in. During low tide they retract their siphons and pull the two shell valves tightly together.

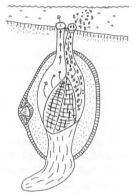

Cross section of a bivalve in filter feeding mode. On the right is the incurrent siphon and on the left is the excurrent siphon. The fine-meshed gills are in between. Note the wide foot extended for use as an anchor.

Many people think that bivalves, with their hard protective shells, are impregnable. Unfortunately for the bivalves, this is not the case at all. A variety of predators have developed techniques for thwarting the bivalves' defenses. Sea stars, or starfish, as they are commonly but incorrectly called, for example, can use their suction-like tube feet to slowly pull the valves apart, while moon snails have sharp drill-like mouth parts that enable them to drill a neat, round hole in the toughest shell.

Some fish have thick teeth and powerful jaws capable of crushing the shells. Even some crabs are able to crush or pry the shells open. Birds swallow the bivalves whole, crushing them with powerful stomach muscles. Adaptable, quick-learning seagulls carry the bivalves high into the air, then drop and shatter them onto the rocks below to get at the soft interior.

The greatest predators of bivalves are human beings. Thousands of years ago, people learned that bivalves could be easily collected in large numbers, especially on tidal flats. The extensive Jōmon-period shell middens, found all around the edge of Tokyo Bay, testify to the zeal with which these early people collected the clams. In fact, in some areas bivalves were clearly the mainstay of the local diet.

Bivalves remain a major commercial fishery resource today. In the Tokyo area, the **short-necked clam** (*asari*) is one of the most common and commercially valuable species. These clams are eaten in a variety of traditional and modern dishes, from miso soup to spaghetti. In early spring, hordes of people flock to the tidal flats to enjoy a day of clamming called *shio-higari*, a popular yearly ritual since the Edo period, two or three hundred years ago.

Other common bivalves include a **razor clam** (*mate-gai*), with a long narrow shell; two species of trough shells (*shiofuki-gai* and *baka-gai*); several cockles (*akagai* and *sarubō*), which can easily be distinguished by their "ribs"; and an oyster (*kaki*).

Local ribbed cockle (*aka-gai*)

Bivalves also play a vital role in maintaining water quality, especially in closed inlets such as Tokyo Bay, where water circulation is slow and secondary organic pollution is always a problem. To begin with, great quantities of nutrient salts, such as nitrogen and phosphorous, are dumped into the bay from agricultural runoff and household discharges (toilet waters are always purified, but kitchen, bath, and laundry waters are usually dumped straight into the rivers). These nutrient salts then provide fuel for tremendous blooms of phytoplankton, especially during the hot summer months. Many of these plankton are reddish in color and, by August, Tokyo Bay water has taken on a reddish tint. These great plankton blooms themselves are not a major problem, but as the plants die they settle down onto the bottom, where they are decomposed by bacteria. Decomposition is a chemical process that requires oxygen, which must be taken from the surrounding water. By summer's end, the bottom meter or so of water is completely deprived of oxygen, and over the years a thick layer of smelly, oxygen-depleted mud, called sludge, builds up on the sea bottom.

In clam beds, millions of filter-feeding bivalves remove tons of excess plankton and organic material from the water, preventing the loss of oxygen and buildup of sludge. A simple experiment can be made to demonstrate this ability. Just fill a bucket with cloudy seawater full of suspended matter, then add a few dozen live clams. In no time at all the bucket water will be sparkingly clear.

POLY-CHAETE WORMS

Lugworm removed from burrow

Anyone who spends a few minutes watching plovers and small sandpipers work a mud flat will notice that the birds frequently pull long, wriggly critters out of the mud. These are marine segmented worms, called **polychaetes** or bristle worms. They are constructed somewhat like our common earthworms but have bristly appendages attached to each segment. In many areas, they form the bulk of the tidal flat biomass.

Many species of polychaetes live in burrows. Some species feed on detritus, while others are carnivores that prey on tiny crustaceans and other small animals. Similar-looking species are difficult to distinguish, but there is one common local species that is easy to spot and study. This is the **lugworm** (*tamashiki gokai*), a dark species with long bristles that lives in a U-shaped burrow, with its head and mouth at one opening and its tail and anus at the other. Lugworms feed in a unique manner. They first swallow some mud, out of which they filter the edible material as it passes through their bodies. The cleaned mud is then expelled from the anus, almost like toothpaste from a tube. The fecal remains can be seen all over the flat and look like little mounds of spaghetti made out of mud. In May, the eggs are laid in a jellylike mass that is deposited alongside the burrow. The lugworm is very common at Funabashi Seaside Park.

Hooked jaws of predatory bristleworms. The jaws can be retracted inside when not in use.

Fecal remains of lugworm

Polychaete worms are important elements in the ocean and shoreline food chains. Shorebirds feed heavily on the worms when the tide is out, and fish take over when the water returns. In addition, the burrows dug by the worms break up and aerate the top layer of the tidal flat, helping to prevent formation of the smelly anaerobic sludge.

Fecal remains (top) and egg mass of lugworm

CRABS

Kome-tsuki gani with *suna-dango* feeding remains

Crabs, along with clams and worms, form the "big three" of small animals that dominate the middle levels of the tidal wetland food chain. Crabs that live in the reed marshes and surroundings are usually omnivores, whereas most of those that live on the open tidal flat itself are anatomically designed for feeding on the algae that grows on the mud while the tide is out.

The easiest local mud crab to study is the tiny ***kome-tsuki-gani***, whose carapace is the size of a one-yen coin. In favorable spots, the flat appears to be carpeted in crabs and little round balls of sand. These balls are the crabs' feeding remains. Mud crabs rake in the surface sand with their spoon-shaped claws, then remove the edible algae with little comblike appendages on their jaws. As they work the sand they roll it into the neat little round balls, which are left on the flat when finished. This process of collecting sand and rolling it into little round balls reminds the Japanese of their own custom of *kome-tsuki*, removing the rice husk and polishing rice. *Kani* or *gani* is the generic word for crab.

Kome-tsuki-gani are prime prey for the smaller shorebirds. They thus never venture far from their burrow and scutter down at the slightest hint of a shadow. With a little practice, they are easily caught for closer inspection. The half-moon carapace, and purplish color on the underside, are good field marks for confirmation.

Four different species of mud crab are fairly common on Tokyo Bay tidal flats. They all feed in essentially the same manner, but each prefers a slightly different microhabitat. From a crab's viewpoint, there are two factors that determine the

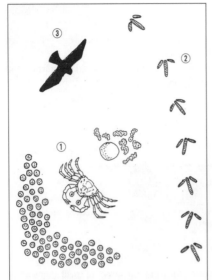

Reconstruction of tidal flat food chain:

1 *Kome-tsuki-gani* mud crab and remains of algae feeding,

2 Tracks of plover hunting crabs,

3 Shadow of raptor hunting plovers.

livability of a tidal-flat habitat. One of these is the composition of the substratum. Some species prefer hard-packed sandy sediments, while others favor soft, muddy areas. The second factor is drainage. Some species choose areas—usually near the high tide line—that drain completely when the tide is out. Others seek habitats where abundant puddles remain even at low tide.

The *kome-tsuki-gani* likes well-drained, sandy habitats. Another species of about the same size, the **chigo-gani** prefers well-drained but muddy areas. A much larger species, the **osa-gani**, usually opts for poorly-drained, sandy habitats, while the larger-still **yamato osa-gani** favors poorly-drained but muddy areas. By choosing to live in slightly different micro-habitats, these four species of mud crab can minimize competition.

The *chigo-gani* can be easily identified even at a distance by its white claws. These crabs are very territorial and proclaim their presence by lifting their white claws up and down in a rhythmical dance.

Chigo-gani mud crab from above (top) and displaying claws (below)

Viewed up close, their carapace is squared off, an easy field mark for distinguishing their species from the *kome-tsuki-gani*, which has a half-moon-shaped carapace.

The two larger species look alike at first glance but can be distinguished by the shape of the carapace, which is almost a perfect square in the *yamato osa-gani*, but in the *osa-gani* is rectangular, noticeably wider from side to side than from front to back. The big *yamato osa-gani* are the favorite prey of curlews, which poke their long, downcurved bill into the crab's burrows. As these crabs are too big to swallow whole, the curlew first whips the crab around, pulling the legs off, then swallows the body. Smaller sandpipers stand by, scarfing up the discarded legs.

Comparison of *osa-gani* (left) and *yamato osa-gani* mud crabs. These two species can be told apart by the shape of their carapaces.

Yamato osa-gani hidden in water. Only long eye-stalks are visible.

The reed marshes and other habitats surrounding the tidal flats also support a great number and variety of crabs. Marsh crabs are more diversified feeders than mud crabs. They do feed on algae and detritus that accumulate on the surface of the flat but also take advantage of other opportunities, such as nibbling on the fresh tender shoots of plants or scavenging on dead fish and birds.

Like the mud crabs, the various species of marsh crab all prefer slightly different microhabitats. Still, they are often found close by one another. Marsh crabs are all fast walkers, and many can spend considerable time out of water. Some can even breathe in fresh water and thus move well inland. Unlike the stream crab discussed in the next section, however, all must return to the sea to spawn.

Male *ashihara-gani*

The **ashihara-gani** is a large, greenish marsh crab with yellowish claws. *Ashihara* is the Japanese word for "reed bed," and indeed these crabs live among the reeds that flourish along the river mouths. They dig huge burrows among the reed clumps but, at low tide, venture out onto the nearby flat. The males have one row of hack-saw–like teeth on the

Female *ashihara-gani* with full clutch of eggs

bottom front edge of the carapace and another along the inside of their long claw segment. By rubbing these together they produce a grating sound which may be either a territorial or mating call.

Another familiar marsh crab is the **kuro benkei-gani**, which seems to have perfectly coordinated its movements with those of the *ashihara-gani*. When the tide is out, the *ashihara-gani* moves out on the open flat, while the *kuro benkei-gani* forages among the reeds. As the tide floods back in, the *ashihara-gani* returns to the reeds, while the *kuro benkei-gani* moves further inland.

Kuro benkei-gani

Both of these marsh crabs are common along the mouths of the Tama and Edo rivers; Rokgo-dote Park along the Tama River mouth is an especially good spot for observing the *kuro benkei* crabs. These marsh crabs have more powerful claws than mud crabs, and should be handled with care.

Heavily armed and armored ishi-gani

Several other crab species can be commonly observed on local flats. The **kefusa iso-gani** is usually found under stones or pieces of debris. The males have a round, hairy pad between the two pieces of their claws. The **ishi-gani** is a huge, powerful swimming crab, with immense claws and flattened, paddlelike segments on the last pair of legs. The paddles are used for swimming and digging into the mud. These crabs will never be found walking across the flat, though they may occasionally be encountered in puddles when the tide is out. Beware of their claws!

Ishi-gani

Another common local tidal-flat crab is the small, round **mame kobushi-gani**, which is about the size of a fifty-yen coin. When disturbed, these crabs quickly burrow out of sight, yet if you catch them, they pretend to be dead. Mating pairs are frequently encountered from late spring through early summer.

Mame kobushi-gani burrowing into sand

RIVER CRABS AND CRAYFISH

Stream crab. This crab has evolved the ability to live totally inland, never having to return to the sea.

Crabs and their close relatives the shrimps are arthropods. They belong to the class Crustacea, and all are usually referred to as crustaceans. Crustaceans are for the most part creatures of the sea, but there are two local fresh-water crustaceans that also deserve special mention.

One of these is the little **stream crab**, called *sawa-gani* in Japanese. This crab is unique in that it lives its entire life in fresh water. Several other species of crab may be found kilometers inland, but these must all return to the sea when it comes time to mate. The stream crab has managed to circumvent this necessity with some unique life-cycle adaptations.

Normally, crab eggs hatch out into planktonic larvae, which look nothing at all like a crab. These larva drift on the ocean currents, growing and molting until they find a place to settle down, upon which they molt into tiny crabs. (Crustaceans, unlike insects, can continue molting and growing even after reaching the adult stage.) The stream crab, however, does not pass through a planktonic larval stage. The eggs hatch out directly into baby crabs, which can then disperse and begin life in the river or canal.

Stream crabs like their water clean and fresh. They are common in the hills and mountains. In the uplands and alluvial plain, they are found only in spots where a steady supply of water naturally seeps out. Ecologists consider abundant stream crabs a sign that the local aquatic environment is in excellent condition.

The **American crayfish** is not nearly as picky. In fact, this crustacean will live in slow-flowing irrigation canals and almost-stagnant ponds. The crayfish was brought to Japan in the postwar years as feed for the bullfrogs that farmers were raising for the export frog-legs market (see Bullfrog in the Amphibians chapter). The hardy crayfish escaped and quickly naturalized all over the Tokyo region as well as in most other parts of Japan.

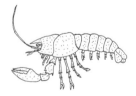

American crayfish

It is hard to assess the impact that American crayfish have had on the countryside ecosystem. Japan's native crayfish prefers very clean, fast-flowing water and is found only in the Tōhoku mountains, so there is probably no direct competition between these two species. The American crayfish are thought to feed heavily on young newts, and native fish and shrimp, but most of these species cannot live in deteriorated aquatic habitats anyway. In many areas, crayfish thus make up a high proportion of the local biomass and provide essential prey for predators such as egrets, shrikes, kingfishers, *tanuki*, and weasels.

Mud skipper

FISH

Tidal flats and shallow shoals are among our most valuable commercial fishing grounds. In Tokyo Bay, commercial fishermen target a variety of species in shallow shoal waters, including **sea bass** (*suzuki*), **halfbeak** (*sayori*), **mullet** (*bora*), **shad** (*kohada*), and several species of **flounder** (*karei*). Young flounders are often seen in puddles on the flats when the tide is out. Stingrays likewise may be hiding in the wet mud. Mullet are primarily fish of the open ocean, but the young spend their first few years around the inner bay shore and even ascend up the rivers. These silver fish move inshore with the flood tide and display a peculiar habit of leaping high out of the water. Look for their jumping show all along the Tokyo waterfront.

The little **goby** (*ma-haze*) is a year-round resident of upper Tokyo Bay, especially around river mouths where fresh and salt water mix. During winter, these fish move offshore to lay their eggs in nest holes and, more recently, in aluminum cans and other hunks of garbage sitting on the bay floor. The male guards the eggs and newly hatched fry. In early spring, the young move inshore and can be caught easily in puddles that form on the tidal flats. From late summer though autumn, the young gobies have grown and begin feeding heavily on bristle worms and other small animals, biting voraciously as well at the worms dangled by the fishermen that line the shore.

Goby

Mud skippers (*tobi-haze*) are superbly adapted to life on tidal flats. They live in nest holes, emerging to feed on small shrimp and other tiny animals when the tide is out. These humorous-looking members of the goby family can breathe in air and can walk slowly about on the flat using

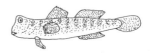

Mud skipper

their tails and chest fins for propulsion and tripodal support. When pressed, they perform great flying flips and leaps that make them most difficult to grab. Tokyo Bay being the northern distribution limit for these skippers, they are not all that common there. Look for them in small numbers on muddy tidal flats along the Tama and Edo river mouths and at the Tokyo Port Wild Bird Park and Gyōtoku Sanctuary.

OTHER
FAVORITES

Tidal flat sea anemone

A naturalist working across a Tokyo Bay tidal flat is likely to encounter a wide variety of strange creatures. Following are a few of my own special favorites.

Sea anemones are usually thought of as rocky-coast denizens, yet this species (*kurogane isoginchaku*) has adapted to life on tidal flats. A suction-cup–like disc at the bottom of the animal is attached to an oyster or clam shell buried in the sand or mud, and the tentacles, which are equipped with poison-tipped darts (not dangerous to humans), are extended into the water. Passing fish and shrimp are stung and paralyzed by the tentacles, then pulled into the cavernous stomach and digested. When disturbed, the anemone can pull itself down into the sand. The green dots sometimes seen on the disc and tentacles are algae that live inside the anemone's tissues. The algae and the anemone have a commensal relationship: the anemone feeds on starches produced by the algae's photosynthesis, while the algae gets a safe home and perhaps some required nutrients.

Scavenger snails (*aramushiro-gai*) have small, thick bodies with rough bumps on their shell. They are the hyenas and jackels of the tidal flat. They make short work of dead crabs and fish and thus help recycle energy and organic matter.

Long, stringy ***ogo-nori*** is a marine algae that grows in clumps on the tidal flats. It is used in making agar-agar, and is also served in sushi shops. ***Ana-aosa*** is a green marine algae that is usually found floating on the water. Wind and tides sometimes pile the floating pieces up on shore, forming deep layers along the high tide line. In the past, this algae was collected by farmers and used to make compost, but today it just piles up and rots, producing a noxious smell. Laver at Funabashi Seaside Park sometimes build up to depths of half a meter or so.

Scavenger snail feeding on dead crab

Thin **mud snails** (*uminina*), about one to two centimeters long, feed on algae that collects on the flat. Their trails can be seen going this way and that. During low tide they often collect around patches of *ogo-nori* or *ana-aosa*, where they can find some protection from desiccation.

Ogo-nori algae and mud snail

Several species of small **mud shrimp** burrow deep into the mud and are only occasionally found on the surface. The ***Nihon sunamoguri*** can be told apart by the relative size of its two claws, the right being several times larger than the left.

A small **hermit crab** (*yubinaga bon-yadogari*) is found, often in large numbers, in tidepools near concrete piers and around stranded driftwood and chunks of garbage out on the flat.

Mud shrimp

Nihon sunamoguri mud shrimp (left) with enlarged claw and two other common mud shrimps, *hasami-shako-ebi* (center) and *ana-jako* (right)

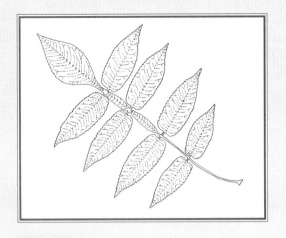

PLANTS

BROADLEAVED EVERGREENS

As November wanes and Tokyo's long autumn draws to a close, the city's zelkovas and ginkgos drop their bright yellow leaves. Winter is on the way, and deciduous trees will display their bare silouettes against the often blue skies. Many other trees will keep their leaves, and most Tokyo parks and gardens will retain a deep green gloss throughout the cold months.

These green-in-winter trees are broadleaved evergreens. As was noted in the introduction, these trees form the Tokyo area's natural climax forest. In terms of classification, they belong to the same families and genera as the broadleaved deciduous trees in the next section, but are adapted to warmer climates with less snow in winter.

Broadleaved evergreen forests are found in a wide swath running across the Asian continent, from the eastern edge of the Himalayas to the South China Sea, including Taiwan, the Ryūkyū Islands, the very southern tip of the Korean Peninsula, and most of southern and western Japan. This area is characterized by mild winters, with an average temperature in the coldest months of a few degrees above freezing, and abundant rainfall brought by monsoons and typhoons. To the north of the swath are drier regions covered by

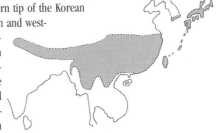

Distribution of Asian broadleaved evergreen forests

147

deserts and steppes. To the south are even warmer and wetter regions that support true tropical rainforests. The broadleaved evergreen forests of Asia are the most extensive in the world, but similar forests of smaller scale can be found in the southeastern corner of the United States.

In Japan, broadleaved evergreen forests are found on Kyūshū, Shikoku, western Honshū, and the coastal area of central Honshū, as far north as Niigata Prefecture on the Sea of Japan side and Ibaraki Prefecture on the Pacific Ocean side. This distribution represents the extreme northern limit of the habitat and is made possible by the warm Japan Current, which ameliorates the archipelago's climate and allows the evergreens to grow much further north than they do on the continent.

A quick examination of a broadleaved evergreen shows that the leaves are much thicker and tougher than those of deciduous trees. The leaves of deciduous trees are designed to work for only half a year or so, while those of the evergreens may be called on to do duty for two or three or as many as six or seven years. The upperside of the evergreen leaf contains a thick waxy layer, called a cuticle, which protects the leaf and produces a beautiful shiny gloss. The common Japanese name for these trees, *shōyōju*, literally means "shiny-leaf tree."

CHINKAPIN

Edible chinkapin acorn

If beech rules Japan's northern forests, **chinkapin** is king in the south. These big, beautiful trees, called *sudajii* (or *shii*) in Japanese, have a round, billowy crown that makes the forest look like it is topped with scoops of ice cream.

The leaves are small (five to ten centimeters long), thick, and leathery, with a distinctive coppery sheen on the underside. Most leaves have entire margins (that is, smooth edges without notches or teeth), but some have a few shallow teeth on the upper half. The bark, especially on older trees, shows deep furrows.

Chinkapins grow wild in the forest. They are also widely planted in parks and gardens, and around Shinto shrines. An impressive stand can be seen along the Imperial Palace Moat just across from Hibiya Park.

Chinkapins belong to the beech family. Trees in this family have a different floral arrangement than roses and most other familiar garden flowers. Most of our typical flowers are "perfect," which means that they have both male parts (stamens) and female parts (pistils) in the same flower. Beech family plants have "imperfect" flowers (separate male and female flowers). Several dozen male flowers, each with numerous stamens, bloom along a twiglike axis. Botanists call this arrangement a catkin. The male catkins grow in the leaf

Chinkapin branch map: female flowers at right and male flowers at left.

joints (where the leaf joins the branch). The female flowers bloom in separate catkins, usually found further out toward the tip of the branch. The stigma (the tip of the pistil, where the pollen is picked up) is split into three segments.

In mid- to late May, the chinkapin's long, bushy male catkins paint the forest edge a beautiful pastel shade of soft greenish yellow. The female catkins are smaller and less conspicuous. Chinkapin flowers are pollinated by insects, which are attracted by the sweet bouquet. Chinkapins, although not true oaks, produce acorns in autumn. These acorns are contained in a sheath, which splits open when ripe, and are edible, even when raw.

EVERGREEN OAKS

Shira-kashi leaves and acorns

Evergreen oaks come in seven species, some of which are difficult to tell apart. Taxonomically, these trees belong to the same genus as the deciduous oaks. The Japanese generic term for evergreen oaks, *kashi* or *gashi*, is thought to derive from *katai-ki* (literally, "hard tree"), which refers to the excellent quality of the wood. The most common native species in the Tokyo area, also the most popular ornamental one, is called ***shira-kashi*** ("white oak") for the color of its wood. The leaf is narrow and spearlike, with several teeth along the upper edge. The trunk is blackish. In mature trees, little crumblike pieces of bark will drop off when the trunk is gently rubbed. The acorn is round, with clearly visible ridges running in parallel lines around the cap (almost all the evergreen oaks have similar-looking acorns).

Aka-gashi, or "red-oak" (so named in Japanese for the color of its wood), is also common in the native forests and around shrines, but is less popular as an ornamental. The *aka-gashi* has a large leaf with a long stalk and entire margins. The bark flakes off, producing raw-looking red scars. In most oaks, the flowers bloom in spring and the acorns mature that same autumn. This species is unusual in that the acorns do not mature until their second year. Less common than the *aka-gashi* or *shira-kashi*, the **urajiro-gashi**, another local species, can be easily identified by a dry whitish green tint on the leaf underside.

Shira-kashi branch

One species of evergreen oak that deserves special mention is the **ubame-gashi**, a shrub that thrives along coastlines from Tokyo southward. The leaves are small (three to five centimeters long) and often curl downward around the edges. The acorn cups show scales rather than parallel ridges. All evergreen oaks have hard wood and make superb charcoal. But this species, in particular, is especially valued as a source of the finest charcoal.

Aka-gashi flowers: the male flowers of oak trees are in long down-hanging catkins, and the pollen is carried on the wind

Oaks, like the chinkapin, belong in the beech family. Their male and female catkins are similar to the chinkapins', but as their pollen is transported by the wind rather than insects, they are more drably colored and lacking in the rich bouquet. All trees in the beech family have simple leaves that are arranged on the branch in an alternating pattern, with spaces between the bases of consecutive leaves.

Ubame-gashi leaves and acorns

For those interested in studying Japan's live oaks in detail, Rinshi no Mori Park has a complete collection with labels.

LAURELS

Tabu-no-ki flowers

The ***tabu-no-ki*** is a giant member of the laurel family that grows well along the coasts of southern and western Japan, not as close to the waves as the *ubame-gashi* oak and *tobera* (see Tobera), but back a little on the sea-facing hills and mountain slopes. It often shares this habitat with the Japanese black pine (see Pines in the Conifers chapter). The *tabu-no-ki* is also planted in parks, especially those near the shore, such as the Hamarikyū Garden. The round marble-size berries are dark green at first but turn purple when ripe. The leaves are long (up to fifteen centimeters) and slightly wider at the top than bottom.

Tabu-no-ki fruit

Shiro-damo is a very common laurel-family member, easily identified by the leaves, which have two large veins running nearly parallel to the center vein and a unique white, waxlike coating on the underside. The tiny yellow flowers bloom in October, about the same time that the bright red berries from the preceding year ripen. The flowers are imperfect, with male and female flowers on separate trees (see Japanese aucuba in the next section). In the inland forests, this tree is usually just part of the undergrowth, dwarfed by oaks and chinkapins. Along the coast, it can grow tall and wide.

Shiro-damo branch (female plant): fruits ripen at the same time flowers come into bloom

Trees of the laurel family have simple leaves arranged in an alternate pattern. The **camphor tree**, also a member of this family, is discussed in the chapter on street and park trees.

Shiro-damo leaves and berries

UNDER-STORY TREES

Yabu-tsubaki flower.
Stamens are fused
into a single structure.

Surprisingly, a number of smaller trees and shrubs have adapted to the dark, damp, and shady habitat underneath the big broadleaved evergreen trees. The most outstanding example is the **Japanese wild camellia** (*yabu-tsub-aki*), which is native to Tokyo-area forests and widely planted in parks and gardens. Several hundred ornamental varieties have been made from this tea-family tree as well as the related *sazanka*, which is not native to the area. These two lineages can be told apart by looking at the mass of pistils in the center of

Sazanka flower. Stamens are separated at the base.

the flower. In the *tsubaki*, these will be fused into a single structure, while in the *sazanka*, they will be separated at the base. Camellia blossoms are greatly prized in flower arrangements that accompany the traditional tea ceremony.

Camellia leaves are especially thick and shiny. In fact, the Japanese name *tsubaki* is thought to derive from *tsuya no ki*, *tsuya* being a bright sheen (the prefix *yabu* means "bush" or "thicket," and indicates a wild species). The edges of the leaves are lined with short, dense teeth, like the blade of a hacksaw. The fruit is a thick, round capsule that at first glance looks like a miniature apple. Split open, it reveals three brown nutlike seeds. Oil pressed from these seeds is used for cooking and as a base for cosmetics.

Another locally common member of the tea family is a neat little shrub called **hisakaki**. The tree is considered sacred to the Shinto gods. Its sprigs are always offered at weddings and other auspicious ceremonies. Tiny white bell-shaped flowers bloom in early spring. The *hisakaki* grows wild in forests and is frequently planted around Shinto shrines. (A closely related species, the **sakaki**, grows in the Kansai area, and is also used in Shinto ceremonies.)

Hisakaki flowers, photographed at the Meiji Jingū Shrine

The **Japanese aucuba**, or *aoki*, may well be the most common tree in the Tokyo area. It is hard to find a stretch of park, garden, or forest edge without at least one or two specimens of this exceptionally strong and prolific member of the dogwood family. The large leaves, as long as an adult's hand, have several big teeth on the upper half. A light green color covers the trunk and branches (the Japanese name means "green tree"). Bright red oval berries, about the size and shape of a large martini olive, brighten up the winter scenery. An escaped ornamental variety, with yellow splotches on the leaves, is also sometimes encountered.

Aucuba male flowers

Aucuba branch (note opposite leaves)

Aucuba male (right) and female flowers. Male and female flowers bloom on separate trees.

The distinctive long-stemmed leaves of the **yatsude**, as large as a basketball and deeply cut into a series of usually eight long fingers, are unmistakable. This short tree, a member of the ginseng family, is common in both natural forests and parks.

Yatsude flowers form at the tip of the branch in dense, round clusters. The small fruit, grayish when ripe, are favorites among birds, which carry them around and drop them here and there. As a result, the *yatsude*, like the aucuba, is a widespread volunteer in most parks and woodlands.

Yatsude leaves

In popular fairy tales, the leaves of the *yatsude* are often portrayed as magic fans used by *tengu*, legendary creatures found deep in Japan's ancient forests. This magic fan can blow up a storm so great that huge boulders are whipped about like straw. In many a story the *tengu* use

Yatsude flowers

their magic to protect the forest from greedy woodcutters. In California, the *yatsude* is called **Japanese aralia**, and is frequently planted around swimming pools.

The **nezumi-mochi** has alternate leaves with entire margins, and is very common along the edge of native forests as well as in parks, gardens, and yards. A dense cluster of white flowers bloom in the heat of summer. In late autumn, grayish fruit, shaped like miniature rugby balls, form at the tip of each branch. This fruit, which looks like mouse scats, gives the tree its Japanese name (*nezumi* means "mouse").

These understory trees native to broad-leaved evergreen forests can thrive even in places that get very little direct sun. They are thus popular ornamentals in the inner city, where narrow streets and small backyards may be in the shade throughout most of the day. In addition, the *yatsude*, aucuba, *nezumi-mochi*, and a **windmill palm**

Nezumi-mochi branch

(*shuro*) that has escaped from cultivation, are so common as volunteers in parks and gardens that groundskeepers often consider them a nuisance.

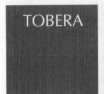

TOBERA

Tobera flowers in full bloom

The **tobera** is a short, dense shrub with spatulate-shaped leaves that often curl under along the edges. White five-petaled flowers bloom in spring, and round capsules ripen in autumn, splitting open to release numerous bright orange seeds. This rugged shrub, able to tolerate high winds and salt spray, is first and foremost a native of the coastline, often found growing perfectly content down to the very edge of the tideline. In the city and suburbs, *tobera* is widely used as a hedge or divider along wide streets.

DECIDUOUS TREES

As was described in the introduction, the classic old-growth forest in the Tokyo area may be broadleaved evergreen, but a wealth of deciduous trees, which drop their leaves in winter, abound in secondary woodlands, coppices, and in parks and gardens. Japanese deciduous trees include oaks, maples, dogwoods, willows, hornbeams, magnolias, snowbells, alders, roses, and cherries—all types familiar to Americans and Europeans. In the past, when the earth was warmer, a great chunk of deciduous forests stretched continuously across the northern Eurasian and American continents. Later, as the earth cooled, these forests were forced southward, eventually breaking up into several isolated fragments. Since then, the trees have evolved into different species, but the basic types (families and genera) remain the same.

BEECH FAMILY

Konara oak leaves and acorn

Oaks form a major component of natural secondary deciduous woodlands and are usually the most common trees in the managed coppice forests. In the past, villagers valued these trees for firewood, charcoal, and compost, made from the leaves. Today they are used mainly as a base for growing *shiitake* mushrooms.

Just like the evergreen oaks discussed in the previous section, the deciduous oaks have wind-pollinated male and female catkins and simple, alternate leaves. The most common native oak in the Tokyo area is the **konara**. Along with the **hornbeam** (*inu-shide*), this oak often dominates stretches of woodlands in the uplands and hills. The leaves have lobes along the edge, and are widest at the upper part, or shoulder, then tapering downward towards the base. The leaf has a short stalk about half a centimeter long. The acorns are usually a little bit longer than those of the evergreen oaks, and the cup shows a scaled rather than parallel ridged pattern.

Konara oak trunk: flat, shiny sections alternate with deep furrows

Konara oak leaf and acorn, with *kunugi* acorn (right) for comparison

The **kunugi** oak is often found growing alongside the *konara*. The leaves are long and lancelike. Each of the side veins ends at a sharp point that sticks out past the leaf edge. Farmers report that this tree grows faster than the *konara*, and that the thick bark is well suited for mushroom cultivation. The huge acorn has a densely fringed cup and matures in the autumn of its second season.

There is some confusion about the origin of the *kunugi*. Some field guides list this tree as native to Honshū,

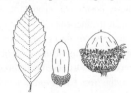

Kunugi acorn. These acorns mature in their second autumn, so can always be found on a bare stretch of branch behind the current year's leaves.

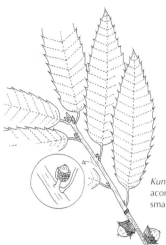

Kunugi trunk shows deep furrows

Kunugi branch. Note large ripe acorns from previous year and smaller acorns from current year.

Leaf of *kashiwa*

but from my observations it does not grow wild in the Kantō area. Some scholars believe it may even be of Korean origin, brought to Japan along with wet-rice agriculture.

The ***abemaki*** oak is sometimes confused with the *kunugi*. The leaves are very similar but can be distinguished by a grayish white tint on the underside. The bark is thick and soft and has been used as a replacement for cork. In the hills and mountains, one also encounters ***kashiwa***, sometimes called daimyo oak in English. This oak has a huge, often deeply lobed leaf with a very short stalk and a big acorn with a fringed cup. The leaves are used to wrap a delicious traditional sweet called *kashiwa-mochi*. Chemicals contained in the leaf act as a preservative and disinfectant.

Oak trunks are often streaked with sweet sap that oozes out in summer. This sap becomes a natural feeding station for various insects, including immense rhinoceros and stag beetles (see Beetles in the Insects chapter). Small owls and hawks, as well as crows and shrikes, are well aware of this bounty.

In autumn, one often sees jays flitting through the oaks. These birds, in collecting and burying the acorns as a winter stash, help disperse the oaks throughout the forest.

Chestnut catkins

Chestnut female flower

Chestnuts on branch

The **Japanese chestnut** (*kuri*) grows wild in the woodlands and is also widely planted in neat orchards. The leaves closely resemble those of the *kunugi* oak, but are not as sharply pointed. Chestnut flowers form in long, yellow-green catkins. The male flowers are arranged like brushes along the axis, with the much smaller female flowers found at the base of the same catkin. The flowers are bee-pollinated and produce a sweet bouquet.

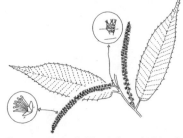
Chestnut, with detail of female flower (right) and male flower (left)

In autumn, the prickly husks, or urchins, grow to the size of a tennis ball. Eventually they fall to the ground and split open to reveal the smooth nuts inside. *Kuri-hiroi*, "chestnut gathering," is a popular pastime in the countryside. The half-opened chestnuts are regularly featured in autumn floral arrangements.

BIRCH FAMILY

Typical hornbeam trunk

Hornbeams are among the most common woodland trees. Their beautiful trunks, with smooth bark marked by contrasting vertical lines of dark and light gray, make them easy to spot. The simple, alternate leaves have very fine teeth along the edges. The male and female flowers bloom in separate catkins, with the female ones further out toward the end of the branch. The flowers bloom in midspring and are wind pollinated. The female catkins then develop into leafy clusters resembling hops. Each seed is attached to a leaflike structure that botanists called a bract. The bracts catch the wind as they fall, and the seeds are swept along the ground for great distances. If you look at the clutter along the side of a farm road you will usually find hundreds of hornbeam bracts.

The most common species in the uplands is **inu-shide**, sometimes called Yedo hornbeam in English, while **aka-shide** increases towards the hills and mountains. The **Japanese hornbeam** (*kuma-shide*) is also found at lower elevations but is not as numerous. All these trees look alike at first glance but can be told apart by the shape of the leaf and bract.

Wind-pollinated flowers of *inu-shide*. The long catkins hanging straight down are male flowers. Female flower clusters are at the tip of new shoot.

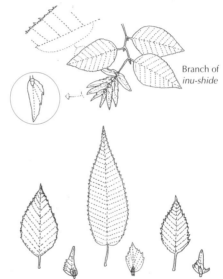

Branch of *inu-shide*

Bract and seed of *inu-shide*

Leaf and seed bract of three local hornbeam species. From left: *inu-shide,* Japanese hornbeam, and *aka-shide*.

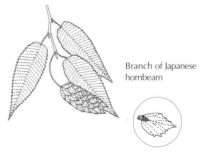

Branch of Japanese hornbeam

Bracts and seeds of Japanese hornbeam

Alders are also members of the birch family, with alternate, toothed-edged leaves and separate male and female catkins. The female flowers develop into little woody structures, called strobiles, that look like miniature pine cones. The strobiles remain on the branch, opening up to release tiny flat seeds.

Several species are found in Tokyo, each with its own habitat preference. The most common is the **Japanese alder** (*han-no-ki*), which loves wet, marshy habitats and is found along streams and around the edges of lakes and ponds. The seeds of this tree have no wings for wind dispersal but can withstand immersion in water for long periods of time. The seeds drop into the stream or pond and are then spread out when the water overflows. In the countryside, alders can quickly take over abandoned rice paddies, growing into a dense forest in a decade or so.

Japanese alder showing male catkins at tip of branch (right) and female flowers at left

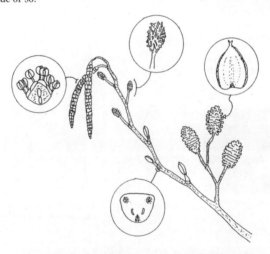

Japanese alder branch in late February. The strobiles from the previous year are still on branch when new flowers come into bloom; close-up sketches of seed (upper right), female flowers (top center), male flower (upper left), and leaf scar (bottom).

Flowers of *kumano-mizuki*

The strange-sounding English name "**dog-wood**" is thought to have originally been called "dagwood"—a "dag" being a term for a sharply pointed instrument (like a dagger). Dogwood produces a hard timber that holds a point very well. In ancient times, this wood was sharpened into skewers for roasting meat and vegetables.

Mizuki. Note alternate leaves.

Several native dogwoods of the genus *Cornus* are found in the Tokyo area, with **mizuki** being the most common. This tree has alternate leaves with veins that start off running towards the edge of the leaf, then turn upward to point toward the tip. Its white flowers are tiny but form a huge, dense clus-

Kumano-mizuki. Note opposite leaves.

ter at the tip of the branch. The berries are round, smaller than a standard marble, and range in color from pink to red to deep purple. The Japanese name *mizuki* means "water tree," referring to a preference for moist soils. A very similar species, the **kumano mizuki**, has opposite leaves.

One of Tokyo's most charming local trees is *hana-ikada*. The flowers, then the berries, grow right out from the center of the leaf itself. The Japanese name, meaning "flower on a raft," is a poetic reference to this unusual variation. This short, shrub-like member of the dogwood family is often found growing along the open, sunny edge of deciduous woodlands.

Flowers of *hana-ikada*

Deep purple berries of *hana-ikada*

Japanese snowbell flowers

The **Japanese snowbell** (*ego-no-ki*) is a tall tree of great interest to flower enthusiasts and ethnobotanists. This tree is common in coppice forests and woodlands. Because of its beautiful white flowers, which bloom in midspring, it is planted widely in parks and gardens. The flowers have five white petals and a bunch of long yellow stamens, and hang down from the branches like clusters of tiny bells.

Japanese snowbell fruit

Little grayish green marble-size fruits develop after the flowers fall off. The fruit consists of a hard brown seed inside a thick rind. In the past, the rinds were employed in a most curious method of catching fish. The rinds were dried, ground into a powder, and mixed with ashes. The resultant mixture was then thrown into a small pond or slow-flowing stream. Fish, temporarily paralyzed by the active chemicals in the rinds, would float to the surface, where they could be easily collected. The fish could then be revived simply by placing them in a bucket of clean water. These same rinds could also be beaten into a froth to be used as laundry detergent. A local name for the snowbell is *shabon-no-ki* (*shabon* means "bubbles" or "froth").

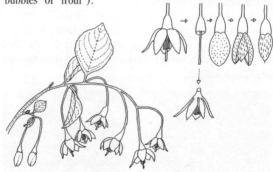

Japanese snowbell, with progression from flower to seed

ROSE FAMILY

Yama-zakura flowers. New leaves (alternate) are reddish when they first appear. Leaves and flowers together identify the tree as *yama-zakura* and not *somei yoshino*.

The famous ***somei yoshino*** cherry, so prominent today during cherry-blossom season, is actually a recently developed ornamental hybrid that became widely popular only about one hundred years ago (see Cherry Trees in the Street and Park Trees chapter). Before that, cherry-blossom viewing centered on a common native species, the ***yama-zakura***. In Japanese *sakura* or *zakura* means "cherry," and *yama* means "mountain," signifying that this is a species that grows in the wild. *Yama-zakura* flowers appear along with the new leaves, while *somei yoshino* flowers bloom before the new leaves emerge, a characteristic which accounts for their stunning appearance. Another fairly common wild cherry is ***uwamizu-zakura***. This tree can be easily identified by the position of the flowers and berries, which form in a long cluster at the tip of the new shoots. Native cherry trees produce fruit in abundance and are a major food source for a variety of wild birds.

Cherry tree trunks show distinctive pattern of horizontal lines and peeling

Flowers of *uwamizu-zakura*

Several wild roses are native to the Tokyo area. The ***no-ibara*** is a common shrub that thrives in sunny thickets and along the edge of the forest. The flowers are small, white, and simple, with only five petals, and sometimes come as a disappointment to those used to gorgeous multipetaled ornamental roses. Wild roses are very hardy. Their stocks are used commercially for developing and growing new ornamental varieties. Another native rose, ***teriha no-ibara***, is a low, spreading vinelike shrub that will grow right out of cracks in the rocks along the wind-swept coastline. The upper side of the leaves has a shiny gloss. While the cherries have simple leaves similar to oaks and beeches, the roses have compound leaves, which means that each leaf is composed of several tiny leaflets. To determine if a leaf is a simple leaf or a compound leaf composed of several leaflets, look for the "auxiliary bud." These buds always form at the spot where the base of a leaf attaches to the branch. They are normally dormant, but if necessary can be activated to grow into a new leaf or branch. A compound leaf will show an auxiliary bud only at its true base, and not at the base of each leaflet.

Berry pickers will want to keep their eyes out for various shrubs of the genus *Rubus*. Their fruit, sometimes called wineberries or blackberries, are sweet and delicious. There are many species, all with white five-petaled flowers, making identification difficult. The most delicious, the **momiji ichigo**, has deeply-cut simple leaves with thorns along the veins and a round yellow-orange fruit about the size of a marble. The flowers form underneath the branch and point downward.

No-ibara with odd pinnate compound leaf

Momiji ichigo flowers

Momiji ichigo fruit

Momiji ichigo (right) and *nawashiro ichigo,* whose bright red fruit is not quite as sweet as that of the *momiji ichigo*

MAGNOLIA FAMILY

Kobushi flower

Magnolias are among the oldest of the true flowering plants, called angiosperms by botanists. (Angiosperm flowers have a special womblike structure called an ovary, which surrounds and protects the developing seeds.) The magnolias we see today have survived essentially unchanged for around one hundred million years. Magnolia flowers are both beautiful and of great interest to the amateur botanist.

Tokyo's favorite magnolia is a hardy native species called the ***kobushi***. The beautiful white flowers, about ten centimeters across, bloom in late March, a week or so before the *somei yoshino*. *Kobushi* flowers consist of six long white petals (three of which are actually sepals). In the center are the pistils, surrounded by scores of pollen-producing stamens. The first day the flower opens, the pistils stick out and are receptive to pollen, but

Winter bud of *kobushi*. Dense covering of soft hairs protects the soft new growth inside.

the stamens continue to remain tightly packed together, not yet being fully matured. From the second day onward the situation is reversed: the stamens separate and begin producing pollen but the pistils now close up and are no longer receptive. Botanists believe this sort of staggered timing is a device for making sure that the flower is not fertilized by its own pollen.

Like all magnolias, the flowers of the *kobushi* open wide, making access for insects easy. The huge petals serve as a sort of landing pad for beetles, which are clumsy and erratic fliers that specialize in dramatic crash landings. The knobby-shaped fruit is actually a collection of pods containing seeds. The black, heart-shaped seeds are coated with a thin skin of bright orange. When ripe, they hang down by a slender white thread.

The *kobushi* is both a common native tree and a popular ornamental. In parks and gardens, it is often confused with the **Yulan magnolia** (*haku-mokuren*), an ornamental species of Chinese origin. The ornamental blooms about a week or

Kobushi seeds. Some seeds form heart shapes.

so earlier and has larger petals that don't open quite as wide. In addition, the *kobushi* can be clearly identified by a small leaf that appears at the base of each flower.

The **Japanese big-leaved magnolia** (*hō-no-ki*) is found only sporadically in the uplands and increases steadily as one moves up into the hills and mountains. The flowers and leaves, though shaped much like the *kobushi*, are much larger. In fact, the flowers are the largest of any native Japanese tree. (The **Southern magnolia**, or *taisan-boku*, an American native with even larger flowers, is widely planted in parks and gardens but is an import and does not grow wild in Japan.) The leaves are big enough for children to make into masks and, like the *kashiwa* oak, are also used to wrap and preserve various foods.

In the magnolia family, leaves are usually egglike in shape, have entire margins (no teeth or lobes along the edge), and are attached in an alternate pattern.

Flower of big-leaved magnolia in late stage. Most of the stamens have dropped off.

Close-up of big-leaved magnolia flower. On the first day (left), pistils are open and stamens closed; by the second day stamens have opened and pistils are closed. Mature fruit at right.

Japanese big-leaved magnolia leaf is large enough to fully hide a child's face

ELM FAMILY

Zelkova, with distinctive inverted broom shape, really stands out in winter

Elms are familiar trees throughout the northern temperate zone, with about 150 species in the family worldwide. All have simple, alternate leaves, usually with fine teeth along the edges. The flowers are small and inconspicuous, but the trees themselves can grow to be immense, often dominating a park or mountain slope.

Zelkova trunk, with scars

Three species in this family are very common in the Tokyo area. One, the **zelkova** (*keyaki*), may be the city's most familiar and easily recognized tree. The shape, like an inverted Japanese sweeping broom, is distinctive. The bark is thin and gray, with horizontal lines in young trees. In mature specimens, the bark falls off in fist-size flakes. As the flake scars heal, the trunk takes on a magnificent silver hue.

Zelkovas grow wild in woodlands and are one of the most popular street and park trees. The inverted-broom shape allows these trees to grow tall without spreading out, making them perfect for narrower streets. Farmers often grow huge zelkovas behind their house. The wood was traditionally used in shipbuilding.

Superficially, the ***muku-no-ki*** appears similar to the zelkova, but it has a more rounded shape and a thick trunk that is often buttressed. The blackish fruits are edible. The **Japanese hackberry**, or *eno-ki*, is a familiar tree in the countryside, where it not only grows wild but was also traditionally planted as a shade tree at strategic spots along heavily used walking routes. Given room to grow, the branches spread out wide into a magnificent rounded crown. The orange berries are edible.

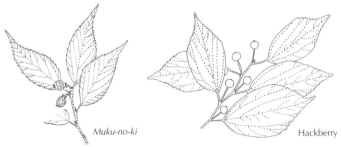

Muku-no-ki

Hackberry

Venerable hackberry at country crossroads

True elms (genus *Ulnus*) are not very common in the Tokyo area woodlands. One native species, ***aki-nire***, is widely planted in parks. The waferlike fruits, called samara, mature in autumn, and are designed to disperse on the wind. The bark flakes off in pieces, and looks a little like the *keyaki*, but a comparison of the leaves shows the difference. Both trees are planted around the big rectangular garden in Hibiya Park just behind the round fountain, across the street from the Imperial Hotel.

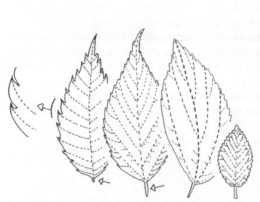

Bark of *aki-nire*

Comparison of elm family leaves. From left: zelkova, *muku-no-ki*, Japanese hackberry, *aki-nire*.

MAPLE FAMILY

Iroha momiji

Maples are the stalwarts of the autumn leaf-viewing parties. Japan is home to a dozen or more species of maple, but almost all of these grow in the higher mountains. Only ***iroha momiji*** (also called ***iroha kaede***) is found occasionally in Tokyo-area woodlands. The small leaves, with rough teeth along the edges, are very deeply cut into only five (or sometimes seven) "fingers." Numerous ornamental varieties have been developed from this species and are greatly prized both here and abroad. A separate subspecies, ***ō-momiji***, has larger leaves with seven fingers and finer teeth. Maple fruits are distinctive winged seeds, usually found in pairs. They disperse on the wind. All members of this family have opposite leaves.

LEGUME FAMILY

Wisteria flowers

The **legume** or **pea family** is known mostly for herbaceous plants, including such important vegetables as beans and peas, but also boasts many species of large trees and heavy woody vines. The **wisteria vine** is a good example. These vines, with their immense hanging clusters of light purple flowers, grow wild along the edge of the woodlands. Few people realize that there are two species, easily told apart by the direction in which they wind. ***Noda fuji*** winds clockwise (from the ground up) while ***yama fuji*** winds in the opposite direction.

Noda fuji (left) and *yama fuji* vines wind in opposite directions

Most members of the legume family keep their seeds in long capsules called pods. Wisteria pods are huge (up to twenty centimeters), heavy structures that ripen in midwinter, when the cold dry weather causes them to dry out and twist. Eventually they burst open with a loud snap and send the round, flat, beautifully-polished mahogany seeds flying in all directions. Wisterias are also planted in many parks and gardens. A typical arrangement has the vines growing up and around a long arbor, forming a tunnel of blooms that viewers can walk through. Like most plants in the pea family, wisteria leaves are compound, with from nine to fifteen leaflets.

Wisteria pod and seeds

Silk-tree flowers

The **silk tree**, or **mimosa**, is a light-loving plant that grows tall along streambeds, roads, and other openings in the woodlands. The leaves are immense double compounds, with each leaf comprising hundreds of tiny leaflets. During the day, the tiny leaflets are held out wide open. At night, or when the plant is roughly handled, they fold up. This gives this tree its Japanese name, *nemu-no-ki*, which means "sleepy tree." The silky flowers that bloom in midsummer do not look at all like typical pea flowers. The flowers lack petals, and the long thin

Silk-tree pods. Note immense double compound leaf.

stamens and pistils stick out unprotected, giving the flowers their silky air.

The **black locust** (*hari-enju* or *nise-akashia*) is a spiny tree native to the mideastern United States that escaped and naturalized throughout Japan. The leaves are compound, with seven to nine pair of oval leaflets and one extra at the tip. Dense drooping clusters of white flowers bloom in midspring.

Flowers of black locust

In autumn, thickets and forest edges are decorated with the delicate pink or purple flowers of various **bushclovers**. There are several native species and also numerous ornamentals, most with trifoliate leaves (compound leaves with three leaflets). Called *hagi* in Japanese, bushclovers are considered one of the traditional "seven flowers of autumn" (see Autumn Wildflowers).

MULBERRY FAMILY

Mulberry fruit

Mulberry trees (*kuwa*) are common inhabitants of thickets and forest edges. The red or dark purple oblong berries are edible, and its leaves are fed to silkworms. The **paper mulberry** (*kaji-no-ki*), with dense soft hair on the leaves, is more common in parks but also escapes and grows on its own. The *kōzo* is native to woodlands, with red berries that are round rather than oblong. Describing the shape of mulberry family leaves is a formidable task. On a single tree one may find leaves with no cuts, simple cuts on only the right or left side, or deep, complicated cuts on both sides, along with every other permutation imaginable. The bark of all three species is used for making traditional Japanese paper (*washi*).

Kōzo male (left) and female flowers

Leaf of paper mulberry, sketched at Shinjuku Gyoen Gardens

SUMAC FAMILY

Nurude

Sumacs are well known throughout the northern hemisphere for the irritating skin inflammations they cause when the leaves or twigs are touched. These irritations are caused by poisonous oils. Several species of the genus *Rhus* are found locally. Fortunately, by far and away the most common is the **nurude**, which contains very little poison and does not affect most people. The leaf is compound, with seven to eleven leaflets. Narrow strips of leafy material, called "wings" are found along the axis. These make a reliable field mark. When hiking in the hills, do beware of the **yama urushi**, with very long compound leaves (thirteen to seventeen leaflets), which has a slightly stronger poison. Perhaps the most dastardly culprit is not a tree at all but the vine **tsuta urushi**, with a very shiny trifoliate compound leaf. Beware of this plant when entering forests or when sitting down on the edge of hiking trails. Japanese lacquerware (*urushi*) is made mostly from the sap of a Chinese species, **urushi**, which is grown on mountain farmsteads.

Large odd-pinnate compound leaf of *nurude*, with distinctive "wings" along central axis. Other sumacs lack these wings.

Yama urushi in winter

Tsuta urushi

THE EDGE OF THE FOREST

Murasaki shikibu

A typical walk in the Japanese countryside takes one along a narrow farm road, just wide enough for a tractor or one of those little white pickup trucks, so popular among local farmers. Often the road is built along the very bottom of a slope, with rice paddies on one side and a coppice forest or mixed secondary forest on the other.

The edge of the forest is a special place, open to the sun and thus providing a superb habitat for many light-loving vines and smaller trees that are unable to grow inside the forest itself. In late autumn, these plants decorate their branches with colorful fruits and berries, vying with one another to attract the attention of local birds, upon which they depend to disperse their seeds. The beautiful colors, however, are as attractive to people as they are to birds. On an afternoon walk one meets not only botanists and birdwatchers, but haiku poets, painters, amateur herbalists, berry pickers, *ikebana* enthusiasts, and craft hobbyists as well.

One of the most captivating fruit belongs to a small tree called *Callicarpa japonica* by botanists, or ***murasaki shikibu***, in Japanese. The genus name *Callicarpa* means "beautiful fruit." The Japanese name is that of a beautiful court lady, the eleventh-century author of *The Tale of Genji*. Botanists point out that the leaves are opposite one another and that the fruit clusters are attached at the leaf joints (between the base of the leaf and the branch), while painters and haiku poets struggle to find the perfect words or brush strokes for the fruit's delicate shade of soft pastel purple.

Kusagi, although also blessed

Murasaki shikibu leaves are opposite, with fruit in leaf joints

Kusagi leaves are opposite, with fruit at tip of branch

DECIDUOUS TREES 173

with beautiful fruit, has not fared quite as well with its Japanese name. The large, heart-shaped leaves exude an unpleasant odor when rubbed or crumpled, thereby inspiring its name, which means simply "smelly tree." The round fruit is deep blue or purple and is surrounded by five red or pink sepals, creating a colorful star pattern.

Gonzui is another common tree with beautiful fruit but a lackluster name. The name *gonzui* originally refers to a small coastal fish that is not only inedible but has poison-tipped spines on its back. The name was extended to this tree because people had trouble finding a use for it. The wood is poor, the fruit inedible, and local farmers say that it doesn't even make decent firewood. Nevertheless, the fruit is a pretty, bright red capsule that opens like a miniature purse to reveal jet-black seeds. A botanist would note that the odd-pinnate-compound leaves are attached opposite one another and that the fruit clusters are at the tip of the branch.

Gonzui odd-pinnate leaves are opposite, with fruit at tip of branch

Siebold's wahoo (*mayumi*) boasts magnificent four-lobed pink capsules that split open to show four dark red seeds.

Siebold's wahoo

The leaves are opposite and the fruits are in the leaf joints. The wood is strong but flexible and is used for furniture and crafts. In the past, this tree was highly valued for making hunting and war bows (*yumi* means "bow" in Japanese). Another common tree in this same genus (*Euonymus*) is the **nishiki-gi**, literally "colorful tree," with bright little orange fruit and "wings" along the branches, all of which allow for easy identification. This tree, a local native, is also widely planted as an ornamental due to its brilliant orange-red autumn color.

The bright red berries of the **gamazumi** are prized both for their beautiful luster and excellent tarty flavor. Local farmers recall stuffing themselves with *gamazumi* berries on their way home from school. This shrub is also planted in parks and gardens, where it attracts birds such as the brown-eared bulbul and azure-winged magpie (see Urban Birds).

Gamazumi flowers

Gamazumi berries

Gamazumi leaves are opposite, with fruit at tip of branch

One of the perennial favorites for use in flower arrangements and handicrafts is the *akebi* vine, which is strong, yet flexible, and thus perfect for crafts. As an added bonus, the large fist-size purple fruit is delicious. In the Kantō area, most people eat only the soft, nearly transparent inner meat, discarding the thick rinds, but in other areas the rinds are used in various dishes. Two species are found in the Tokyo-area countryside: the *akebi*, with five fingerlike leaflets in each compound leaf, and the *mitsuba akebi*, with a trifoliate leaf. Wisteria vines are also used to weave wreaths and baskets.

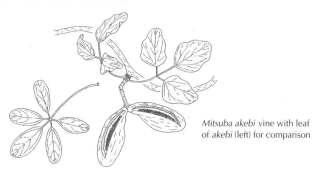

Mitsuba akebi vine with leaf of *akebi* (left) for comparison

The fruit of another tough vine, the **karasu-uri**, is picked for decoration. In English, this vine is sometimes called "snake-gourd," while the Japanese name means "crow [*karasu*] gourd." The fruit of the *karasu-uri*, about the size of a chicken's egg, is bright orange, resembling miniature pumpkins. A similar species with smaller fruit is called **suzume-uri**, or "sparrow-gourd." The terms *karasu* and *suzume* are often used to distinguish between two closely related species of different sizes, *karasu* (the "crow") being the larger.

The **smilax vine** is also a popular ornament. This is a thin yet strong vine, armed with sparse sharp thorns. The Japanese name, *saru-tori ibara*, means "monkey-catcher rose," although the plant actually belongs to the lily family. The round berries, which form in a dense cluster in the leaf joints, are the glossiest red imaginable. The leaves are antiseptic and traditionally used to wrap and preserve sweets made with pounded rice.

The autumn countryside is a popular gathering spot for birds and all sorts of people. Unfortunately, in many areas adjacent to heavily populated residential districts, there are simply not enough fruit and berries to go around. If you are a harvester-type admirer, a good rule is to take but a small portion of vines or berries, and these only from areas where plenty is available. Remember that the birds want their share too.

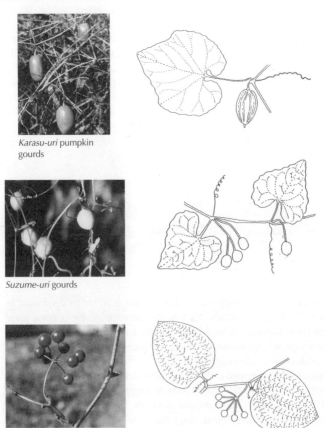

Karasu-uri pumpkin gourds

Suzume-uri gourds

Smilax vine

CONIFERS

Many people equate the terms "conifer" and "evergreen." Evergreen, as was noted earlier, refers only to leaf persistence, denoting plants that keep leaves on their branches throughout the year, in contrast to deciduous plants, which drop all their leaves in winter. Evergreen and deciduous are not true taxonomic categories, as both types may occur within a single family (the *mizuki* dogwood, for example, is deciduous, while the aucuba is evergreen), or even with a single genus (like *Quercus*, the oaks).

Conifers, on the other hand, form a taxonomic category, containing trees that grow their seeds in cones. Most are evergreen, but some, such as the Japanese larch and the dawn redwood (see Conifers in the Street and Park Trees chapter), are deciduous.

Conifers are an ancient group. Their lineage goes back to the Mesozoic period, some two hundred million years ago, when dinosaurs ruled the earth. They were among the first plants to reproduce by seeds rather than spores. Botanists usually divide seed plants into two great groups: the angiosperms ("covered seeds"), which have an ovary that surrounds and protects the growing seeds; and the gymnosperms ("naked seeds"), which lack this protective ovary. Conifers are classified as a subgroup within the gymnopserms. Yews, podocarps, cycads, and ginkgos also belong to other subgroups in the gymnosperms.

Conifers have simple flowers and fruit. Male and female flowers are separate, and the wind is used to carry pollen from one tree to the next. The female flowers develop into the cones, which contain hard, naked seeds usually fitted with wings to help them disperse on the wind. The leaves are either needlelike, as in pines and spruces, or flat and scalelike, as in cypresses and junipers.

Temperate-zone Japan is chiefly a land of broadleaf forests, with evergreen chinkapins and oaks in the warmer regions, and deciduous beech and oaks in areas where it is cooler. In these natural habitats, conifers play a minor role, inhabiting mostly marginal areas, such as wind-swept coastlines, subalpine zones, ridges, and volcanic outcrops, all of which have poor soil. Only in subarctic western and northern Hokkaidō are there extensive natural conifer forests.

In the postwar years, national forestry policy, emphasizing productivity over all else, encouraged villagers to strip off the native broadleaves and replace them with dense plantations of fast growing conifers such as cryptomeria, cypress, and Japanese larch. These plantations now cover entire mountainsides and regions.

Neat rows of perfectly matched conifers may look pretty but are an ecological disaster. As the ground under the densely planted trees is dark all year round, very few plants other than the conifers can survive. Without insects, fruits, or tubers, these plantations offer no food to native birds and mammals. Deprived of their natural food sources, animals such as macaques, bears, wild boars, and deer take to raiding crops. They are then killed as varmints.

The conifer plantations have messed up entire watershed ecosystems as well. These shallow-rooted trees hold little water compared to the deeper-rooted broadleaves. During heavy rains, the deeply rooted broadleaves will soak up and hold most of the water, releasing it slowly and steadily during dryer weather. In the shallow-rooted conifer plantations, however, most of the rainwater is washed immediately downslope as runoff, swelling the streams and rivers and causing floods in the valleys and plains. On the other hand, as soon as the rains stop, the watershed dries up, resulting in severe water shortages. In an attempt to counteract these problems, the government has built hundreds and thousands of large and small dams throughout the country and lined the rivers with steep-sided concrete walls, thus further degrading the watershed ecosystems. Still another problem caused by the conifer plantations is heavy attacks of asthma and allergies. In early spring, millions of conifers planted on the mountainsides surrounding Tokyo release their pollen. A haze of yellowish green pollen fans out across the Kantō Plain, almost like some "killer mist" from an over-the-top science fiction movie. People sensitive to the pollen suffer from breathing problems and other symptoms.

PINES

Close-up of black pine female flower cones in bloom

Pine trees are among the most familiar and highly valued conifers. Their long needles are tied together in bundles. The length of the needles and the number in each bundle are good field marks for identifying species. Two species, the **Japanese black pine** (*kuro matsu*) and the **Japanese red pine** (*aka matsu*), are common in the Tokyo area.

The black pine thrives along the coastline, even in thin, sandy soil. The classic mature coastal forest of central and southern Japan is a mixed stand of huge black pines and ***tabu-no-ki*** laurels. Unfortunately, extensive groves of these old-growth forests have become extremely rare, though black pines are still frequently encountered on top of sandy cliffs or clinging desperately to wind- and wave-battered rocks.

In extreme environments, powerful winds sculpt the black pine trunk and branches into wild, twisted shapes. The Japanese have long appreciated these great natural works of art and try to re-create them in planned environments, especially along the edges of ponds in stroll gardens. Sculpted black pines can be seen in any of Tokyo's formal gardens. The black pine, a favorite among bonsai enthusiasts, is also planted behind sandy beaches to help stabilize the dunes. The strong wood, with beautiful grain, is used in pillars and flooring. The needles burn at a very high temperature and, in the past, were used to fire ceramic roof tiles.

The black pine's name comes from the dark color of its rough, deeply furrowed bark. The needles grow up to fifteen centimeters long, with two per bundle. The female flowers are usually bright red and form at the tip of the branch in early winter. The cones are slightly larger than a ping-pong ball, but smaller than a tennis ball.

Black pine in flower, female cones on top and males below

The red pine was once one of the most widespread trees in the Tokyo area, found in groves from the uplands well into the middle mountain slopes. In the postwar years, most of these trees were wiped out by a disease thought to have been spread by a species of longhorn beetle. As a result, this pine has become rare in natural forests and woodlands, and is found mostly in parks and gardens instead.

The name of this conifer comes from the reddish gray tint on the bark. The leaves are in bundles of two but are shorter and softer than those of the black pine. The trunk tends to grow straighter, especially in natural forests. The wood is excellent and makes superb charcoal and firewood, favored by potters and blacksmiths. At the base of these pines grow the greatly prized *matsutake* mushrooms, a parasitic fungi.

Bark of red pine

Another species of native pine, **goyō matsu**, is found in Tokyo parks and gardens. This tree can be easily identified by its bundles of five short needles.

RED-WOODS

Cryptomeria trunk

The **Japanese cryptomeria** (*sugi*) is, far and away, the most common conifer in the Tokyo area. Although often called "**Japanese cedar**" in English, this tree is actually a member of the redwood family, related to the great coastal redwoods and giant sequoias of California. The Japanese name *sugi* is thought to have evolved from *massugu ki* (literally, "straight tree"). Indeed, the cryptomeria grows straight and tall, sometimes to a height of fifty meters or more. Many cryptomeria live to a ripe old age. Famous specimens on the island of Yakushima, off the southern coast of Kyūshū, are estimated to be more than five thousand years old.

In its natural mountain habitat, often growing alongside great old beeches, the cryptomeria is a magnificent tree. Tall, stately, sacred specimens planted around Shinto shrines are also awe-inspiring. Unfortunately, most of the trees seen today are stunted caricatures growing in tightly packed plantations. Fast growing and hardy, with beautiful, fragrant wood, the crytomeria has long been the tree of choice for foresters.

The bark of the cryptomera is reddish-brown and peels away lengthwise in long strips. The needles are short and sharp and cover the branches on all sides, like a test tube brush. The small round cones contain numerous tiny brown seeds with narrow wings around the edges.

CYPRESSES

Hinoki cypress seed cones

Next to the Japanese cryptomeria in popularity as a forestry tree is the ***hinoki*** cypress. This tree has a small round cone, about the size of a marble, which is divided into sections like a miniature soccer ball. The reddish gray bark peels off in lengthwise strips. Often planted together with cryptomeria, the *hinoki* can be easily distinguished by its flattened, scalelike needles. The heartwood is fragrant, with a beautiful sheen. In some areas, the wood is cut into thin strips for traditional crafts such as straw hats and fans. The bark is extremely resistant to rot and was traditionally employed as a roofing material.

The *hinoki* cypress grows naturally along mountain slopes and ridges, where it is often the locus of forest fires. The wood contains a pitch that burns readily and is said to catch fire just by the friction of branches rubbing together in the wind. The Japanese name *hinoki* literally means "tree of fire." A closely related species, the ***sawara***, is also widely planted in the Tokyo area. The needles of the *sawara* have sharp edges, while those of the *hinoki* are rounded. Both these trees are in the genus *Chamaecyparis*, and although in the cypress family, are not true cypresses (genus *Cupressus*). A botanical stickler would insist that they be called **false cypress** instead.

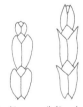

Hinoki cypress (left) and *sawara*. *Sawara* has sharper leaf points, which can be seen with a loupe, as well as felt.

STREET AND PARK TREES

For many hurried city dwellers and commuters, street trees provide the only chance to interact with living creatures on a daily basis. They are nature's front-line troops, bringing a touch of green and a sense of changing seasons into areas which would otherwise be devoid of natural interest. Street trees also permit animals such as insects and birds to inhabit downtown and heavily populated areas.

The Japanese have been planting trees along major travel routes and approaches to shrines and temples for over a thousand years. Japanese native cherries and zelkovas, as well as pines and cryptomeria, are among the historical favorites. The Japanese hackberry, too, a magnificent summer shade tree, was traditionally planted at crossroads and at fixed intervals along the old highways (see page 168).

Systematic planting of trees along ordinary city streets began in the early Meiji period. These initial efforts were strongly influenced by European and American urban design concepts, and Tokyo's first official street trees are said to have been planted on the Ginza.

During the following decades, Tokyo planners experimented with popular street trees from around the world. Seeds and seedlings were grown in local parks, and species best adapted to Tokyo were chosen and planted throughout the city. Unfortunately, most of these original trees were destroyed in the Great Kantō Earthquake of 1923, and, what was left, in the bombings of World War II.

Today, street trees are planted for scenic value, for shade, to help shut out noise and traffic pollution, and to support local biodiversity. Tokyo currently boasts about half a million street trees. Street trees are chosen for their adaptability, resistance to disease and air pollution, ease of transplanting and maintenance, and potential for steady growth. Many of Tokyo's popular street trees, such as the American sycamore, London plane, flowering dogwood, and tulip tree, are thus the same species familiar to city folk living in temperate zones throughout the world.

In addition to these European and American stalwarts, various trees of Chinese origin, including the ginkgo, Tang maple, weeping willow, and tallow tree, also grace Tokyo's streets; whereas zelkovas, elms, cherries, and horse chestnuts are natives that have been brought into the city from the surrounding mountains and countryside.

While street trees are limited by the harsh demands of the urban landscape, parks and gardens provide plenty of open space for planting. Almost all of the native trees discussed in the previous three sections can be enjoyed in the larger urban parks. Parks also include many species of nonnative origin, and their convenient location and ease of access makes them ideal spots for amateur botanists and tree lovers. Time spent studying trees in an urban park will surely enhance later trips into the hills and countryside.

PLANE TREES

Bark of London plane

One way to learn street trees is to start off on those with leaves bigger than your hand. The most common tree in this category is the **platanus**, or **plane tree**. The Japanese name *suzukake-no-ki* (literally, "tree with hanging bells") refers to the little round clusters of flowers and later seeds that hang down from the branches. These trees grow a new layer of thin bark each year. As the trunk expands, the older outer layers of bark burst apart, like a child that has outgrown his clothes. The result is a beautiful pattern on the trunk that looks like an uncompleted jigsaw puzzle.

Platanus are popular street trees throughout the world and were brought to Japan in the late nineteenth century. Most people lump all plane trees together, but a close inspection reveals that there are actually three separate species. The **American plane tree** (*Amerika suzukake*) is also called **sycamore**, which causes many people to confuse it with the sweetgum, which is also called sycamore.

(This sort of inconsistency in use of common names shows why the formal scientific names are so important.) The American plane tree is an immense tree—old giants can reach thirty meters in height, with a trunk diameter of three meters or more. It is native to the eastern United States, from the Mississippi River to the Atlantic Ocean. The huge leaves have very shallow lobes and coarse teeth, and the hard, clean wood is traditionally used for butchers' carving blocks. The **Oriental plane** (*suzukake-no-ki*), known to live more than a thousand years, grows wild in southeastern Europe and western Asia, between the Balkans and the Himalayas. The leaves have much deeper lobes than the American species. The third species, the **London plane** (*momijiba suzukake*) is actually a hybrid of the two wild species, said to have occurred naturally from parent trees planted at Oxford in the late seventeenth century. As is often the case, the hybrid turned out to be more frost-resistant and adaptable than either of its parents and is now by far the most popular of the three. Also, as might be expected in a hybrid, the leaf shape shows lobes that are intermediate in depth between the American and Oriental species.

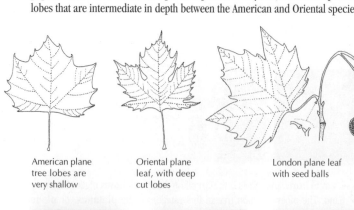

American plane tree lobes are very shallow

Oriental plane leaf, with deep cut lobes

London plane leaf with seed balls

Seed ball of American plane

Seed balls of Oriental plane

Seed balls of London plane

The London plane can be enjoyed throughout the city and suburbs. For those who enjoy fieldwork and want to learn to distinguish the three species, a visit to the Koishikawa Botanical Gardens or the Rinshi no Mori Park is in order. A fun task is to compare not only the leaves and trunks but the seed balls as well. The American plane usually has only a single ball on each stalk, often a very large one. The Oriental species has several balls, all attached directly to a single main stalk. The London plane, ever the compromiser, has several balls hanging together, some of which are attached to the main stalk by their own short ministalks.

In winter, these seed balls break up, sending thousands of little seeds, each with a tuft of fluffy hair, flying away on the wind.

OTHER
BIG-LEAF
TREES

Akame-gashiwa growing
along Shibuya sidewalk

Another very popular street tree with big leaves is the **American sycamore**, also called **sweetgum** (*Amerika-fū* or *momijiba-fū*). With fingerlike lobes, this tree is sometimes mistaken for a maple. Yet the leaves of all maples are attached in an opposite pattern, while those of the sycamore are alternate. The thick, deeply furrowed bark allows one to distinguish these from the plane trees at a glance. The seeds form spiked woody balls. The **Chinese sycamore** (*fū*) is also found planted around Tokyo, but in lesser numbers. The leaf of the Chinese species is divided into three lobes, as compared to five or seven for the American. Both produce beautiful red, orange, and purple leaves in autumn.

Tulip trees are members of the magnolia family (see Magnolia Family in the Deciduous Trees chapter) and are native to eastern North America. They, too, have big leaves that are easily recognized by their shape. A line of tulip trees is planted along the Sakurada Moat, between the sidewalk and Uchibori Dōri, and huge specimens can be ogled at Shinjuku Gyoen Gardens. The Japanese name, *yuri-no-ki*, means "lily tree."

A bag of big leaves collected from street trees will inevitably include the **phoenix tree** (*ao-giri*), a native of China easily identified by its green-tinted bark, and the ***akame-gashiwa***. The *akame-gashiwa* is unique in that it is a true Tokyo native. Oddly enough, it probably wasn't planted where you found it. The seeds of this hardy tree are dispersed by birds and will establish a foothold even in sidewalk cracks. A close look at the leaves shows little openings at the base, on either side of the stem. A sweet nectar is exuded from these openings and, in summer, the leaf will be swarming with tiny ants. The ants collect the nectar but do not eat the leaf itself. Instead, they chase away would-be herbivores such as shield bugs and caterpillars and, in doing so, repay their debt to the tree. Look for the *akame-gashiwa* in empty lots or along any poorly tended patch of hedging or border. In the countryside, this tree is a fixture along the edge of the woodlands.

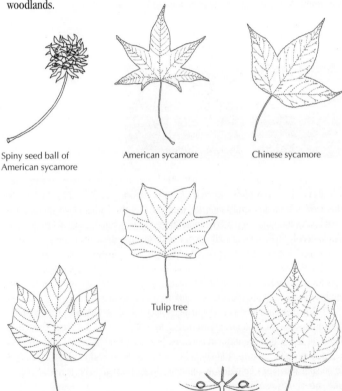

Spiny seed ball of
American sycamore

American sycamore

Chinese sycamore

Tulip tree

Phoenix tree

Akame-gashiwa leaf showing
nectar vents

GINKGO

London plane and ginkgo leaves

The most popular street tree in Tokyo, numbering about sixty-five thousand plantings, is the **ginkgo**, or **maidenhair tree**. In fact, the ginkgo leaf is the official symbol of the Tokyo municipality and, as such, is seen frequently on signposts, pamphlets, and the sides of government vehicles. The fan-shaped leaf turns deep yellow in autumn and has a unique pattern of veins. Hundreds of narrow veins run in parallel lines from the base of the leaf out to the top margins.

Ginkgos, called *ichō* in Japanese, are native to China. They were once thought to be extinct in the wild, but the most recent news is that some native Chinese groves have been discovered. Ginkgo trees were brought to Japan centuries ago and were traditionally planted around shrines and temples.

Botanists believe that the ginkgo is a living relic of ancient trees that flourished more than one hundred million years ago. It has no contemporary relatives and is classified all by its lonesome in a special division within the gymnosperms.

Ginkgo trees are dioecious, with separate male and female trees. The fruit, which consists of a hard kernel surrounded by a fleshy skin, forms only on the female trees and ripens in early autumn. The skin gives off an unpleasant odor as it disintegrates and contains chemicals which can cause an itchy rash. The kernel, however, is edible. These "ginkgo nuts," called *ginnan* in Japanese, are eaten skewered and grilled, and also appear in hot egg custard (*chawan-mushi*) and other traditional Japanese dishes. Experienced fans caution not to eat too many nuts at once, at risk of developing abdominal pain.

In recent years, extracts and herbal teas made from ginkgo leaves have become enormously popular in Europe and America. These herbal remedies are said to reduce mental stress and improve concentration.

Ginkgo trees can be seen along streets and in parks throughout the city and around shrines, temples, and farmhouses in the countryside. Famous spots for viewing the beautiful yellow leaves in fall include the University of Tokyo and the Jingū Outer Gardens (along the approach road leading from Aoyama Dōri).

MORE CHINESE IMPORTS

Leaves of *tō-kaede* maple (left), *nankin haze* (center), and ginkgo

In addition to the ginkgo, other popular street trees of Chinese origin include the ***tō-kaede***. The *tō* in the Japanese name refers to China's Tang Dynasty, and *kaede* is a general term for maple. One theory holds that the word *kaede* originally was *kaeru-no-te*, or "frog's feet," referring to the splayed, fingerlike shape of maple leaves, though the *tō-kaede* leaves are usually cut into only three sections. The light brown bark peels off in lengthwise strips. These maples, with thirty-five thousand plantings, are the third most popular tree on Tokyo's streets, slipping between the plane trees (forty-three thousand), in second, and the flowering dogwoods (thirty-three thousand), in fourth. The much-celebrated cherry comes in fifth place, at thirty-one thousand plantings.

The leaves of the ***nankin haze*** are immediately recognized by shape: with a width as great or greater than the length, it resembles an English teakettle without a spout. The fruit is a woody capsule that splits open to reveal round white seeds. Autumn reds and scarlets are magnificent.

WEEPING WILLOWS

Weeping willows along Inner Moat of Imperial Palace

Weeping willows (*shidare yanagi*) are native to China but have been planted all around the world. These trees were brought to Japan more than a thousand years ago. In Japan, they have a strong association with water and are planted along the edges of rivers and canals. They will also grow quite well in a park meadow. The Inner Moat of the Imperial Palace, just across from Hibiya Park, has a row of fine willows on the water side.

DOG-WOODS

Flowering dogwood

Flowering dogwoods (*hana mizuki*) are natives of the eastern United States and are sometimes referred to as goodwill ambassadors. In 1912, the governor of Tokyo presented the United States with *somei yoshino* cherry trees, which were planted along the Potomac River, in Washington, D.C. Several years later, the United States reciprocated with a gift of flowering dogwoods. These trees are appreciated for their flowers, little orange fruit, and beautiful fall colors. They are now very common, especially in apartment complexes and other suburban residential areas.

Close-up of individual dogwood flower

Flowering dogwoods bloom in late April. At first glance, the flowers appear as large single flowers with four white or pink petals and a mass of greenish yellow stamens in the center. A closer look shows that each "flower" is really a cluster of tiny flowers, called an inflorescence (a botanical term for a cluster of flowers). The "petals" are, in reality, bracts, structures which surround and protect the growing inflorescence, then spread out when the flowers are ready to bloom. Botanists assume that the conspicuous bracts help attract insects. The leaves turn deep crimson in autumn and are accompanied by clusters of bright orange cylindrical-shaped fruit.

Yama-bōshi dogwood flowers, with sharply pointed bracts. Flowering dogwood have bracts with rounded edges

The flowering dogwood is sometimes confused with **yama-bōshi**, a native Japanese species that is also occasionally planted in parks and gardens. The *yama-bōshi* blooms a few weeks later and has sharply pointed bracts, in contrast to the rounded and slightly puckered bracts of the American species.

CHERRY TREES

Somei yoshino cherry blossoms

As spring moves northward along the Japanese archipelago, television weather casters breathlessly track the progression of the "cherry-blossom front" (*sakura zensen*), while office workers and old classmates meet to map out strategies for securing a choice spot to hold their annual flower-viewing party (*hana-mi*). The whole nation seems caught up in cherry-blossom fever.

Cherry blossoms are not only this nation's favorite flower but a familiar symbol of Japan throughout the world. A picture postcard of cherry trees in full bloom, with snow-covered Mount Fuji in the background, is perhaps the most widely recognized image of the Japanese landscape.

When people today use the words *sakura*, or "cherry blossom," they are almost inevitably referring to a single ornamental variety of cherry tree, known as the **somei yoshino** (see also Rose Family in the Deciduous Trees chapter). In truth, Japan is home to about ten native species of cherry, and a thousand years of horticulture has produced over three hundred ornamental varieties. The *somei yoshino*, undoubtedly the most popular park cherry today, is actually a relative newcomer on the Japanese cherry scene.

A great deal of controversy still surrounds the origin of the popular *somei yoshino*. One theory holds that a horticulturist in the Somei district of Tokyo developed this variety in the mid-nineteenth century, towards the end of the Edo period, by crossing the **Edo higan**, a huge native cherry species, with the **Ōshima-zakura**, a local species found on the Izu Islands and near the tip of the Bōsō and Izu peninsulas. Other researchers believe that the *somei yoshino* was originally an older, naturally occurring hybrid.

Japanese appreciation of cherry blossoms dates back to the ninth or tenth century, perhaps farther. At that time, however, the Japanese plum (*ume*), which blooms in early February, was the more popular tree. Only later on did the cherry gradually replace the plum as the most revered and admired spring blossom.

By the end of the twelfth century, *yae-zaki*, ornamental varieties with extra petals (like a rose), had developed. Cherry blossom appreciation quickly spread from the court nobility to the emerging military class. From the early seventeenth century, cherry trees from all over the country were collected and raised at the *daimyō yashiki* (Edo mansions of the feudal lords). Documents published in 1711 list about 70 ornamental varieties, but by the mid-nineteenth century, this number had risen to around 250.

As horticulture technology progressed, great numbers of cherry trees were planted in public areas, and cherry-blossom fever spread to both the merchant and commoner classes. In spring, the banks of the Sumida River, and the temples and shrines around what is now Ueno Park became popular *sakura-meisho* "cherry spots," places where people gathered in large numbers to drink, eat, dance, and enjoy the blossoms. The parties that fill the city's parks and blossoming avenues during the two weeks of spring when the trees bloom can be traced directly back to these gatherings.

Whatever the *somei yoshino*'s origins, there is no doubt that it took Tokyo, then the entire nation, by storm. The tree is hardy, fast-growing and easy to care for, while the delicate pinkish white flowers bloom in great numbers, covering the leafless branches in masses of soft color. When a breeze blows, the petals break loose and drift slowly to the ground, creating *sakura fubuki*, a magical blizzard of blossoms.

The peak of the *somei yoshino* season usually comes in late March and early April. Other species bloom much earlier. In fact, early blooming species begin flowering in mid-January, well before the plums. There are also species, such as **sato-zakura**, that bloom well after the *somei yoshino*. The *sato-zakura* blossoms have multiple crowns and look almost like soft pink roses.

The park along the Chidorigafuchi Moat is Tokyo's most popular cherry-viewing spot today, but Ueno Park, with various early-blooming varieties, is deeply appreciated by more sophisticated aficionados. Rikugien Gardens are visited for their magnificent **shidare-zakura**, or "weeping cherry," a beautiful ornamental variety with downswept branches, derived from the *Edo higan*. For those who want to delve even deeper into the fascinating history and variety of ornamental cherries, Shinjuku Gyoen Gardens have 1,500 trees representing 75 different varieties.

Somei yoshino in full bloom

HORSE CHESTNUT

Japanese horse chestnut flowers

Japanese horse chestnuts (*tochi-no-ki*) are native to mountain forests and do not grow wild in the Tokyo countryside. Nevertheless, they do quite well in parks and even along streets. A row of fine old horse chestnuts can be enjoyed along Sakurada Dōri, in the middle of the Kasumigaseki government district (across the street from the Sakurada Gate).

The leaves of the horse chestnut are immense compound affairs, with five or seven leaflets attached in a palmate pattern to a single central node. The tiny white flowers bloom in a long, dense cluster that sticks straight up. Leathery capsules, equal in size or slightly larger than a ping-pong ball, split open to reveal the chestnutlike seeds. The winter bud is reddish-brown and covered with a sticky resin that protects the new growth inside from the cold. One street in

Japanese horse chestnuts

the Ginza area, Marronnier Dōri, is planted with the closely related **European horse chestnut**. "Marronnier" is French for "horse chestnut."

Winter bud of Japanese horse chestnut is covered with sticky resin, and the triangular leaf scar, where the huge compound leaf dropped off, can be clearly seen. Bumps in the scar show the position of tubular canals that carry water into the leaf and starches out.

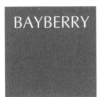

BAYBERRY

Bayberry leaves and fruit

The **bayberry**, or **wax myrtle** (*yama-momo*), is a broadleaved evergreen, native to southern Japan, that grows well in the Tokyo area. It is popular in city parks and suburban housing complexes. Given room to expand, it assumes a short but nicely rounded shape. The leaves have an attractive wrinkled appearance. Above all, this tree is valued for its bright red berries, which ripen in summer and are mixed with *shochu* (a distilled liquor) and rock candy to make a delicious restorative liquor called *yama-momo-shu*. Japanese fruit liqueurs, also made from plums and wild cherries, are drunk as aperitifs and restoratives. The bayberry is dioecious, the fruit thus appearing only on the female trees. To assure yourself a share of the bounty, pick out likely trees in advance, then get up early in order to beat the local birds and berry pickers, all of which are probably closely watching the same tree.

OAKS

Tan oak flowers, with small acorns from previous year

Chinkapins and ***shira-kashi*** ("white oak") are planted liberally as park and street trees. Another oak relative, the **tan oak** (*mateba-shii*), is also very common in parks. The flowers of this tree are like the chinkapin, but the acorns are protected by caps rather than sheaths. In fact, this tree is the best acorn producer in the city, and the acorns are considerably longer and fatter (with scaled rather than lined caps) than those of the regular live oaks.

The leaf is thick and a soft green color, with no teeth on the edge and almost no stalk. The acorns take two years to mature. Immature acorns from the previous year are therefore visible at the same time (mid-May) that the flowers are blooming. This tree is native to Kyūshū but has been planted in dense woodlots along the Miura and Bōsō peninsulas. Tan oak acorns are edible but not as tasty as those of the chinkapin. One interpretation of the Japanese name is *mateba oishii* ("If you wait a little bit, it will be delicious"). In other words, as long as the chinkapin acorns last, no one wants to eat the tan oaks', but once the chinkapin nuts run out, then the tan oaks can pass muster!

CONIFERS

Dawn redwood

Native cryptomeria, pines, and cypress are widely planted in city parks. In addition, the **Himalayan cedar** (*Himaraya sugi*), with large, heavily foliaged branches that spread out wide and begin to incline downward, is popular, especially in and around open lawns. Native to the northwestern Himalayas, this conifer is also planted frequently on school and company grounds. Magnificent specimens can be enjoyed at Shinjuku Gyoen Gardens.

Several Tokyo parks also feature the **dawn redwood** (*metasekoia*) and **swamp cypress** (*numa sugi*), both members of the redwood family. The redwoods are considered to be one of the most ancient families of conifer,

Himalayan cedar at Shinjuku Gyoen Gardens

formerly widespread but now reduced to marginal habitats. The dawn redwood was long known only as fossil remains, until live specimens were discovered in southwest China. The tiny, flat needles are arranged on either side of short branches, which in turn are attached in an opposite pattern. The swamp cypress, a native of the North American southeast, resembles the dawn redwood except for the short branches, which are arranged in an alternate rather than opposite pattern. Mizumoto Park has a fine stand of dawn redwoods. Rinshi no Mori Park offers a great variety of trees in this family, including the **California redwood**.

Other local gymnosperms include the **podocarp** (*inu-maki*), which is the official tree of Chiba Prefecture. Podocarps have wide leaves (for a gymnosperm) and are dioecious. The male flowers are in yellow catkins. The female flowers have a most extraordinary shape. This species prefers warm climates and in the Tokyo area grows wild only on the Miura and Bōsō peninsulas. The podocarp does very well when planted and is a popular ornamental and hedge tree.

Podocarp female flowers

CAMPHOR TREE

Camphor tree leaves and flowers

The **camphor tree** (*kusu-no-ki*) is a popular laurel family evergreen that grows well in the Tokyo area. The origin of this tree is in some doubt. Some researchers feel it was native to Kyūshū and the Ryūkyū Islands, but others believe it came from Taiwan and areas even farther south. The camphor tree is long-lived and, given room to grow, stands tall with a beautiful rounded shape.

The bark is dark, rough, and deeply furrowed. The leaves, just about big enough to fit in the palm of one's hand, are shiny, with smooth (no teeth) edges. Two large veins run almost parallel to the midvein. If in any doubt as to the identity of this tree, just crumple a piece of leaf and hold it up to your nose. You will immediately recognize the smell of camphor, a scent like those little white mothballs used when storing clothes in the dresser or closet. If you happen to be waiting for a late date at the Hachikō Entrance to Shibuya Station, check out the two camphor trees facing the street, just to the right of the main crossing.

Camphor tree trunk

SPRING WILDFLOWERS

The Tokyo area is a paradise for wildflower lovers. Flowers bloom almost throughout the year, in a great variety of habitats, including grassy fields, roadsides, the rice-paddy dikes, forest floors, rice paddies and irrigation canals, the edges of ponds and lakes, and coastal rocks and sands.

The wildflower season kicks off very early in spring. In fact, dandelions, groundsels, and speedwells may bloom on the occasional warm afternoon even in midwinter. From April through May, several new species come into bloom almost every day, enough to keep even a dedicated botanist busy from dawn till dusk. Keeping track of all the local wildflowers would be a virtually impossible task, but there are many species that are easy to identify and great fun to investigate.

EARLY SPRING GRASS-FIELDS

Common field speedwell

Quite frequently, people stop and ask me, "Did you lose something?" For many years, I couldn't understand why this should happen to me so often until one day a friend pointed out that I always seem to be staring at the ground as if searching for lost keys or contact lens. Then I understood!

When we human beings began to walk upright some four or five million years ago, we gained several great advantages. We were able to see far into the distance and our hands were freed for using tools and for other useful tasks. But by going upright, we lost sight of the ground. Our eyes are now a meter and a half off the earth and positioned to look forward, rather than down. Thus we tend to search for objects at mid-range or longer distances and usually miss tiny things right beneath our feet.

A good example are the tiny flowers that bloom in grassy fields and along the side of the road in late winter and early spring. Many of these are only a few millimeters wide. They are designed to catch the eye of a low-flying bee or horse fly and simply do not register in the pupil of a briskly walking human. The only way to find and enjoy them is to deliberately look downward, at the risk of attracting the assistance of well-meaning passersby.

The first flower to look for is the tiny sky-blue **common field speedwell**. This plant is one of the true cosmopolitans. Originally a Eurasian and African species, it has managed to spread around the entire world and can now be seen all over Japan as well as on lawns and empty lots throughout most of North America.

From a slight distance, the speedwells look like almost ridiculously short plants, but a little poking around shows that the stems are actually quite long. As the stem grows, it spreads out laterally along the ground rather than vertically. This strategy provides some protection against the late winter wind and also enables the plant's leaves to take maxi-

Common field speedwell, with detail of flower (top) and capsule

mum advantage of the few hours of strong sunlight available early in the season.

Speedwells belong to the snapdragon family. The flowers appear to have four petals but actually consist of a single crown united at the base and divided into four lobes. Each lobe has a series of purple or dark blue lines against a lighter blue background. In the yellowish center are a single pistil and two stamens.

Speedwell flowers attract small bees and horseflies, which are surprisingly active on sunny days, even in late winter. These insects carry pollen from one flower to the next, performing the essential cross-pollination service that prevents inbreeding and maintains the genetic diversity necessary for long-term adaptability and survival.

Speedwells get their common English name from their habit of growing along roadsides, where they are said to speed travelers along their way. The genus name *Veronica* derives from Saint Veronica, a woman who wiped the sweating face of Jesus while he was struggling to carry his cross on the road to Calvary. The image of Jesus' face was miraculously preserved on the cloth. The speedwell's light blue corolla with yellow center and stamens is thought to have reminded people of this miracle cloth.

The generic Japanese name for speedwells, *inu-no-fuguri*, is not nearly so evocative. In fact, the term literally means "dog's testicles"! This name comes from the shape of the plant's capsules, which resemble the private parts of a male canine as seen from behind. These capsules, containing the plant's seeds, split open when ripe. They are visible along the stem below the flowers. The common field speedwell, which is thought to have arrived in Japan around the end of the nineteenth century is called *ō-inu-no-fuguri*. The prefix *ō* means "large," and is used to distinguish this species from Japan's slightly smaller native species *inu-no-fuguri*. Unfortunately, the native speedwell appears to be virtually extinct, at least in the southern Kantō area. It is hard to say if its decline is due to competition from the introduced species or to deterioration of habitat.

Two other very common early-spring roadsiders belong in the mint family, which is one of the most important plant families both in terms of biodiversity and usefulness. About 250 genera and nearly 7,000 species are found around the world, mostly in temperate zones. These include many of our most honored medicinal and culinary herbs, such as spearmint, peppermint, sage, rosemary, thyme, basil, marjoram, and lavender.

In early spring, roadsides and empty lots are covered with pink and purple dead-nettle flowers, typical members of the mint family. These flowers, although basically short, low-growing species, sometimes form wide, dense carpets that cover an entire field.

At a casual glance, the clusters appear to be all the same plant, but a closer look shows two distinct species, the **henbit dead-nettle** and the **purple dead-nettle**. Like the common speedwell, both of these species are European in origin but cosmopolitan in distribution. They are thought to have arrived here in Japan around the end of the nineteenth century, and have increased to the point where they are now one of this country's most common roadside weeds.

Henbit dead-nettle

The henbit dead-nettle has larger, deep pink, almost purplish flowers. The leaves on the upper stem are sessile (attached directly to the stem without a stalk). Two leaves are arranged opposite one another in pairs, and the effect created resembles a soft, comfortable seat cushion. The Japanese name for this plant, *hotoke-no-za*, literally means "the Buddha's seat cushion."

Purple dead-nettle

The purple dead-nettle has smaller flowers of a lighter shade of pink (sometimes even white). The leaves are heart-shaped, and have fairly long stems. At the very top of the plants, the leaves overlap one another in a distinct pattern. This species is called *hime-odoriko-sō* in Japanese, as the shape of the flower resembles a little dancing girl (*odoriko*). The *sō* means "weed" or "herb," and the *hime* literally means "princess" but carries the connotation of something small or delicate. A separate species of deadnettle, with much larger white flowers, is called just plain ***odoriko-sō***. Unfortunately, this native species is far rarer than the two exotics.

In examining these mints, the first step is to twirl the stem between your thumb and forefinger. The stems are distinctly square in cross-section, a characteristic which is very common in the mint family. Mints are not the only family of flowers with square stems, but if you come across an unknown square-stemmed plant, the first place to begin searching is in the mint family section of your local wildflower field guide.

Comparison of henbit (left) and purple dead nettle (right). Detail of normal henbit flower (top), and nonopening "insurance" flower (left).

As these two dead-nettles are common weeds, don't be afraid to pick some and take them home for closer examination. Flower architecture is often amazing. Color patterns as well as the structure of the various parts may at first seem random but are actually a product of millions of years of coevolution between the plant and the insects that pollinate it. Discovering the "functional" aspects of a flower enhances one's appreciation of its natural beauty.

The henbit dead-nettle, with its larger flowers, is most useful for this purpose. The flower structure is typical of the mint family, with an upper lip formed into a hood, and a wide, flat lower lip that extends downward and outward at the mouth of the flower.

The wide, flat lower lip serves as a landing platform for visiting insects. Seen through a magnifying glass, the lip is pale pink with a series of darker markings. These markings, called nectar guides, help orient visiting insects by showing them the correct way to crawl into the flower. Nectar guides on flower petals function like landing lights at an airport. An insect that follows the guides will not only get a reward of nectar but will be ideally positioned to cross-pollinate the flower.

Finding the henbit's stamens and pistil is a fun exercise. Most people look for them deep inside the flower and are disappointed. They are actually hidden underneath the hood of the upper lip. As an insect follows the nectar guides and forces its way into the flower, the stamens and pistils are pulled down to touch the insect's head or thorax. A good magnifying glass shows a single pistil in the center surrounded by four stamens, two of which are long and two are short. By staggering the length of its pistils, a flower is able to spread them out over a wider area, rather than having them all bunched up together in a single clump. This is most likely a strategy designed to increase the probability of at least one or two of the stamens coming into contact with a visiting insect.

A thorough check of a healthy henbit dead-nettle usually reveals several flowers that are much shorter than the others. The lips are indistinct, and the tip resembles a purple pin cushion. These are flowers which do not open. They fold inward and pollinate themselves, pushing their own stamens against their own pistil. Normal flowers can be pollinated only by visiting insects, and these special flowers thus serve as a sort of insurance policy, ensuring that the plant will produce at least a few seeds, even if no insects show up.

Mixed in with the speedwells and dead-nettles will be several plants with very tiny white flowers. One of these is the **shepherd's purse**. This little mustard-family plant is thought to be native to the Mediterranean area but, like the

Shepherd's purse

speedwells and dead-nettles, has achieved a worldwide distribution. In fact, the shepherd's purse may have been the first wild plant to spread across wide areas, carried to Asia by early caravans trading along the famous silk route. The shepherd's purse probably reached Japan via the first contacts with China, nearly two thousand years ago.

The shepherd's purse is called *nazuna* in Japanese, but children know it as *pen-pen-gusa*. The little capsules, which to the early Mediterraneans resembled a purse or bag carried by shepherds, remind the Japanese of the pluck used to play the *shamisen*, a traditional stringed instrument. In addition, children twirl the stems rapidly in their fingers, enjoying the *pen-pen* rattling sound made by the capsules hitting against each other. Like all mustard-family plants, the flowers have four petals arranged like a Maltese cross, one pistil, and six stamens, four of which are long and two are short.

Tiny **chickweeds** of the genus *Stellaria* are among the first flowers of spring. Seen with the naked eye, the flowers appear like miniature ten-petaled stars. Through a loupe, one sees that there are really only five petals. Each petal is divided in two at the base and shaped like a pair of rabbit ears. In early spring, the most common species is ***ko-hakobe***, a cosmopolitan weed as familiar to Europeans and Americans as to the Japanese. As spring comes on, several other closely related chickweeds will come into bloom.

Ko-hakobe chickweed

Shunran

Deciduous forests provide a special window of opportunity for wildflowers. In early spring, the air and ground have begun to warm up and insects are flying. What's more, the leaves of the deciduous trees have not yet grown into a canopy that shuts out the light. Many wildflowers have adapted their seasonal rhythms to take advantage of this unique chance. They emerge, grow, bloom, and seed in this short period when light is available. Because these flowers bloom in such a rush and seem to be here one day and gone the next, they are collectively referred to as the spring ephemerals.

Many members of the spring ephemerals are perennials; that is, they store energy in underground tubers and root systems and send out leaves and flowers year after year. **Orchids** are typical employers of this strategy. In the Tokyo region, the most common forest orchid is a Cymbidium. The Japanese name *shunran* simply means "spring orchid." The leaves are long and thin, with fine serrations along the edge. Usually only one flower blooms at the tip of each pedicel, or flower stalk. Each flower has three green sepals. One of these sticks straight up and the other two project out to the sides, giving the flower a dynamic wind-mill-like appearance. There are also three petals, two of which are green and look just like the sepals. As is the case in most orchids, the third or central petal is transformed into a curling structure called the "lip." The *shunran* lip is usually reddish.

Spontaneous mutations sometimes produce reddish or yellow flowers as well as striped or mottled patterns on the leaves. These natural mutations are eagerly sought by enthusiasts.

The *shunran* closely resembles the plants used in botany textbooks for illustrating the unique structure of orchid flowers. The male reproductive parts, or stamens, and female reproductive parts, or pistils, are fused into a single structure called the column. At the tip of the column are pollinia, little bags of sticky pollen that adhere to a visiting insect. Behind the pollinia is a cavity which contains the stigma, or receptive part of the pistil.

Orchid seeds, like orchid flowers, insist on being totally unique. The seeds of most plants consist of an embryo surrounded by a layer of nourishing endosperm. The embryo utilizes the energy in the endosperm to fuel growth

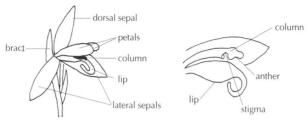

Structure of *shunran* flower, with detail of column and lip

during germination. Orchid seeds, however, lack this layer of endosperm. By eliminating the space-consuming endosperm, orchids have been able to reduce the size of their seeds and pack thousands into a single capsule. Yet, without an endosperm, they cannot germinate on their own and must land on a certain type of fungus from which they obtain nutrients during the germination process.

Other once common local forest orchids include the tall, multiflowered *ebine* and the **Japanese lady slipper** (*kumagai-sō*). Unfortunately, these two beauties have been virtually wiped out by irresponsible collecting, a problem shared by many of the attractive forest-floor perennials.

Ebine

The lily family is also well represented in the spring ephemerals. In Tokyo-area woodlands, two species of small greenish white **Solomon's seal lily** (*amadokoro*) are quite common. The leaves and flowers, which hang down like cute little bells, are always on a single undivided stem. *Amadokoro* has short wide leaves and a stem that is chevron-shaped in cross-section. *Naruko yuri* has longer, thinner leaves and a round stem. The dried root of both is used as a restorative in traditional Japanese herbal folk medicine.

Fairy bell lilies look just like Solomon's seals, but have stems that divide into branches as they grow. Look for tall *hōchaku-sō* throughout the hills and uplands, and tiny *chigo yuri* in the hills. The petals of the *chigo yuri* open much wider than all the other species.

One doesn't have to be a botanist to be familiar with **violets**. These perennial herbs are cosmopolitan in distribution, with an estimated five hundred species worldwide. Japan, alone, supports about one hundred species and subspecies. Some of these are rare alpine or coastal species, while others are a common part of the spring fauna in urban parks and gardens.

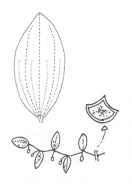

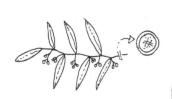

Two common Solomon's seal lilies: *amadokoro* (left) and *naruko yuri* (right). The two species can be distinguished by the shape of the leaves and the shape of the stem in cross-section.

Amadokoro

Most people assume that the violet's name comes from its purplish color. In actuality, the exact opposite is true. *Viola* was originally a generic Latin term for small, sweet-smelling flowers. Only later did the meaning evolve to describe colors near the blue end of the blue-red spectrum. Although most violet flowers come in shades of blue or purple, there are also many species with pink, white, or even deep-yellow flowers.

Hōchaku-sō

Violets are mostly small, ground-hugging plants. Seen from a standing perspective, they appear as nothing more than splashes of color, spilled paint staining the forest floor. A close look reveals that a violet flower is composed of five petals, two on top, one on each side, and one in the center. The center petal is usually a little bit wider than the others, and often has attractive streak marks near the base. These are the nectar guides, designed to show insects the route into the deep parts of the flower, where the nectar is hidden. The central petal also has a projection, called a "spur," that juts back behind the flower. The length of the spur varies from species to species.

Tachi-tsubo sumire

The violet's reproductive parts are located in the

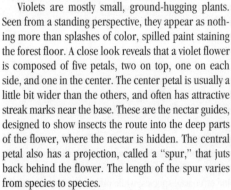

center of the petals. You have to look closely to see them. Five pollen-producing stamens, the male parts, are arranged in a ring around a single pistil, the female part. The two lowermost stamens project backwards into the spur and have at their base special glands that secrete sweet nectar. Insects follow the nectar guides deep into the spur, coming in contact with the pistil and stamens before reaching these nectaries. It is in this manner that the violet flowers are cross-pollinated.

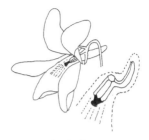
Structure of violet flower, with detail of stamens and pistil

Violet flowers have another neat trick up their sleeves. As the days lengthen towards summer, the plant begins producing a second type of flower bud. These inconspicuous buds, called cleistogamous flowers, never open. Inside, the stamens are pressed directly against the pistil, allowing self-pollination. Cleistogamous flowers are thought to be a sort of insurance policy. Like the henbit dead-nettle, the violet is assured of producing at least some seeds, even if no insects are available to cross-pollinate the regular flowers.

Once pollinated, the ovary of the violet swells into a capsule, packed with tiny seeds. When ready, the capsule splits open into three parts, exposing the seeds. To each seed is attached a little outgrowth, called a caruncle, that is coated with a sweet, sticky substance greatly favored by ants. Ants carry the seeds back to their nest, consuming the caruncle but leaving the seed to germinate.

In the Tokyo area, the most common violet is *tachi-tsubo sumire*. The petals are a soft purple, with dark veinlike streak marks outlined against a white background. The tips of the stamens are orange and can be clearly seen in the center of the flower. The leaves are heart shaped. In mature specimens, the flowers and leaves are attached to the same stalk.

While most of the spring ephemerals are widely loved and appreciated, there is one group of local plants whose blooms often evoke as much apprehension as admiration. These are the tall, spreading plants of the genus *Arisaema*, commonly called **jack-in-the-pulpit** in English.

Jack-in-the-pulpit flowers show a unique construction. The actual flowers are very tiny and are arranged around a barlike axis, called a spadix. The spadix, in turn, is covered and protected by the spathe, a large leaflike structure. In most species, the spathe ends in a sinuously curved triangular hood which, at a quick glance in a dark forest, can appear very much like a poisonous snake raised up and ready to strike. In fact, the Japanese name for one common species is ***mamushi-gusa***, *mamushi* being the name of a small but potentially dangerous pit viper, and *kusa* (or *gusa*) meaning "grass" or "herb." This species even has a sheath which closely resembles the markings on a pit viper. The English name refers to the image of the tip of the spadix enclosed in the hood of the spathe, which is thought to resemble a preacher standing in a pulpit.

The flowers are located at the base of the spadix, hidden inside the spathe, and thus cannot be seen from outside. To inspect the flowers, one must gently pull open the folds of the spathe and take a peek inside. Most of the Japanese species are dioecious (with male and female flowers appearing on separate plants).

Mamushi-gusa

Female *mamushi-gusa* with spathe removed to show flowers

Male *mamushi-gusa* with spathe removed to show flowers

Japanese jack-in-the-pulpits are pollinated by tiny flies, which are easily overlooked but just big enough to be seen with the naked eye. The flies are thought to be attracted by unpleasant odors, which in some species resemble that of rotting meat. Flies enter the male plant from the top of the spathe, crawl over the flowers picking up pollen, then exit from a special curtain opening at the very base of the spathe. Female plants lack this opening, and many flies appear to die inside the spathe after pollinating the flowers. The exact nature of the relationship between these insects and plants still remains a mystery.

Another amazing feature of Japanese jack-in-the-pulpits is their ability to change sex. A plant that is female one year may be male the next. Botanists believe that the sex of a plant is determined by the amount of energy stored up in the underground rhizome at the start of the year. A plant with plenty of stored energy will be female for that year, but one with less energy will be male. A plant with very little or no stored energy for that year will send out leaves but no flowers, concentrating on building up its reserves.

Japan is home to a great variety of jack-in-the-pulpits. Although botanists frequently disagree on their division, around twenty species or subspecies can be found nationwide. Only a few of these are native to the Tokyo area. The most common is called ***Urashima-sō*** in Japanese. This charming name refers to the long, stringlike tip of the spadix, which reminds people of the fishing pole used by Urashima Tarō, the hero of a popular fairy tale. Urashima Tarō saves a sea turtle from some mischievous boys and, as a reward, is dined and entertained at a fabulous undersea palace. The story ends with a sort of Rip van Winkle twist. Urashima returns home, opens a forbidden box given to him at the undersea palace, and finds out that he has become an old man.

The *Urashima-sō* is common in Tokyo parks as well as in coppices in the nearby countryside. Another local species, the *mamushi-gusa*, has a spadix that ends in a club rather than a long string. The *Urashima-sō* has a single compound leaf that arises directly from the base of the plant, while the *mamushi-gusa* has two compound leaves that are bound together with a sheath. In autumn, the fruit of both species, which resembles a corncob, ripens into an eye-catching bright orange.

Most of the spring ephemerals can be found in open woodlands and coppice forests throughout the countryside. The Institute for Nature Study, in Meguro, also has a nearly complete collection, including orchids, lilies, arums, violets, anemones, and irises.

Urashima-sō

Berries of *Urashima-sō*

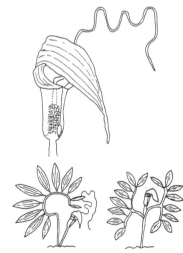

Urashima-sō flower and plant (top and bottom left) and *mamushi-gusa*. Note difference in structure of leaves and flower stalks.

Bittercress (left) and shepherd's purse

In the southern Kantō region, the rice paddies are usually turned over and filled with water in late April, and the rice seedlings transplanted during the Golden Week holidays in early May. There is thus a period from mid-March, when the air warms up, through mid-April when the paddies are available to spring wildflowers. Several species take advantage of this, flowering and seeding before the plows come in. The seeds are then plowed into the paddies, where they lay dormant until the following spring.

One common early spring rice-paddy flower is the **bittercress** (*tane-tsuke-bana*). *Tanetsuke*, in Japanese, refers to the practice of soaking the rice seeds in water before planting them in the seedling mats, a task that is usually accomplished about the same time that this flower comes into bloom (*hana* or *bana* means "flower"). Bittercress is in the mustard family. Its tiny white four-petaled flowers closely resemble those of the shepherds's purse, but the seed capsules are long and thin, shaped like miniature bean pods, rather than a heart. The bittercress is often mixed in with a tough little yellow **buttercup** called *ta-garashi*, literally "rice-paddy mustard" (see Five-Petaled Yellow Flowers).

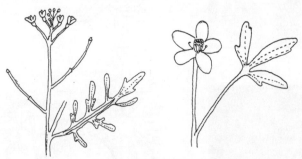

Bittercress (left) and *ta-garashi*

Horsetail

Early spring walkers in the Japanese countryside often encounter small groups of women armed with plastic bags and little garden trowels. These women are engaged in the ancient Japanese outdoor pastime of *sansai-tori*, collecting edible wild greens. Their bags are full of a variety of local plants, including the *tsukushi*, or **horsetail**. Horsetails are primitive plants, related to ferns, that reproduce by spores rather than seeds. They have two distinct stems, a brown stem for reproduction and a green vegetative one for photosynthesis. The green stem, called *sugina*, looks like a miniature Christmas tree. The brown stem, which is the edible part, is topped by a cluster of small baglike structures, filled with yellowish green spores that are released on the wind when ready.

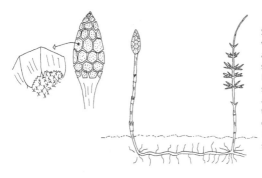

Structure of horsetail, with reproductive stem at left and vegetative stem (*sugina*) at right. Note that these two stems are connected by an underground system and are two parts of the same plant. Detail of spore capsules at left.

The bittercress, too, is edible, as is **seri**, another small green that grows along the edge of the paddies and in the nearby irrigation ditches.

The new shoots and flower buds (*fuki no tō*) of **Japanese butterbar** (*fuki*) are also prized by *sansai* enthusiasts, as are those of **mugwort** (*yomogi*). The latter are my own special favorite, especially when mixed with pounded rice to make the delicious traditional *kusa-mochi* sweets. The new shoots of several ferns, especially **warabi** and **zenmai**, are also delectable targets of the local gatherers.

Japanese butterbar   Mugwort   *Zenmai* fern sprout

Seri, along with shepherd's purse and chickweed, is one of the "seven herbs of spring" (*haru no nanakusa*) mentioned in the *Man'yōshū*, an anthology of ancient poetry. The young shoots of these herbs are traditionally used to make a warming gruel, which is eaten during the cold, raw weather of late winter and early spring.

RAPE

Close-up of rape flowers

In April, some areas of the countryside blaze bright yellow with fields of **rape** (*seiyō aburana*) flowers. Once cultivated for the oil squeezed from their seeds, these tall mustard-family plants are now grown mostly as edible greens or for cut flowers. They have also escaped and grow wild along upland fields and roadsides. Likewise, similar-looking **wild mustards** (*seiyō karashina*) have escaped and now grow wild. Generically called *na-no-hana* in Japanese, these tall yellow blooms are frequently celebrated in song and poem, and, when flowering en masse, are considered a staple spring image in the countryside landscape.

Along country roadsides and fields, rape blossoms are often joined by another tall mustard-family plant, *ō-ara-seitō* with light purple or, sometimes, white flowers. The slopes along the inner moats are also carpeted with this combination, and both plants grow wild along the right of way on the JR Yamanote and other inner-city train lines.

Close-up of *ō-ara-seitō*

These two tall plants have much larger flowers than the tiny white shepherd's purse and bitttercress and are thus better suited for botanical study. Their structure—with four petals arranged in a crossed pattern, one pistil, four long stamens, and two shorter stamens—can be clearly seen. The mustard family includes not only mustard itself, but cabbage, turnip, cress, rocket, radish and many other familiar vegetables. The long white Japanese *daikon* radishes, *nozawa-na* pickles, and the green *wasabi* paste used to flavor sushi and *sashimi* also come from mustard-family plants.

Structure of mustard-family flower. Note Maltese-cross shape of four petals plus four long and two short stamens.

DANDE-LIONS AND RELATIVES

Side view of Kantō dandelion. Bracts lay neatly against base of flower.

Dandelions are perhaps the most numerous wildflowers in the Tokyo area. They are typical members of the sunflower (or daisy) family. Each dandelion contains hundreds of tiny flowers, called florets, all blooming together on a single head. A close look at an individual flower shows an ovary, containing the seed, at the base. The ovary is surrounded by thin silken hair that will fluff out and serve as a parachute when the seed is ready to go for a ride on the wind. The rest of the flower is composed of a tubelike crown with a wide tongue, a long thin pistil that splits into two and curls at the tip, and a stamen that surrounds the pistil at a lower level.

Almost all of the dandelions seen along the city streets are the common European species *seiyō tanpopo*, which was introduced to Japan in the Meiji period, around the end of the nineteenth century. The dandelion is one of the toughest weeds imaginable, perfectly at home on gravel driveways or in sidewalk cracks. Along country roads and on the dikes between the rice paddies, one also finds two of Japan's original native species: the **Kantō dandelion** (*Kantō tanpopo*) and the **white-flowered dandelion** (*shiro-bana tanpopo*).

The Kantō dandelion and the common dandelion look alike, but can be easily told apart by the bracts in their side profile. The bracts, a ring of leaflike structures, surrounds the flower head in the bud stage and remain even after the bud opens and the flower comes into bloom. In the common dandelion, the bracts spread outward and then hang down in a messy pattern, while in the native species they remain neatly pressed against the base of the head.

Side view of common dandelion with bracts spread out and down

The common European dandelion is a hardy plant, able to bloom throughout the year in the Tokyo area. In addition, it is resistant to air, water, and soil pollution and is able to fertilize its own flowers and produce seeds even without the benefits of cross-pollination by visiting insects. These adaptive characteristics have allowed this dandelion to flourish in urban environments all over the world.

Mature seeds of common dandelion ready for flight

Japan's native dandelions, on the other hand, are far less resistant to pollution and are unable to produce seeds without cross-pollination. Thus they have disappeared from most of the cities and have even become scarce in the surrounding countryside. Japan is home to about twenty species of native dandelion, many of which are in the process of being replaced by the common European import.

Ecologists often use dandelions as rough indicators of how healthy a habitat is. Relatively undisturbed areas, whose air, water, and soil are clean, will support the native species, while habitats that are polluted or frequently disturbed will harbor only the common European dandelion. Surprisingly, the large municipal cemeteries in central Tokyo, such as Aoyama and Yanaka, are reliable spots for locating the native species.

Another very common member of the sunflower family is **butterweed**, or **groundsel** (*noboro-giku*), a cosmopolitan roadside and urban weed that blooms from late winter onward. The flower heads are much smaller than dandelions, and several heads bloom at the tip of each stem branch. The florets, as well, are slightly different and worth a close look. Dandelion-style florets, also called lingulate or ray florets, have a tonguelike shape, while those of the butterweed, called tubular florets, are shaped like a vase. Some members of the family, such as sunflowers and daisies, have both types, with the tubulars in the center and the lingulates around the edge.

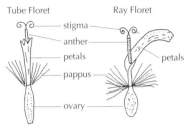

Tube Floret

Ray Floret

stigma
anther
petals
petals
pappus
ovary

Common butterweed, with details
of flower head (top) and seed

Comparison of butterweed tubular florets
(left) and dandelion lingulate (ray) florets

Even tough dandelions and butterweeds's
cow in the presence of fierce **sow thistles** of
the genus *Sorbus*. These big, heavy urban
weeds can grow as tall as a child. The flowering heads are composed of lingulate florets
but do not open as wide as the dandelions.
The stems of sow thistles branch out like
small trees, with dozens of flowers per plant.
Two species are common: ***no-geshi***, with
rough but touchable leaves that lightly clasp
the stem, and ***oni no-geshi***, with wicked, un-
touchable spines, and leaf bases that make a
180-degree rounded curve where they clasp
the stem. The Japanese prefix *oni* means "devil"
or "monster" and is often used to describe large
or heavily armored plants. Both species of sow
thistle are cosmopolitan urban roadsiders.

A naturalist could spend quite a few days
just studying the various yellow sunflower-
family flowers that bloom in spring. Another
tall weed of this family is ***oni tabirako***, with
dozens of smaller flowering heads (about the
diameter of a one-yen coin) in a dense cluster.
Out in the countryside, various species of the
genus *Ixeris* are also found. The ***jishibari***
and ***ō-jishibari*** grow along rice-paddy dikes.
These look like dandelions but have much
fewer lingulate florets in each head. The former

Sow thistle

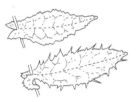

Comparison of *no-geshi* (top) and *oni
no-geshi* sow thistle leaves

Ō-jishibari (left) and dandelion.
Note difference in density of
lingulate florets.

is a small, low plant with roundish spoon-shaped leaves, while the latter is taller, with longer oval leaves. ***Nigana*** is a common roadside and open-field plant with only five florets. A subspecies, called ***hana nigana***, has ten or so florets.

Hana nigana with about eight to ten lingulate florets

Nigana with five lingulate florets

FIVE-PETALED YELLOW FLOWERS
An Exercise in Identification

Botanists employ systematic charts to help them identify plants. Sometimes the charts themselves are enormous complicated affairs, but the system employed is logical and easy to understand. To begin with, some characteristic of a plant is used to place it in a basic group, such as a family or genus. Once this is accomplished, other characteristics are used to determine the species. To a beginner, this may seem like an impossible task. Yet, it is really not as difficult as it looks and can even be a fun and rewarding exercise, almost like solving a mystery in Sherlock Holmes fashion.

Mid- through late spring is a perfect time to try out this technique, using a wide variety of small (one- to two-centimeter-wide) yellow flowers with five petals. The first step is to locate such a flower, then sit down and begin examining it closely. Almost all the flowers seen in the Tokyo area will fall into one of three groups: wood sorrel, buttercup, or rose family.

To determine which group the plant is in, use the following steps.

STEP 1 Look at the leaf. If it looks like a classic shamrock, with three heart-shaped leaflets, then the flower is a wood sorrel. If not, then it is either a buttercup or a member of the rose family.

Fleabanes of the genus *Erigeron* are roadside weeds with tall stems topped by dense clusters of small daisylike flowers. The florets, which vary in color from pure white to pinkish or even light purplish, are extremely thin and tightly packed, almost stringy in appearance. Two species, both North American in origin, have escaped and naturalized here in the Tokyo area. The ***haru jo-on*** blooms from April into mid-

Fleabane flowers. Lingulate florets are very thin.

May, then the ***hime jo-on*** takes over. As there is some overlap in blooming periods, the best way to tell these two apart is to pinch or cut a part of the stem. If the stem is hollow, it is the *haru jo-on*; if solid, *hime jo-on*.

STEP 2 Assuming the flower is not a wood sorrel, turn it over and count the petals. If there are only five, it is a buttercup. If there are ten, then it is in the rose family.

Some observers might want to stop here, but others might want to take the process further. Here are a few more steps for breaking down each of the three groups.

GROUP 1—WOOD SORREL: There are only two sub-species in the Tokyo area: *katabami*, with green leaves, and *aka katabami*, with reddish leaves (*aka* means "red"). The wood sorrel is a tough little cosmopolitan plant, quite happy growing on gravel roadeds or even in sidewalk cracks in central Tokyo.

Leaf of wood sorrel

GROUP 2—BUTTERCUP: There are four species found in the Tokyo area. Most of these can be told apart by the shape of their leaves. The big basal leaves, which arise directly from the root, are more useful for this purpose than the smaller leaves that attach to the stem. Compare the shape of these leaves. This should allow you to identify the *uma-no-ashigata* (also called *kinpōge*) and *ta-garashi* (see Early Spring Rice Paddies). The other two species, *kitsune-no-botan* and *ke-kitsune-no-botan*, have leaves that look alike, and are thus very difficult to tell apart. The latter species, however, is overwhelmingly common in the Tokyo area, and for all practical purposes you can assume that this is what you are looking at.

Once you've learned to identify the three common buttercups, you are ready to do some basic fieldwork in plant ecology. These three very similar species can coexist peacefully in the same area because, just like the tidal-flat mud crabs, each prefers a slightly different habitat. The *ta-garashi* likes very wet habitats, with standing water, and thus grows directly in marshes and rice paddies (the Japanese name means "rice-paddy mustard"). The *ke-kitsune-no-botan* (literally, "hairy fox's peony") likes moist but not truly wet habitats and is common on the rice-paddy dikes or along the sides (but not in the water) of irrigation canals. The *uma-no-ashigata* prefers even drier areas and is found in empty lots and along the edge of upland vegetable fields.

Basal leaves of three common buttercups. From left: *uma-no-ashigata*, *ta-garashi*, and *ke-kistune-no-botan*

GROUP 3—ROSE FAMILY: This is a more diverse group of plants and takes some time to get to know. Start by looking at the ten sepals. Note that these are actually two sets, an inner and an outer, of five each. If the sepals in both sets are basically the same shape and size, then the plant is in the genus *Potentillia*; but if the outer sepals are much wider and rougher than the inner, then the plant is in the genus *Duchesnea*.

When viewed from above, the extra sepals of rose-family flowers can be seen between and behind the petals (left). The next step is to turn the flower over and view the underside. Genus *Duchesnea* (center) will show five wide outer petals and five narrow inner petals, while genus *Potentillia* (right) will show five narrow outer petals and five narrow inner petals.

Three species of *Potentillia* are common in the Tokyo area and can be told apart by studying the compound leaves: three leaflets (the shape of each leaflet is very different from the wood sorrel) means it is *mitsuba-tsuchiguri*; five leaflets in a fingerlike pattern shows *hebi-ichigo*; and five, nine, or seven leaflets, arranged in a herring bone pattern denotes *kiji-mushiro* (literally "pheasant's straw cushion").

Leaves of three common *Potentillia* species: *mitsuba-tsuchiguri* (left), *hebi-ichigo,* and *kiji-mushiro*

Plants in the genus *Duchesnea* are commonly called cinquefoils in English. Two species are readily located in the Tokyo area. The most common is *hebi-ichigo*, or "snake strawberry." The Japanese name refers to the little strawberrylike fruits (unfortunately not edible) that form after the flowers wilt. This cinquefoil is found on lawns, rice-paddy dikes, and just about any place where the weeds are cut regularly. The second species, *yabu hebi-ichigo*, is not nearly as common. The *yabu* has larger leaves, and the fruit is slick and shiny, compared to the dull and wrinkled fruit of the first species. Both cinquefoils can be observed and compared at the Institute for Nature Study, in Meguro.

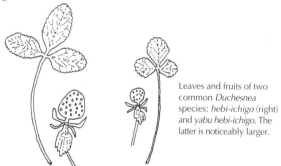

Leaves and fruits of two common *Duchesnea* species: *hebi-ichigo* (right) and *yabu hebi-ichigo.* The latter is noticeably larger.

217

SUMMER WILDFLOWERS

As the days warm and lengthen, the competition for light and space along the roadsides and in open fields really heats up. The tiny, ground-hugging plants of spring are overwhelmed by taller weeds that get both their leaves and flowers high up in the air—the better to ensure access to light and attract insects. Speedwells and dead-nettles are replaced by tall evening primroses and goldenrods. Only on the rice-paddy dikes and on well-tended lawns, where the grass is regularly cut, can low-growing plants continue to compete.

Tough vines take the struggle for light one notch higher, climbing up over fences or other plants, always striving to get their leaves just an extra notch above those of the competition. In the Tokyo area, any untended fence or border hedge is summarily taken over by tough summer vines like bindweed and kudzu.

Summer is also the best season for botanizing around the water. The irrigation ditches and shallow ponds become choked with cattails, irises, and water lilies. Waterside botanizing is also considered a good strategy for beating the summer heat.

HOUTTUY- NIA

Houttuynia

From late May through the rainy months the **Houttuynia** (or **lizard's tail**) is one of the most frequently encountered flowers in the Tokyo area, easily identified by its distinctive heart-shaped leaves, white-and-yellow flower clusters, and a powerful odor that once experienced is never forgotten. Look for this hardy herbaceous plant in shady or at least partially shady habitats, such as underneath trees in parks and forests. In central Tokyo, it can even be seen growing in the little patches of dirt around street trees.

The flowers are similar in structure to those of the flowering dogwood (see Dogwood in the Street and Park Trees chapter). What first appears as a single flower with four white petals and a yellow center is actually a whole bunch of tiny yellow flowers arranged on a central axis. Each flower has a pistil and three stamens, but no petals or sepals. The four white structures originally mistaken for petals are bracts. They surround and protect the flower in the bud stage, then flair out to help attract insects. The white bracts are especially effective in the shady habitats that this plant prefers.

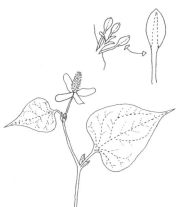

Houttuynia with details of single flower

The plant's odor, which can be overwhelming in the vicinity of a large cluster, is not so much revolting as medicinal; and indeed, this is one of the area's most famous medicinal herbs. The Japanese name, *doku-dami*, has several interpretations. *Doku* means "poison," and *dami* may be a corruption of "*tameru*" (literally, "to stop"). Some researchers believe the *dami* to stem from *itami*, or "pain," meaning that the plant can be used to treat poison and pain. A common nickname is *jūyaku* (literally, "ten medicines"), which alludes to the plant's applicability for treating a wide variety of symptoms.

The entire plant, including the roots, is harvested and dried in the sun. The dried product is then used to make a tea for treating such problems as constipation and high blood pressure. Between five and fifteen grams, steeped in half a liter of hot water, is the recommended dose. The *doku-dami* is a relatively safe herb and can thus be harvested and utilized by beginners and amateurs.

In addition to treatment of specific problems, *doku-dami* is also popular as a general restorative and health drink. Some of the commercially bottled health teas advertised on television use this plant in combination with other leaves. You can also buy boxes of *doku-dami* tea bags in any supermarket or drugstore.

DAY FLOWERS

Wide open bisexual day flower. Note two long stamens, one long pistil (in center), and four shorter pistils.

From mid- to late summer, **day flowers** (*tsuyu kusa*) surpass the houttuynia as the area's most common roadside flower. These little flowers are also worth taking a close look at. At the bottom of the flower are two long stamens with up-curved tips. These are the working stamens that produce pollen. Above these are four more stamens, yellow in color. Three of these are short and X-shaped, while the fourth is a little bit longer and Y-shaped. These yellow stamens produce little or no pollen and are thought to serve mostly as advertising aids, contrasting with the deep purple petals and catching the eyes of passing insects. A close examination of a few dozen flowers will show that although most are perfect (bisexual) flowers with a single coiled-tip pistil between the two long stamens, there are also male-only flowers that lack a pistil.

As their name suggests, these flowers are short-lived, wilting by late afternoon. During the day, the flowers wait patiently for insects to come and cross-pollinate them, but if none come by evening they fold in and pollinate themselves, pushing their own pistil and stamens together.

Plants often seem to be unsure of their reproductive strategies. On the one hand, exchanging genetic material through cross-pollination is clearly the ideal. This sort of reproduction gives the species as a whole more genetic diversity, which allows a population of plants to adapt to changes in the environment.

A plant that regularly self-pollinates itself produces nothing but genetic clones and thus suffers a loss in long-range adaptability. On the other hand, cross-pollination must rely on the wind or on animal pollinators such as insects, birds, and bats, and as such does not always go as planned. Self-pollination, in contrast, is much more reliable and offers an enticing if short-sighted strategy.

The day flower is the ultimate realist, embracing cross-pollination as the ideal but perfectly willing to settle for self-pollination as preferable to producing no seed at all. Considering how widespread this plant is, this strategy has obviously been a great success.

Cayratia vine flowers

Tokyo, with its warm climate and abundant precipitation, offers excellent conditions for plant growth. Any area left untended for even a few weeks in summer is soon covered with dense foliage. An open field will be packed with tall weeds, and a fence or border will be overrun by tough volunteer vines.

Vines are not true parasites. Most have roots and leaves of their own and thus do not steal water or sugars directly from their host. By climbing up and over fences or other plants, however, they are able to position their leaves up high without investing in a thick trunk or stem.

The **cayratia vine**, which grows wild along roadside thickets, fences and planted borders, is one of Tokyo's commonest weeds. The compound leaves have a unique birdfoot shape (the leaf first branches into three, then each of the side branches fork out into

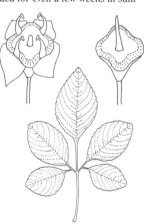

Cayratia leaf and flower: male stage of flower (left), female (right)

two leaflets). The tiny flowers, no more than a few millimeters wide, are arranged in dense clusters that protrude from the leaf joints. Often the flower cluster will be buzzing with honey bees and other insects that come to collect the nectar.

Seen up close, cayratia flowers are colorful works of pop art. Each tiny flower is based on a squarish receptacle that looks like a miniature pedestal. A quick survey shows two distinct flower types. One type has four green petals arranged around an orange base and four yellow stamens sticking straight up along the edge, with a single small pistil located in the very center. The other type of flower shows only a tall pistil in the center of a pinkish base.

These two types are actually the same flower in different stages of its cycle. Newly opened flowers are male, with mature stamens ready to attach pollen to visiting insects. In this stage, the pistil, or female reproductive part, is small and immature and not yet ready to accept pollen. After about three or four hours, the stamens and petals drop off, while the little pistil begins to grow like a magic crystal. This is the female stage of the flower, when the pistil is ready to accept pollen from incoming bees. By staggering the maturation of the male and female parts, the cayratia flower is able to ensure that it doesn't pollinate itself.

Cross-pollinated flowers soon develop into juicy berries typical of the grape family. These are eaten by birds, which disperse the seeds in their scats and pellets. In addition, the cayratia vine is able to spread asexually by extending new shoots from its underground root system. This combination of sexual and asexual reproduction makes the cayratia a formidable and aggressive competitor.

The standard Japanese name for the cayratia vine, *yabu-garashi*, refers directly to this aggressive nature: *yabu* means "thicket," and *karasu* (the "k" becomes a "g" in some combinations) means "to cause to wilt." The image conjured up by this name is that cayratia vines can cover the outer edge of a roadside thicket so completely that the other plants, deprived of sunlight, soon wilt and die.

A common nickname, *binbō-kazura* ("pauper vine"), offers two more colorful nods toward the vine's aggressiveness. One interpretation implies that farmers whose land this vine invades will lose all their plants and be driven into poverty. Another suggests that a border or fence overrun by cayratia is proof that the owner cannot afford to keep his grounds properly maintained.

Another very prominent summer vine is the **bindweed**, a member of the morning glory family. The large pink funnel-shaped flowers are so pretty that most people think they were planted

Bindweed flowers: the corolla is twisted like a pretzel in the bud stage, but straightens out as the flower blooms

on purpose to decorate a hedge or border. Local caretakers will tell you in no uncertain terms that, despite the pretty flowers, these tough vines have arrived on their own and are almost impossible to get rid of.

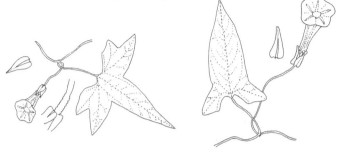

Comparison of *ko-hiru-gao* bindweed (left) and *hiru-gao*

Butterflies and other insects that visit bindweed flowers first land on the wide-spreading corolla lip, then disappear into the long tube. The nectar is hidden near the bottom of the tube, and the stamens and pistils are positioned directly in the path of any insect that crawls or reaches in.

Two species of bindweed, ***hiru-gao*** and ***ko-hiru-gao***, are common in the Tokyo area. The flowers of the latter are smaller, and the leaf usually has a wider base and deeper lobes. The surest way to tell them apart is to closely compare the stalk that connects the flower to the vine. In the *hiru-gao*, the stalk is smooth and round, while in *ko-hiru-gao* it is somewhat flattened, with scalloplike wrinkles along the edge.

Bindweed is a medicinal herb that can be used right in the field to soothe itchy insect bites. Just crumple a leaf in your hand and squeeze the juice onto the sensitive area.

The **paederia vine** is saddled with an uncomplimentary yet descriptive Japanese name, *hekuso-kazura. Kazura* is a common word for "vine," but *hekuso* means "fart!" As might be expected, the leaves and especially the light brown berries, produce an uncomfortable odor. The berries, however, are actually a natural skin cosmetic. In the past, mountain villagers would crush them and rub the juice onto their hands and face to prevent frostbite. The small, tubular flowers of this "fart vine," whitish gray on the outside but deep reddish purple inside, bloom in midsummer. The berries stay on the vine well into the winter.

Paederia vine flowers

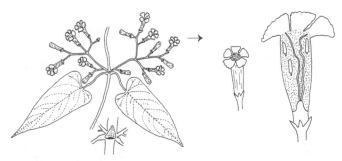

Paederia vine and flowers

A plant's name often reflects its popular image. The ***kana-mugura*** vine, for example, is a thin but strong annual that by midsummer can completely take over the edge of a sunny thicket or planting. The *kana* in the name conjures up the image of a "steel wire." The stems and leaves of this tough vine are lined with millions of short but sharp downward-pointing spikes. These serve as small hooks and anchors, allowing the plant to climb and cling tenaciously. You can see the spines with a loupe, or feel them by rubbing the vine between your fingers in the upward direction.

Kana-mugura vine. Note down-turned spikes.

No discussion of tough vines would be complete without mention of the toughest of all, the **kudzu** (*kuzu*). Although listed as one of the "seven flowers of autumn" (see Autumn Wildflowers), the big peaflowers, purple with yellow centers, begin blooming in late summer. The compound leaves have three leaflets each. The two side leaflets rotate on their stalks, turning themselves perpendicular to the sun's rays on hot summer afternoons. Japanese call this action *kuzu no hirune* ("the kudzu's afternoon nap"), but botanists suggest it is a strategy to minimize moisture loss due to evaporation. The vines are as thick and strong as mountain-climbing ropes, and the pods are densely coated with long hairs that cling to passing animals.

Kudzu vines were brought to the southeastern United States in the 1930s and planted to help stabilize eroding slopes. Since then they have naturalized and now grow like wildfire, earning them the nickname "the vine that ate the south." In Japan,

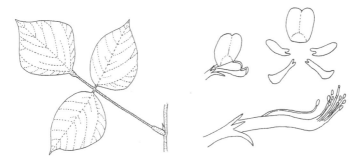

Kudzu trifoliate compound leaf and flower structure

too, the kudzu can be a pesky vine but is also highly valued for its beautiful flowers, which promise that the hot, humid summer is nearly over and that cool autumn weather is on its way. The kudzu once had many traditional uses: the roots were pulverized to make an edible starch, the leaves fed to horses, and the vines used as ropes or woven into cloth. An herbal tea made from the dried flowers is still used to treat hangovers and to stop a cold from coming on. I have even met people who claim to make delicious jam from the fresh flowers. Small children love the winter bud and the leaf scar, which looks like a little bunny rabbit.

Kudzu vines offer a superb chance to study the structure of pea family flowers, which consist of five petals. The large, wide petal on top is called the standard, the two side petals the wings. The two bottom petals fold together to form the keel. There are usually ten stamens, one of which is separated from the rest. Presumably this helps ensure that an insect crawling into the flower touches at least one stamen. Typically, the single pistil is longer than the stamens. This helps ensure that the insect touches the pistil first and the stamens later, lessening the chance of self-pollination.

IRISES

Kaki-tsubata

One way to survive the heat of summer is to spend some time around the water, and while you are there, you may as well do a little botanizing. The summer waterside show starts off with irises in June. The flower's name comes from Iris, the Greek goddess of the rainbow, and the genus contains more than two hundred species distributed throughout the northern temperate zone.

Aside from being an object of great beauty, the iris flower is a finely tuned device for attracting insects and ensuring that pollen is carried from one flower to the next. The iris bloom may look like three separate flowers arranged at 120-degree intervals, but is really a single immense flower composed of six tepals (a botanical term used in plants in which the sepals and petals both have color). The three wide outer tepals, also called the "falls," usually hang downward and are decorated with vivid patterns that serve as nectar guides for visiting insects. In contrast, the three inner tepals, or "standards," are usually narrower and stand erect.

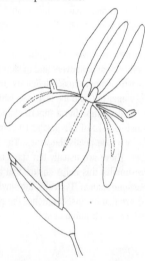

The pistil is split into three branches, each of which lies tight against one of the outer tepals. These pistil branches are often as showy and colorful as the tepals. The stigma, the part of the pistil that receives pollen from visiting insects, is located at

Structure of iris flower. The pistil branch at right is lifted up to show the stamen hidden underneath. The receptive stigma is on the outside surface of the pistil tip.

the outer tip of each pistil branch, while the pollen-producing stamens are found hidden underneath the branches. You have to lift the branches up with the tip of your finger to see them. The nectar is located in the central tube, deep at the base of the flower.

A visiting insect first lands on one of the falls, then follows the bright and attractive nectar guide markings into the flower. As the insect squeezes between the tepal and the pistil, it first comes into contact with the stigma, and in so doing, pollinates the flower with pollen already on its head from a previous flower. Continuing inwards, the insect then brushes up against the stamen, picking up new pollen for the next flower it visits. As the insect emerges after feasting on nectar, it touches only the nonreceptive inner edge of the pistil branch. This arrangement is thought to be another strategy for preventing self-pollination.

Three species of native iris and one introduced exotic species can be found in the Tokyo area. The **kaki-tsubata**, with bluish purple tepals and white nectar guides, is native to sunny, shallow marshes. The **no-hana-shōbu** also likes wet habitats, but can be told from the first species by its tint, which is closer to true purple, its yellowish nectar guides, and slightly wider tepals. A third native species, the **ayame**, prefers drier habitats and is easily recognized by its beautiful falls, with a complicated net pattern against a blue background.

The most common wild-growing iris is the **yellow flag** (*ki-shōbu*), a hardy species native to Europe and central Asia that escaped here from cultivation. The stalks can reach a meter high. Yellow flags grow in dense clusters along the edge of ponds and irrigation canals.

In addition to wild irises in the countryside, there are dozens of parks with ornamental iris gardens, including Meiji Jingū and the Imperial Palace's East Gardens. Most of Japan's cultivated iris varieties are derived from the *no-hana-shōbu*.

Yellow flag iris

WATER LILIES

Water lily

Tokyo parks and garden ponds, as well as countryside irrigation ponds and ditches, are fine habitats for enjoying plants in the water-lily family, which in the Tokyo area includes the **water lilies** themselves as well as **lotus**, **spatter-docks**, and **water shields**.

Most of the water lilies seen in Tokyo are the large, ornamental varieties, called *suiren* in Japanese. These come in various colors, but the most popular combination has white tepals and a yellow center. The huge leaves, commonly known as lily pads, float on the surface of the water. When the new leaves first emerge from the base of the plant they are rolled up tightly, like small scrolls. After they break through the surface and into the sun they unfold. Lily pads provide shade and hiding places for fish, frogs, and various aquatic insects. Egrets and king-fishers are well aware of this bounty and can often be seen hunting among the pads.

Lotus with flower and newly emerging leaf (bottom right)

In addition to the ornamentals, Japan is also home to a small native water lily with white petals and yellow center. The Japanese name is ***hitsuji-gusa***, and derives from the time of day that the flower opens, about two in the afternoon, or the hour of the sheep (*hitsuji* means "sheep") in the traditional reckoning. In the Tokyo area, this species is found mostly in nature parks, such as the Institute for Nature Study, in Meguro.

Lotus flowers are native to India and China but were brought to Japan a very long time ago. Lotus seeds found in archeological sites thought to be two thousand years old have been planted and germinated. The image of pure, beautiful flowers springing from the dirty muck at the bottom of a pond is highly symbolic in Buddhist theology, and thus lotus flowers are frequently planted around temples. The lotus root, called *renkon* in Japanese, is eaten in pickles and tempura, and the plants are grown commercially on a small scale.

The huge leaves of the lotus also emerge rolled up but, when expanded, do not actually float. The flowers, usually light pink, consist of numerous sepals and petals surrounding a central receptacle with several dozen little compartments. After the flower wilts, the receptacle expands, and a small brown nutlet forms in each of the compartments. *Hasu*, the Japanese name for the plant, is thought to derive from *hachi-no-su* ("bees' nest") and refers to this compartmentalized receptacle.

Spatterdocks have long, slightly pointed floating leaves and small cuplike yellow flowers on thick stems. One native species, ***kōbone***, was formerly common in ponds and irrigation canals but is now rare in the Tokyo area.

Lotus flower just before opening

Lotus flower in full bloom

Receptacles of lotus floating at Shinobazu Pond in Ueno. Each little compartment contained a single nutlet.

Spatterdock

Many of the other natives in the water-lily family are also regionally endangered, including the **water shield** (*junsai*) and the ***oni-basu***, which has enormous round floating leaves a meter or more in diameter. The beautiful yellow ***asaza*** is a rare native plant that has floating leaves like a water lily but actually belongs in the gentian family.

Dense lotus beds can be enjoyed at Shinobazu Pond in Ueno and Meiji Jingū Shrine. Mizumoto Park features lotus, *oni-basu*, and *asaza*, while Shakujii Park is famous for spatterdocks.

CATTAILS

Gama

Cattails are tall plants that grow in dense colonies along the shallow edges of ponds and canals. They usually are found standing right in the water, rather than up on the bank. The leaves are long and thin, and the flowers bloom on a high central stalk that sticks straight up. The male and female flowers hug the stalk in separate clusters, with the female below. Later, the female cluster turns into a brown velvety cylinder. In America, this is sometimes called a "punk" and is burned to repel mosquitoes. In late fall and winter, the cylinder becomes a mass of white cotton, which is actually the seeds. Each seed is equipped with fluffy white hairs that float on the wind.

Three species are found in the Tokyo area. *Gama* is up to two meters tall, with thick leaves about two centimeters wide and a long thick cylinder between fifteen and twenty centimeters long. *Ko-gama* is smaller in all dimensions, only a meter or so tall, with leaves less than one centimeter wide, and a cylinder less than ten centimeters long. *Hime-gama* shows long, very thin cylinders. A reliable field mark is a noticeable gap between the female and male flower clusters (in the other two species, the male cluster begins right on top of the female).

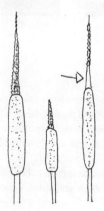

Comparison of local cattails: from left, *gama, ko-gama, hime-gama*. Note gap between male and female flowers in *hime-gama*.

SUMMER LILIES

Yama yuri

O ne of the most impressive flowers of summer is the ***yama yuri***, an immense lily that blooms in the forest shade. Lilies have six tepals (three sepals and three petals), six very long stamens, and a single long pistil with a three-sectioned stigma at the tip. The flowers' wide open stance and long stamens and pistils are designed to allow butterflies easy access to the interior. The butterfly hovers in front of the flower, or actually perches on the stamens and pistil, and sticks its long hoselike mouthpiece deep into the tube. As this happens, the stigma and anthers (stamen tips) come in contact with the insect's head and belly, and the flower is pollinated.

Structure of lily flower: six tepals, six long stamens, and one long pistil with a stigma that is divided into three lobes

Yama yuri tepals are white with reddish purple dots and yellow center lines. The anthers are brownish red. The fruit is a capsule with three compartments, each stacked with dozens of flat seeds surrounded by thin winglike membranes. The capsules split open and the seeds are dispersed on the wind. The *yama yuri* is also grown as an ornamental and is very popular in flower arrangements for weddings and parties. In these cases, the huge anthers are usually cut off to avoid spilling the bright red pollen all over the guests' fine clothes.

Two species of tall orange **day lily** are frequently encountered on the rice-paddy dikes and along sunny farmroads. One of these (***no-kanzō***) has only six tepals, and the other (***yabu-kanzō***) has up to twelve. Both of these day lilies are found only around farmland and do not produce seeds of their own. They are probably of Chinese origin and were originally planted for their flower buds, which are edible when dried, and their medicinal herbal qualities.

Another tall orange flower that blooms in summer is the ***kitsune-no-kamisori***, literally "the fox's shaving razor." This plant is often mistaken for a lily but is actually in the spider-lily family (see Spider Lilies in the Autumn Wildflowers chapter). In lilies, the ovary, the cushioned nest in which the seeds develop, is superior. This means that the ovary sits above the spot where the tepals attach and is thus hidden inside the flower. In spider lilies, the ovary is inferior, which means it is located below the tepals and can thus be seen as an inflated bead at the very base of the flower. This plant is named for its thin, sharp leaves. It grows wild but is also planted around cemeteries and old graves.

No-kanzō: orange with only six tepals

Yabu-kanzō: orange with more than six tepals. In many flowers some of the stamens mutate into petals.

Kitsune-no-kamisori

SUMMER ROAD-SIDERS

Red clover

In summer, the frequency of mowing is a major factor in determining which plants can grow where. Untended roadsides and abandoned fields are the domain of tall weeds. Among the most common are stately **evening primroses**. Several species, all originally American natives, were brought here as ornamentals and escaped. The pretty yellow flowers wilt during the day but come into full bloom at night. The Japanese name, *machiyoi-gusa*, means "wait-for-night weed." Night-blooming flowers are generally pollinated by moths rather than butterflies. The capsules ripen in late autumn and winter and contain thousands of incredibly tiny seeds, the favorite food of siskins and other seed-loving birds.

On well-tended lawns one finds shorter plants. Clovers of the genus *Trifolium*, once simple European pasture flowers, are now summer standards in city and suburban parks. The **white clover** (*shiro tsume-kusa*) arrived here during the

Edo period as packing for glass and other fragile trade items imported from the Netherlands (*tsume-kusa* means "packing weed"). Another, slightly larger species is the **red clover** (*aka tsume-kusa*), which was brought here around the end of the nineteenth century as pasture for the developing dairy industry.

Blue-eyed grass

Yellow **wood sorrels** continue blooming throughout the summer, when they are joined by a beautiful purple relative, ***murasaki katabami***. Little **blue-eyed grass** (*niwa-zekishō*), with purplish six-petaled flowers the size of one-yen coins, are American natives that belong to the iris family. One of the most interesting weeds of well-manicured lawns is the neat little **lady's tresses orchid**. Although only a foot or so tall, the stalk is lined with tiny pink blooms arranged in corkscrew fashion. Seen through a loupe, each bloom is a perfect little pink orchid with a fluffy white lip.

Lady's tresses orchid

If you like your roadside weeds tough, then you'll love the **Carolina nightshade** (*waru-nasubi*). This plant, a relative of the famous deadly nightshade, is native to the southern United States. Covered with wicked, painful spines, it flourishes in the least-promising habitats, including the little squares of dirt surrounding street trees on busy central Tokyo avenues. The flowers, about the size of a ten-yen coin, have five lobes and are either white or pale purple with yellow centers.

Carolina nightshade

Balloon flower in final bud stage, looking exactly like a little purple balloon

Over long centuries, Tokyo city folk have developed many traditional methods of coping with the stifling heat and humidity of summer. These include taking an evening stroll on a bridge or along a riverbank, eating lean, protein-rich fish such as eel and sea bass, listening to insects singing, enjoying a fireworks display or chilling horror play, and keeping a few potted plants around the house.

Tokyoites are among the world's most ardent gardeners. Even narrow alleys, barely wide enough for two people to walk abreast, will often be lined with pots and planters. The most popular plants of the midsummer season are balloon flower, morning glory, and Chinese lantern plants.

The balloon flower (*kikyō*) is a hardy perennial that grows wild on all four of Japan's main islands. The name in English comes from the flower bud, which swells and takes on a light purple color just before opening, looking for all the world like a miniature purple hot air balloon ready to take off.

The big, open balloon flowers are perfect for studying flower structure. When the flower first opens, the five stamens are pressed tight around the pistil, which is not yet fully developed. As the stamens slowly push off they leave copious amounts of pollen in the center of the flower. After a while the stamens drop off and the pollen is blown or carried away. The pistil then matures and splits into five thin sections. This staggered timing of the reproductive parts, already seen in the magnolias and the cayratia vine, is thought to be a simple mechanism for assuring that the flower does not pollinate itself.

Balloon flower in male stage

The root of the balloon flower is skinned, washed, and dried as a medicinal herb. An infusion made from the resulting powder is then gargled and drunk to relieve severe coughs and sore throats. In Korea, where the same species is also native, the roots are made into a pickle.

Balloon flower in female stage

Morning glories rival the balloon flowers in popularity. These twisting vines are usually grown in pots fitted with a small trellis for the plants to climb on. The large round flowers open in the morning but close in the afternoon, giving the plant both its English name "morning glory" and Japanese appellation, *asagao* (literally "morning face").

Morning glories are not native to Japan but were brought here from the continent, originally as a medicinal herb. In the early nineteenth century, horticulturists in Edo began developing ornamental varieties. A sort of craze ensued, with individual plants featuring highly unusual flowers or leaves fetching small fortunes for the horticulturists who developed them. One catalogue dating back to this period depicts 180 formally recognized varieties. Today, morning glories already in flower can be bought at any garden shop. Elementary school children raise them from seeds, recording the plant's growth and seasonal changes as part of their summer science projects.

Japanese morning glory coverd with dense white fuzz

Chinese lantern plants (*hōzuki*) are members of the nightshade family. They are also referred to as **strawberry tomato** and **winter cherry**, while species of the same genus native to the United States are usually termed ground cherry. The main attraction is not the flowers but the amazing fruit. After the flowers drop off, the five sepals expand, turn bright orange, then coalesce to enclose the growing fruit in a tightly sealed case that resembles a miniature paper lantern.

Some botanists believe that the lantern plant is native to Japan, but others suggest that it was brought here from the Asian continent a very long time ago. Originally the plant was valued as a medicinal herb. The leaves, stem, and roots, which contain a chemical compound called physalin, are sun dried and used to make an infusion prescribed for a severe cough, sore throat, or fever. The fruit contains vitamin C and citric acid and is used as a diuretic and laxative. In the past, the fruit was pickled, preserved, and used as a vitamin supplement for children.

Chinese lantern plant

Young girls and women also use the lantern plant fruit as a sort of toy whistle. The seeds and juice are carefully removed, and the emptied-out fruit is placed in the mouth and blown through. Depictions of court women whistling in this manner date to the Heian period. The Japanese name is thought to come from an association with a young girl's cheeks (*hō* is Japanese for "cheek").

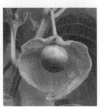

The bracts removed to show the small tomato-like fruit

Morning glories and lantern plants are available in any garden shop or nursery but are also sold at special markets, called *asagao-ichi* or *hōzuki-ichi*, usually held near Buddhist temples, especially those dedicated to Kannon, a Buddhist goddess of mercy. Some temples even set aside two or three days for these markets. Believers who visit the temple during these days are said to accumulate special blessings. The Asakusa Kannon temple (Sensō-ji) has the most famous *hōzuki-ichi*, with devotees annually estimated at about half a million over the two-day market period (usually during the second week in July). One visit to the temple during the *hōzuki-ichi* is said to allow a devotee to accumulate blessings equivalent to forty-six thousand visits on a regular day!

Chinese lantern plant in autumn. The bracts have weathered away to a fine netting, and the fruit is visible inside.

Similar but smaller markets are held at the Genkaku-ji temple, near Kōrakuen Station on the Marunouchi Line, and the Bishamon-ten Zenkoku-ji temple, near Kagurazaka Station on the Tōzai Line. The most popular morning glory market is held in the Iriya neighborhood (Hibiya Line), just east of Ueno, usually during the first week of July.

● ●

AUTUMN WILDFLOWERS

Autumn in Tokyo is a long, drawn out affair, running from the first appearance of high cirrus clouds in early September to the arrival of the cold, dry winds in late November or even early December. During this period, there is a sort of minirush of wildflowers coming into bloom. Roadsides are taken over by tall plume grass and even taller goldenrods. The rice-paddy dikes, which were mostly solid green during the hot summer months, become splashes of color again. Bright red spider lilies bloom around temples and graveyards, and color the slopes of the Imperial Palace Inner Moat.

SUSUKI

Susuki plumes

If cherry blossoms are the symbol of spring, then a field of silver-and-gold **plume grass**, waving gently in the breeze, is the classic symbol of autumn in the Japanese countryside. *Susuki* plume grass is widely celebrated in art and verse. Cut stalks are placed on small tables along with pounded rice cakes and other autumn offerings, set out on verandas or in the garden at night as the central altar for autumn moon-viewing parties. Such parties are traditionally conducted on or near the full moon during the months of September and October.

Susuki is a native Japanese grass, found throughout most of the country, from sea level well up into the mountains. It prefers well-drained habitats and often forms great colonies covering entire fields and hillsides. It is this landscape, especially with the silver plumes backlit by a slowly sinking sun, that is so dear to Japanese artistic and natural sensibilities.

Originally, *susuki* grew primarily in areas where forest fires or slash-and-burn agriculture had opened up the landscape. As such, the *susuki* field was a transitional plant community which, in the course of a decade or so, would be overwhelmed by a new growth of secondary woodland.

As agriculture became more settled, Japanese farmers found many uses for *susuki* stalks. They were used as livestock fodder and bedding, and as fertilizer in upland fields and rice paddies. The stalks were also valued for making brooms and other implements and for thatching the roof of farmhouses and outbuildings.

Eventually, farmers found the *susuki* so useful they began to artificially maintain fields on the outskirts of the village. An annual burning would prevent the forest trees from regaining a foothold, and the field could thus be maintained in *susuki* for decades at a time. These fields, called *kaya-ba* (*kaya* is a general word for tall, stiff grasses that can be used as thatching, and *ba* means "place" or "area"), were often kept as communal property, with all the village households sharing the right to harvest the necessary amount of stalks.

Today, *susuki* has been completely replaced by commercially available feed and fertilizer, and farming communities no longer maintain their *kaya-ba*. Still, *susuki* is a hardy and aggressive colonizer, quick to take advantage of newly opened habitats, which are always in high supply in development-intensive Japan.

Small patches of *susuki* can thus often be found surrounding suburban housing developments and even in empty lots and loosely maintained parks in the inner city.

Susuki plumes are composed of numerous ripening seeds, each with a tuft of fine hair attached. These hairs catch and reflect the sunlight, giving the landscape its distinctive silver-and-gold glow. The seeds are designed to be dispersed by the wind, dandelion style.

A few minutes spent searching around the edges of the plume grass clumps is often rewarded with the discovery of a beautiful parasitic **broomrape flower**. This plant is called *nanban-giseru* in Japanese for the flower's close resemblance to the old long-stemmed tobacco pipes (*kiseru* or *giseru*) used by the early European traders (*nanban*, or "southern barbarians") that lived in Nagasaki during the Edo period. The broomrape has no leaves of its own and taps directly into the roots of the plume grass.

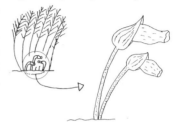

Parasitic broomrape flowers

Many people confuse the *susuki* with *ogi*, a similar looking plume grass that grows in wet or swampy habitats. The *ogi* stalks are taller than the *susuki*'s and grow singly rather than in dense clumps. *Ogi* seeds have far longer hairs, with an even deeper silver luster.

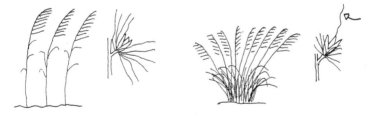

Ogi (left) and *susuki* plume grasses, with detail of individual flowers

GOLDEN-ROD

Goldenrod flowers. Each flower produces a seed that disperses on the wind.

In many open and disturbed habitats, the *susuki* finds itself in fierce competition with tall **goldenrod**, an erect member of the sunflower-family that can grow to heights of close to three meters. The goldenrod is a native of North America. Brought to Japan as an ornamental, it escaped and naturalized. Like the plume grass, the goldenrod is an aggressive opportunist, filling the late autumn air with windborne seeds.

Goldenrods, which produce tens of thousands of seeds per plant, can usually outperform the plume grass in the early stages of the fight for a newly created or disturbed habitat. Once established, the goldenrod releases a special chemical from its roots that prevents the growth of other plants. Thus, a new empty lot or bulldozed slope will often be quickly covered with a solidly packed colony of tall goldenrod.

After a period of five or six years, the goldenrod starts to weaken, and the plume grass begins moving in, setting up in dense clumps of several dozen stalks. Once these clusters have been established, it is only a matter of time before the plume grass reclaims the territory lost to the foreign invader.

Goldenrod is called *seitaka-awadachi-sō* in Japanese. *Seitaka* means "tall," and *awadachi* conjures up an image of bubbling foam, referring to the fluffy seeds that follow the flowers. In Europe, goldenrod was traditionally used to make a medicinal salve applied to cuts. In fact, the genus name *Solidago* is thought to imply a stitching or welding of two objects together.

"SEVEN FLOWERS OF AUTUMN"

Nadeshiko pink

Japanese aesthetics are imbued with a keen sense of the changing seasons, often marked by the appearance of different plants and flowers at different times of year. This custom can be traced back to the *Man'yōshū*, Japan's first anthology of poetry. This anthology was compiled in the late eighth century, but many of the actual poems are thought to be much older.

The *Man'yōshū* consists of twenty volumes written by many authors in various styles over a span of several centuries. Plants play a frequent role in the compositions, not only to symbolize a particular place or season, but to convey the mood of the poet or symbolize the relationship between the poet and a loved one. One of the most famous flower verses, which comes from the eighth volume, is known as the *Aki no nanakusa*, or "Seven Flowers of Autumn." A rough translation would be as follows. Keep in mind that the Japanese count by first extending all their fingers then bending them back down one-by-one.

> *Flowers blooming*
> *In the autumn countryside*
> *Bending my fingers, counting*
> *Seven different kinds*

The famous seven flowers described in this text include the balloon flower, kudzu vine, and *susuki* plume grass. The first two actually begin blooming in late summer (see Summer Wildflowers). Another member, a beautiful native pink, the **nadeshiko**, grows wild in slightly moist habitats, such as along irrigation canals and the edges of the rice-paddy dikes. The flower is pinkish white with five petals that are fringed along the edge. It is these fringed or "pinked" edges (think pinking shears), and not the color of the petals, that give this group of flowers their English name.

Also in this celebrated group are the **ominaeshi**, a tall plant with dense clusters of tiny yellow flowers, that grows in the gaps among the clumps of *susuki* plume grasses; **bush clover** (*hagi*), a short bush in the pea family that flourishes along the sunny edge of the woodlands and coppice forests; and *fujibakama*, a tall sunflower-family plant that is thought to be a native of China. Clusters of white flowers adorn the tips of the stems. Long pistils give these flowers a unique stringy appearance, and the leaves and stems produce a pleasant fragrance that was traditionally used as a bath perfume and in aromatic sachels worn by little girls. A bath infusion is also useful for easing the itch from insect bites and other minor skin irritations.

Bush clover

The plants chosen by the old poets are all species that would have been common on the outskirts of any village or manor. They were picked not only for their beauty but for their usefulness as medicinal herbs. There is a also a corresponding *haru no nanakusa* ("seven herbs of spring") for the springtime. These are all plants chosen not for their flowers but for their new spring shoots, which are edible greens used in soups, gruels, and other traditional health-food dishes served in late winter and early spring.

With the exception of the *fujibakama*, all of these plants can be found blooming wild in the Tokyo area. One would be very hard-pressed to find them all blooming together at the same time and place. The Mukōjima Hyakka-en Gardens, however, makes a gallant effort and usually has at least six or so (minus the pink) on display around mid to late September.

AUTUMN FAVORITES

Nohara azami

Some additional autumn favorites include ***ohara azami***, a tall purple thistle with spiky leaves (another purple thistle, ***no azami***, blooms from late spring through summer), and a strange rose-family plant called ***waremokō***. The flower clusters look almost like little red pine cones but are actually collections of tiny flowers. Each flower has four sepals and very short stamens and pistil.

The ***tsurigane ninjin*** is a tall plant in the bellflower-family, with dozens of one-centimeter-long

Waremokō

purple bell-shaped flowers. The long pistil sticks out below the lip of the tube, making the flower look like a miniature version of the great bronze hanging bells seen at Buddhist temples. ***Akino-no-geshi*** is a tall daisy-family plant with numerous lingulate florets colored a distinctive shade of creamy yellow. Several asterlike plants, with white or purple ray florets, are also among the autumn favorites.

Typical autumn aster

RICE-PADDY DIKES

Mizo-soba

The narrow dikes that separate the rice fields are called *aze* in Japanese. In autumn, these dikes are often sprinkled with the bright red leaves and reddish pink flowers of the ***inu-tade*** knotweed. The tiny flowers are in long clusters. *Inu* in Japanese means "dog." As a prefix it is often attached to plants that have little or no direct value to man.

Mizo-soba, another knotweed, has roundish rather than long, thin clusters, and very distinctive leaves shaped like the head of a fox, with two dark markings that look just like eyes. This species prefers slightly wetter habitats and is

Inu-tade

usually found along the edge of the irrigation canals rather than actually on top of the *aze* dikes. The ***mamako-no-shiri-nugui*** knotweed looks similar to *mizo-soba* but is covered with wicked spines. The Japanese name combines elements not often associated with flower lovers. *Mamako* means "adopted child," and *shiri-nugui* is a cloth used to wipe one's bottom! Several other tall plants of the same genus, *Polygonum*, can be found along roadsides and in other disturbed habitats.

Scattered here and there among the pink and red knotweeds is a delicate little native **geranium** (*gen-no-shōko*), with soft white or pinkish white petals. The long, thin capsules, shaped at first like a rolled-up umbrella, later split into five sections, and the seeds are catapulted outwards when ripe. An infusion made from sun-dried leaves of this herb was traditionally used to treat diarrhea.

SPIDER LILY

Cluster of red spider lily flowers

Japanese visitors and residents cannot fail to notice the tall, bright red lilylike flowers that bloom in carpets along the edges of rice paddies, roadsides, and river dikes, and also around temples and cemeteries. These are **spider lilies**, called *higan-bana* in Japanese. The Japanese name means "flowers [*hana* or *bana*] that bloom around the time of the autumn equinox [*higan*]."

A close inspection around the base of these flowers reveals an interesting situation. The flower stalks rise directly out of the ground, with no leaves present. The leaves of this plant will not appear until late autumn. They photosynthesize throughout the winter months, storing up energy in an underground bulb, then wilt the following spring. The energy stored in the bulb is used to produce the tall flower stalks and flamboyant flowers.

The bulb of the spider lily contains alkaloids and other ingredients that cause sickness and vomiting if consumed directly. In the past, a concoction made from the bulb was used to induce vomiting when necessary, and a paste was made that could be applied to sore and tight muscles in the shoulder and back. Furthermore, if the bulb is thoroughly soaked in water for a long time, the alkaloids can be removed, leaving a large quantity of edible starches. In some districts, it is said that the bulbs of the spider lily were always kept in reserve as a last ditch source of food when the rice and other crops failed.

Although swallowtail butterflies can often be observed flitting among the spider lilies, these plants do not produce viable seeds. Once a plant is established, it can spread asexually by extending the underground system of roots and bulbs, but no new plants can be produced from the flowers and seeds. For this reason, all the Japanese *higan-bana* began as cultivated plants and as such are usually found only in and around human habitations.

The spider lily originated in China but is thought to have been brought here more than two thousand years ago, following the same route as wet-paddy rice. Whether these plants were originally imported as medicinal herbs or for their food value is uncertain. Today they are strictly ornamental, with some pink and white varieties also available.

The bright red color of the spider lily is actually a rarity here in Japan. A quick perusal of Japanese field guides shows that, with the exception of the **Japanese camellias**, there are almost no true red flowers native to this country. One possible explanation for this lack involves the different ways in which birds and insects perceive color.

Red is thought to fall outside the color spectrum seen by most insects. Many red flowers are thus pollinated by birds, especially hummingbirds, which can see the red colors. Yet hummingbirds are not found in Japan, and red flowers might therefore have a hard time getting pollinated here. The Japanese camellia gets around this problem by bringing out its big, red blooms in midwinter, when food is scarce and birds such as the white eye and the brown-eared bulbul are happy to feast on pollen.

This theory is nevertheless complicated by the large swallowtail butterflies, which are able to distinguish colors at the red end of the color spectrum. Indeed, these butterflies are frequently seen visiting the red spider lilies.

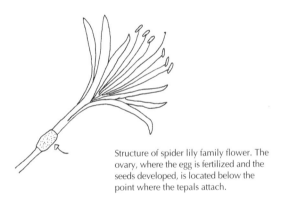

Structure of spider lily family flower. The ovary, where the egg is fertilized and the seeds developed, is located below the point where the tepals attach.

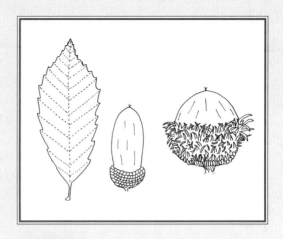

PART
III

NATURE SITES

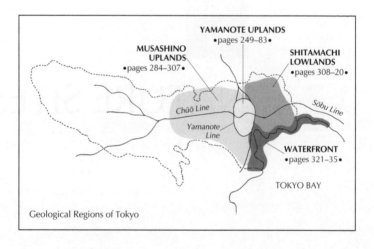

YAMANOTE UPLANDS
•pages 249–83•

MUSASHINO UPLANDS
•pages 284–307•

SHITAMACHI LOWLANDS
•pages 308–20•

Chūō Line

Sōbu Line

Yamanote Line

WATERFRONT
•pages 321–35•

TOKYO BAY

Geological Regions of Tokyo

THE YAMANOTE UPLANDS

As was noted in the introduction, the area of Tokyo called the Yamanote, or "High City," is actually the easternmost extension of the Musashino Uplands. The Yamanote is formed by several long narrow fingerlike sections of high ground that stand about twenty to twenty-five meters above the alluvial plain. The top of the uplands are relatively flat, but the whole system is laced with narrow, branching river valleys, called *yato* (map 1). Unfortunately, most of the rivers that once flowed through the *yato* valleys are now filled in or buried underground, and a walker has great difficulty envisioning the original topography.

For those readers who, like me, never feel quite comfortable without at least a rudimentary feel for the lay of the land, I suggest spending an hour or so riding the JR Yamanote Loop Line, which runs in a rough circular course around the central city area, and the JR Sōbu Line, which cuts right through the center of the loop. A typical place to begin this exploration is at Tokyo Station, taking the Yamanote inner loop counterclockwise from Tokyo toward Ueno and Ikebukuro:

• From Tokyo to Ueno, the tracks are on an elevated platform high above the alluvial plain. From the window, you can look down on the city streets. The loop line crosses the Kanda River just before arriving at Akihabara.

• From Ueno north through Uguisudani, Nippori, Nishi Nippori, and Tabata, the tracks are built right up against the cliffs that form the edge of the uplands, which are visible from the west (left) window. The top of the uplands here is occupied mostly by Ueno Park, Yanaka Cemetery, and associated temples. To the east (right), the land runs perfectly flat out to the Sumida River and beyond.

• After Tabata, the Yamanote tracks make a sharp turn to the west (left), and pass through a manmade cleft cut into the wall of the uplands. Gradually the tracks climb up toward the higher level, but just before Komagome Station the land suddenly drops away again. This is a *yato* valley, through which a river called the Yata once flowed. The river itself no longer exists, but the valley continues well northward, indicating that the Yata River was originally the final downstream stretch of the long Shakujii River.

• After Komagome, the tracks again cut through a narrow finger of the high ground called the Hongō Uplands.

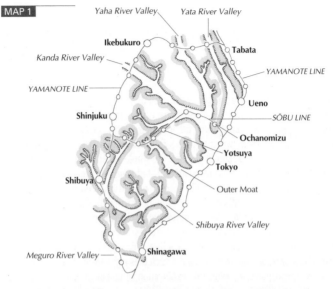

MAP 1

Yaha River Valley   Yata River Valley

Ikebukuro

Tabata

Kanda River Valley

YAMANOTE LINE

YAMANOTE LINE

Ueno

Shinjuku

SŌBU LINE

Ochanomizu

Yotsuya

Tokyo

Shibuya

Outer Moat

Shibuya River Valley

Meguro River Valley   **Shinagawa**

A basic map of the Yamanote terrain, showing the many complicated branches of the narrow *yato* valleys. The valley sides are usually steep except in areas where they have been cut away by bulldozers. Many of the patches of green that can be seen here and there are along the slopes of the valleys. The Sumida River alluvial plain and Tokyo Bay are to the right of the map, and the Musashino Uplands are to the left.

• BETWEEN SUGAMO AND ŌTSUKA STATIONS, another valley opens up. This valley was once cut by the Yaha River. Like the Yata, it too no longer exists. The opposite side of the valley appears just as the train leaves Ōtsuka.

• FROM ŌTSUKA PAST IKEBUKURO AND ON TO MEJIRO the train moves over basically high ground, but there also appears to have once been a very narrow side valley, a tributary of the Kanda River, that reached close to where the tracks now run.

• BETWEEN MEJIRO AND TAKADANOBABA a distinct valley opens up. This rather wide valley has been cut by the Kanda River, and the river itself can be seen running through a concrete channel just before reaching Takadanobaba.

• FROM TAKADANOBABA PAST SHINJUKU, the land is basically high ground though, around Shinjuku Station, development is so intense that one has trouble seeing the topography.

• BETWEEN SHINJUKU AND YOYOGI, the tracks cross a very narrow side valley, probably a small tributary near the headwaters of the Shibuya River.

• JUST BEFORE HARAJUKU, the tracks begin running right along the edge of the Meiji Jingū Shrine grounds. Though mostly high ground, the land is split by a small side valley of the Shibuya River, which once flowed from a pond in the shrine grounds down through what is now the crowded, narrow shopping arcade in Harajuku.

• BETWEEN HARAJUKU AND SHIBUYA, the land suddenly drops off into the main valley of the Shibuya River itself. Today this river begins as a tiny channel on the south side of Shibuya Station, then flows over a winding course to empty into Tokyo Bay. Originally, however, the Shibuya had several highly branched tributaries that reached up, not only into the Meiji Jingū Shrine, but also to the Shinjuku Gyoen Gardens as well as the Aoyama Cemetery.

• JUST BEFORE REACHING EBISU, the tracks encounter another section of high ground, then climb through a steep-sided cleft up to Meguro Station. The National Science Museum's Institute for Nature Study is located just a five-minute walk east from this station.

• RIGHT AFTER MEGURO, the land again drops steeply, this time into the valley of the Meguro River.

• BETWEEN GOTANDA AND ŌSAKI STATIONS the tracks cross the Meguro River, which flows here from right to left.

• ON THE APPROACH TO SHINAGAWA, the tracks appear to cut through the very tip of an upland locally known as Gotenyama.

• FROM SHINAGAWA ALL THE WAY BACK TO TOKYO, the tracks are again running on an elevated trestle over the lowlands. The original Tokyo Bay coastline was along the south side of the tracks between Shinagawa and Shinbashi. Continue on past Tokyo to Akihabara, then change trains to the JR Sōbu Line bound for Yotsuya and Shinjuku. At this point, you are still on the alluvial plain.

• BETWEEN AKIHABARA AND OCHANOMIZU high ground can be seen on both sides of the track. This high ground is part of the Hongō Uplands. The Outer Moat of the Imperial Palace (see maps 2, 3, and 7) appears on the north (right) side. The moat here does not follow a natural valley. Instead, it is actually a great ditch cut right through the tip of the high ground in the mid-seventeenth century.

• BETWEEN OCHANOMIZU AND SUIDŌBASHI, the land falls away again as the tracks enter the lowermost stretch of the Kanda River Valley, with the moat still on the right side.

• BETWEEN IIDABASHI AND YOTSUYA, the edge of the high ground can be seen on the left. Sotobori Park runs right along the tracks at the top of this slope.

• AFTER YOTSUYA, the tracks enter a short tunnel, which cuts though a swatch of high ground to emerge over a narrow valley just before reaching Shinanomachi. This valley is part of the watershed that once formed the south western part of the outer moat. (See Hie Shrine entry and map 4.)

• BETWEEN SHINANOMACHI AND SENDAGAYA, another narrow patch of high ground separates this valley from the next. The narrow valley that can be seen around SENDAGAYA is the uppermost stretch of the Shibuya River and leads into the ponds of the Shinjuku Gyoen Gardens.

This little adventure ends at Shinjuku Station. A rough approximation of the topography described here is shown on map 1. The positions of the valleys were reconstructed, with great difficulty, from years of field research and study of topographic and historical maps. The major valleys are all in the right place, but the smaller side valleys are more difficult to situate accurately. Just keep in mind that Tokyo's famous *saka* (sometimes *zaka*), or slopes, usually occur along the edge of the *yato* valleys. Most slopes are thus steep but short, rising twenty or twenty-five meters in a few-minutes' walk and leaving out-of-shape strollers short of breath. Many of the city's remaining patches of greenery, including parks, gardens, and temple and shrine grounds, are found on the edge of the high ground or along the slopes of the valley sides, areas which have been a little more difficult to develop intensively.

Once you have familiarized yourself with the basic topography, there are plenty of spots in the Yamanote to explore. Some of these, like Kitanomaru Park, the East Gardens, and the various shrines and temples, can be enjoyed on a lunch-hour break, while others, like Meiji Jingū Shrine and Ueno Park, require a few solid hours to fully appreciate. First-time visitors and beginning naturalists might want to start off with the moat walk, whereas horticulture and flower enthusiasts should check out the various gardens. Serious botanists and naturalists will definitely benefit from detailed study at the Koishikawa Botanical Gardens and the Institute for Nature Study.

The following entries introduce a few of my favorite Yamanote spots. There are numerous other places not listed here, including shrines, temples, and smaller parks and gardens, where nature abounds. Once you get started, you are sure to discover favorite spots of your own.

INNER PALACE MOATS (皇居内濠 ✳ Kōkyo Uchibori)

SEE MAPS 2 AND 3

For nearly three hundred years, from 1603 to 1867, Tokyo was called Edo and served as the military and administrative capital of the Tokugawa shoguns that ruled Japan during this period. The grounds of the current Imperial Palace were originally the site of Edo Castle, the shogun's residence and stronghold. The castle grounds now constitute an immense block of greenery right smack in the center of the city. The surrounding moats, built to protect the somewhat paranoid shoguns, provide a vital habitat for many species of wintering waterfowl. The moat water may look dirty but actually harbors a large number of minnows and other small fish that provide prey for cormorants, terns, grebes, and egrets. Shoveler ducks feast on the abundant algae and plankton that float in the water.

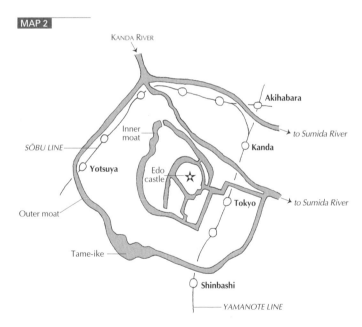

MAP 2

The original position of the Edo Castle moats, about the time of their completion in the mid-seventeenth century. The overall structure is more like a clockwise spiral than a set of concentric rings. Modern-day train lines are overlayed for orientation.

Edo Castle was built near the edge of the high ground overlooking the mouth of the Sumida River and the northern reaches of Tokyo Bay. The castle grounds were surrounded by a series of moats that, at first glance, appeared to be arranged in two concentric rings but actually formed a clockwise spiral, sort of like the unfolding coils of a nautilus shell. The approximate position of the moats at their completion in the mid-seventeenth century is shown in map 2.

The innermost coil of moats originally surrounded the main and west castle donjons and are now completely contained within the palace grounds. The next coil, now called the Uchibori, or Inner Moat, surrounded the north donjon and several smaller donjons as well as areas given over to various administrative buildings.

The Hibiya Moat and other moats that still remain along the edge of the Marunouchi and Ōtemachi business districts formed the southeastern section of

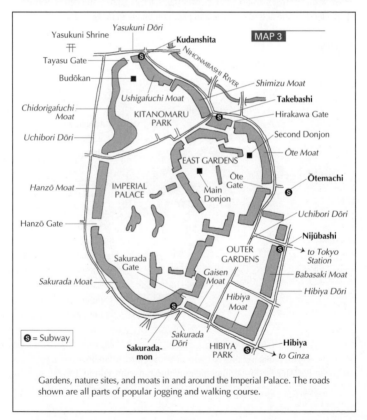

Gardens, nature sites, and moats in and around the Imperial Palace. The roads shown are all parts of popular jogging and walking course.

this inner coil (see map 3). These moats were dug out of the alluvial plain and are thus shallow-sided and perfectly rectangular. The western moats (Sakurada, Hanzō and Chidorigafuchi) utilized a natural *yato* valley that still runs along the edge of the high ground upon which the castle was built. These moats curve to follow the natural contours and have much higher sides. The northeastern side of the spiral, occupied by the Ushigafuchi and Shimizu moats, follows the natural contours between the high ground and the lowlands near the mouth of the Kanda River.

Today, the sidewalks along the inner moats form one of the few stretches in central Tokyo where one can walk or run for a substantial distance without being constantly held up by traffic lights. As a result, they are immensely popular with joggers and fitness walkers. Flower and birding enthusiasts are easily identified by their more leisurely pace.

The Hibiya Moat, just across the street from Hibiya Park and a few-minutes' walk from the busy Ginza shopping district, is a natural spot to start exploring the inner moats. At this point, you are still on the alluvial plain, so the sides of the moats are not very high. Weeping willow trees are planted all along the water side of the sidewalk, with tulip trees on the street side. On the other side of the moat is a dense grove of chinkapins. Huge carp—and in the winter, tufted ducks—often gather at the corner of the moat waiting for handouts from tourists.

As you walk north along the sidewalk, beautiful stone work can be seen on the opposite side of the moat. The moat stones were cut from cliffs along the coast of the Izu Peninsula. They were loaded in boats and brought to Edo. After unloading at quays along the river and canals, the huge stones were then dragged to the castle walls. Stories abound of heavily laden vessels traveling from Izu to Edo being sunk by typhoons!

The outer Sakurada Gate separates the Gaisen and Sakurada moats. All the entrances to Edo Castle were protected by huge gates like this, called *mon* in Japanese. After crossing the bridge, attackers had to break through the first door, then make a ninety-degree right turn and pass through a second door.

As you leave the gate and continue along the course, the Diet Building can be seen straight ahead. Just across the wide street that borders the moat (Uchibori Dōri) is Sakurada Dōri, with its rows of big Japanese horse chestnuts.

The high, steep sides of the Sakurada Moat are covered with grass and pine trees. Rapeseed blossoms color the slopes yellow in April. Spider lilies then color them red in September. Look for little terns fishing in summer, and mute swans, little grebes, and spot-billed ducks throughout the year.

Chidorigafuchi Park begins right after the Hanzō Gate, which leads directly into the Imperial Palace and is not open to the public. Originally, this was the gate where the Kōshū Kaidō—a long highway that ran from Edo to through Kōfu in Yamanashi Prefecture to Shimo Suwa in Nagano Prefecture—entered Edo Castle.

The area on the other side of the moat, where the emperor now resides, is a solid block of green called the Fukiage Forest. This forest is a legacy of the Emperor Shōwa (formerly known as Emperor Hirohito), a trained biologist and ardent nature lover. Concerned with loss of forest acreage on the Musashino Uplands, the emperor had this forest planted as a reserve for local plants and animals. Although off-limits to the public, the Fukiage Forest, along with the well-preserved Akasaka Goyōchi (the Crown Prince's Palace Grounds) are the central city's most vital wildlife habitats. Rare and endangered goshawks are seen in the Fukiage Forest all year round and are probably nesting there.

From the Hanzō Gate all the way to the Yasukuni Shrine runs Chidorigafuchi Park, one of the city's most popular spots for flower-viewing parties (*hana-mi*). The beautiful *somei yoshino* cherries are in full bloom in late March and early April. At that time, all the spots under the cherry tress are filled with celebrating Tokyoites. In August, *abura-zemi* cicadas provide a free open-air concert and, in winter, large rafts of widgeons and shovelers bob on the water. Rowboats are available along the Chidorigafuchi Moat. Yasukuni Shrine, just off the moat, is surrounded by some immense ginkgos and chinkapins.

At the foot of the bridge leading to the Tayasu Gate stands a huge tower of stone and wood. This is a great lantern that was built in 1871. The structure was originally a devotive lantern dedicated to Yasukuni Shrine, but it was so high and bright that it also served as a lighthouse. At that time, Kudan Slope was higher and steeper than today, and the light of this lantern could be seen not only by ships coming into Tokyo Port, but as far away as the Bōsō coast in Chiba Prefecture. After the Great Kantō Earthquake of 1923, the top of Kudan Slope was bulldozed into the Ichigaya Valley.

Access: The centrally located Inner Moat can be accessed from any number of stations, including Kudanshita and Takebashi on the Tōzai Line. For details refer to the map.

KITANOMARU PARK　(北の丸公園 ✳ Kitanomaru Kōen)

SEE MAP 3

The Tayasu Gate, between the Chidorigafuchi and Ushigafuchi moats, leads into Kitanomaru Park, a veritable paradise for tree lovers. Plantings include most of the Tokyo area's broadleaved evergreens as well as a host of local deciduous trees. Many of the colorful berry trees described in the Edge of the Forest section can be enjoyed here as well, along with the various birds attracted to them. The western edge of the park, along the Chidorigafuchi Moat, is the wildest and most serene. This park was originally the site of the castle's north donjon (*Kitanomaru*) and contains the Nippon Budōkan, the National Archives, Science Museum, and Tokyo National Museum of Modern Art.

Access: Take the Tōzai Line to Kudanshita Station, exit 2, which brings you right to the Tayasu Gate.

THE EAST GARDENS (東御苑 ✳ Higashi Gyoen)

SEE MAP 3

The East Gardens originally housed the main castle donjon. Today, they feature collections of trees from around the nation and a traditional Japanese water garden planted with azaleas, hydrangeas, and irises. For Tokyo naturalists, the real gem here is the Shōwa Forest (Shōwa no Mori), a block of typical Musashino Upland deciduous woodland planted by the Emperor Shōwa. Here are oaks, hornbeams, and most of the other native deciduous trees as well as forest wildflowers such as the light pink Japanese bellflowers (*hotaru-bukuro*) that bloom in early summer. The Shōwa Forest is located near the Hirakawa Gate, just east of the water garden.

The East Gardens are built right into the edge of the uplands, with the water garden and Shōwa Forest on the plain, and short but steep slopes, Shiomi-zaka (Seaview Slope) and Bairin-zaka (Plum Grove Slope), leading up to the top of the rise, upon which the main donjon stood. English maps and pamphlets are on sale at refreshment stalls.

Access: The closest subway access is Takebashi Station (exit 12) on the Tōzai Line.
  ❖ Kōkyo Gaien, Chiyoda-ku, Tokyo 東京都千代田区皇居外苑

THE OUTER GARDENS (皇居外苑 ✳ Kōkyo Gaien)

SEE MAP 3

The numerous moats along the eastern edge of the palace grounds are good spots for viewing typical waterfowl, and the sidewalks are lined with weeping willows, camphor trees, and ginkgos. The Outer Gardens, located alongside Uchibori Dōri and the Hibiya and Babasaki moats, are planted with almost two thousand black pines. There are also some fine zelkova specimens and extensive grassy areas that are sure to harbor some dusky thrush in winter. This whole area was originally part of an inlet of Tokyo Bay but was filled in the early seventeenth century.

ACCESS: Take either the Toei Mita Line to Hibiya Station, or the Chiyoda Line to Nijūbashi-mae Station (exit 2).

❖ Kōkyo Gaien, Chiyoda-ku, Tokyo 東京都千代田区皇居外苑

HIE SHRINE (日枝神社 ✳ Hie Jinja)

SEE MAP 4

The Outer Moat, or Sotobori, formed the first defensive line of Edo Castle, with the area in between this and the Inner Moat occupied by the shogun's staunchest allies. The bridges crossing the moat were all equipped with manned checkpoints, called *mitsuke*, thus ensuring that the flow of people and goods in and out could be tightly controlled.

The southeastern section utilized a natural valley that led from the Shinbashi area up as far as Yotusya. This valley was wide in the central part, but broken into a maze of narrow branches futher upstream. Unfortunately, very little of this section of the moat remains today. Sotobori Dōri avenue, from Shinbashi Station to Akasaka-mitsuke, closely follows the original course. The wide part of the valley was once covered by a marsh and holding pond, called a *tame-ike*. This place name is still used today to designate the area around the intersection of Sotobori Dōri and Roppongi Dōri.

Hie Shrine occupies the tip of high ground that once overlooked this section of the Outer Moat. Actually, the shrine was originally located closer to Edo Castle but was moved to its present location in 1659. As is often the case in Tokyo, the heavily forested shrine grounds form a welcome relief from summer heat, and during the coldest months the abundant broadleaved evergreen trees add a splash of warmth and color to the gray winter landscape. The steep stairs leading up from Sotobori Dōri pass through a tunnel of vermillion Shinto shrine gates (*torii*). The slope here is especially rich in understory trees and shrubs.

Tōtenkō, traditional domesticated fowl from the mountains of northwestern Shikoku, roam the inner shrine grounds. These fowl have been bred for their long crow, which lasts up to twenty-five seconds. A second breed of traditional fowl are kept in cages behind the shrine office. One side of the inner plaza is covered with a fine grove of *mōsōchiku* bamboo.

ACCESS: Take the Nanboku Line to Tameike Sannō Station (exit 5).

❖ 2–10–5 Nagatachō, Chiyoda-ku, Tokyo 東京都千代田区永田町2–10–5

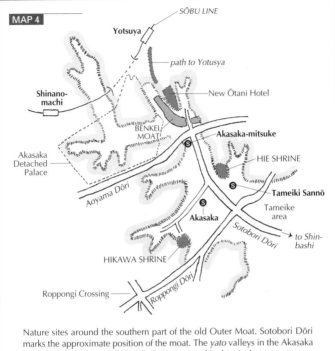

MAP 4

SŌBU LINE

Yotsuya

path to Yotusya

Shinano-machi

New Ōtani Hotel

BENKEI MOAT

Akasaka-mitsuke

Akasaka
Detached
Palace

Aoyama Dōri

HIE SHRINE

Tameiki Sannō

Tameike
area

Akasaka

Sotobori Dōri

to Shin-bashi

HIKAWA SHRINE

Roppongi Crossing

Roppongi Dōri

Nature sites around the southern part of the old Outer Moat. Sotobori Dōri marks the approximate position of the moat. The *yato* valleys in the Akasaka Detached Palace Grounds are the best preserved in the city but are not open to the public.

HIKAWA SHRINE (氷川神社 ✳ Hikawa Jinja)

SEE MAP 4

Hikawa Shrine is located on the opposite side of the moat valley. The site contains a solid block of old trees. Big camphors and chinkapins are planted on the level ground near the top along with an immense ginkgo that is thought to be more than four hundred years old. A fine *aka-gashi* evergreen oak stands just to the right at the top of the main set of stairs.

Access: Take the Chiyoda Line to Akasaka Station (exit 6).
    ❖ 6–10–12 Akasaka, Minato-ku, Tokyo 東京都港区赤坂6–10–12

BENKEI MOAT (弁慶濠 ✳ Benkeibori)

SEE MAP 4

The Benkeibori is the only part of the southwestern section of the Outer Moat remaining today. It starts at Akasaka-mitsuke and curves along between the New Ōtani Hotel and the Akasaka Detached Palace Grounds, which contains the residences of the Imperial princes and their families. Although off-limits to the public, this Imperial residence is preserved in a very natural state.

The sides of the Benkei Moat are densely forested, with some *somei yoshino* cherries and many huge specimens of camphor tree. A short but pleasant (and little-known) walking path runs along the bottom of the Benkei Moat wall, along the water's edge on the New Ōtani Hotel side. The path starts near the entrance to the New Ōtani Hotel, then descends a set of steep steps down to the water's edge. Huge tree branches hang over the path and moat, providing desperately needed shade in summer. The path emerges near the Benkei Bridge, where rowboats can be rented. On top of the rise is the garden of the hotel itself, a beautifully designed and meticulously maintained traditional Japanese garden with varied terrain and abundant water features, including a pond, stream, and small waterfall. From the northern terminus of the Benkei Moat, a path leads along the heavily forested dike to Yotsuya Station, with the campus of Sophia University on one side and athletic grounds on the other. This path allows a walker to connect with Sotobori Park, the next destination.

ACCESS: For the east end of the moat (Benkei-bashi Bridge), use Akasaka-mitsuke Station (exit 9) on Ginza or Marunouchi lines, or Nagatachō Station (exit 9) on the Hanzōmon Line. For the Sophia University, use Yotsuya Station on JR Sōbu Line or Marunouchi Line.

❖ Kioi-chō, Chiyoda-ku, Tokyo 東京都千代田区紀尾井町

SOTOBORI PARK (外濠公園 ✳ Sotobori Kōen)

SEE MAP 5

The outer moat originally consisted of valleys belonging to separate watersheds. The Benkei Moat was the final section of the river valley that came up from Shinbashi. From Yotsuya eastward, the moat utilized a narrow side valley in the Kanda River system. These two valleys were connected by a manmade trench.

The top of the dike along the southern (inner) edge of the Kanda tributary section of the moat, all the way from Yotsuya to Iidabashi, has been set aside as a public park. Strollers here enjoy venerable old *somei yoshino* cherries and fine groves of black pines, mixed with typical street trees such as ginkgo, platanus, and Tang maples. Remains of old stonework from the *mitsuke* guardhouses can be seen near the bridges at Yotsuya, Ichigaya, and Iidabashi.

The park ends at Iidabashi Station, but anyone interested in history and topography will enjoy a short walk east to Ochanomizu Station. The Kanda River joins the Outer Moat just after Iidabashi Station. A little to the east, it splits into two branches. One branch continues flowing east past Suidōbashi Station and on to Ochanomizu to eventually empty into the Sumida River, near Ryōgoku Bridge, while the other branch, called the Nihonbashi River, flows south, then turns east to join the Sumida near Eitai Bridge.

This southern branch of the Kanda River is actually closer to the original river course. The eastern branch, which forms the last section of the Outer Moat, is a manmade cleft dug in the mid-seventeenth century by the shogun's engineers. To start with, the shogun excavated a deep, wide ditch, cutting right through the southern tip of the Hongō Uplands. Once this ditch was completed, the waters of the Kanda were diverted eastward.

The river diversion was an engineering marvel for its day and was a vital project in the overall design of central Edo. Not only did the project complete the Outer Moat but, by diverting most of the Kanda River's water eastward and away from the central part of the city, it helped prevent floods and allowed the land between the castle and the Sumida River to be filled in and laced with a network of canals and wharfs that were used to transport goods and materials right where the shogun needed them. In addition, the sand from the excavation work was used to fill in some of the salt marshes around the mouth of the Sumida, creating the areas now known as Marunouchi and Ginza (see the chapter on Shitamachi).

Today, Ochanomizu Station sits right in the middle of the shogun's great ditch, with high ground on both sides of the station. To the north of the station is the bulk of the Hongō Uplands, dominated by Tokyo University. To the south is the small remaining part of the severed tip. Meidai Dōri starts at the west side of the station and runs down past Meiji University to Yasukuni Dōri, descending the steep slope at the very edge of the uplands.

ACCESS: Sotobori Park can be reached via Iidabashi, Ichigaya, or Yotsuya station on the JR Sōbu Line. Various subways also let out at these stations.

❖ Yotsuya, Shinjuku-ku, Tokyo 東京都新宿区四谷

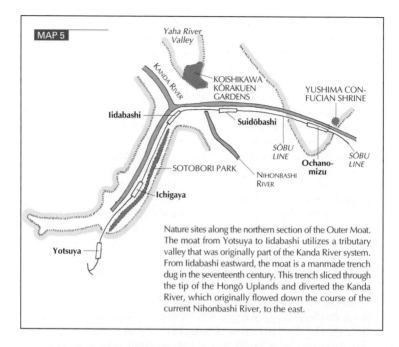

Nature sites along the northern section of the Outer Moat. The moat from Yotsuya to Iidabashi utilizes a tributary valley that was originally part of the Kanda River system. From Iidabashi eastward, the moat is a manmade trench dug in the seventeenth century. This trench sliced through the tip of the Hongō Uplands and diverted the Kanda River, which originally flowed down the course of the current Nihonbashi River, to the east.

KOISHIKAWA KŌRAKUEN GARDENS

(小石川後楽園 ✳ Koishikawa Kōrakuen)

SEE MAPS 5, 6, AND 7

The Koishikawa Kōrakuen Gardens were originally built in 1629 as the Edo mansion, or *daimyō yashiki*, of the Mito clan. The Mito were closely related to the ruling Tokugawa shogunate family and among their staunchest allies. The mansion guarded the approach to Edo Castle from the north and was also strategically placed to protect the Kanda Aqueduct, a vital source of water for the castle and city. After 1867, the area was used as an arsenal. In 1952, it was designated as a public park and national historical site.

The gardens are typical of the *kaiyū-shiki* style favored by the old samurai class. Some writers have characterized these traditional strolling gardens as the world's first theme parks. Landscapes are designed to re-create famous scenic places in Japan and China. As visitors stroll slowly around the prescribed course, they enjoy views suggestive of these famous scenery spots. At the Koishikawa Kōrakuen, for example, strollers can imagine coastal rocks along the Bōsō Peninsula, rushing streams and waterfalls in the mountains surrounding Kyoto, and even the banks of famous lakes in China.

The gardens almost magically manage to pack an amazing amount of nature and scenery into a limited area. You could walk around the perimeter in ten or fifteen minutes, but a thorough exploration of all the winding, twisting paths inside can easily take an hour or two. The paths continuously circle and double back, creating the illusion of a long stroll through constantly changing landscapes.

Flowering plants start with plums in February, then move on to cherries in late March. An immense weeping cherry, thought to be more than a hundred years old, dominates the central plaza just inside the main gate. The long, downswept branches covered with pink blossoms are especially beautiful when viewed from across the small pond. Facilities also include a lotus pond, wisteria trellis, azalea bushes, and iris garden. A unique feature is a small rice paddy, planted and harvested by local elementary school children. In midsummer these gardens are prized as a refuge from the stunning heat and humidity of summer in the city and, in autumn, for the beautiful colors of their abundant maples.

Access: Located just north of the Outer Moat, between Iidabashi and Suidōbashi stations on the JR Sōbu Line. A seven-minute walk from Iidabashi Station, south exit (*minami-guchi*). Open every day from 9:00 to 16:30. Admission is ¥300. Children of elementary-school age or younger are free. ☎ (03) 3811–3015 (in Japanese).

❖ 1 Kōraku, Bunkyō-ku, Tokyo 東京都文京区後楽1丁目

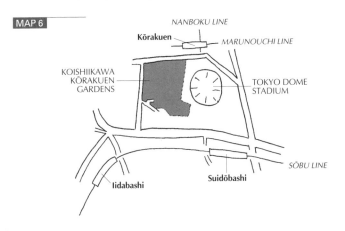

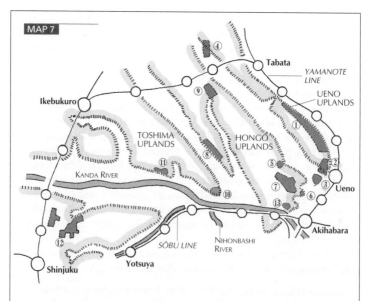

MAP 7

Tabata

YAMANOTE LINE

UENO UPLANDS

Ikebukuro

TOSHIMA UPLANDS

HONGŌ UPLANDS

KANDA RIVER

Ueno

Akihabara

NIHONBASHI RIVER

SŌBU LINE

Yotsuya

Shinjuku

Nature sites along the "fingers" of the high ground north of the Kanda River. From east (right) to west, the fingers are the Ueno Uplands, the Hongō Uplands, and the Toshima Uplands. The *yato* valleys separating the fingers are the Yata River, the Yaha River, and the Kanda River. The numbered sites are:

1 Yanaka Cemetery
2 Ueno Park
3 Shinobazu Pond
4 Kyū-Furukawa Gardens
5 Nezu Shrine
6 Yushima Tenjin Shrine
7 Tokyo University

8 Koishikawa Botanical Gardens
9 Rikugi-en Gardens
10 Koishikawa Kōrakuen Gardens
11 Edogawa Park
12 Toyama Park
13 Yushima Confucian Shrine

YUSHIMA CONFUCIAN SHRINE (湯島聖堂 ✳ Yushima Seidō)

SEE MAPS 5 AND 7

Located on the Hongō Rise just north of Ochanimizu Station, this temple devoted to Confucius is heavily wooded, with some fine chinkapins and other broadleaved evergreens. There is also a row of *ao-giri* in the rear. A venerable specimen of the Chinese pistachio tree (*kaino-ki*) stands just before the statue of Confucius.

A tree of this species was planted on the grave of Confucius in China, and the Chinese pistachio tree is thus considered sacred to Confucian devotees.

Access: Take the Hijiribashi exit at Ochanomizu Station on the JR Sōbu or JR Chūō line.

❖ 1 Yushima, Bunkyō-ku, Tokyo 東京都文京区湯島１丁目

YANAKA CEMETERY (谷中霊園 ✳ Yanaka Reien)

SEE MAPS 7 AND 8

North of the Sōbu Line, the Yamanote Uplands are cut by the river valleys into narrow strips, appearing almost like a hand with ghostly fingers extending down from the edge of the Musashino. Unfortunately, with the exception of the Kanda, none of the interspersing rivers exist anymore. One has to look carefully to understand the pattern of valleys and narrow strips of high ground.

Starting from the east, the first and narrowest finger of high ground (Ueno Uplands) is found between the valley of the Yata River and the Sumida River plain. This finger runs all the way north to Higashi Jūjō Station (off the map). Originally, when the Shakujii was flowing through the bed of the Yata, this was a long, incredibly thin peninsula but now it is cut off from the rest of the upland by the redirected course of the Shakujii.

A sizable portion of this finger is taken up by Yanaka Cemetery which, to my friends' surprise, I often recommend as an ideal spot for enjoying wildflowers. The key to a rich wildflower fauna in urban areas is just the right amount of weed control. If the grounds are fastidiously weeded or sprayed with herbicide, only the ornamental plants will survive. On the other hand, if the grounds are completely abandoned, tall weeds such as evening primroses, fleabanes, and goldenrods will crowd out everything else.

Yanaka Cemetery is simply too expansive to be completely weeded, but a minimum of groundwork keeps the tall invaders under control. In addition, the cemetery is heavily planted in both deciduous and evergreen trees and is shut off from the busy, main thoroughfares by steep slopes on one side and quiet residential neighborhoods on the other. The result is an excellent wildflower habitat.

One indication of the cemetery's richness is the dandelions. Ecologists often use dandelions as rough indicators of how healthy a habitat is. Relatively undisturbed areas, with clean air, water, and soil, will support the native species, while habitats that are polluted or frequently disturbed will harbor only the common European dandelion. Among the Yanaka tombstones, one finds two of Japan's native species, the Kantō dandelion and the white-flowered dandelion.

Avoid loud and boisterous behavior, and carry back your own litter, including cans and cigarette butts. Also confine your botanizing to the paths that wander among the gravesites. Do not trespass on any of the sites themselves. A map is available at the Administrative Office, but the cemetery is so laced with narrow paths that visitors inevitably become temporarily lost!

ACCESS: Yanaka Cemetery can be reached easily from the north exit (*kita-guchi*) of JR Nippori Station, on the Yamanote and Keihin Tōhoku Lines. The private Keisei railway also stops here. The cemetery managers welcome visitors but ask that all respect the gravesites and conserve the habitat.

❖ 7–5–24 Yanaka, Taitō-ku, Tokyo 東京都台東区谷中7–5–24

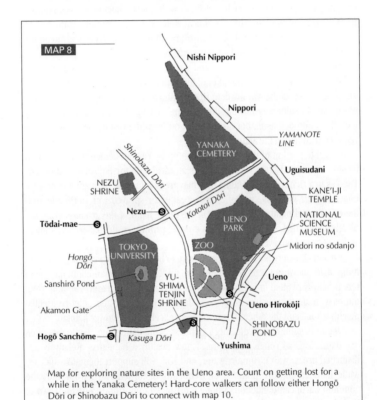

Map for exploring nature sites in the Ueno area. Count on getting lost for a while in the Yanaka Cemetery! Hard-core walkers can follow either Hongō Dōri or Shinobazu Dōri to connect with map 10.

UENO PARK (上野公園 ✳ Ueno Kōen)

SEE MAPS 7 AND 8

Ueno Park sits on the very tip of the narrow finger of high ground, an area often called the Ueno-dai, known also as the Ueno Uplands (or the Ueno Rise) in English. In 1868, when the shogun's government was in the final stages of collapse, the last supporters of the old regime gathered their forces on Ueno Rise. A fierce battle took place, lasting all day and producing hundreds of casualties, before the high ground was finally breached and the last holdouts subdued.

The Ueno Rise used to offer a commanding view of the Sumida Delta area which, during the Edo period, was the heart of the Shitamachi, or "Low City," and where most of the commoners lived. In fact, this strategic location has made Ueno an attractive spot for thousands of years. A prehistoric village existed here during the Jōmon period, when the delta area was still part of a shallow sea. The inhabitants of this village left behind artifacts and mounds of discarded shells.

The Tokugawa clan immediately recognized the strategic importance of the Ueno Rise. In 1624, in keeping with the city's carefully laid out geomancy, the Kan'ei-ji temple was constructed and charged with guarding the northeastern gate from bad luck and evil spirits. Several of the later shoguns were buried here.

The slope leading up from Shinobazu Pond supports a dense forest of native broadleaved evergreen trees, including chinkapins, evergreen oaks, camellias, and aucubas as well as some large *tabu-no-ki* laurels. These laurels are primarily coastal trees and are thought to be remnants of former times when Tokyo Bay extended further inland than today.

On top of the rise are various types of cherry trees. Legend holds that the Buddhist monk who founded Kan'ei-ji temple was a great lover of cherries and that he brought trees from his native Wakayama Prefecture to be planted around the temple. Today, Ueno is considered a must-visit for cherry enthusiasts. The popular *somei yoshino* varieties won't show until the end of March, but early-flowering varieties begin blooming from late January.

Another Ueno specialty is winter peonies, grown in a garden attached to Tōshōgū Shrine. Peonies usually bloom in April, but horticulturists have developed methods that trick the flowers into blooming much earlier. Blossom colors are delicate hues of white, pink, and yellow, and each plant is protected from the cold by its own little shed made of rice straw.

During the first years of the new Meiji government, there were several plans to fill in Shinobazu Pond and cut down the trees on nearby Ueno Rise to use in building materials. Fortunately, these ideas were never realized, and the whole area was designated as a public park. Today, Ueno remains one of the most popular recreational areas for Tokyo residents.

Access: A first-time visitor to Ueno Park should stop in at the botanical study room (*Midori no sōdanjo*), located just across from the Park Entrance (Kōen-guchi) of JR Ueno Station. The friendly and helpful staff will direct you to blooming trees and other items of interest to nature enthusiasts. Take the JR Yamanote or Keihin Tōhoku Line to Ueno Station.

❖ Ueno Kōen, Taitō-ku, Tokyo 東京都台東区上野公園

NATIONAL SCIENCE MUSEUM
(国立科学博物館 ＊ Kokuritsu Kagaku-hakubutsukan)

SEE MAP 8

This museum of natural history is Japan's most prestigious and contains all the exhibits and facilities expected of a first-rate urban museum. Exhibit halls cover evolution and fossils, ecology, conservation, and adaptation to environment. Several halls are devoted to the flora and fauna of Japan, and two new halls feature dinosaurs and ocean wildlife.

The Discovery Room concentrates on nature in the Tokyo-area countryside. The room is packed with hands-on interactive exhibits covering local trees, insects, birds, and mammals. Volunteer staff are on hand to help out, and a unique service allows visitors to make their own sealed plastic herbariums using pressed specimens of leaves and flowers.

Access: Follow the directions for Ueno Park. ☎ (03) 3822–0111 (weekdays), ☎ (03) 3822–0114 (weekends and holidays). Open 9:00 to 16:30, closed Mondays. Entrance fee is ¥420 for adults, ¥70 for students.

❖ 7–20 Ueno Kōen, Taitō-ku, Tokyo 東京都台東区上野公園7–20

UENO ZOO (上野動物園 ✳ Ueno Dōbutsuen)

SEE MAPS 7 AND 8

This urban zoo has tigers, elephants, gorillas, hippopotami, and all the other usual children's favorites. The giant pandas are always a popular attraction. In addition, a section devoted to Japanese birds will help out visiting birdwatchers. The new Vivarium has an excellent collection of reptiles and amphibians, including estuarine crocodiles from northern Australia, which are the world's largest reptiles, and Japanese giant salamanders, the world's largest amphibians.

ACCESS: Follow the directions for Ueno Park. ☎ (03) 3828–5171. Open 9:30 to 16:30, closed Mondays. Entrance fees are ¥600 for adults and high school student, and ¥200 for junior high school students. Children of elementary school age or younger are free.

❖ 9–83 Ueno Kōen, Taitō-ku, Tokyo 東京都台東区上野公園9–83

SHINOBAZU POND (不忍池 ✳ Shinobazu-no-ike)

SEE MAPS 7 AND 8

Shinobazu Pond is a shallow body of water located at the spot where the Yata River used to flow out onto the alluvial plain, and is probably a remnant of the extensive salt marshes that once covered the Sumida River Delta. As the city of Edo expanded, the pond grew in importance as a recreation area, and by the mid-nineteenth century was one of the city's most famous landmarks.

The current pond is divided into three sections. The northern section is within Ueno Zoo and is home to a small colony of cormorants, while the western section is given over to rowboats and paddleboats and is thus kept free of vegetation. Naturalists spend most of their time watching birds on the large southern section, which is filled almost bank to bank with lotus plants and has a clump of reeds near the northern edge. These plants provide superb feeding and nesting habitat for a wide range of waterfowl.

In winter, Shinobazu Pond is packed with ducks that are fed by tourists and locals alike. While there is little enjoyment in watching birds massed up for free handouts, this is a great chance to see the different duck species up close. The same winter handouts attract large flocks of black-headed gulls, which can be viewed from morning through early afternoon. Night herons arrive in late afternoon. Although these birds are strict carnivores, they have learned to snap up minnows and other small fish that are attracted to the free bread.

In summer, the immense expanse of lotus leaves completely covers the pond. Spot-billed ducks, little grebes, coots, and gallinules nest among the reeds and lotus leaves. Huge *ao-daishō* rat snakes occasionally swim by, looking for a chance to raid the birds' nests for eggs or chicks.

By autumn, the lotus flowers have wilted, and their floating seed cups start drifting along the pond edges. These cups are composed of numerous compartments, each holding a seed. The Japanese name for lotus, *hasu*, is thought to be derived from *hachi-no-su* (literally, "bee hive"), referring to the appearance of these seed cups.

Access: Take the Shinobazu or Chūō exit at Ueno Station on the JR Ueno Line, or exit Ueno Hirokōji Station on the Ginza Line.

NEZU SHRINE (根津神社 ✳ Nezu Jinja)

See maps 7 and 8

The next finger of high ground, rising on the opposite side of the Yata Valley is called the Hongō-dai, or Hongō Uplands (sometimes translated into English as the Hongō Rise). This finger is much wider than the Ueno Uplands, and is bounded on the west by the valley of the Yaha River.

Nezu Shrine is located on the opposite side of the Yata Valley from Ueno Park. Built right into the eastern edge of the Hongō slope, the grounds are attractive at any time of year for their rich tree fauna and the shrine itself, but really come into their own in late April, when the entire slope is covered with pink, red, purple, and white azaleas.

Access: Nezu Shrine can be reached by taking the Chiyoda Line to Nezu Station (exit 1).
  ❖ 1–28–9 Nezu, Bunkyō-ku, Tokyo 東京都文京区根津1–28–9

YUSHIMA TENJIN SHRINE (湯島天神 ✳ Yushima Tenjin)

See maps 7 and 8

If Nezu is the city's premier destination for azaleas, then Yushima Tenjin Shrine, also along the eastern slope of the Hongō Uplands, is the choice of plum blossom fans. The plum blossom festival is held annually, usually in late February. The shrine is also popular among students studying for entrance exams.

ACCESS: The shrine is a two-minute walk from Yushima Station (exit 3) on the Chiyoda Line or a five-minute walk from Ueno Hirokōji Station (exit 3) on the Ginza Line.

❖ 3–30–1 Yushima, Bunkyō-ku, Tokyo 東京都文京区湯島3–30–1

TOKYO UNIVERSITY (東京大学 ✳ Tōkyō Daigaku)

SEE MAPS 7 AND 8

The sprawling campus of Tokyo University dominates the central section of the Hongō Rise. From the local topography, it appears that one or perhaps two small, very narrow side valleys once cut into the campus. Today, however, these are difficult to trace. The entire campus, which is open to the public, is heavily wooded with typical park and street trees and abundant native broadleaved evergreens. Right smack in the center of the campus is a rare gem, Sanshirō Pond, surrounded by an excellent sloping forest of native cherries, oaks, dogwoods, and elms. In early December, visitors flock to the Akamon gate to view the line of spectacular ginkgo trees.

ACCESS: Take the Marunouchi Line to Hongō Sanchōme Station (exit 2) or the Nanboku Line to Tōdai-mae Station (exit 1).

❖ 7 Hongō, Bunkyō-ku, Tokyo 東京都文京区本郷 7 丁目

KOISHIKAWA BOTANICAL GARDENS
(小石川植物園 ✳ Koishikawa Shokubutsuen)

SEE MAPS 7 AND 9

These gardens, owned by the Tokyo University Faculty of Science, are a must-see for both beginning and serious botanists and ethnobotanists. The land runs along the western slope of the Hongō finger. In the past, it would have overlooked the Yaha River valley. The terrain is rugged, with a maze of steep trails climbing up and down the slope. The grounds were first established during the Edo period, in 1684, as a medicinal herb garden and continued to be used to test-grow new crops, such as sweet potatoes, during the same period.

The park is divided by forest type, including broadleaved deciduous, broadleaved evergreens, and conifers. At the bottom of the slope is a Japanese water garden with irises, water lilies, and a fine grove of native alders. One whole section is devoted to platanus trees, with all three species available for study and comparison. Taxonomic and medicinal plant gardens provide opportunities for in-depth research.

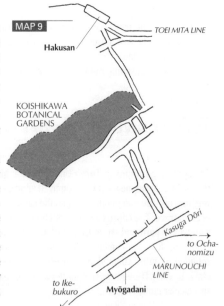

Of special scientific interest are the direct decendents of Sir Isaac Newton's famous apple tree and Gregor Johann Mendel's grapevine. A ginkgo tree near the entrance was used in experiments conducted here that first identified how the female eggs are fertilized by spermatozoids in gymnosperm seed plants.

ACCESS: Located about a ten-minute walk from Hakusan Station on the Toei Mita Line or a fifteen-minute walk from Myōgadani Station on the Marunouchi Line. Entrance tickets are sold at the little store across from the gate. Admission is ¥330 for adults, ¥110 for children. Open daily, except Monday, from 9:00 to 16:30. ☎ (03) 3814–0138.

❖ 3–7–1 Hakusan, Bunkyō-ku, Tokyo 東京都文京区白山3–7–1

KYŪ-FURUKAWA GARDENS
(旧古河庭園 ✳ Kyū-Furukawa Teien)

SEE MAPS 7 AND 10

This small garden is built right into the western slope of the Ueno Uplands and is best known for its classic western-style brick bulding and terraced rose garden. The lower part of the garden is landscaped in traditional Japanese style, with a densely wooded slope and small pond.

ACCESS: About a ten-minute walk from either Komagome Station on JR Yamanote

Line, Kami Nakazato Station on JR Keihin Tōhoku Line, or Nishigahara Station on the Nanboku Line. Very crowded when roses are blooming in June and October. Open daily from 9:00 to 17:00. Admission is ¥150 for students of junior high school age and older. ☎ (03) 3910–0394.

❖ 1–27–39 Nishigahara, Kita-ku, Tokyo 東京都北区西ヶ原1–27–39

RIKUGI-EN GARDENS (六義園 ✳ Rikugi-en)

SEE MAPS 7 AND 10
The Rikugi-en Gardens, located a few minutes' walk from Komagome Station on the JR Yamanote or Nanboku Line, were laid out in the late seventeenth century and are considered to be a textbook example of formal landscape gardens enjoyed by the samurai military class of the Edo period. During the Edo period, the Tokugawa shoguns awarded tracts of desirable land to loyal supporters and faithful retainers. The land on which the Rikugi-en Gardens stand was deeded in 1695 to Yanagisawa Yoshiyasu, a minister in the cabinet of the fifth Tokugawa shogun.

Yanagisawa was an avid horticulturist and a great lover of art and literature. He laid out a landscape garden based on a central pond surrounded by pine trees and dotted with artificial islands. A circling watercourse features high, rounded bridges and small waterfalls. Points along the garden path, marked with little gazebos and tea spots, were designed to represent scenes made famous in various traditional *waka* poems.

After the Meiji Restoration of 1867,

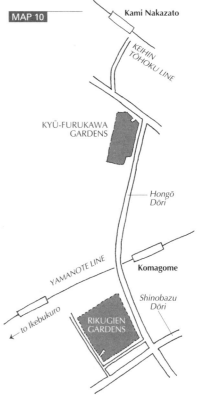

Rikugi-en Gardens and Kyū-Furukawa Gardens can both be reached on a short walk from Komagome Station

the gardens were obtained by the Iwasaki family, the founders and owners of the Mitsubishi Group. The land served as a villa and, for a while, as the temporary residence of the prime minister, before being donated to the city and opened as a public park in 1937.

The Rikugi-en Gardens are small and can be enjoyed in a few hours. In addition to plums and *somei yoshino* cherries, *shidare-zakura* ("weeping cherries"), with their sinuous cascading branches, are quite spectacular. Several species of maple make fall leaf-viewing a popular activity, and there are very old specimens of native *inu-shide* hornbeam and *keyaki* elms.

Behind the formally landscaped and meticulously maintained water garden is a small but rich area given over to a natural forest, with native oaks and hornbeams. This part of the park is always serenaded in birdsong. Look for flocks of great tit and Japanese white eyes.

ACCESS: The Rikugi-en Gardens are open every day from 9:00 to 17:00. Admission is ¥300, but children of elementary school age and under and seniors over 65 enter free. A small snack bar sells drinks, including a sweet fermented saké called *ama-zake* and a few light dishes. If you come on the JR Yamanote Line, take the south exit (*minami-guchi*) of Komagome Station; subway passengers on the Nanboku Line should use exit 2. ☎ (03) 3941–2222.

❖ 6–16–3 Honkomagome, Bunkyō-ku, Tokyo 東京都文京区本駒込6–16–3

EDOGAWA PARK (江戸川公園 ✳ Edogawa Kōen)

SEE MAP 7

On the other side of the Yaha Valley is another finger of high ground, called the Toshima Uplands (Toshima-dai). This upland stretches over to the main valley of the Kanda River itself. The Kanda, which flows through the central city, has always been fondly thought of as the Yamanote's river. Edogawa Park sits along the Kanda Valley side of the Toshima Uplands and features a heavily wooded stretch of slope. In addition to typical park and street trees, the park has some good-size broadleaved evergreens, understory shrubs, and even a few *konara* oaks and native hornbeams. This is a good spot to cool off in summer or to do a little botanizing if you happen to be in the area. A little bit to the east are two fine gardens with ponds, one at the Chinzansō Restaurant and the other at Shin Edogawa Park.

ACCESS: The park is close to Edogawabashi Station on the Yūrakuchō Line. Take exit A, walk under the expressway, and turn left.

❖ 2–1 Sekiguchi, Bunkyō-ku, Tokyo 東京都文京区関口2–1

TOYAMA PARK (戸山公園 ✳ Toyama Kōen)

See maps 7 and 11

South of the Kanda River is a large, thick chunk of upland that leads on to Shinjuku. Toyama Park is situated along the northern edge of the rise, on a short valley of the Kanda. (Shinjuku Gyoen Gardens are also located on these uplands but are at the headwaters of the Shibuya River watershed.)

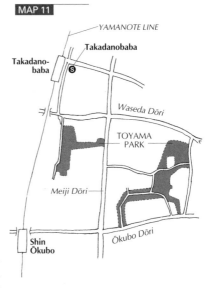

MAP 11

Laid out among Waseda University and several huge housing developments, Toyama Park has assumed one of the wierdest shapes imaginable. The park is split into two sections, the Nishi Ōkubo section to the west and the Hakone-yama section to the east. The western section contains the ward gymnasium and the central municipal horticulture library. The eastern section was formerly a strolling garden built by a daimyo in the late seventeenth century. Strollers were treated to miniature reconstructions of the fifty-one rest stops of the Tōkaidō Highway. One of these, representing Mount Hakone, was at the time a high hill which dominated the garden. Today, this hill, at forty-four meters above sea level, is the highest "natural point" in the central city! Toyama Park is good for viewing trees, especially azaleas, and also for wildflowers that flourish along the numerous winding paths. Japanese toads breed in a small manmade pond in the eastern section.

Access: The western section of the park is a fifteen-minute walk from Takadanobaba Station on the Yamanote Line, Toyama exit, or the Tōzai Line, exit 3. Some time spent wandering back and forth is needed to explore the different park sections, which are separated by about a ten-minute walk.

❖ 3–5–1 Ōkubo, Shinjuku-ku, Tokyo 東京都新宿区大久保3–5–1

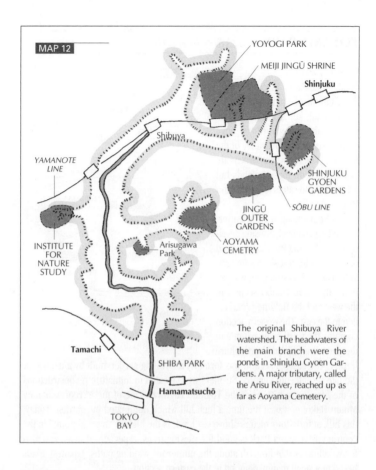

The original Shibuya River watershed. The headwaters of the main branch were the ponds in Shinjuku Gyoen Gardens. A major tributary, called the Arisu River, reached up as far as Aoyama Cemetery.

SHINJUKU GYOEN GARDENS (新宿御苑 ＊ Shinjuku Gyoen)

SEE MAPS 12 AND 13

The Shibuya River today appears at the southern side of Shibuya Station, looking more like sewer drainage than a river. From there, it flows southeast, later turning east, then north, then east again before emptying into Tokyo Bay, just south of Takeshiba Wharf. Along most of this short journey, the Shibuya is flowing beneath elevated portions of the Shuto Expressway, out of sight and out of mind to most people.

This modern-day Shibuya River is only a shadow of the original river system (see map 1), which reached all the way up into the ponds of the Shinjuku Gyoen Gardens and included tributaries coming down from Meiji Jingū Shrine, Yoyogi Park, and Aoyama Cemetery. Dōgenzaka and the many steep slopes encountered around Shibuya Station as well as those leg-stretchers along Omotesandō and in the Harajuku district are all part of the Shibuya River drainage.

Shinjuku Gyoen Gardens sit at the very headwaters of the Shibuya River system. Like so many other Tokyo parks, they were originally the manor grounds of a feudal lord. The basic Tokugawa defense policy was to locate the estates of loyal daimyo at strategic points that could guard the castle and the entrances into the city. The Naitō clan, one of the shogun's most loyal allies, was established on the northwestern edge, in the area close to what is now called Shinjuku. Several major roads, including the Ōme Kaidō and Kōshū Kaidō as well as the Tamagawa Aqueduct entered the city at this point.

Following the Meiji Restoration of 1867, much of the old Naitō manor was first converted into an agricultural experimental station and technical training center, then later into a botanical garden that included duck ponds and the city's zoo. The zoo was soon moved to its present site at Ueno, and the Shinjuku Gardens began serving as a center for importing western horticultural technology.

Orchids and other ornamental flowers were raised in greenhouses. Potential street trees, especially platanus, tulip trees, and Himalayan cedars, were grown and used to supply cuttings and seedlings for plantings throughout the city.

Today, Shinjuku Gyoen Gardens are administered by the Environment Agency and offer a surprising natural sanctuary in proximity to the great shopping and entertainment districts of Shinjuku and Kabukichō. The park includes a French-style promenade lined with platanus trees and a traditional Japanese garden built around a few small ponds. The ponds are dammed at the head of several narrow *yato* valleys that form the top of the Shibuya River watershed. There is also an English landscape garden and large stretches of open grassfields, which are punctuated with shade trees and superb for picnicking or just relaxing and reading a book.

Botanists come here to enjoy some of the largest and oldest trees in the city. Look for immense cedars, platanus, tulip trees, and ginkgos. Some of these are the original parents from which many of the city's street and park trees were raised. In addition, there are several areas planted in native oaks and a small section just inside the main gate called the *Haha to Ko no Mori* ("Mother and Daughter Forest"), where a visitor can wander through native forests that are allowed to follow their natural pattern of succession. The greenhouse contains an outstanding collection of subtropical and tropical plants.

A tour through the Shinjuku Gyoen should begin at the Shinjuku Gate, a ten-minute walk from the south exit (*minami-guchi*) of Shinjuku Station or a five-minute walk from either Shinjuku Gyoen-mae Station on the Marunouchi Line or Shinjuku Sanchōme (exit C5) on the Toei Shinjuku Line. A small education center located just outside the gate contains displays, specimens, and reference materials. A staff member from the Environment Agency is usually on hand to answer questions and provide guidance.

The gardens are open from 9:00 to 16:30 daily except Monday. Admission is ¥200. Snacks and guide maps can be purchased at the center, and several teahouses and a small cafeteria are available within the park grounds. ☎ (03) 3350–0151.

❖ 11 Naitōchō, Shinjuku-ku, Tokyo 東京都新宿区内藤町11

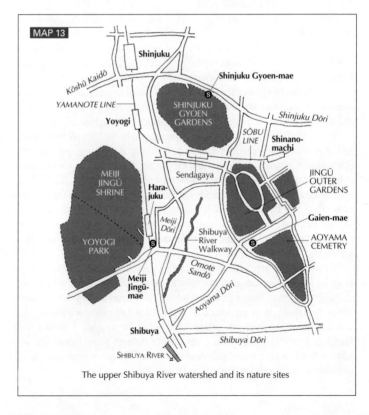

The upper Shibuya River watershed and its nature sites

MEIJI JINGŪ SHRINE (明治神宮 ✻ Meiji Jingū)

SEE MAPS 12 AND 13

The Meiji Jingū Shrine is second only to the Imperial Palace as a must-stop for both foreign and domestic tourists visiting Tokyo. The heavily wooded shrine complex is also a haven for tree lovers and birdwatchers.

Emperor Meiji died in 1912, and although he was buried in his native Kyoto, a great shrine in his memory was constructed in Tokyo as well. A total of forty sites vied for the honor. The present Meiji Jingū Shrine, which already belonged to the Imperial Household Agency, was chosen.

Fortunately, the botanists and architects commissioned to design the park showed great vision. Although they visited various parks in Europe and America, they eventually decided on a uniquely Japanese concept. The new park was to contain some open, grassy areas that would be surrounded by dense, dark groves of native broadleaved deciduous trees. The park designers knew from the outset that they would never live to see their dream completed in its full glory, for the Meiji Jingū Shrine forests would not attain full maturity until the twenty-second century.

To begin with, the shrine grounds were planted with fast-growing conifers such as pines, cryptomeria, and cypress. At the same time, a large number of broadleaved tree saplings, including both deciduous and evergreen species, were added. The designers envisioned that the park would gradually evolve through a typical forest succession, leading to the dense, dark, native climax forest of chinkapins and evergreen oaks. This process was estimated to require about two hundred years.

Today, the succession is well under way, and the shrine grounds are superb for studying trees, especially the big broadleaved evergreens and their understory species. Some parts of the park still contain many deciduous trees. One such area is near the South Pond, which is formed around a natural water seep at the head of a narrow side valley that once flowed through the Harajuku area to join the upper Shibuya River. This pond is also a favorite spot for birdwatchers. Look for common kingfishers, little egrets, and little grebes in the vicinity of the pond, and great and varied tits in the trees. This is perhaps the best spot in the city for enjoying great tits close up. About four thousand huge jungle crows roost in the trees throughout the winter months.

The northern part of the South Pond features a popular iris garden, and both sliders and soft-shelled turtles live in the water. The North Pond, near the Shinjuku side of the grounds, is surrounded by marshlands, dense forests, and some open grasslands.

ACCESS: Meiji Jingū Shrine is open from dawn to dusk. The park is free, but entrance to the South Pond section is ¥500. The shrine grounds are at Harajuku Station on the Yamanote Line or Meiji Jingū-mae (exit 2) on the Chiyoda Line.

❖ 1–1 Yoyogi Kamizono-chō, Shibuya-ku, Tokyo
東京都渋谷区代々木神園町1–1

YOYOGI PARK (代々木公園 ✳ Yoyogi Kōen)

SEE MAPS 12 AND 13

Yoyogi Park is adjacent to Meiji Jingū Shrine, and together these two heavily wooded areas form one of the most extensive patches of forest habitat in central Tokyo. In contrast to the solemn darkness of Meiji Jingū Shrine, Yoyogi is a wide-open urban park with grassy lawns and recreational facilities.

Yoyogi Park was originally a Japanese army practice ground. In the postwar years it was taken over by the U.S. Occupation troops and used as a barracks and housing base. During the Tokyo Olympics of 1962, the area served as a dormitory for athletes. Afterwards, it was opened to the public as a park.

Yoyogi Park is used primarily by joggers, cyclists, roller skaters, and picnickers but is also a great spot for studying native and street trees. In the southeastern part of the park, near the Harajuku Gate, is a bird sanctuary that abuts Meiji Jingū Shrine, and a small botanical garden with specimen trees donated by Olympic athletes from around the world.

ACCESS: The park is accessible from three stations: Harajuku Station on the JR Yamanote Line, Meiji Jingū-mae (exit 2), or Yoyogi Kōen-mae (exits 2, 3, and 4) and on the Chiyoda Line .

❖ 2–1 Kamizono-chō, Shibuya-ku, Tokyo 東京都渋谷区神園町2–1

MEIJI JINGŪ OUTER GARDENS
(明治神宮外苑 ✳ Meiji Jingū Gaien)

SEE MAPS 12 AND 13

The Meiji Jingū Outer Gardens are situated on the Aoyama Uplands, between the valley of the Shibuya River and the valley that used to form the Outer Moat. Various sports stadiums, including the Jingū Stadium—home grounds of the Yakult Swallows professional baseball team—are surrounded by heavily wooded stretches of park and abundant street trees. The approach from Aoyama Dōri is lined with huge ginkgo trees that are famous for their magnificent yellow in late autumn.

Access: The closest station is Aoyama Itchōme (exits 1 and 2) on the Hanzōmon and Ginza lines.

❖ Kasumigaoka-machi, Shinjuku-ku, Tokyo 東京都新宿区霞岳町

AOYAMA CEMETERY (青山霊園 ✳ Aoyama Reien)

SEE MAPS 12 AND 13

This municipal cemetery was catapulted into the limelight in the mid 1990s, when it became known that groups of expatriates were using the secluded area as a sanctuary for smoking marijuana. The cemetery grounds occupy a finger of high ground that was originally surrounded on both sides by narrow *yato* valleys. These valleys were at the head of the Arisugawa River, a major tributary that joined the Shibuya River a little south of Hiro-o Station.

Situated on dry land overlooking a rich valley, the Aoyama Uplands have always been an attractive place to live. Pieces of Jōmon-period pottery have been excavated from among the tombs, proving that villages have been here for at least several thousand years. During the Edo period, the tip of the uplands was part of the manor of the Aoyama clan, but after the Meiji Restoration of 1867 the land reverted to the government. In 1872, it was designated as a public cemetery. Buried here are many famous people, including General Nogi Maresuke, a war hero who joined his leader in death by committing suicide when Emperor Meiji died in 1912.

Like the other municipal cemeteries, these grounds are dotted with large trees, including some big camphors, and are also excellent sites for native dandelions and other small wildflowers that flourish among the tombstones.

The grounds of the Nezu Art Museum and Chōkoku temple occupy the head of another narrow *yato* valley that used to branch off the Arisugawa near its headwaters. Arisugawa Memorial Park itself, with a fine pond and walking paths along heavily wooded slopes, is built into the edge of the high ground along the lower eastern edge of the *yato* valley. The French Embassy and Tengen-ji temple stand on the very edge of the uplands, where the Arisugawa joined the Shibuya.

Access: The cemetery grounds can be reached by taking the Chiyoda Line to Nogizaka Station (exit 5).

❖ 2–32–2 Minami Aoyama, Minato-ku, Tokyo 東京都港区南青山2–32–2

SHIBA PARK (芝公園 ✳ Shiba Kōen)

See map 12

This highly fragmented park is located on high ground along the very edge of the Yamanote, where the Shibuya River empties out onto the coastal plain. Several long, thin park segments completely surround the grounds of the Zōjō-ji temple. The western section of the park, just below Tokyo Tower, is heavily wooded with native broadleaf trees, including abundant maples that put on a nice show in autumn. The southeastern section, behind the golf driving range and bowling alley, is a steep, densely forested slope with a monument to Inō Tadataka (1745–1818) on the top level. Inō is famous for making the first accurate maps of the Japanese islands. Beginning this long task after fifty, he walked all over the country, surveying and mapping as he went. A copy of these maps was carried back to Europe. For many decades, they formed the basis for the depiction of Japan on world maps as well. During the Jōmon period, there was a village on the slope. If you search carefully at the base of the stairs you can find shells that have washed down from the midden.

Access: The park can be reached from Shiba Kōen Station (exit A4) on the Toei Mita Line.

❖ 4–10–17 Shiba Kōen, Minato-ku, Tokyo 東京都港区芝公園4–10–17

INSTITUTE FOR NATURE STUDY (国立科学博物館付属自然教育園 ✳ Kokuritsu Kagaku-hakubutsukan Fuzoku Shizen-kyōiku-en)

See maps 12 and 14

Tokyo nature enthusiasts will definitely want to spend a half day or so botanizing in this heavily wooded central city nature reserve, which specializes in native woodland wildflowers and trees and shrubs of the Musashino Uplands. Along the shaded main path are planted a selection of local anemones, lilies, orchids, irises, arums, and poppies. The earliest spring flowers appear in late February, and autumn blooms last into November. A small nature center posts pictures of

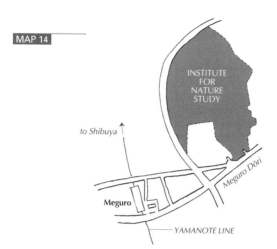

MAP 14

INSTITUTE FOR NATURE STUDY

to Shibuya

Meguro Dōri

Meguro

YAMANOTE LINE

plants currently in bloom, and provides background information on topics such as forest succession, bird life, butterflies, and seed dispersal.

The area covered by this park was originally the site of a fort built in the thirteenth or fourteenth century by a local chieftan. The fort was surrounded by earthworks, on top of which were planted huge chinkapin trees. Many of these old giants survive today, the largest having a trunk circumference of almost seven meters. The park is also famous for ancient black pines, which were planted as part of a formal Japanese garden during the Edo period, when the area was a manor belonging to the Matsudaira clan.

Like Meiji Jingū, this park is home to a roost of several thousand jungle crows. The crows favor parks that are closed to the public after dark. A small pond provides opportunities to view mandarin ducks in winter, and turtles and little grebes all year round. During spring and summer, a succession of water plants bloom along the edges of the pond. Although the topography is very hard to see, the pond is located at the head of a narrow *yato* valley. The original river flowed north to join the Shibuya.

ACCESS: The institute is a part of the National Science Museum and is open from 9:00 to 16:30 (winter) or until 17:00 (summer). Closed Mondays and days following national holidays. Admission is ¥210 for adults and ¥60 for children. A seven-minute walk from the east exit (*higashi-guchi*) of Meguro Station on the JR Yamanote Line. ☎ (03) 3441–7176.

❖ 5–21–5 Shiroganedai, Minato-ku, Tokyo 東京都港区白銀台5–21–5

THE MUSASHINO UPLANDS

The Musashino Uplands stretch from Tokyo westward to the mountains, are bordered by the Tama and Ara rivers, and appear relatively flat and feature-less. This area, fondly and nostalgically called the Musashino by local people, was originally covered with well-tended oak woodlands and open fields of plume grass. Today, urban sprawl seems to go on forever, as cramped riders on the JR Chūō, Odakyū, and Keiō lines know all too well. What little nature remains is often along the rivers or on terrace and valley slopes that are too steep for intensive development.

Fortunately, some of the remaining natural spots have been set aside as parks or protected as temple or shrine grounds. One way of exploring these spots and of understanding their relationship to the topography is to follow the courses of the rivers that lace the Musashino. These rivers are contained completely within the Musashino and thus have their sources not in steep mountain ravines but in natural seeps at the base of slopes along the *yato* valleys or edges of the terraces.

The rivers of the Musashino are all relatively short, with gentle gradients. Most have several tributaries, each with its own natural seeps as water sources. The seeps are usually near the headwaters of the narrow valleys, and in many cases the fresh water collects in a small holding pond, either natural, manmade or a combination of both. This type of holding pond, called *tame-ike*, can be seen at Shakujii Park, Zenpukuji Park, and Inokashira Park.

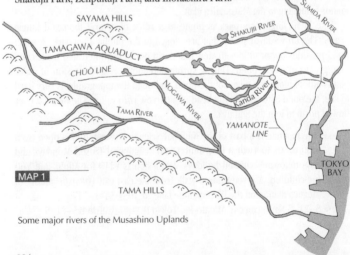

Some major rivers of the Musashino Uplands

There are dozens of small rivers that drain through the Musashino Uplands. For the purpose of nature exploration, the Shakujii, Kanda, and Nogawa rivers are good choices to start off with. The relative position of these three rivers is shown in map 1. As can be seen, the Shakujii and Kanda flow eastward and empty into the Sumida River. These two are typical *yato* valley rivers. The Nogawa, on the other hand, flows along a cliff separating two river terraces, and is a tributary of the Tama. The Tamagawa Aqueduct (Tamagawa Jōsui) is also shown on the map. Although this is a manmade canal dug in the seventeenth century, it has been restored along much of its length, and now offers good opportunities for nature hiking.

The Shakujii River, shown in map 2, has its source way out in western Tokyo, near the Koganei Country Club, in Kodaira City. From there it flows for about twenty-five kilometers, in an almost due easterly direction, picking up water from the Fujimi Pond in Musashiseki Park and Sanpōji Pond in Shakujii Park.

The course of the Shakujii River. The headwaters are found around Koganei Park, but the best spot for nature watching is Shakujii Park, located on a short side valley at about the middle of the watershed. Walking paths and a series of small nature parks line the river along the lower reaches inside the Yamanote Line, near Asukayama Park.

The Shakujii passes between Itabashi and Jūjō stations on the Saikyō Line, then flows across the city, nearing Ōji Station on the Keihin Tōhoku Line. The river appears to vanish east of the station then reappear on the other side, but it actually passes through a long underground tunnel. East of Ōji Station, the Shakujii breaks out of the uplands and flows a short distance across the alluvial plain before joining the Sumida between the Horifune and Toshima neighborhoods, at the point where the Sumida makes a sharp curve.

This last portion of the river is artificial. Originally, the Shakujii turned sharply south and flowed down along the inside of the Ueno Cliffs, eventually emptying out onto the alluvial plain in the vicinity of Shinobazu Pond. The Yata River, discussed in the Yamanote Uplands section, can be thought of as the old final segment of the Shakujii.

Koganei Park is located along the Shakujii near its headwaters, and Musashi-seki Park (not discussed below, but a short walk from Higashi Fushimi Station on the Seibu Shinjuku Line) straddles the river a little further downstream. Shakujii Park, the prime natural destination along the river, is actually at the head of a short tributary valley. The very edge of the Musashino Uplands, where the river currently flows out onto the plain, is set aside as Asukayama Park.

The Kanda River is the best known of the Musashino rivers (see map 3).

The three main branches of the Kanda River, each with headwaters at a holding pond. The pond at Inokashira Park, at the head of the main branch, is the most famous.

Millions of people see it every day from the windows of the JR Yamanote Line, which crosses the river just north of Takadanobaba Station. A little bit downstream, the river passes by Edogawa Park, then serves as part of the Outer Moat before flowing across the alluvial plain to pass under Asakusa Bridge and empty into the Sumida just north of Ryōgoku Bridge. As was noted in the chapter on the Yamanote Uplands, this lowest section is not the original river course.

Upstream, the Kanda has several major sources. One of these is the pond at Inokashira Park in Mitaka, and the other, the pond at Zenpukuji Park (the section of river flowing out of this pond is called the Zenpukuji River). Just west of Shinjuku, the Kanda is joined by the Myōshōji River, which has its source at a pond in Myōshōji Park, near Kami Igusa, in Suginami Ward.

Excellent nature destinations on the Kanda River system include Inokashira Park, at the headwaters of the main branch; Zenpukiji Park, at the headwaters of the Zenpukiji branch; and Zenpukijigawa and Wadabori parks, along the middle reaches of the Zenpukiji branch.

The Nogawa river and nearby Kokubunji Cliff offer some of western Tokyo's best natural areas (see maps 4 and 5). The Nogawa differs from the Shakujii and Kanda in that it flows not through a narrow valley of its own, but along the base of a cliff dividing two terraces. Also, the Nogawa is a major tributary of the Tama River rather than the Sumida.

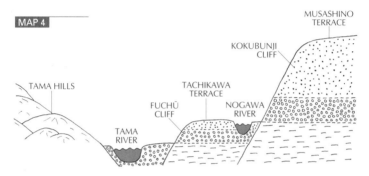

A cross-section showing the geology along the Nogawa river. The river flows along the base of a cliff that marks the boundary between two ancient terraces of the Tama River. A smaller cliff marks the boundary between the Tachikawa Terrace and the current plain of the Tama River. The three geological strata shown are (from the top) the volcanic deposits, called the Kantō Loam; the old river gravels; and marine sediments.

The Nogawa's uppermost source lies in a holding pond at the head of a narrow *yato* valley in Kokubunji. From there, the river winds for about twenty-five kilometers in a southeastern direction, almost paralleling the course of the Tama.

Throughout most of its course, the Nogawa is flowing near the base of a steep cliff that is between fifteen and twenty meters high. This Kokubunji Cliff, called the Kokubunji Gaisen by Japanese geologists, is always on the north or northeast side of the river, and also runs in a basically parallel southwest direction. Here and there narrow *yato* valleys, tributaries of the Nogawa, break up the line of the cliff, which continues well down into Setagaya Ward.

Kokubunji Cliff is the boundary between two ancient terraces. Over tens of thousands of years, the Tama River has cut a series of terraces into the surrounding uplands. Each terrace marks the level of the riverbed at that time, so the higher terraces are always the older. The Kokubunji Cliff occurs where the land drops off steeply from the Musashino Terrace down to the Tachikawa Terrace. Another smaller and less clearly defined cliff, called the Fuchū Gaisen, marks the boundary between the Tachikawa Terrace and the modern flood plain of the Tama River.

The steep Kokubunji Cliff often shows up as a line of trees and greenery amidst a sea of heavy residential development. In addition, natural water seeps (*hake*) dot the base of the cliff, creating rich aquatic habitats between the cliff and the river. The top of the Musashino Terrace is covered with weathered volcanic loam, blown there on the prevailing westerly winds from eruptions of Mount Fuji and volcanoes in the Hakone mountains. This loam is porous and allows water to seep down into it. The fossil river gravels that underlie the loam are also porous, but the marine deposits at the very base are made of tightly packed silt that blocks the flow of water. Rainwater falling on the Musashino Terrace seeps down through the loam and gravel, then flows horizontally along the top of the silt layer, eventually emerging at the base of the cliff as natural springs.

MAP 5

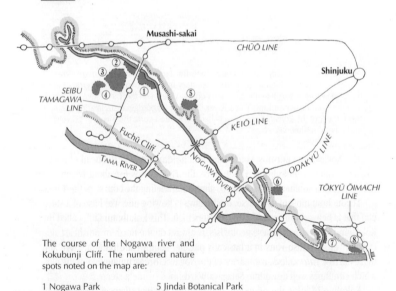

The course of the Nogawa river and Kokubunji Cliff. The numbered nature spots noted on the map are:

1 Nogawa Park
2 Musashino Park
3 Tama Cemetery
4 Sengenyama Park
5 Jindai Botanical Park
6 Kinuta Park
7 Todoroki Keikoku
8 Tamagawadai Park

An adventurous walker can trace the entire course of the Nogawa river and Kokubunji Cliff in a few days (or one very long day). The river starts off just north of the Chūō Line, between Kokubunji and Nishi Kokubunji stations. For a while the river and cliff run almost parallel to the Chūō Line, then begin sloping southeast to pass through Musashino Park and Nogawa Park (between Shin Koganei and Tamabochi-mae stations on the Seibu Tamagawa Line). The cliffs at this point are only a few dozen meters behind the river, and the campus of the International Christian University sits right on top of the Musashino Terrace, just above Nogawa Park.

A few kilometers downstream, the river passes by the Jindai Metropolitan Botanical Park. The cliff line here is indented by several narrow *yato* side valleys that once held small tributaries of the Nogawa. The river crosses the Keiō Line between Shibasaki and Kokuryō stations, then makes a short detour loop to the east before continuing southeast again. The line of the Kokubunji Cliff intersects the Keiō Line between Tsutsujigaoka and Shibasaki stations.

Between the Keiō and Odakyū lines are more *yato* valleys, including one that carries a fairly substantial tributary. Riders leaving the city on the Odakyū Line will see the cliff and river between Seijō-Gakuen-mae and Kitami stations. Finally, the Nogawa accepts the water of the Senkawa, another typical Musashino river, before dumping into the Tama in western Setagaya Ward, near Futako-Tamagawaen Station on the Tōkyū Ōimachi Line. The cliffs continue on a little further then peter out.

KOGANEI PARK (小金井公園 ✳ Koganei Kōen)

SEE MAPS 2 AND 6

This wide-open, extensive park is full of tennis courts, cycling roads, and other recreational facilities. Flower enthusiasts appreciate the cherries, azaleas, and an immense magnolia that stands next to the park office. Naturalists usually head for the extensive deciduous woodlands in the north-central part of the park. Here are oaks, zelkovas, and other native woodland trees. Part of the woodlands are set aside as a nature reserve, with good birdwatching, especially for tits and other forest birds in winter.

The Shakujii River flows along the northern edge of the park but actually begins in the golf course, a little further to the east. Unfortunately, these upper reaches of the river are sorely polluted, and trapped inside a steep, narrow concrete channel. On the opposite side, the Tamagawa Aqueduct flows along the southern edge of the park. An outdoor historical museum, with reconstructed dwellings from all periods of Japanese prehistory and history, is adjacent to the park on the west.

MAP 6

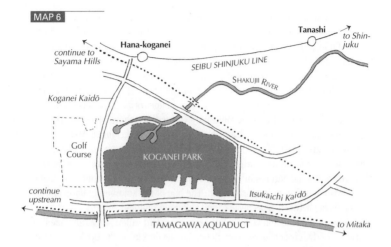

ACCESS: To get to Koganei Park, take a bus or walk from Musashi Koganei or Higashi Koganei station on the JR Chūō Line. One enjoyable way to reach this park is to walk along the Tamagawa Aqueduct from Mitaka Station on the JR Chūō Line (about a twenty-five minute walk). Strong walkers will want to continue trekking after perusing the park. Just to the north of the park is a walking path that leads all the way out to the Sayama Hills, about a ten-kilometer jaunt. The Tamagawa Aqueduct can also be followed upstream for as far as one likes.

❖ 1–13–11 Sekino-chō, Koganei-shi, Tokyo
東京都小金井市関野町1–13–11

SHAKUJII PARK (石神井公園 ✳ Shakujii Kōen)

SEE MAPS 2 AND 7

Shakujii Park, located along a short tributary valley, is a must stop not only for naturalists but also for artists and poets who want to appreciate the beauty of traditional Japanese landscapes.

The park consists of two ponds surrounded by steep slopes. The long, narrow eastern pond (Shakujii-ike) is popular with fishermen, and is primarily a recreational resource. The slopes along the southern side, however, are heavily wooded.

The western pond (Sanpōji-ike) is the gem of this park, and is perhaps the region's best-preserved and most beautiful traditional-style holding pond (*tame-ike*). The pond is completely surrounded by dense woodlands, including a good mix of broadleaved evergreens, deciduous oaks, and ornamental cherries. A small island sits in the center of the pond, and a shrine and temple are located on promontories along the southern shore. This southern shore is especially famous for kingfishers and clusters of yellow *kōhone* spatterdock blossoms. A wooden-slat walking path leads completely around the pond. The marshlands in the northeastern corner are set aside as a reserve for local species of rare and endangered aquatic plants.

ACCESS: The park is a ten-minute walk from Shakujii Kōen Station on the Seibu Ikebukuro Line. A little further to the east (upstream) is Musashiseki Park, a smaller park with pond and wooded sections. Musashiseki is a short walk from Higashi Fushimi Station on the Seibu Shinjuku Line.

❖ 1–26–1 Shakujiidai, Nerima-ku, Tokyo 東京都練馬区石神井台1–26–1

ASUKAYAMA PARK (飛鳥山公園 ✳ Asukayama Kōen)

SEE MAPS 2 AND 8

This park is located along the edge of the Musashino Cliffs and can be seen on the west (left) windows of the JR Keihin Tōhoku Line as the train comes into Ōji Station from the south. The park is wooded with ornamental cherries and broadleaved evergreens as well as camellias that bloom in late winter.

The Asukayama Museum, located in the southern section of the park, has a wide range of exhibits that will help the visitor or beginning naturalist interpret the natural history of the Tokyo area. Exhibits cover the geology, prehistoric cultures, history, and plants and animals of the Tokyo Shitamachi alluvial plain.

After viewing the park and museum, a short jaunt upstream is well worth the effort. Well-maintained strolling paths line both sides of the river, which flows through a very deep, straight channel, made by cutting across the many sinuous curves and bends of the original river course. In several spots, the old river bed is preserved as small but heavily wooded U-shaped parks. The second park upriver, at a spot where water once cascaded out of the slope, has a little pond that, for some reason, is a favorite wintering spot among the city's pintail ducks.

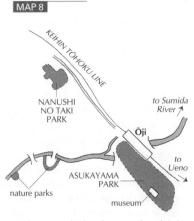

MAP 8

KEIHIN TŌHOKU LINE

NANUSHI NO TAKI PARK

to Sumida River ↗

Ōji

to Ueno

ASUKAYAMA PARK

nature parks

museum

If time allows, a five-minute walk north along the western side of the train tracks will bring you to Nanushi no Taki Park. This little-known park, consisting of a pond and heavily wooded backslope, is a real surprise. A maze of narrow paths wind up and down the slope, past several

Asukayama Park, along lower reaches of Shakujii River

waterfalls and some huge specimens of *inu-shide* hornbeam.

ACCESS: Take the JR Keihin Tōhoku Line to Ōji Station. The museum is open from 10:00 to 17:00, and closed Mondays. The entrance fee for the Asukayama Museum is ¥300, or with a ticket for adjacent Paper Museum, ¥600. ☎ (03) 3916–1133.

❖ 1–1–3 Ōji, Kita-ku, Tokyo 東京都北区王子1–1–3

INOKASHIRA PARK (井の頭公園 ＊ Inokashira Kōen)

SEE MAPS 3 AND 9

Inokashira Park, located in western Tokyo a half hour or so from the central city, is famous for its pond, which is said to have originally been fed by seven separate natural seeps. These seeps were a major source of the Kanda River, which flows out of the park in a southeast direction.

The Inokashira Park Zoo is small but very well stocked with local Japanese birds and mammals. In one consecutive row of cages, for example, live the four medium-size mammals found in the Kantō area: the Japanese red fox; the *tanuki*, or raccoon dog; the Japanese badger; and the *hakubishin*, or masked palm-civet.

The zoo also has a colony of macaques, some Japanese martens, both deer and serows, and even Ryūkyū wild boars. The real stars, however, are the Japanese squirrels. Although they look like other squirrels throughout the world, the Japanese squirrel is actually an endemic species found only in Japan. The squirrels are native to Honshū, Shikoku, and Kyūshū (the squirrel found on Hokkaidō is a completely different species).

Squirrels, like foxes, were once common in the Tokyo area but are now very rare. One reason for their decline is loss of forest habitat. An epidemic that wiped out the Tokyo-area pines several decades ago may also have played a major role. Squirrels depend heavily on pine nuts, which they harvest in autumn and bury in the leaf litter for their winter larder.

The squirrels at Inokashira are part of a project to artificially restore the species. Squirrels born and raised in the enclosures are being experimentally released in other parts of the park. So far, the project has not been successful, most likely due to the huge jungle crows, which find the young, inexperienced squirrels an easy target. Squirrels raised in a captive environment don't learn to fear and avoid the crows as wild ones do.

One of the squirrel houses is open to the public, and the tame animals are happy to receive food from the hands of children. The zoo also has an Ural owl, Tokyo's most common local owl species, and a series of cages with most of the Tokyo-area songbirds.

MAP 9

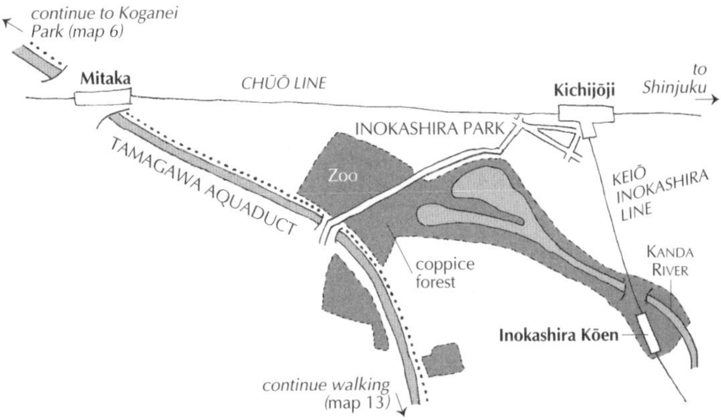

continue to Koganei Park (map 6)

Mitaka   CHŪŌ LINE   Kichijōji   to Shinjuku

TAMAGAWA AQUADUCT   Zoo   INOKASHIRA PARK   KEIŌ INOKASHIRA LINE   KANDA RIVER

coppice forest

Inokashira Kōen

continue walking (map 13)

Inokashira Park and vicinity. The pond and surroundings are always crowded, but few people go as far as the coppice forest and Tamagawa Aqueduct. Walkers can follow the aqueduct downstream (see map 13) or upstream to Mitaka Station or Koganei Park.

A separate aquatic zoo is located near the pond, which is the center of the park. The pond offers superb birdwatching for all of our local winter ducks, including colorful mandarin ducks, which are provided with wooden nesting boxes. Mandarin ducks usually nest in tree holes, but with few nesting sites available, they have disappeared from most of the Tokyo area. And as is the case with the squirrels, young ducks raised in the nest boxes often fall prey to the jungle crows.

In the aquatic zoo, one can also closely compare the two species of swan that winter in Japan. The specimens are all injured individuals brought here from other areas. A small aquarium houses most of Tokyo's common freshwater fish and amphibians.

Botanists will enjoy the southern part of the park, which is covered with a fine coppice of native deciduous trees. The Tamagawa Aqueduct, which cuts through the southern tip of the park, is also densely wooded, with labels that include scientific names on many trees. A walking path runs alongside the aqueduct in both directions. An hour or so spent walking and observing will familiarize one with many of our local deciduous woodland trees.

ACCESS: Inokashira Park is a five-minute walk from Kichijōji Station on the JR Chūō Line, or a one-minute walk from Inokashira Kōen Station on the Keiō Inokashira Line. A ticket good for entrance to both the main zoo (*shizen bunka-en hon-en*) and aquatic park (*bun-en*) costs ¥400 for adults and ¥150 for junior high school students. Children of elementary school age and younger enter free. Open from 9:30 to 16:30. Zoos closed Mondays and the day following national holidays. ☎ (0422) 47–6900.

❖ 1–18–31 Gotenyama, Musashino-shi, Tokyo
東京都武蔵野市御殿山1–18–31

ZENPUKUJI PARK (善福寺公園 ＊ Zenpukuji Kōen)

SEE MAP 3

The central branch of the Kanda is called the Zenpukuji River, with its source at two ponds in Zenpukuji Park. The upper (western) pond has row boats for rent and is popular with flower enthusiasts. The northern edge of this pond is lined with cherries and willows, backed by hydrangeas and azaleas. Behind these is a bamboo grove. In the northeast corner of the park is a fine stand of huge chinkapins and evergreen oaks.

The lower (eastern) pond is smaller but kept in a more natural state. Much of the pond edge is covered with reeds, and water lilies and other aquatic plants are in abundance. Waterfowl are also prevalent, and the section of the river between the two ponds has been restored to support fireflies.

Sort of inconveniently located midway between Nishi Ogikubo Station on JR Chūō Line or Kami Shakujii Station on Seibu Shinjuku Line. A twenty-minute walk from either station, or take the Kantō Bus (which runs between the two stations) to the Zenpukuji Kōen-mae stop.

❖ 3–9–10 Zenpukuji, Suginami-ku, Tokyo 東京都杉並区善福寺3–9–10

ZENPUKIJIGAWA PARK (善福寺川緑地 ✳ Zenpukujigawa Ryokuchi)
WADABORI PARK (和田堀公園 ✳ Wadabori Kōen)

SEE MAPS 3 AND 10

MAP 10

Further downstream, the Zenpukuji River goes into a tight horseshoe bend. The river here is straddled by Zenpukujigawa Park, a two-kilometer stretch of pleasant parkland, with a wooded cycling and walking path running along the river. The path is famous for cherry trees and, in the clear river water, colorful carp.

Just downstream, the green belt widens as the river enters Wadabori Park. Much of the surrounding slopes feature deciduous woodlands with typical trees such as zelkova and oak. A conifer-covered rise on the north side of the river gives a good overview of the park and is the ancient barrow grave of a local chieftain that lived here about two thousand years ago, during the Yayoi period.

Wadabori Pond, in the center of the park, is home to spatterdocks and other aquatic plants. A large grove of tanbark oaks has been planted at the eastern edge of the park, to the north of the river, while the southeast corner is blanketed by a stand of *hinoki* cypresses and red pines.

SEE MAPS 5 AND 11

Access: Wadabori Park is about a fifteen-minute walk from Nishi Eifuku Station on the Keiō Inokashira Line. Zenpukigawa Park is about twenty-five-minute walk from Hamadayama Station, one stop after Nishi Eifuku on the same line.

❖ 1–30–27 Narita Nishi, Suginami-ku, Tokyo 東京都杉並区成田西1–30–27

NOGAWA PARK (野川公園 ＊ Nogawa Kōen)

The best place to begin exploring the Nogawa River and Kokubunji Cliff is at Nogawa Park, where the entire slope of the cliff as well as the wetland area between the river and the cliff has been set aside as a nature reserve. Raised wooden boardwalks allow visitors to stroll through the marsh to view the alders and other aquatic plants up close. Dense clusters of Japanese daffodils bloom in late January, and fireflies can be seen in early summer.

Displays in the small nature center explain the local geology and ecology, especially the fireflies that breed in the marshlands at the base of the cliff. There are also specimens of various local plants and a showcase featuring natural plant dyes.

The southern part of Nogawa Park is devoted primarily to open space and recreational facilities but also has an extensive grove of deciduous oaks, many of which have been coppiced. From the main entrance of Nogawa Park, one can either walk to Sengenyama Park, passing through Tama Cemetery, or follow the river downstream to Jindai Botanical Park.

Adjacent Musashino Park, a solid working park with woodlands, supports a municipal nursery where many of the city's street and park trees are grown. In mid-April, visitors flock to enjoy a tunnel of *sato-zakura*, an ornamental variety of cherry with large, multipetaled blossoms. In addition, nearby Tama Cemetery is densely planted with a variety of old trees, including some venerable zelkovas and cherries. The International Christian University (ICU), which sits on the top of the Musashino Terrace, is also heavily forested.

Put together, these parks and grounds form a large, concentrated cluster of high-quality habitats that supports a great variety of plants and animals. It would take a bit of walking to see them all in one day. Nogawa Park, with its marshland reserve and little nature museum, is the first stop for naturalists.

Access: Nogawa Park is about a fifteen-minute walk from Shin Koganei Station on Seibu Tamagawa Line. This line connects with the JR Chūō Line at Musashi-sakai. Just follow the tracks south (the direction you were heading in if you came from Musashi-sakai) until you run into the Nogawa River. Nogawa Park will be on your left, and Musashino Park on your right.

❖ 6–4–1 Ōsawa, Mitaka-shi, Tokyo 東京都三鷹市大澤6−4−1

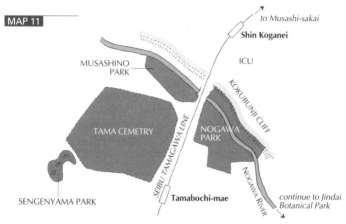

Nature spots along the upper Nogawa river

SENGENYAMA PARK (浅間山公園 ✳ Sengenyama Kōen)

SEE MAPS 5 AND 11

Sengenyama is a unique park. Although often mistaken for part of the Kokubunji Cliff, this set of three rounded hills is actually an isolated section of an old series of hill lands, the rest of which has eroded away. The top of the hills are only about eighty meters above sea level and some thirty meters above the surrounding plain, yet the slopes are covered entirely with secondary oak woodland, much of which is still maintained as working coppice forest in the traditional manner.

Late January or early February is a good time to visit Sengenyama. You are almost sure to meet local farmers raking in leaves and hauling them off in immense basket-style backpacks. The leaves are mixed with rice bran (*nuka*) and allowed to ferment for a year or so, after which the mixture is used as compost in upland fields and seedling soil for vegetables such as tomatoes, cucumbers, and eggplants. About twenty farmers have concessions to collect the leaves in different sections of the park.

Throughout the park are many fine examples of coppiced oaks, hornbeams, and cherries, some with newly cut trunks that are already starting to grow back with double or triple trunks. Piles of cut oak trunks and branches can also be seen here and there. These are destined for use as a base for cultivating *shiitake* mushrooms.

Sengenyama Park is especially famous for its *musashi kisuge*, light orange-yellow day lilies that bloom from mid- to late May. These rare plants are considered an endemic subspecies of the famous *nikkō kisuge* day lilies found at Nikkō, Oze, and other alpine areas.

ACCESS: A long walk (twenty-five minutes) from Tamabochi-mae Station on the Seibu Tamagawa Line (one stop after Shin-koganei). If you keep the Tama Cemetery on your right you will run right into Sengenyama Park.

❖ 2–24–1 Tamachō, Fuchū-shi, Tokyo 東京都府中市多磨町2–24–1

JINDAI BOTANICAL PARK （神代植物公園 ✳ Jindai Shokubutsu Kōen）

SEE MAP 5

The Jindai Botanical Park is one of the most popular destinations for Tokyo-area amateur botanists and flower enthusiasts. As a botanical park rather than a formal garden, the sections are laid out in a clearly defined, easy-to-use pattern. Ornamentals, for example, are displayed in separate gardens for roses, tree peonies, azaleas, bush clovers, cherries, plums, wisterias, magnolias, flowering dogwoods, and camellias. Jindai's collection of azaleas and rhododendrons is especially rich. While most gardens concentrate on stunning visual displays, Jindai focuses on presenting a wide array of different species and varieties, with all specimens separated for ease of access and labeled for easy identification and study.

The park also features special sections devoted to conifers and bamboos and a superb stretch of native oak and hornbeam woodland. Some of the trees in this section have been coppiced with two or three trunks.

In winter, just before the plum buds start to open, flower enthusiasts look for wintersweet (*rōbai*). These unusual trees, native to China, are covered with spectacular waxy yellow flowers that emit a sweet bouquet. The blossoms open wide in the morning but start to close in the afternoon.

Jindai is also equipped with an immense greenhouse packed with tropical and desert plants. One section is devoted entirely to begonias and another to orchids. Pools display a wide variety of tropical water lilies. One pool re-creates a subtropical coastal intertidal forest, providing visitors an opportunity to see some of the mangrove trees native to Japan's Ryūkyū Islands.

The park is situated at the edge of the Musashino Uplands, just above the Tachikawa Terrace and the Nogawa River. From the park's southeast entrance (Jindai-ji Gate), the land drops off very steeply into the precincts of Jindai-ji temple, a Tendai sect Buddhist temple, said to have been founded in the early eighth century. The temple is built right into the cliff and is surrounded by venerable cryptomerias and pines.

Inside the temple grounds, just to the right of the main temple building, stands a magnificent soapberry tree. In midwinter, the tree is bare of leaves, but the branches are decorated with thousands of yellow-orange fruit the size of large marbles. The outer rind of these fruits contain a chemical substance called saponin, which produces a froth when beaten. These fruit were once used as a natural detergent for washing clothes. Inside each fruit is a single hard, round, black seed, which forms the core of the feathered birdie used in *hanetsuki*, a traditional badminton-like game with wooden paddles played during the New Year.

As is often the case in Japan, Jindai-ji temple is situated around a natural water seep. Water seeping out of the slope is collected in a small holding pond, then sent down to the Nogawa River in moss-covered stone channels. Just below the temple is an area where the seep overflow has created a small marsh, which is now managed by the Jindai Botanical Park as an aquatic plant garden and reserve.

Across the street from the main entrance is a separate section of the park devoted to perennials. Again, layout and labeling makes this a superb field for amateur botanists to expand their knowledge and field experience. A small botanical study room, *midori no sōdanjo*, contains botanical specimens, books, and field guides. There is usually a ranger on duty who can answer questions and show you how to identify plants.

ACCESS: The best way to get to Jindai Botanical Park is to take the Keiō Line to Tsutsujigaoka Station. Go out the north exit (*kita-guchi*) and turn left to the bus loading area. The bus costs ¥200 and takes about fifteen minutes. The park can also be reached by bus from Mitaka, Kichijōji, or Fuchū stations on the JR Chūō Line. Open 9:30 to 16:30, except Mondays and days following national holidays. The entrance fee is ¥500 yen for adults and ¥200 for junior high school students. Children of elementary school age and younger and seniors over sixty-five enter free. There is a small coffee shop in the park, and the Jindai-ji temple neighborhood is famous for *Jindaiji soba* noodles. ☎ (0424) 83–2300.

❖ 5–3–10 Jindaiji Motomachi, Chōfu-shi, Tokyo
東京都調布市深大寺元町5–3–10

KINUTA PARK (砧公園 ✳ Kinuta Kōen)

SEE MAPS 5 AND 12

Kinuta Park is located along the eastern edge of the uplands, overlooking the valley of the Sengawa River, which joins the Nogawa just before it empties into the Tama. The park is famous for its magnificent specimens of magnolias (*kobushi*), located near the small kiosk in the center of the park. Flower enthusiasts flock here in early April to enjoy the immense white blossoms.

In the northern corner of the park is an area set aside as a bird sanctuary. Just to the north of the bird sanctuary is a mixed forest of deciduous and broadleaved evergreen trees, while directly east is an excellent secondary woodland. Bicycles can be borrowed free of charge.

ACCESS: The park is about a ten-minute walk from Yōga Station on the Tōkyū Shin Tamagawa Line.

❖ 1–1 Kinuta Kōen, Setagaya-ku, Tokyo 東京都世田谷区砧公園1–1

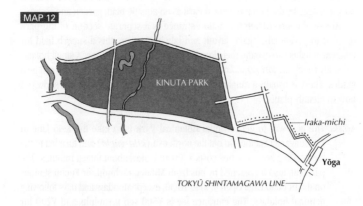

TAMAGAWA AQUEDUCT
(玉川上水緑道 ＊ Tamagawa Jōsui Ryokudō)

SEE MAPS 6 AND 13
One problem facing the first Tokugawa shoguns was how to secure an abundant supply of fresh water. The local wells and natural seeps along the Yamanote *yato* valleys simply did not produce enough water to meet the needs of the entire city. To alleviate the water shortage, the shoguns designed and built a clever system of aqueducts.

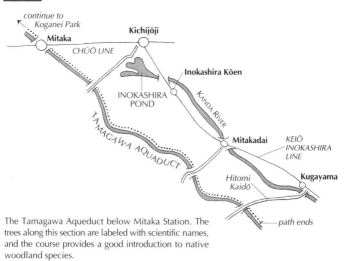

MAP 13

The Tamagawa Aqueduct below Mitaka Station. The trees along this section are labeled with scientific names, and the course provides a good introduction to native woodland species.

The most ambitious water suppy project was the Tamagawa Aqueduct, completed in 1654. This aqueduct drew off water from the Tama River and sent it forty-three kilometers to Shinjuku. The aqueduct had to flow across the relatively level Musashino Uplands, and its completion is considered a great feat of engineering for those days, when accurate surveying equipment was not available.

In the postwar years, the Tamagawa Aqueduct was abandoned, but in the mid 1980s much of its length was restored and refurbished as a long walking course. Both sides of the waterway are heavily wooded with oaks (*kunugi* and *konara*), dogwoods, hornbeams, wild cherries, snowbells, zelkovas, hackberries, and most other native broadleaved trees. The trees are labeled throughout in Japanese characters, but in the stretches around Inokashira Park the labels have scientific names as well. Forest birds such as tits and pygmy woodpeckers, as well as spot-billed ducks and common kingfishers, are common. The slopes of the aqueduct, which are fenced off from the walking paths, is a superb habitat for violets and other tiny wildflowers.

One way to start exploring the Tamagawa Aqueduct is to walk either upstream or down after visiting Inokashira Park. Mitaka Station on the JR Chūō Line is another popular access point. From there the route passes by Yachō no Mori Park, with a fine stand of red pines, and runs along the southern edge of Koganei Park.

Many walkers start off further upstream at Higashi Yamatoshi or Tamagawa Jōsui stations on the Seibu Haijima Line. Right next to Higashi Yamatoshi Station is the Tokyo Metropolitan Medicinal Plant Garden, a unique ethnobotanical park with sections covering plants used in traditional Japanese folk medicine, Chinese herbal medicine, and natural cloth dyes. For those interested in the mysterious and occult, there is a special garden full of poisonous plants and even a section, double-fenced with high pointed spikes, with hemps and poppies.

A little more than thirty kilometers of the aqueduct are currently open to walkers. The aqueduct connects with several other long-distance walking and cycling courses, such as the path that runs out to the Sayama Hills (discussed in the entry on Koganei Park). This network of paths allows serious walkers to really stretch their legs.

Access: See directions for Inokashira Park and Koganei Park.

　　　1–13–1 Sekino-chō, Koganei-shi, Tokyo

❖ 東京都小金井市関野町1–13–1

TODOROKI GORGE (等々力渓谷 ✳ Todoroki Keikoku)

See maps 5 and 14

This narrow, steep-sided valley is one section of the Yazawa River, a short tributary of the Tama River with its source up around Kinuta Park. The Todoroki Keikoku is at the downstream end of the river, where it cuts through the last sections of the Musashino Uplands before flowing out onto the plain of the Tama River.

Wooden and stone paths lead along the bottom of the slope and are often wet with water oozing out of the valley sides. The slopes are covered with a dense woodland, including many native alders, oaks, elms, dogwoods, and cherries. At the downstream end of the park, at the base of a set of stairs leading up to the Todoroki Fudō temple, is a small waterfall, still used by pilgrims in purification ceremonies.

The grounds of the temple, on top of the uplands along the eastern side, are also beautifully wooded, with a small holding pond. All in all, a good place to cool off in summer.

Access: The northern entrance to the park is just a three-minute walk from Todoroki Station on the Tōkyū Ōimachi Line. The distance involved here is not great, but there is a lot to see, so figure on at least two hours out and back.

❖ 1 Todoroki, Setagaya-ku, Tokyo 東京都世田谷区等々力1

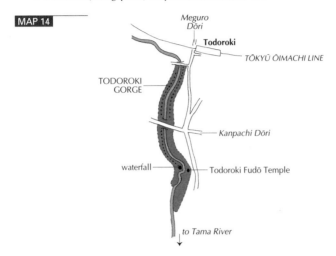

TAMAGAWADAI PARK (多摩川台公園 * Tamagawadai Kōen)

Sᴇᴇ ᴍᴀᴘ 5

Tamagawadai Kōen is situated along the edge of the Musashino Uplands, overlooking the Tama River. This heavily wooded park is actually built on several immense barrow tombs (*kofun*). The keyhole shape of the tombs is clearly visible. Some parts of the park are wooded with broadleaved evergreens, while others show typical deciduous woodland trees. Look for cattails in the small water garden, abundant *yama yuri* summer lilies, and flocks of rose-ringed parakeets. As mentioned in the chapter on birds, these big green beauties, with reddish beaks and neck rings, were originally kept as pets. Some birds escaped, while others were released when their owners could no longer care for them. The naturalized flock is now breeding in the park.

Access: The park is a ten-minute walk from Tamagawaen Station on the Tōkyū Tōyoko or Tōkyū Mekama Line.

❖ 1–63–1 Denenchōfu, Ōta-ku
東京都大田区田園調布1–63–1

AKATSUKA PARK (赤塚公園 ＊ Akatsuka Kōen)

SEE MAP 15

Located in the northern part of the Musashino Uplands, this park is really a network of parkland, shrine, and temple sites, along with a historical and art museum, each interesting in its own right.

The main (northern) section of the park is a long, narrow slope that parallels the Shuto Expressway No. 5. The slope is heavily wooded, with good groves of oaks (*konara* and *kunugi*), hornbeams, snowbells, and hackberries. Among these are many typical broadleaved evergreens and some fine Japanese horse chestnuts. The area at the base of the slope is fenced off, serving as a sanctuary for native anemones.

In the northwest section of the complex is a rise that once supported a small castle. Although little of the castle remains, the slope here is heavily forested with oaks and hornbeams. At the base of the slope is a small holding pond and the

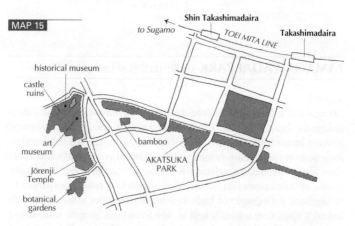

An explorer's map for the Akatsuka Park area. There is more than enough here to merit a full day of strolling around. The little botanical park is a true gem.

Itabashi Ward art and history museums. Behind (south of) these is a slope with a fine stand of broadleaved evergreens, Jōren-ji temple (with an enormous statue of Buddha said to be the largest in the city), and finally the Akatsuka Botanical Gardens. These small grounds are packed with local trees, including Musashino woodland species, fruit trees, and a fine collection of Japanese conifers. A separate garden, a favorite with local haiku poets, is devoted to plants noted in the *Man'yōshū*. Next to the office is a small room with books and specimens.

ACCESS: Best access is from Shin Takashimadaira Station on the Toei Mita Line. The botanical gardens are open every day from 9:00 to 16:30 (16:00 from December through February). Admission is free.

❖ 3–1 Takashimadaira, Itabashi-ku, Tokyo
東京都板橋区高島平3–1

MAKINO MEMORIAL GARDENS
(牧野記念庭園 ＊ Makino Kinen Teien)

SEE MAP 16

For amateur naturalists and botanists, the trek out to the Makino Memorial Gardens is more of a pilgrimage than an expedition. Makino Tomitarō is considered to be the founding father of modern botany in Japan. His long years of indefatigable field research and accurate and detailed but still highly attractive drawings, have inspired several generations of Japanese plant lovers.

Makino was born in 1862 into a wealthy family of saké brewers living on the island of Shikoku. From early childhood, he was fascinated with plants, collecting and studying species in the mountains behind his home. In 1881, young Makino left his home island for Tokyo, hoping to obtain books on botany, a microscope, and other instruments that he needed to continue and expand his hobby.

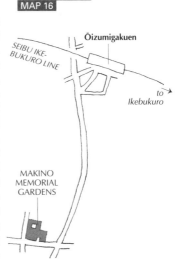

MAP 16

This was an exciting time for the natural sciences in Japan. Throughout most of Japanese history, botany was closely related to medicine and horticulture. Scholars studied plants for their value as medicinal herbs or worked to develop new varieties of vegetables, fruit, and ornamental flowers. After the Meiji Restoration of 1867, interest in the natural sciences began growing at an explosive pace. To young Makino, Tokyo in 1881 must have seemed like a veritable fairyland of new ideas and opportunities.

From that moment on, Makino began to devote his life to botany. He trekked all over Japan in search of specimens, climbing mountains to study rare alpine plants and often venturing out on unstable cliffs to make a vital observation or collection. Makino also devoted long hours to making detailed yet attractive sketches of the plants he collected. When put together, these formed some of the most thorough and beautiful field guides in the world. The *Makino Field Guides*, in both standard and handy pocket versions, are still immensely popular today.

The Makino Memorial Gardens are located at the site where Makino lived from 1926 until his death in 1957. The gardens are tiny but packed with an amazing 340 species of trees and herbaceous plants. Some of these are rare species that Makino transplanted to his garden so that he might observe them at his leisure. Makino's study is preserved as it was when he worked here, and a small museum houses the implements he used in collecting and analyzing plants as well as some fine examples of his sketches.

Access: The gardens, managed by Nerima Ward, are a ten-minute walk from Ōizumigakuen Station on the Seibu Ikebukuro Line. Hours run from 9:00 to 17:00 (closed Tuesdays). Admission is free.

❖ 6–34–4 Higashi Ōizumi, Nerima-ku, Tokyo
東京都練馬区東大泉6–34–4

RINSHI NO MORI PARK (林試の森公園 ✽ Rinshinomori Kōen)

See map 17

For nearly eighty years, this park was a research station operated by the Forestry Agency. Trees from different parts of Japan as well as foreign countries were raised here. The research station has been moved to Mount Tsukuba, but the great diversity of trees now make the park a prime destination for amateur botanists. In addition to all the common street and park trees, many native species appear with labels for easy study. A special feature is the placement of all of the difficult evergreen oaks in one convenient spot. Abundant trees from Europe and America, including maples, oaks, ashes, and even California redwoods, attract both Japanese fans looking for something exotic and expatriates seeking a nostalgic taste of their native fauna.

ACCESS: Slightly off the beaten track and rarely visited by tourists, Rinshi no Mori Park is a ten-minute walk from Musashi Koyama Station on the Tōkyū Mekama Line. Nearby Meguro Fudōson (ten-minute walk from Fudō-mae Station) is also a heavily forested oasis worth a side trip. Those confident using local maps can walk from Meguro Station on the JR Yamanote Line, stopping to enjoy the Meguro River on the way.

❖ 5 Shimo Meguro, Meguro-ku, Tokyo 東京都目黒区下目黒 5 丁目

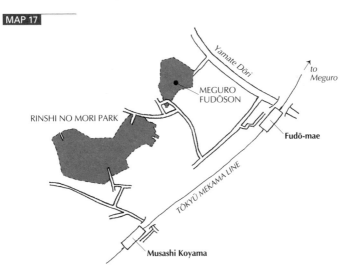

MAP 17

Rinshi no Mori Park and the Meguro Fudōson temple. The park, although a little difficult to find, is a must stop for tree lovers. More confident explorers can walk from Meguro Station, crossing the Meguro River.

THE SHITAMACHI LOWLANDS
The Alluvial Plain

Tokyo's alluvial plain is a flat, low-lying region, only a meter or so above sea level, that stretches from the cliffs of Ueno eastward to the Shimōsa Uplands of Chiba Prefecture. This flatland is actually the delta, or flood plain, created where two major river systems, the Ara and the Tone, deposit their sediments as they slow down on the approach to Tokyo Bay.

The Ara River has its source deep in the Chichibu Mountains of western Saitama Prefecture, while the Tone starts even further to the north, in the Mikuni Mountains along the boundary between Gunma and Niigata prefectures. These two great rivers are responsible for creating the Kantō Plain, one of Japan's largest and most fertile lowlands.

Today, the Tone River flows eastwards, picks up the Kinu River flowing down from the Nikkō Mountains in Tochigi Prefecture, then empties into the Pacific Ocean near the port of Chōshi. Historians, however, believe that the Tone originally flowed southward and emptied into Tokyo Bay. The commonly accepted theory is that around the middle of the seventeenth century, the shogun's engineers dug a long canal, diverting the course of the Tone into what was then a tributary of the Kinu (see map 1).

Japanese historians are justly proud of the shogun's civil engineering accomplishments. They like to point out that, in contrast to today's ill-conceived pork-barrel–style public works construction, the shoguns' projects were always well thought out in advance and often produced multiple benefits.

The diversion of the Tone is a typical example. One reason for this project was to reduce the amount of water flowing down into the alluvial delta area. Like most river deltas, the Tokyo alluvials were really seasonal marshlands that flooded during the heavy rains of spring and summer. By diverting the waters of the Tone eastward, the government was able to control this flooding to some degree.

Another major benefit of this project was to establish a river transport network for bringing goods from the northern regions of Tōhoku and Hokkaidō to Edo (present-day Tokyo). Originally, coastal sailing vessels bound for the shogun's capital had to sail south, round the Sunosaki Cape at the tip of the Bōsō Peninsula, then work their way northward through the Strait of Uraga and on into

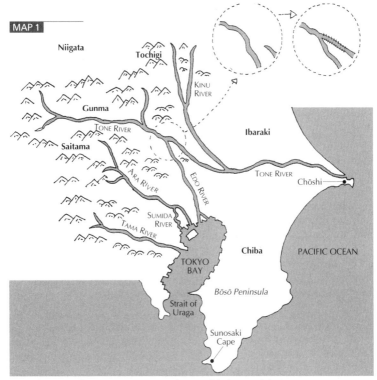

The Ara and Tone river systems, with a simplified view of the Tone River diversion at upper right.

Tokyo Bay. This route around the cape was not only time consuming but a dangerous maneuver, as the waters off the southern Bōsō are known for their treacherous winds and currents.

With the new river system, sailing vessels could dock at Chōshi port, where their cargo was transshipped to sleek river crafts that could be sailed up the Tone, then down the Edo, and finally across the canals to the landing wharfs of the capital. Small stopover and supply ports, called *kashi*, sprung up along the rivers at intervals of a day's travel. This water transport system flourished throughout the Edo period and even into the Meiji Period.

Another typical multiple-benefit project was the canal dug through the tip of the Hongō Uplands, diverting the Kanda River eastward into the Sumida (map 2). Again, one reason for this project was flood control, especially in the low-lying

MAP 2

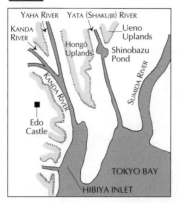

The drawing at left shows the lower alluvial plain when the shogun first took over Edo Castle, around the start of the seventeenth century. The Kanda River empties into the head of the Hibiya Inlet (approximately the area from current-day Marunouchi to Yūrakuchō). The drawing at right shows the same area a few decades later, when the Kanda River was diverted eastward to the Sumida and the Hibiya Inlet was filled in. The lower stretches of the original Kanda form the basis for a network of canals and wharves. The Shakujii River was also diverted further to the north and, by this time, no longer flowed into the bay.

areas just below Edo Castle. As was noted in the Yamanote chapter, the diverted Kanda also served as a portion of the Outer Moat, completing the castle defenses.

Moreover, the silt obtained from digging the canal was used to fill in the shallows just east of the castle. When the shogun first moved into Edo Castle, there was a long arm of Tokyo Bay, called the Hibiya Inlet, that reached northward along the edge of the high ground upon which the castle was built. The shogun filled this inlet with dirt from the canal and used the original lower course of the Kanda (later renamed the Nihonbashi River) as the base for a network of canals and wharfs leading in from Tokyo Bay. Seagoing vessels coming up the bay were unloaded in the offing and their goods transshipped up the canals to the landing wharfs.

In the first decades of the Edo period, the common people lived on the alluvial plain between the uplands and the Sumida. This area is the original Shitamachi, or "Low City." As the city grew the Shitamachi spread across the river, where people lived and worked along an expanding network of canals (map 3).

The most vital of these eastern canals was the Onagi, which lead eastward, almost paralleling the coast and connecting the city with the Edo River. This canal was originally dug to carry salt from Gyōtoku to the castle and later became a part of the Tone-Edo water transport system.

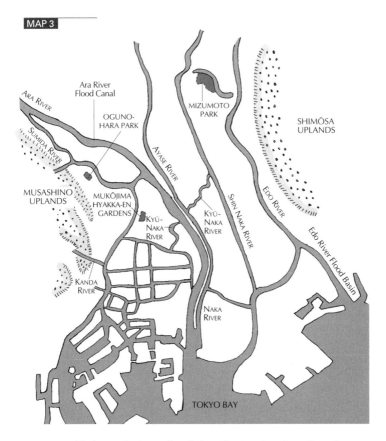

MAP 3

A simplified map of Tokyo's alluvial plain. The rivers have been diverted and rerouted so much that it is almost impossible to guess their original formation. Here and there a section of river with sinuous curves, such as the Kyū-Naka River, preserves its native shape. Keep in mind that the wide body of water called the Ara river is a flood control canal excavated early in this century. Most of this water originally flowed through the Sumida, which was a much bigger river than it is today.

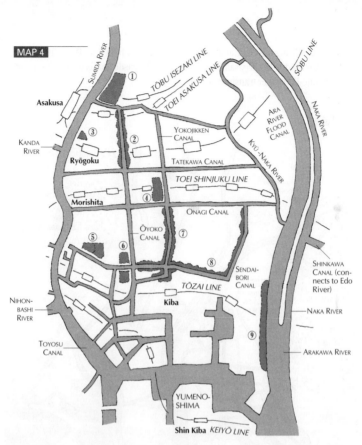

MAP 4

SUMIDA RIVER

① TOBU ISEZAKI LINE

Asakusa

TOEI ASAKUSA LINE

SŌBU LINE

NAKA RIVER

YOKOJIKKEN CANAL

ARA RIVER FLOOD CANAL

③

②

KANDA RIVER

KYŪ-NAKA RIVER

Ryōgoku

TATEKAWA CANAL

TOEI SHINJUKU LINE

Morishita

④

ONAGI CANAL

ŌYOKO CANAL

⑦

⑤

⑥

⑧

SENDAI-BORI CANAL

SHINKAWA CANAL (connects to Edo River)

TŌZAI LINE

Kiba

NIHON-BASHI RIVER

NAKA RIVER

TOYOSU CANAL

⑨

ARAKAWA RIVER

YUMENO-SHIMA

Shin Kiba KEIYŌ LINE

An explorer's map of the eastern Shitamachi canals today. Following the waterways is the best way to familiarize yourself with this area. Many of the canals have been turned into waterside parks. The following numbered sites are marked on the map:

1 Sumida Park. Urban parkland along the Sumida River. The western side is famous for cherry blossoms.

2 Ōyokogawa Waterside Park. Greenery and waterside habitats along a walking path.

3 Kyū-Yasuda Gardens. Formal Japanese Gardens.

4 Sarue Park. Expansive urban parkland.

5 Kiyosumi Park and Kiyosumi Gardens. See separate entry in this chapter.

6 Kiba Park. Urban parkland.

7 Yokojikken-gawa Waterside Park. Greenery and waterside habitats along a walking path.

8 Sendaibori-gawa Waterside Park. Greenery and waterside habitats along a walking path.

9 Arakawa Sunamachi Riverside Park. Open parkland along the Arakawa River.

The Tokugawa shoguns were always a bit paranoid and thus were not particularly fond of bridges. As a result, both goods and people moved through the Shitamachi by boat. The residents of the Yamanote walked up and down their hills, but the Shitamachi burghers truly lived in the "Venice of the Orient."

Today, the eastern canals have lost most of their original function. In fact, due to land subsidence, much of the eastern Shitamachi is actually below the level of Tokyo Bay and must be protected from flooding by a system of water gates. Still, many of the canals now have walking courses along much of their length, and others have been converted into waterside parks.

The rich native wetland habitats of the alluvial plain have mostly disappeared, and most of the greenery is in the form of urban parks, such as Hibiya Park and Sarue Park, or formal gardens, such as the Kyū-Yasuda, Kiyosumi, Hamarikyū, and Kyū-Shibarikyū gardens. Mizunomoto Park does preserve some superb wetland habitats, and the Ogunohara Park along the Sumida is a happy surpise, full of dragonflies and aquatic plants (map 4).

MIZUMOTO PARK (水元公園 ✳ Mizumoto Kōen)

SEE MAPS 3 AND 5
Mizumoto Park is the best spot to get a feeling for the rich wetland habitats that once covered the alluvial plain. The main park is built around a large pond, called Koai-dame, that was dug in 1729 to both prevent flooding and provide irrigation water to the surrounding rice paddies. Narrow canals lead from the Koai-dame into various sections of the park, creating typical wetland habitats, such as reed beds, iris gardens, lotus and water-lily ponds, cattail marshes, willow thickets, and alder forests. These habitats are ideal for studying wetland plants, waterfowl, frogs, and dragonflies.

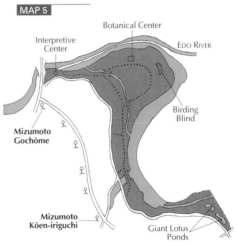

Mizumoto Park. Only the widest strolling paths are shown. This is an extensive park where children can play all day long.

The park has a small nature center at the eastern corner and a botanical study center a little bit to the west. The northwestern section of the park along the Koaidame is set aside as a wildbird reserve. Wooden blinds with observation slits allow watchers to look out on a marsh and pond. In addition to various ducks, look for little grebes and common kingfishers. Muskrats, brought from America as fur-bearers, have also naturalized in the pond and can sometimes be seen from the observation point.

Other features include a sizable grove of metasequoia dawn redwoods and a series of small experimental ponds, located in the southern corner, in which giant lotus plants are being raised. The flowers bloom in midsummer and the stalks thrust right through the huge, floating leaves.

ACCESS: Take the JR Jōban or Keisei Kanamachi line to Kanamachi Station. Board a bus and get off at either Mizumoto Kōen Iriguchi or Mizumoto-gochōme.

❖ 3–2 Mizumoto Kōen, Katsushika-ku, Tokyo 東京都葛飾区水元公園3–2

OGUNOHARA PARK (尾久の原公園 ✳ Ogunohara Kōen)

SEE MAPS 3 AND 6

This park is a little-known gem right along the Sumida River. The site was originally a chemical factory built in 1917 to manufacture caustic soda. In the early 1970s, the factory was found to be discharging dangerous levels of mercury into the Sumida, and the operations were eventually moved to more modern and efficient facilities in Chiba Prefecture. The land was purchased by the city, and the factory itself was torn down. The natural habitat was allowed to reassert itself, eventually giving

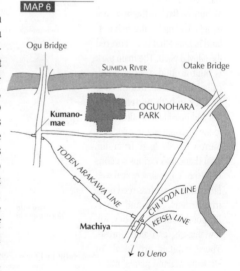

way to a superb ecosystem. Grassy meadows, dotted with shallow marshes, support an amazing variety of butterflies and dragonflies. This small but ecologically rich park is a tribute to nature's ability to rejuvenate when given half a chance.

Access: The park is a little hard to find. Getting there requires a twenty-minute walk from Machiya Station on the Keisei or Chiyoda Line. Or take the Toden Arakawa (trolley) Line to Kumano-mae for a shorter five-minute jaunt.

❖ 7–1 Higashi Ogu, Arakawa-ku, Tokyo 東京都荒川区東尾久7–1

MUKŌJIMA HYAKKA-EN GARDENS
(向島百花園 ✳ Mukōjima Hyakka-en)

See maps 3 and 7

Flower and horticulture enthusiasts, as well as amateur botanists, will definitely want to take a trip out to see these gardens. Local specialties here include the "seven herbs of spring," a group of young shoots and new leaves traditionally eaten in gruel on January 7; and the "seven flowers of autumn," which are based on a poem in the *Man'yōshū*, a collection of ancient verses written in the eighth century and earlier. Among the autumn flowers are *susuki* plume grasses, which make a nice contrast with the apartment buildings bordering the park. The gardens also include a small collection of early spring perennials and a bush clover "tunnel," where autumn visitors can stroll right through a long tube of purple peaflowers.

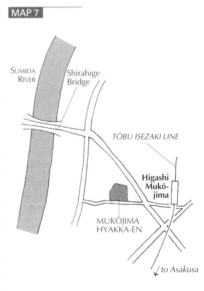

Unlike most of Tokyo's formal gardens, the Mukōjima Hyakka-en was not originally a daimyō estate but was instead built by literate commoners in the early nineteenth century. In addition to the flowers and insects, there are moon-viewing parties during the full moons of autumn, and insect-listening gatherings in late summer, when participants learn to identify and appreciate the songs of various cicadas, crickets, and katydids.

Access: The park is an eight-minute walk from Higashi Mukōjima Station on the Tōbu Isezaki Line, which departs from Asakusa. Open every day, 9:00 to 17:00 (except December 29 to January 3). Entrance is ¥150. ☎ (03) 3611–8705.

❖ 3 Higashi Mukōjima, Sumida-ku, Tokyo 東京都墨田区東向島3

HIBIYA PARK (日比谷公園 ∗ Hibiya Kōen)

SEE MAP 3 IN THE YAMANOTE CHAPTER

Just across the street from the Hibiya Moat is Hibiya Park. Although not very large or wild, the importance of this expanse of greenery is exaggerated by its location. Squeezed in between the shopping and tourist attractions of the Ginza-Hibiya area and the government offices of Kasumigaseki, Hibiya Park is one of the most heavily used public parks in the city.

During the Edo period, this area was a manor belonging to the Matsudaira clan. After the Meiji Restoration of 1867, it was used as an army training field. In 1902, the space was opened as one of Japan's first western-style public parks. Today, with two lakes and over four thousand trees belonging to 170 species, the park attracts naturalists as well as tourists and harried workers.

Shinji Pond, at the Ginza corner of the park, is home to spot-billed ducks and *shiokara* dragonflies. Japanese toads breed here in late March, and little egrets occasionally stop by to try their luck at small fish. In the area behind and around the large rectangular flower bed near the fountain, you can learn to distinguish among the elms and zelkovas as well as the three species of plane tree. A maze of narrow, winding paths surrounds Unkei Pond. These paths are seldom crowded and are planted with a great variety of Japanese and foreign trees. In the corner of the park opposite the Hibiya shopping district is a botanical study room (Green Salon), which has exhibits and specimens that help visitors identify the park trees and flowers. The second floor holds a well-stocked library, with some books and free pamphlets in English.

Access: See directions for Inner Moat.

❖ Hibiya Kōen, Chiyoda-ku, Tokyo 東京都千代田区日比谷公園

HAMARIKYŪ GARDENS (浜離宮恩賜庭園 ✳ Hamarikyū Onshi Teien)

SEE MAP 8

These beautiful gardens are located along the coast just below Shinbashi Station. They were originally constructed in the mid-seventeenth century and served as a sort of seaside holiday resort for the shoguns and their relatives, who enjoyed tea ceremonies and falconry around the landscaped ponds. At the start of the eighteenth century, the sixth shogun made some major additions and improvements and planted a black pine in commemoration of the work. This pine still stands today, just to the left inside the gate, and is one of the most magnificent specimens in the country, with long, spreading branches that swoop nearly to the ground. Be sure to take a few minutes to study and appreciate this tree from botanical, aesthetic, and spiritual standpoints.

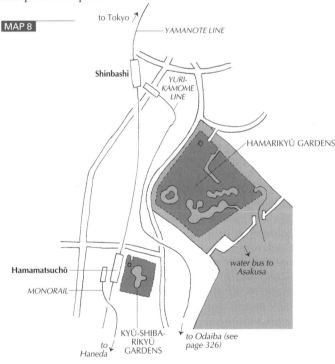

Locations of Hamarikyū Gardens and Kyū-Shibarikyū Gardens

These gardens are well stocked with trees and flowers, and are especially famous for their rape blossoms and peonies, which bloom in spring. Throughout the grounds are fine specimens of the Machilus laurel which, along with the black pine, is a stalwart of southern Japan's native coastal forests.

One of the ponds has an outlet to the sea and tide and is a good spot to look for great gray herons and great egrets fishing in the shallows. The other ponds are set up for duck hunting. After the Meiji Restoration of 1867, the gardens were turned over to the Imperial Family. Emperor Meiji and his guests engaged in a very peculiar method of hunting ducks. Narrow, steep-sided canals were dug around the edges of the pond, where domestic ducks were kept and fed. Attracted by the seemingly happy domestic birds, wild ducks also moved into the canals and were then scooped up with nets! The canals have been reconstructed, along with little blinds where hunters can keep a watch on the ducks through narrow slits in the wall. After the war, the grounds were donated to the Tokyo government, and today they are managed as public gardens.

Access: Hamarikyū Gardens are a fifteen-minute walk from Shinbashi Station on the Toei-Asakusa subway and JR Yamanote and Keihin Tōhoku lines. Open every day, 9:00 to 17:00 (except December 29 to January 3). The entrance fee is ¥300. ☎ (03) 3541–0200.

❖ 1–1 Hamarikyū Teien, Chūō-ku, Tokyo 東京都中央区浜離宮庭園1–1

KYŪ-SHIBARIKYŪ GARDENS
(旧芝離宮恩賜庭園 ✳ Kyū-Shibarikyū Onshi Teien)

Sᴇᴇ ᴍᴀᴘ 8

This small but superbly laid-out park consists of a pond surrounded by a typical formal stroll garden. Famous scenic spots from Japan and China are re-created in miniature. Although popular mostly with garden and flower enthusiasts (several venerable wisteria vines decorate a trellis just inside the entrance), the gardens are worth a short stop if you happen to be in the Hamamatsuchō area, especially in winter, when the pond will be filled with ducks and black-headed gulls.

The Shibarikyū are one of the oldest formal gardens in the city, having been laid out on filled-in marshlands around the middle of the seventeenth century. Like the Hamarikyū, these gardens became the property of the Imperial Family before they were later donated to the city.

Access: Kyū-Shibarikyū Gardens are a few minutes' walk from JR Hamamatsuchō Station on the JR Yamanote and Keihin Tōhoku lines. Open every day from

9:00 to 17:00 (except December 29 to January 3). The entrance fee is ¥150. ☎ (03) 3434–4029.

❖ 1–4–1 Kaigan, Minato-ku, Tokyo 東京都港区海岸1–4–1

KIYOSUMI GARDENS (清澄庭園 ✳ Kiyosumi Teien)

SEE MAPS 4 AND 9

Kiyosumi Gardens are a must stop for horticulture fans and also offer some fine birdwatching, with ducks and other waterfowl in winter and flocks of azure-winged magpies all year round. The formal garden is famous for its *ishi-watari*, a path of stepping stones that runs along the edge of the pond, and a section that re-creates in miniature the scenery of the Nagatoro Gorge in western Saitama Prefecture, where the Ara River cuts a steep, rocky channel through the Chichibu Mountains. In late autumn, when the gardens' abundant maple trees are in full color, the effect is truly amazing. This is a good spot and time to really appreciate the genius of traditional Japanese garden design.

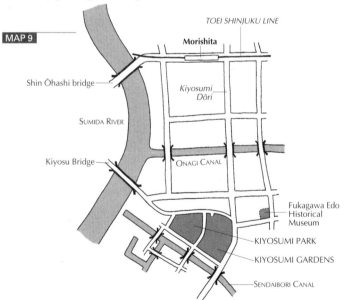

Location of Kiyosumi Gardens and eastern canals

Nearby are abundant trees at Kiyosumi Park, and the Fukagawa-Edo Historical Museum, in which life along a typical Edo-period canal has been reconstructed. The area around the eastern mouth of the Sumida is also a logical place to begin exploring the network of canals. Walkers can start here and follow either the Onagi or Sendaibori-gawa canals westward.

Access: The gardens can be reached from Morishita Station (exit A4) on the Toei Shinjuku Line or Monzen-nakachō (exit 3) on the Tōzai Line. Kiyosumi Gardens are open every day, 9:00 to 17:00 (except December 29 to January 3). The entrance fee is ¥150. ☎ (03) 3641–5892.

❖ 3–3–4 Kiyosumi, Kōtō-ku, Tokyo 東京都江東区清澄3–3–4

AROUND THE WATERFRONT

Tokyo Bay is a shallow body of water with a flat, gently sloping bottom of sand or mud. Many big rivers, including the Tama, Ara, and Tone (see the introductory section of the Shitamachi chapter), flow from the mountains down across the Kantō Plain to empty into the bay.

These rivers transport enormous loads of silt. Over thousands of years, silt carried seaward by the rivers built up huge deltas at their mouths and created incredibly rich tideland ecosystems along the coast. Until only a half-century ago, a nearly continuous ring of tidal flats and salt marshes stretched from Kawasaki on the west all the way around to Kisarazu on the east.

These tidal wetlands made Tokyo Bay one of the most productive wildlife habitats in the world. The wetlands were home to enormous banks of crabs, clams, fish, and bristleworms. Great flocks of migratory shorebirds, numbering in the hundreds of thousands or even millions, hunted on the flats at low tide. Geese, cranes, and egrets foraged among the salt marshes, and rafts of ducks and other waterfowl bobbed in the shallow offshore shoals.

The local residents of the south Kantō have also had their eyes on Tokyo Bay's abundant marine resources for thousands of years. By about five thousand years ago, the Jōmon people were collecting clams and other tidal flat resources intensively. The resources were so plentiful that these hunter-gatherers were able to live in large, settled villages. Edo, which reached a population of over one million in the early eighteenth century, depended heavily on the largess of the bay's aquatic resources. *Nigiri-zushi*, those melt-in-your-mouth morsels of seafood on vinegared rice that have conquered the world's taste-buds, were originally invented using fresh fish, clams, shrimp, and crabs from Tokyo Bay.

Today, one can only imagine what Tokyo Bay was like when its shores teemed with wildlife. Unfortunately, almost all of the tidelands fell victim to landfill schemes within a few short decades after World War II. The Keihin Industrial Zone, Haneda Airport, the entire Tokyo Port and waterfront district, Makuhari Messe, and even Disneyland are all built on landfilled tidelands.

Still, a few tattered remnant tidelands have been preserved or restored. Ironically, migratory birds now crowd into these few remaining habitats in great numbers, much as harried city workers—starved for greenery—mob Hibiya Park on weekday lunch hours. This concentration in a narrow area often makes the birds easy to locate and observe.

Clamming is also possible on several tidal flats, and the intrepid explorer can find plenty of spots for up-close hands-on study of fascinating tideland creatures such as mud crabs, sand anemones, bristleworms, and sand dollars.

MAP 1

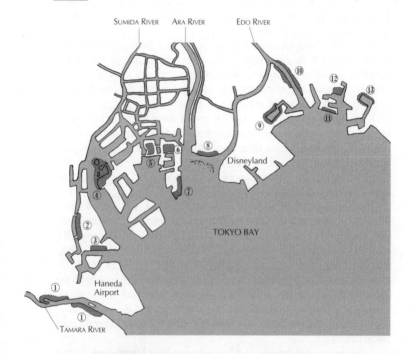

1 Tama River Mouth (Rokugō-dote)
2 Ōi Futō Chūō Seaside Park
3 Tokyo Port Wild Bird Park
4 Odaiba Marine Park
5 Tatsumi Seaside Park
6 Yumenoshima Seaside Park
7 Wakasu Seaside Park

8 Kasai Seaside Park
9 Gyōtoku Sanctuary
10 Edo River Flood Basin
11 Funabashi Seaside Park
12 Funabashi Fishing Port
13 Yatsu Tidelands

TAMA RIVER MOUTH (六郷土手 ✳ Rokugō-dote)

SEE MAPS 1 AND 2

The Tama River has its source high in the Okutama Mountains to the west of Tokyo. The river then flows southeast along the border between the Tama Hills and the Musashino Uplands, emptying into Tokyo Bay just south of Haneda Airport. The bay's tides push a few kilometers up the river, creating a brackish water environment, with scattered sections of salt marsh and mud flat. These tidelands form a small but precious wildlife habitat. In addition, this is one of the few places near central Tokyo where one can explore a salt marsh first hand.

The best place to begin exploring the Tama River tidelands is along the Rokugō-dote Bank, which stretches along the north bank of the river from Rokugō Bridge on the west to Daishi Bridge on the east. A 3.6-kilometer nature study trail runs along the edge of the reeds. There are also side trails, some with elevated wooden slats to walk on, that lead down into the marsh. The best of these are in the western part of the park, right behind the baseball fields. At high tide, the marsh is inundated with seawater, and you have to be content to watch from the edge.

Kuro benkei-gani marsh crabs are plentiful here, from late spring through midautumn, and often leave the protection of the reeds to forage on the paths and even at the edge of the fields. When threatened, they scurry back into the reeds, but they can be easily herded and cornered. Once a crab sees there is no escape, it assumes a defensive posture, with claws raised and pointed toward the towering enemy.

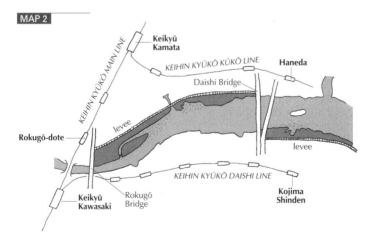

MAP 2

Keikyū Kamata

KEIHIN KYŪKŌ MAIN LINE

KEIHIN KYŪKŌ KŪKŌ LINE

Haneda

Daishi Bridge

levee

Rokugō-dote

levee

KEIHIN KYŪKŌ DAISHI LINE

Keikyū Kawasaki

Rokugō Bridge

Kojima Shinden

Deeper in the marsh, in areas that are inundated regularly by the tide, live *ashihara-gani* marsh crabs. Unlike the adventurous *kuro benkei-gani* crabs, these crabs never stray too far inland from the huge holes that they dig deep into the mud among the reed stalks.

Along the offshore edge of the reed marsh are found small patches of mud flat occupied by dense colonies of bristleworms and mud crabs, the favorite prey of sandpipers and plovers, which from late summer through spring can be seen feeding on the flat at low tide. Little egrets also hunt along the water's edge and, as the tide rises, great egrets arrive to fish the shallows. Ducks and cormorants bob in the deeper water offshore.

The Rokugō-dote nature trail ends at the foot of Daishi Bridge. If you have enough time, cross this bridge and explore the salt marshes and mud flats on the opposite (southern) downstream bank. Here the reeds grow up to the very edge of the levee, and a small sand spit, locally called Nezumi-jima (Mouse Island), sits in the middle of the river. *Kuro benkei-gani* crabs come right up on the paved bike path that runs along the top of the levee, and at low tide the flats are filled with mud crabs. Sometimes even a few mud skippers can be spotted among the reeds when the tide is out.

Access: The Rokugō-dote Bank can be accessed easily from Rokugō-dote Station on the Keihin Kyūkō Line (only local trains stop at this station, so change at Keihin Kamata if you are on an express). After completing the course, you can return from Haneda Station on the Keihin Kyūkō Line or cross over to the south bank and return from Kojima Shinden Station on the Keihin Daishi Line.

❖ Minami Rokugō, Ōta-ku, Tokyo 東京都大田区南六郷

ŌI FUTŌ CHŪŌ SEASIDE PARK
(大井ふ頭中央海浜公園 ＊ Ōi Futō Chūō Kaihin Kōen)

See map 3

Ōi Wharf (Ōi Futō) is a massive manmade island off the coast just south of Shinagawa, separated from the rest of the city by the Keihin Canal. The western edge of the wharf can be seen from the window of the monorail between Tennōzu Isle (Airu) and Ōi Keibajō-mae stations. When the tide is out, two distinct lines appear along the seawall, a whitish one on top and a blackish one below. The top line is composed of barnacles, and the black one of mussels.

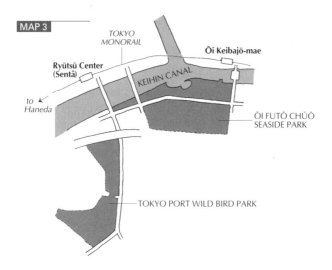

MAP 3

TOKYO MONORAIL

Ōi Keibajō-mae

Ryūtsū Center (Sentā)

KEIHIN CANAL

to Haneda

ŌI FUTŌ CHŪŌ SEASIDE PARK

TOKYO PORT WILD BIRD PARK

From Ōi Keibajō-mae Station, cross a footbridge to reach Ōi Futō Chūō Seaside Park. Start off by looking for barnacles, mussels, and crabs among the intertidal stone blocks that have been placed along the shore. Next, check out the small manmade sand flat, which is set aside as a wild bird reserve, and is thus off-limits, but can be viewed either from the main path or from inside a small observation hut equipped with a spotting scope. Look for shorebirds, gulls, ducks, cormorants, and waders. (The hut is often closed when the caretaker is making his rounds.)

A second small manmade nature reserve, containing a diverse forest and shallow freshwater pond sits just north of the observation hut. This reserve is fenced and gated, and only open during daylight hours.

Just south of the sand flat is a small beach open to the public. Look for *kefusa iso-gani* marsh crabs under stones and for barnacles covering the iron fence that separates the beach from the sand flat reserve.

Access: Take the monorail from Hamamatsuchō Station on the JR Yamanote or Keihin Tōhoku Line to Ōi Keibajō-mae Station. If time permits, continue on to the Wild Bird Park (next entry). Both of these sites can be enjoyed on a single half-day walking trip. Allow about fifteen minutes from the Seaside Park to the Wild Bird Park, then another fifteen minutes returning to Ryūtsū Center (Sentā) Station on the monorail.

❖ 4 Yashio, Shinagawa-ku, Tokyo 東京都品川区八潮 4 丁目

TOKYO PORT WILD BIRD PARK
(東京港野鳥公園 * Tokyo-kō Yachō Kōen)

SEE MAP 3

Also located on Ōi Wharf is the Tokyo Port Wild Bird Park, which is a must see for all birdwatchers and tideland explorers. The heart of this park is an impressive Observation Center, with two stories of windows that overlook a manmade tidal flat and fresh-water reed marsh. Spotting scopes line the windows, and knowledgable rangers and volunteer docents are always on hand to help visitors spot and identify the birds. The basement floor of the center allows a close-up view of the flat and is perfect for learning about crabs and other intertidal animals. Several smaller sheltered observation huts are strategically located along the paths, and the western half of the park contains a small freshwater pond and an ecology workshop.

The park is well worth a visit any time. Cormorants, common kingfishers, egrets, and herons are year-round residents. Winter is duck season and lucky observers might see a marsh harrier, or a long-eared or short-eared owl. From late summer through the following spring, shorebirds are the stars. The number of shorebird species is few in winter but increases dramatically during the spring (April–May) and autumn (late August–September) migrations. Little terns and reed warblers are common summer visitors.

ACCESS: A fifteen-minute walk from Ryūtsū Center (Sentā) Station on the monorail. Open from 9:00 to 17:00 (February to October) and 9:00 to 16:30 (November to January). Closed Mondays. ☎ (03) 3799–5031

❖ 3–1 Tōkai, Ōta-ku, Tokyo 東京都大田区東海3–1

ODAIBA MARINE PARK (お台場海浜公園 * Odaiba Kaihin Kōen)

SEE MAP 4

In the 1850s, at the very end of the Edo period, American steamships commanded by Commodore Perry were waiting off the coast of Edo. To protect his city, the shogun set about building a series of manmade islands (called *odaiba* in Japanese) to be used for cannon batteries. The original scheme called for eleven islands, but due to budget problems only five were completed. Today, Battery Islands No. 3 and No. 6 remain. Odaiba Seaside Park includes Battery Island No. 3 and a rim of sandy beach.

MAP 4

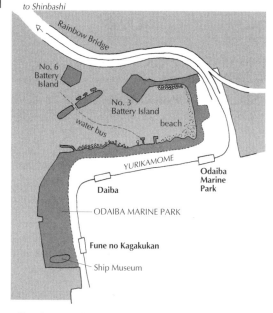

to Shinbashi

Rainbow Bridge

No. 6 Battery Island

No. 3 Battery Island

beach

water bus

YURIKAMOME

Daiba

Odaiba Marine Park

ODAIBA MARINE PARK

Fune no Kagakukan

Ship Museum

This small park is popular with sunbathers and marine recreation enthusiasts, and on summer weekends may be too crowded to enjoy. The sandy tidelands support clams and *kome-tsuki-gani* mud crabs, and birdwatching is good both on the water and on the actual battery island, which is well forested and open to the public. From summer through autumn, fishermen line the shore, casting for little gobies. These are deep-fried as tempura.

A coastal park continues around the edge of the island all the way to the Ship Musuem. Look for mullet leaping high out of the water, and for terns in summer and ducks in winter.

Access: Odaiba Park can be reached on the Yuri Kamome skyrail leaving from Shinbashi Station, or by water bus from Asakusa or the Hamarikyū Gardens. If you have the time and energy, walking across the Rainbow Bridge is a worthwhile experience. To the south of the bridge you can see Battery Island No. 6, which has recently been taken over as a roosting and nesting site by the city's large cormorant population. Abundant food stands and popular restuarants nearby.

❖ 1–4–1 Daiba, Minato-ku, Tokyo 東京都港区台場1—4—1

YUMENOSHIMA SEASIDE PARK
(夢の島海浜公園 ＊ Yumenoshima Kaihin Kōen)

TATSUMI SEASIDE PARK
(辰巳の森海浜公園 ＊ Tatsuminomori Kaihin Kōen)

WAKASU SEASIDE PARK (若洲海浜公園 ＊ Wakasu Kaihin Kōen)

SEE MAP 5

Several seaside parks have been built among the endless acres of manmade islands south of Tokyo. Most of this parkland is devoted to sports and recreational facilities, but the area is heavily planted with trees, and there are a few patches of interesting forest and coastline.

Yumenoshima (literally, "Island of Dreams") Seaside Park occupies the central position. A rich variety of park and street trees includes several species of eucalyptus, natives of Australia. The most natural area, with such native trees as *konara* oaks and Japanese alders, is tucked away in the southwest corner, between the big athletic stadium and the bridge leading over to Tatsumi Island.

A major attraction here is the Yumenoshima Tropical Greenhouse Dome, an indoor botanial garden where a tropical mood is maintained throughout the year. The immense floating leaves of giant lotus plants flourish underneath tall palms that stretch to the ceiling. One section focuses on plants of the Ogasawara Islands, a grouping found a thousand kilometers south of Tokyo. Most impressive is *tako-no-ki*, literally "octopus tree," an oddly shaped subtropical tree distinctive for its numerous adventitious roots that jut down from the trunk like the arms of an octopus. Actually, these roots allow the tree to spread out over a stretch of mountain slope. Another small section is filled with nothing but carnivorous plants with various diabolical mechanisms for trapping insects.

To the west is Tatsumi Seaside Park, divided into eastern and western sections. The eastern part features a double row of *somei yoshino* cherries, which form a tunnel of pinkish white blossoms in late April and also serve as a natural sound chamber for the abundant cicada song, which lasts well into September. The western part is more natural, with dense plantings of black pine, weeping willows, and tanbark oaks that reliably produce a heavy crop of huge acorns.

To the south is Wakasu Seaside Park, with a golf course, fishing pier, cycle rental center, and even a campground. The southern edge of the island is fitted with stone blocks that support large colonies of barnacles and mussels. A cycling-walking path runs around the golf course and along the eastern shore, and offers great vistas of Tokyo Bay. On a fine day, you can see clear across to the Bōsō Peninsula.

Access: Tatsumi and Yumenoshima seaside parks can be reached directly from Tatsumi or Shin Kiba Stations on the Yūrakuchō Line, or Shin Kiba Station on the JR Keiyō Line. Wakasu Seaside Park is a little more difficult: a bus runs out from Shin Kiba (loading platform No. 2), but there are very few departures, especially on weekends. The walk out takes about thirty minutes. The Yumenoshima Tropical Greenhouse Dome is open from 9:30 until 16:00; closed Mondays. The entrance fee is ¥250 for adults, ¥100 for junior high school student and under. ☎ (03) 3522–0281~2

❖ **Yumenoshima Seaside Park:** 3–2 Yumenoshima, Kōtō-ku, Tokyo
東京都江東区夢の島3–2

❖ **Tatsumi Seaside Park:** Tatsumi, Kōtō-ku, Tokyo 東京都江東区辰巳

❖ **Wakasu Seaside Park:** 35 Wakasu, Kōtō-ku, Tokyo 東京都江東区若洲35

MAP 5

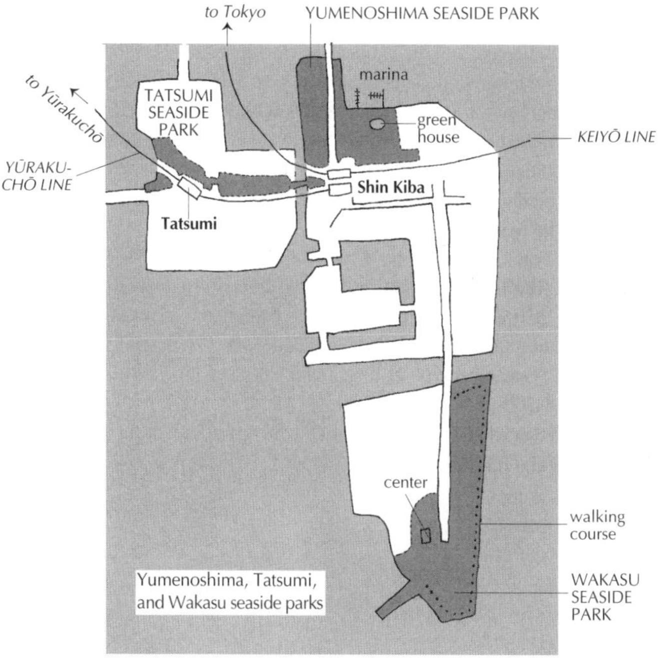

Yumenoshima, Tatsumi, and Wakasu seaside parks

KASAI SEASIDE PARK　(葛西臨海公園 ＊ Kasai Rinkai Kōen)
TOKYO SEA LIFE PARK　(葛西臨海水族園 ＊ Kasai Rinkai Suizoku-en)

SEE MAP 1

This is a huge, sprawling complex along the shore between the mouths of the Ara River Flood Control Canal and the Edo River, with plenty of spacious, open parkland, and is popular with dating couples. Two manmade sand flats have been constructed along the southern (seaward) edge. The eastern flat is closed off as a wildlife reserve, but the western flat is open to the public and is a good place to stroll while birding or looking for various burrowing clams and mud crabs.

The western part of the park features two artificial ponds, one fresh water and the other brackish. A raised bird observatory provides a strategic vantage point for observing both ponds. A walking path runs around the brackish pond and along the coast, looking across the mouth of the Edo River to Disneyland.

In the center is the Tokyo Sea Life Park, a municipal aquarium with a huge doughnut-shaped tank full of tunas and sharks (including ferocious-looking hammerheads) and various thematic exhibits, such as the Deep Sea, Antarctic Ocean, Caribbean Sea, and the Izu Islands. One upper-level exhibit is devoted to the fish of Tokyo Bay, with the popular *ma-haze* gobies and a neat collection of mud skippers. The park also has a superb exhibit of waterfowl and is deeply involved in efforts to conserve and propagate the endangered Humbolt penguin. A detached underground section provides a valuable introduction to Japanese freshwater fish and wildlife, including trout, chub, sweetfish, river crabs, and the red-bellied Japanese newt.

ACCESS: Kasai Rinkai Kōen Station on JR Keiyō Line. Tokyo Sea Life Park is open from 9:30 to 17:00; closed Mondays. Entrance is ¥700 for adults, ¥250 for junior high school students and under. ☎ (03) 3869–5152.

❖ **Kasai Seaside Park:** 6–21 Rinkai-chō, Edogawa-ku, Tokyo
東京都江戸川区臨海町6–2

❖ **Tokyo Sea Life Park:** 6–2 Rinkai-chō, Edogawa-ku, Tokyo
東京都江戸川区臨海町6–2

GYŌTOKU SANCTUARY
(行徳野鳥観察舎 ＊ Gyōtoku Yachō Kansatsusha)

SEE MAP 6

This small sanctuary, located right in the midst of congested reclaimed land between the Edo River and the Edo River Flood Control Canal, is a must stop for birding fans. The park contains both freshwater and tidal marshlands, and although the habitats themselves are normally off-limits, there is a small nature center with a wide second-floor window that over-looks the entire area. Spotting scopes are arranged along the window, and friendly and knowledgeable staff members are always on hand to provide expert guidance. Good for ducks and other waterfowl in winter, shorebirds during the migrations, and hunting raptors at any time of year. Just out-side the center is a series of cages where local birds injured in acci-dents are nursed back to health. The

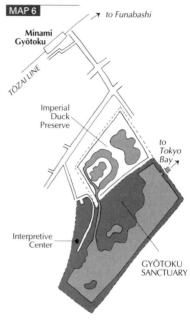

Imperial Duck Reserve is adjacent to the sanctuary but is closed to the public. Those with time left over can work their way over to the Edo River Flood Basin, where narrow tidal flats develop along the shoreline on both sides. This canal, although usually called a river, is actually an arm of the sea. The floodgates, located where the canal meets the old Edo River, are usually kept closed. Under normal conditions, the flow of the Edo River thus stays in the main channel. During heavy rains, the floodgates are opened, dumping the water directly into the bay and thus protecting the low-lying communities to the west.

ACCESS: A twenty-minute walk from Minami Gyōtoku Station on the Tōzai Line. Open from 9:00 to 16:30; closed Mondays, and the last Friday of each month. Occasional docent-led hikes are offered inside the sanctuary. ☎ (047) 397–9046.

❖ 4–22–11 Fukuei, Ichikawa-shi, Chiba 千葉県市川市福栄4–22–11

FUNABASHI SEASIDE PARK
(船橋海浜公園 ✻ Funabashi Kaihin Kōen)

SEE MAP 7

This park includes tennis courts and a huge outdoor pool but is fronted by an extensive sand flat. This is the closest place to Tokyo where one can directly explore a substantial tidal flat. Part of the flat is fenced off during the spring *shio-higari* clamming season (April 1 to June 30). During this period, you have to pay an entrance fee to dig *asari* short-neck clams, which are brought in and seeded by the truckload. The eastern part of the flat, outside the clamming areas, is always open to the public. The flat is composed of firm sand and is safe to walk across. Small *kome-tsuki-gani* mud crabs abound in the

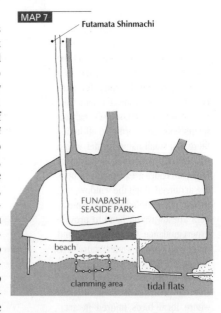

MAP 7

Futamata Shinmachi

FUNABASHI SEASIDE PARK

beach

clamming area

tidal flats

upper intertidal area, and great colonies of *tamashiki gokai* polychaete worms are found further out, along with *mamekobushi-gani* crabs and *kurogane isoginchaku* sea anemones.

To the south of the flat extends a wide stretch of shallow shoals called the Sanbanze. An ambitious and poorly formulated plan called for filling in these shoals to make another coastal subcity. This plan, which met with strong opposition from local conservationists, was fortunately scrapped in 1999. Hopefully, future plans for the Sanbanze will include environmental education facilities and extensive restoration of the salt marsh habitat.

The Sanbanze is one of Tokyo Bay's major fishing grounds. Bottom trawlers, gill netters, and purse seiners fish for sea bass, flatfish, and mullet, while smaller boats concentrate on clams. In winter, the offshore waters are filled with a veritable forest of bamboo poles. These are for hanging the nets on which *nori* (laver) is grown. The Sanbanze is the last major *nori* ground along the northern coast of the bay.

Access: A little difficult to reach by public transportation. A bus runs from the front of Funabashi Station on the JR Sōbu Line, right out to the park (get off at Funabashi Kaihin Kōen, the last stop).

❖ 40 Shiomi-chō, Funabashi-shi, Chiba 千葉県船橋市潮見町40

FUNABASHI FISHING PORT

SEE MAP 8

Although there are no natural areas in this port, a walk along the piers is worthwhile for learning about Tokyo Bay fisheries. The fishermen of Funabashi proudly trace their history back more than three hundred years, to when the shogun granted them exclusive fishing rights in return for having a portion of the catch delivered directly to his castle's kitchens. Today the men farm *nori*; scoop up *asari* and other bivalves in small metal cages that are slowly dredged through the sand; catch flounder and other fish with gill nets

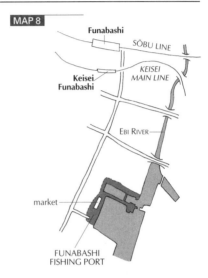

MAP 8

Funabashi

SŌBU LINE

KEISEI MAIN LINE

Keisei Funabashi

EBI RIVER

market

FUNABASHI FISHING PORT

and bottom trawls; and surround sea bass, sardines, and other free swimming fish with purse seines. The smaller boats—those outfitted, for farming *nori*, clamming, and gill netting—will be in the inner (northern) part of the harbor. A narrow pedestrian bridge spans this section of the port then leads on to the outer harbor, where the bigger vessels—bottom trawlers and purse seiners—are docked. The local wholesale fish market is also found in the outer harbor and is teeming with energy when the catch comes in.

Access: Funabashi Fishing Port is about a ten- to fifteen-minute walk due south of Funabashi Station on the JR Sōbu Line or Keisei Funabashi Station on the Keisei Main Line. If time permits, walk eastward to the Ebi River, then follow the water southward into the port. Do not touch fishing gear without permission, and when visiting the market, be careful to stay out of the way of busy trucks and forklifts.

❖ 23 Minatomachi, Funabashi-shi, Chiba 千葉県船橋市湊町23

YATSU TIDELANDS （谷津干潟 ＊ Yatsu-higata）

SEE MAP 9

The Yatsu Tidelands never cease to amaze visitors. Somehow this small wetland was left untouched in the middle of a huge expanse of landfill, surrounded on all sides by elevated freeways and densely packed residential areas. Checking the location on a map, Yatsu looks more like an inland pond than a tidal wetland. Two narrow canals maintain the vital link with Tokyo Bay, allowing the tides to enter and leave. Yatsu Tidelands is a protected site registered under the Ramsar Convention on Wetlands, an international agreement to preserve wetland habitat used by migratory birds. Indeed, when the ebbing tide leaves the flats high and dry, the mud will be packed with shorebirds, especially during the spring migration season of April and May. A spacious nature center (Kansatsu Center) overlooks the flat from the southern shore. Inside are various interactive displays introducing coastal-wetland ecology and rows of spotting scopes along the windows. Staff and volunteer docents assist visitors in finding and identifying birds.

The tidal flat itself is off-limits, but a walking path leads clear around the sanctuary. The best way to enjoy this park is to first stop off at the nature center to study ecology and learn which birds are present, then spend an hour or two circumnavigating the flat. Be sure to check out the black-necked stilts, which can usually be found in the small pond next to the nature center, and to use the scopes to observe crabs as well as birds. Especially numerous here are the large *yamato osa-gani* mud crabs and the smaller *chigo-gani*, which will put on a great dancing show during ebb tide. A large number of great egrets are usually on hand and will show off their superb fishing skills when the tide begins to flood back in.

ACCESS: The tidelands are a little difficult to reach. The best approach is a twenty-minute walk from either Minami Funabashi or Shin Narashino stations on the JR Keiyō Line. The nature center is open from 9:00 to 17:00, and closed Mondays. Entrance is ¥200 for high school students and adults, ¥100 for elementary and junior high students. ☎ (0474) 54–8416

❖ 5–1–1 Akitsu, Narashino-shi, Chiba 千葉県習志野市秋津5–1–1

MAP 9

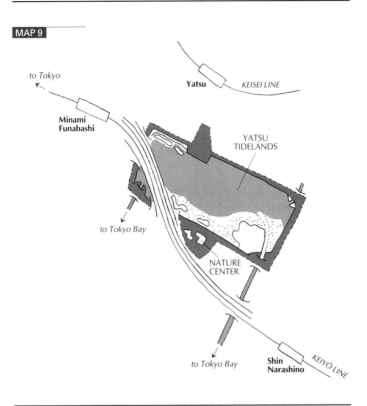

to Tokyo

Yatsu   *KEISEI LINE*

Minami
Funabashi

YATSU
TIDELANDS

to Tokyo Bay

NATURE
CENTER

to Tokyo Bay   Shin
Narashino   *KEIYŌ LINE*

GLOSSARY

Alluvial plain Low-lying plain composed of mud and sand deposited by rivers. Found along the lower reaches of the major rivers.

Alluvial sediments Mud, sand, or gravel deposited by the action of running water.

Alternate An arrangement of leaves on a stem or branch, in which the right and left leaves are attached at staggered intervals. See also Opposite.

Alternate leaves

Anaerobic Mud or water from which the oxygen has been depleted. Layers of anaerobic mud, called sludge, form in parts of Tokyo Bay, as well as at the bottom of some ponds and shallow lakes. This condition develops when large amounts of algae and other organic material pile up on the bottom and are decomposed by bacteria. The decomposition process requires oxygen, which is taken from the surrounding water, resulting in depletion.

Angiosperm A seed-bearing plant with a true flower. The seeds of these plants develop inside a protective room called the ovary, which is found at the base of the pistil. Gymnosperms, the other division of seed-bearing plants, lack an ovary, so are technically not considered to have true flowers. See also Flower, Pistil.

Anther The tip of the stamen, from which pollen is released. See also Stamen.

Arthropod A group of invertebrate animals with jointed bodies covered by a hard exoskeleton. Includes insects, spiders, scorpions, millipedes, centipedes, shrimp, and crabs. Some zoologists classify all these animals in a single phylum called the Arthropoda. Others, however, divide them into several phyla based on body structure characteristics such as number of legs.

Auxiliary bud

Auxiliary bud A bud that forms at the base of a leaf, where the leaf is attached to the branch or stem. This bud may be activated by hormones if the leaf falls off, or if the plant decides to grow a new branch from that spot. As the auxiliary bud is always located at the true base of the leaf, its position can be used to determine if a leaf is simple or compound. See Simple leaf, Compound leaf.

Aze **dike** The narrow dikes used to separate rice paddies.

Basal leaf A leaf that arises directly from the base of a plant, as opposed to leaves that are attached to the stem or branches.

Basal leaf

Broadleaved (or broadleaf) A general, rather than technical, term for trees with wide, flat leaves, as opposed to those with narrow, needlelike leaves (conifers). From the standpoint of formal taxonomy, broadleaved usually refers to trees in the gymnosperm as opposed to the angiosperm category. The ginkgo tree, however, presents an exception. This tree, because of its flower structure, is classified as a gymnosperm, but its leaves are wide and flat and look just like those of typical broadleaved trees. Be careful not to equate the terms "broadleaved" and "deciduous." Broadleaved trees may be either.

Catkin A long, thin cluster of flowers, usually hanging down from the branch.

Clasping leaf A leaf that appears to clasp or scissor the stem or branch. The base of the leaf extends backwards beyond the stem or branch.

Class A formal taxonomic category below phylum. See Taxonomy.

Climax forest The most mature and stable stage of a forest succession, as opposed to the younger or secondary stages. Also called "old growth forest."

Clasping leaf

Compound leaf A leaf that is composed of several connected blades, called leaflets, as opposed to a simple leaf, which consists of only one blade. An auxiliary bud is found at the base of the leaf, but not at the base of the individual leaflet. If the leaflets are all attached to a single node in a fingerlike pattern the leaf is a "palmate compound." Palmate compound leaves with only three leaflets are referred to as "trifoliate." If the leaves are lined up on both sides of a long axis, the leaf is a "pinnate compound." If there is a leaflet at the tip of the axis, the leaf is an "odd pinnate compound" (referring to the number of leaflets); but if there is no leaflet at the tip it is an "even pinnate compound." If the leaflets are arranged on side axes that in turn are attached to the main axis, the leaf is a "double compound." See also Simple leaf.

Compound leaf, palmate   Compound leaf, trifoliate   Compound leaf, even pinnate   Compound leaf, odd pinnate   Compound leaf, double compound

Conifer A taxonomic division of gymnosperm trees with cones that contain the seeds. Includes many familiar trees, such as pines, firs, spruces, cypresses, redwoods, and larches. Be careful not to equate this term with "evergreen." Although most conifers are evergreens, there are some, like the larch and the dawn redwood, that are deciduous.

Coppice A managed forest, usually composed mostly of deciduous oaks, in which the trees are cut down every few decades. New trunks grow straight out of the cut stumps. In Japan, these forests were managed for firewood, wood for making charcoal, leaves for compost, and logs for growing mushrooms on.

Daimyō yashiki A large manor, usually consisting of house and gardens, which each daimyo (a feudal lord) was required to build and maintain in Edo. Some of the daimyō's family members were required to live at the *daimyō yashiki*, a system that historians interpret as a sort of hostage program. Many of the large parks and gardens seen in Tokyo today were originally the grounds of the *daimyō yashiki*.

Deciduous A tree that drops its leaves in response to cold or drought, as opposed to an evergreen tree, which keeps its leaves all year round. See also Evergreen.

Dioecious A plant with imperfect flowers, where the male and female flowers are on separate plants. Each individual plant is thus either male or female. As opposed to a monoecious plant, which has separate male and female flowers blooming on the same individual plant. See also Monoecious, Flower, Imperfect flower, Perfect flower.

Dioecious male plant | Dioecious female plant

Edo The old name for Tokyo, and also for the historical period from 1600 to 1867, when Japan was ruled by the Tokugawa shoguns.

Escapee A species of plant or animal that has escaped from captivity or cultivation and naturalized (begun reproducing on its own) locally. See also Volunteer.

Exoskeleton The hard outer layer of chitin on an arthropod, secreted by glands in the skin. Once excreted the exoskeleton stays the same size, so in order to continue growing, the animal must periodically shed the old exoskeleton and secrete a new one.

Exotic A species of plant or animal that originated outside an area, but has established itself and begun reproducing locally. As opposed to native.

Evergreen A tree that keeps leaves on its branches throughout the year, as opposed to deciduous trees, which drop their leaves in response to cold or drought. Both broadleaved trees and conifers may be evergreen. See also Deciduous, Broadleaved, Evergreen.

Flower The reproductive structure of an angiosperm plant. A typical flower consists of a base, several sepals, several petals (which may be independent or fused together to form a cup or tube), stamens (the male reproductive parts), and a pistil (female reproductive part). See also Stamen, Pistil, Perfect flower, Imperfect flower.

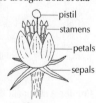

pistil
stamens
petals
sepals

Flower

Green Centers Small nature centers operated by the Tokyo municipal government in public parks. Called "*Midori no sōdanjo*" or "Green Salon" in Japanese.

Habitat The type of environment which a particular plant or animal favors: tidal flat, secondary woodland, open grassfield, dense thicket, shallow pond, et cetera.

Holding ponds Small, shallow ponds made by damming the upper reaches of a *yato* valley. Called "*tame-ike*" in Japanese. Originally functioned as water storage for the rice paddies. See also *Yato* valley.

Honshū The largest island of the Japanese archipelago.

Imperfect flower A flower which has only male parts (stamens) or female parts (pistils), as opposed to a "perfect flower," which has both. See also Flower, Monoecious, and Dioecious.

Kansai A general term for western Honshū, especially the area around Osaka and Kōbe. Contained within the Kinki Region.

Kantō See map. The region of central Honshū to which Tokyo belongs, including the Kantō Plain and surrounding mountains, and the Boso and Miura peninsulas.

Kantō Plain The large flat alluvial plain created by the Ara and Tone river systems. See also Alluvial plain.

Kawa The Japanese word for "river." In formal place names the "k" sometimes changes into a "g," as in Tonegawa, the Tone River.

Ki General Japanese word for tree. In common names the "k" sometimes changes into a "g," as in *kusa-gi*, literally "stinky tree." The "*ki*" or "*gi*" is also sometimes rendered as *boku*, as in *taisan-boku*, the southern magnolia.

Leaf scar The mark left on a branch by a leaf that has fallen off. The bumps in the scar are the remains of the tubelike structures that carried water into the leaf and starches out. The auxiliary bud is usually seen above the scar.

Loam A general term for volcanic sediments that were carried in on the wind. Loam comprises the upper layers of the uplands in the Tokyo area. See Uplands.

Leaf scar

Man'yōshū An anthology of ancient poetry. The poems were collected and recorded in the eighth century, but many are thought to have been written much earlier. Many of the poems portray plants in an allegorical sense.

Margin The edge of a leaf, which may be smooth (entire) or lined with teeth.

Molt The process of shedding an old outer skin and forming a new one. All arthropods, including insects, spiders, and crabs, must molt in order to grow. Snakes and lizards, however, also molt. See Exoskeleton.

Monoecious A plant with imperfect flowers. The male and female flowers are separate, but bloom on the same individual plant. As opposed to dioecious, in which the male and female flowers bloom on separate plants. See also Imperfect flower, Dioecious.

Imperfect monoecious

Nectar guides Marks on the petals or crown of a flower that guide a visiting insect into the spot where the nectar is. These marks are designed to position the insect so that it will come in contact with the stamens and pistil, thus pollinating the flower.

Old growth forest See Climax forest.

Opposite An arrangement of leaves on a stem or branch in which the right and left leaves are directly opposite one another, as opposed to alternate.

Opposite leaves

Order A formal taxonomic category between class and family, very useful in the study of insects. See also Taxonomy.

Ovipositor The egg-laying organ of a female insect, located at the tip of the abdomen. In cicadas it is shaped like a sharp, serrated knife blade, and in katydids like a sword or sickle. Worker bees, wasps, and hornets are all females, but they do not lay eggs. Their ovipositor has evolved into the stinger.

Palmate A simple leaf with veins that spread out in a fingerlike pattern, with several veins originating from a single node at the base of the leaf; or a compound leaf with leaflets arranged in a fingerlike pattern. See also Compound leaf, Pinnate.

Palmate leaf

Perfect flower (bisexual flower) A flower that has both male parts (stamens) and female parts (pistils), as opposed to an imperfect flower, which has only one or the other. See also Stamen, Pistil, Flower, Imperfect flower, Dioecious, and Monoecious.

Phylum A formal taxonomic category below kingdom, very useful in the study of coastal animals. See also Taxonomy.

Pinnate A simple leaf with side veins branching out from a single central vein; or a compound leaf with leaflets arranged along a central axis. See also Compound leaf, Palmate.

Pinnate leaf

Pistil The female reproductive part of a flower. Consists of the stigma, or tip, a long, thin style, and an ovary at the base. Pollen is received by the stigma, then travels down through the inside of the hollow style to the ovary, where it fertilizes the eggs. Once fertilized the eggs develop into seeds inside the protective ovary. See also Perfect Flower, Flower, Angiosperm.

Sacred grove A grove of trees surrounding a Shinto shrine or Buddhist temple. As it is forbidden to cut the trees down, these groves often contain many venerable old trees. Called *chinju no mori* in Japanese. See also Shrine, Temple.

Scientific name The formal designation of a plant or animal, consisting of genus and species. Use of the scientific name helps prevent confusion resulting from regional and cultural differences in common names. See also Taxonomy.

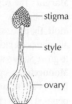

— stigma

— style

— ovary

Pistil

Secondary woodland A young forest of fast-growing deciduous trees that springs up in the gap left by a fire or windstorm. This is one stage in the forest succession, and is eventually replaced by climax forests, also known as old growth forests. See also Climax forest.

Sepal Leaflike structures usually seen just below the petals on a typical flower. The sepals surround and protect the flower in the delicate bud stage, then open up to allow the flower to bloom. See Flower.

Shinto Japan's native religion that existed before Buddhism was brought here from China and Korea. See also Shrine, Sacred grove.

Shogun A powerful samurai lord authorized to govern Japan. Throughout history, Japan was officially ruled by an emperor. Since the eleventh century, however, the emperor became primarily a figurehead, and actual control was always in the hands of the samurai. To preserve the façade of imperial rule, the emperor appointed the most powerful samurai lord as shogun, and authorized him to maintain law and order in the land.

Shrine A religious edifice associated with Shinto beliefs; "*jinja*" in Japanese. See also Shinto, Sacred grove.

Simple leaf A leaf that is composed of only one blade, as opposed to a compound leaf, which has several blades. See also Compound leaf, Auxiliary bud.

Species The basic unit for classifying plants and animals. As a general rule, a species represents all individuals that are able to reproduce with each other and produce viable offspring. See also Taxonomy.

Stigma The receptive tip of the pistil. See Pistil.

Simple leaf

Stamen The male reproductive part of the flower. Consists of a supporting stem, called the filament, and the tip, or anther. Pollen is released from the anther, and is either carried away on the wind or clings to a visiting animal, such as an insect or bird. See also Flower.

Subspecies A population of a species that is unable to exchange genes with other populations of the same species due to geological isolation. For example, the badger that lives in Japan is the same species as that found on the Eurasian continent. But because Japan is an island, the Japanese badgers never have a chance to exchange genes with populations of mainland badgers, and are thus considered a subspecies. Subspecies that are isolated from one another for a long time will eventually evolve into separate species.

anther

filament

Stamen

Tame-ike Small irrigation pond. See Holding pond.

Taxonomy The formal system employed by scientists for classifying living organisms. The system starts at the level of Kingdom. Currently five kingdoms are recognized: animals, plants, fungi, single-celled organisms, and viruses and bacteria. Each kingdom is then subdivided into phyla (singular, phylum). All the species in a phylum share basic design characteristics. For example, all animals with internal skeletons, including fish, amphibians, reptiles, birds, and mammals, are placed in the Phylum Chordata. Phyla are then further subdivided into class, order, and family. Finally, each unique "type" of plant or animal is placed in a genus and given a species name. These last two names form the scientific name of the species. As an example, the formal taxonomy for two common species is given below:

	JAPANESE TOAD	JAPANESE CAMELLIA
KINGDOM	Animal	Plant
PHYLUM	Chordata	Tracheophyta
CLASS	Amphibia	Angiospermae
ORDER	Salientia	Theales
FAMILY	Bufonidae	Theaceae
GENUS	Bufo	Camellia
SPECIES	japonicus	japonica

Although evolutionary relationships are often far from clear, the basic premise of taxonomy is that the categories represent common ancestries. All the species in a phylum, for example, should theoretically be traced back to a single common ancestor. Also, keep in mind that the classification of individual species is constantly being reviewed and updated, and changes are frequent. Feuds among scientists over the fine points of taxonomy are legendary!

Temple A religious edifice associated with Buddhism; "*otera*" in Japanese. See also Shrine, Sacred grove.

Thorax The middle, or chest part of an insect's body, located between the head and the abdomen. In spiders, thorax and head are fused into a single structure called the cephalothorax.

Understory Shrubs and other smaller plants that grow underneath the large trees in a forest.

Uplands Plateaulike high ground composed mostly of wind-blown volcanic loam. Called "*daichi*" in Japanese.

Volunteer An informal term for a plant that has invaded a park or garden on its own, rather than having been deliberately planted.

***Yato* valley** Narrow, highly-branched valleys cut into the uplands.

LIST OF SPECIES NAMES

All Japanese mammals, birds, reptiles, and amphibians have formally recognized English common names. Most plants, insects, marine invertebrates, and crabs, however, do not. Many of these species are unknown outside of Japan and are being introduced in English for the first time in these pages. In some cases, there is thus no English name given. In others, only a general term, such as "orchid" or "day lily" is offered as guidance. In still other cases, an English name has been created from the scientific name, so that a name like "Arisaema japonica" would be rendered as "Japanese jack-in-the-pulpit."

JAPANESE NAME	SPECIES NAME	ENGLISH NAME/EQUIVALENT
MAMMALS •Pages 39–46•		
abura-komori	Pipistrellus abramus	Japanese pipistrelles
azuma-mogura	Mogera minor	small Japanese mole
himizu	Urotrichus sp.	shrew-mole
togari nezumi	Sorex sp.	shrew
hakubishin	Paguma larvata	masked palm-civet
itachi	Mustela itatsi	Japanese weasel
ten	Martes melanpus	Japanese marten
amami no kuro-usagi	Pentalagus furnessi	Amami black rabbit
Nihon-risu	Sciurus lis	Japanese squirrel
aka-nezumi	Apodemus speciosus	large Japanese field mouse
kaya-nezumi	Micromys minutus	harvest mouse
no-usagi	Lepus brachyurus	Japanese hare
tanuki	Nyctereutes procyonoides	raccoon dog
ana-guma	Meles meles anakuma	Japanese badger
BIRDS		
URBAN BIRDS •Pages 48–54•		
do-bato	Columba livia	pigeon
suzume	Passer montanus	tree sparrow
hashibuto-garasu	Corvus macrorhynchos	jungle crow
muku-dori	Sturnus cineraceus	gray starling
kiji-bato	Streptopelia orientalis	rufous turtledove
tsugumi	Turdus naumanni	dusky thrush
hiyo-dori	Hypsipetes amaurotis	brown-eared bulbul
onaga	Cyanopica cyana	azure-winged magpie

JAPANESE NAME	SPECIES NAME	ENGLISH NAME/EQUIVALENT
tsubame	Hirundo rustica	barn swallow
kawasemi	Alcedo atthis	common kingfisher
haku-sekirei	Motacilla alba	white wagtail
seguro sekirei	Motacilla grandis	Japanese wagtail
shijū-kara	Parus major	great tit
mejiro	Zosterops japonica	Japanese white-eye
yama-gara	Parus varius	varied tit
shime	Coccothraustes coccothraustes	hawfinch
kawara-hiwa	Carduelis sinica	Oriental greenfinch
hōjiro	Emberiza cioides	Siberian meadow bunting
kashira-daka	Emberiza rustica	rustic bunting
enaga	Aegithalos caudatus	long-tailed tit
kakesu	Garrulus glandarius	jay
jōbitaki	Phoenicurus auroreus	daurian redstart
wakake-honsei-inko	Psittacula krameri	rose-ringed parakeet

CORMORANTS   •Pages 54–56•

kawa-u	Phalocrocorax carbo	great cormorant
umi-u	Phalocrocorax filamentosus	Temminck's cormorant (Japanese cormorant)

SEAGULLS   •Pages 57–60•

yuri kamome	Larus ridibundus	black-headed gull
umi-neko	Larus crassirostrus	black-tailed gull (Japanese gull)
seguro kamome	Larus argentatus	herring gull
ko ajisashi	Sterna albifrons	little tern

WATERFOWL   •Pages 61–65•

ma-gamo	Anas platyrhynchos	mallard
hashibiro-gamo	Anas clypeata	shoveler
ko-gamo	Anas crecca	green-winged teal
hidori-gamo	Anas penelope	widgeon
karu-gamo	Anas poecilorhyncha	spot-billed duck
oshidori	Aix galericulata	mandarin duck
onaga-gamo	Anas acuta	pintail
okayoshi-gamo	Anas strepera	gadwall
yoshi-gamo	Anas falcata	falcated teal
tomoe-gamo	Anas formosa	Baikal teal
kinku hajiro	Aythya fuligula	tufted duck
hoshi hajiro	Aythya ferina	pochard
suzu-gamo	Aythya marila	greater scaup
ō-ban	Fulica atra	coot
ban	Gallinula chloropus	common gallinule (moorhen)
kaitsuburi	Podiceps ruficollis	little grebe

ō hakuchō	Cygnus cygnus	whooper swan
ko hakuchō	Cygnus columbianus	whistling swan
kobu hakuchō	Cygnus olor	mute swan

SHOREBIRDS   •Pages 66–69•

daishaku shigi	Numenius madagascariensis	curlew
hama shigi	Calidris ferruginea	dunlin
daizen	Pluvialis squaterola	black-bellied plover
shiro chidori	Charadrius alexandrinus	Kentish plover (snowy plover)
miyako-dori	Haematopus ostralegus	oystercatcher
oguro shigi	Limosa limosa	black-tailed godwit
ō-sorihashi shigi	Limosa lapponica	bar-tailed godwit
chūshaku shigi	Numenius phaeopus	whimbrel
tōnen	Calidris ruficollis	rufous-necked stint
ko chidori	Charadrius dubius	little ringed plover
medai-chidori	Charadrius mongolus	Mongolian plover
munaguro	Pluvialis dominica	golden plover
ta shigi	Gallinago gallinago	common snipe
ta geri	Vanellus vanellus	lapwing
seitaka shigi	Himantopus himantopus	black-winged stilts
sorihashi seitaka shigi	Recurvirostra avocetta	avocet
sorihashi shigi	Xenus cinereus	terek sandpiper
kyōjo shigi	Arenaria interpres	ruddy turnstone
kiashi shigi	Tringa brevipes	gray-tailed tattler

WADERS   •Pages 69–71•

ko sagi	Egretta garzetta	little egret
dai sagi	Egretta alba	great egret
chū sagi	Egretta itermedia	intermediate egret
ama sagi	Bubulcus ibis	cattle egret
yoshi-goi	Ixobrychus sinensis	Chinese little bittern
sasa-goi	Butorides striatus	green-backed heron
ao sagi	Ardea cinerea	gray heron
goi sagi	Nycticorax nycticorax	black-crowned night heron
toki	Nipponia nippon	Japanese crested ibis
kōnotori	Ciconia boysiana	Oriental white stork

COUNTRY BIRDS   •Pages 72–75•

fukurō	Tyto capensis	Ural owl
aoba-zuku	Ninox scutulata	brown hawk-owl
ko-gera	Dendrocopos kizuki	Japanese pygmy woodpecker
aka-gera	Dendrocopos major	great spotted woodpecker
ao-gera	Picus awokera	Japanese green woodpecker
hibari	Alauda arvensis	skylark
sashiba	Butastur indicus	gray-faced buzzard-eagle
ō-taka	Accipiter gentilis	goshawk
chūhi	Circus aeruginosus	marsh harrier

JAPANESE NAME	SPECIES NAME	ENGLISH NAME/EQUIVALENT
hayabusa	Falco peregrinus	peregrine falcon
chōgenbō	Falco tinnunculus	kestrel
mozu	Lanius bucephalus	bull-headed shrike
kiji	Phasianus colchicus	common pheasant
hashiboso-garasu	Corvus corone	carrion crow

REPTILES •Pages 76–84•

ao-daishō	Elaphe climacophora	Japanese ratsnake
shima-hebi	Elaphe quadrivirgata	Japanese four-lined rat snake
jimuguri	Elaphe conspicillata	burrowing ratsnake
hibakari	Amphiesma vibakari	Japanese keelback
shiro-madara	Dinodon orientalis	oriental odd-tooth snake
mamushi	Agkistrodon blomhoffi	*mamushi* pit viper
yama-kagashi	Rhabdophis tigrinus	back-fanged keelback
yamori	Gekko japonicus	Japanese gecko
Nihon tokage	Eumeces latiscutatus	Japanese five-lined skink
Nihon kana-hebi	Takydromus tachydromoides	Japanese grass lizard
akamimi-game	Trachemys scripta	Mississippi red-eared slider
ishi-game	Mauremys japonica	Japanese pond turtle
kusa-game	Chinemys reevesii	Reeves' pond turtle
suppon	Pelodiscus sinensis	Chinese softshell turtle
kamitsuki-game	Chelydra sertentina	American snapping turtle

AMPHIBIANS •Pages 85–92•

ama-gaeru	Hyla japonica	Japanese tree frog
shurēgeru ao-gaeru	Rhacophorus schlegelii	Schlegel's green tree frog
mori ao-gaeru	Rhacophorus arboreus	forest green tree frog
Nihon aka-gaeru	Rana japonica	Japanese brown frog
yama aka-gaeru	Rana ornativentris	Montane brown frog
ushi-gaeru	Rana catesbieiana	bullfrog
Tōkyō daruma-gaeru	Rana porosa	Tokyo daruma pond frog
azuma hiki-gaeru	Bufo japonicus formosus eastern	Japanese toad
Tōkyō sanshō-uo	Hynobius tokyoensis	Tokyo salamander
imori	Cynops pyrrhogaster	Japanese fire-bellied newt

INSECTS
BUGS •Pages 95–96•

akasuji-kin kame-mushi	Poecilocoris lewisi	shield bug (stink bug)
taiko-uchi	laccotrephes japonensis	water scorpion
mizu kamakiri	Ranatra chinensis	water scorpion
amenbō	Gerris sp.	pond skater

JAPANESE NAME	SPECIES NAME	ENGLISH NAME/EQUIVALENT

CICADAS •Pages 97–99•
nii-nii-zemi   Platypleura kaempferi
higurashi   Tanna japonensis
tsukutsuku-bōshi   Meimuna opalifera
minmin-zemi   Oncotympana maculaticollis
abura-zemi   Graptopsaltria nigrofuscata
kuma-zemi   Cryptotympana japonensis

SUMMER DRAGONFLIES •Pages 100–2•
shiokara tonbo   Orthetrum albistyrum
ō-shiokara tonbo   Orthetrum triangulare
koshiaki tonbo   Pseudothemis zonata
oni-yanma   Anatogaster sieboldii

AUTUMN DRAGONFLIES •Pages 103–4•
aka tonbo zoku   Genus Sympetrum   red skimmer dragonflies
noshime tonbo   S. infuscatum
miyama akane   S. pedemontanum
aki akane   S. frequens
natsu akane   S. darwinianum
maiko akane   S. kunckeli
mayutate akane   S. eroticum

DAMSELFLIES •Page 105•
ajia-ito tonbo   Ischnura asiatica
haguro tonbo   Calopteryx atrata

GRASSHOPPERS •Pages 106–8•
shōryō batta   Acrida cinerea
shōryō batta-modoki   Gonista bicolor
onbu batta   Atractomorpha lata
kobane inago   Oxya yezoensis
tonosama batta   Locusta migratoria   migratory locust
kuruma batta-modoki   Oedaleus infernalis

KATYDIDS AND CRICKETS •Pages 109–10•
kubikiri-gisu   Euconocephalus thunbergi
kutsuwa-mushi   Mecopoda nipponensis
suzu-mushi   Homeogryllus japonicus   bell cricket
ao-matsu-mushi   Calyptotrypus hibinonis

MANTIS •Pages 111–12•
ō kamakiri   Tenodera aridifolia
chōsen kamakiri   Tenodera angustipennis
harabiro kamakiri   Hierodula patellifera
ko kamakiri   Statilia maculata

JAPANESE NAME	SPECIES NAME	ENGLISH NAME/EQUIVALENT
HORNETS •Pages 113–16•		
suzume-bachi zoku	Genus Vespa	hornets
kiiro suzume-bachi	V. xanthoptera	
kogata suzume-bachi	V. analis	
ō suzume-bachi	V. mandarinia	
PAPER WASPS •Pages 116–17•		
ashinaga-bachi zoku	Genus Polistes	paper wasps
futamon ashinaga-bachi	P. chinensis	
BUTTERFLIES •Pages 117–22•		
monshiro-chō	Pieris rapae	cabbage white
sujiguro monshiro-chō	pieris melete	black-veined white
ki-chō zoku	Genus Eurema	yellows
ki-chō	E. hecabe	
monki-chō	Colias erate	orange sulfur
janome-chō zoku	Genus Mycalesis	browns
hime janome	M. gotama	
misuji-chō zoku	Genus Neptis	gliders
ko misuji	N. sappho	common glider
beni shijimi	Lycaena phlaeas	small copper
aka tateha	Vanessa indica	admiral
hime aka-tateha	Cynthia cardui	painted lady
yamato shijimi	Pseudozizeeria maha	blue
ki tateha	Polygonia c-aureum	
ageha-chō zoku	Genus Papilio	swallowtails
ki ageha	P. machaon	common swallowtail
ageha-chō	P. xustus	
monki ageha	P. helenus	
kuro ageha	P. protenor	
karasu ageha	P. bianor	
aosuji ageha	Graphium sarpedon	blue triangle
maimai-ga	Lymantria dispar	gypsy moth
iraga	Cnidocampa sp.	
tonbo-edajaku	Cystidia sp.	inchworm
BEETLES •Pages 122–24•		
kabuto-mushi	Allomyrina dichotoma	rhinoceros beetle
nokogiri kuwagata	Prosopocoilus inclinatus	stag beetle
miyama kamikiri	Mallambyx raddei	longhorn beetle
shirosuji kamikiri	Batocera lineolata	longhorn beetle
gomadara kamikiri	Anoplophora malasiaca	longhorn beetle
hotaru zoku	Genus Luciola	fireflies
heike-botaru	L. lateralis	
genji-botaru	L. cruciata	
tentō-mushi	Coccinella sp.	ladybug beetle
hime-gengorō	Rhantus pulverosus	water beetle

JAPANESE NAME	SPECIES NAME	ENGLISH NAME/EQUIVALENT
ANT LION •Pages 125–26•		
usuba kagerō (ari-jigoku)	Hagenomyia micans	lacewing insect (ant lion)
SPIDERS •Pages 126–30•		
jorō-gumo	Nephila clavata	orb web spider
kogane-gumo	Argiope amoena	orb web spider
naga kogane-gumo	Argiope bruennichii	orb web spider
kusa-gumo	Agelena sp.	sheet-web spider
iō-iro hashiri-gumo	Dolomedes sulfureus	hunting spider
kabaki komachi-gumo	Chiracanthium japonicum	hunting spider

TIDAL FLATS

CLAMS •Pages 133–36•		
asari	Tapus philippinarum	short-necked clam
mate-gai	Solen strictus	razor clam
shiofuki-gai	Mactra veneriformis	trough shell
baka-gai	Mactra sinensis	Asian trough shell
akagai	Scapharca broughtonii	cockle
sarubō-gai	Scapharca subcrenata	cockle
kaki	Crassostrea sp.	oyster
kagami-gai	Dosinorbis sp.	Japanese dosinia

POLYCHAETE WORMS •Pages 136–37•		
tamashiki gokai	Arenicola brasiliensis	lugworm

CRABS •Pages 137–40•		
kome-tsuki-gani	Scopimera globosa	
chigo-gani	Ilyoplax pusilla	
osa-gani	Macropthalmus dilatatus	
yamato osa-gani	Macropthalmus japonicus	
ashihara-gani	Helice tridens	
kuro benkei-gani	Holometopus dehaani	
kefusa iso-gani	Hemigraspus penicillatus	
ishi-gani	Charybdis japonica	
mame kobushi-gani	Philyra pisum	

RIVER CRAB AND CRAYFISH •Pages 141–42•		
sawa-gani	Geothelphusa dehaani	stream crab
amerika zarigani	Procambarus clarki	American crayfish

FISH •Pages 142–43•		
suzuki	Lateolabrax japonicus	sea bass
sayori	Hemiramphus sajori	halfbeak
bora	Mugil cephalus	mullet
kohada (konoshiro)	Clupanodon punctatus	shad
karei	Family Pleuronectoidae	flounder

JAPANESE NAME	SPECIES NAME	ENGLISH NAME/EQUIVALENT
ma-haze	Acanthogobius flavinanus	goby
tobi-haze	Periophthalmus cantonensis	mud skipper

OTHER FAVORITES   •Pages 143–44•

kurogane isoginchaku	Anthopleura kurogane	sea anemone
aramushiro-gai	Reticunassa festiva	scavenger snail
ogo-nori	Gracilaria verrucosa	
ana-aosa	Ulva sp.	
uminina	Batillaria sp.	mud snail
nihon sunamoguri	Callianassa japonica	mud shrimp
anajako	Upogebia major	mud shrimp
hasami-shakoebi	Laomedia astacina	mud shrimp
yubinaga hon-yadogari	Pagurus dubius	tidal flat hermit crab
aka-kurage	Chrysaora melanaster	
mizu-kurage	Aurelia aurelia	moon jelly

BROADLEAVED EVERGREENS   •Pages 147–54•

sudajii	Castanopsiscuspidata	chinkapin
kashi zoku	Genus Quercus	oaks (evergreen)
shira-kashi	Q. myrsinaefolia	
aka-gashi	Q. acuta	
urajiro-gashi	Q. salicina	
ubame-gashi	Q. phylliraeoides	
tabu-no-ki	Machilus thunbergii	
shiro-damo	Neolitsea sericea	
yabu-tsubaki	Camellia japonica	Japanese wild camellia
sazanka	Camellia sasanqua	
hisakaki	Eurya japonica	
aoki	Aucuba japonica	Japanese aucuba
yatsude	Fatsia japonica	Japanese aralia
nezumi-mochi	Ligustrum japonicum	
tobera	Pittosporum tobira	

DECIDUOUS TREES   •Pages 155–76•

nara zoku	Genus Quercus	oaks (deciduous)
konara	Q. serrata	
kunugi	Q. acutissima	
abemaki	Q. variabilis	
kashiwa	Q. dentata	
kuri	Castanea crenata	Japanese chestnut
shide (soro) zoku	Genus Carpinus	hornbeams
inu-shide	C. tschonoskii	
aka-shide	C. laxiflora	
kuma-shide	C. japonica	Japanese hornbeam

JAPANESE NAME	SPECIES NAME	ENGLISH NAME/EQUIVALENT
hannoki-zoku	Genus Alnus	alders
han-no-ki	A. japonicus	Japanese alder
yama han-no-ki	A. hirsuta	
mizuki	Cornus controversa	dogwood
kumano mizuki	Cornus brachypoda	dogwood
hana-ikada	Helwingea japonica	
ego-no-ki	Styrax japonicus	Japanese snowbell
yama-zakura	Prunus jamasakura	
uwamizu-zakura	Prunus grayana	
no-ibara	Rosa multiflora	
teriha no-ibara	Rosa wichuriana (or Rosa luciae)	
momiji ichigo	Rubus palmatum	
nawashiro-ichigo	Rubus parvifolius	
mokuren zoku	Genus Magnolia	magnolias
kobushi	M. kobus	kobus magnolia
haku-mokuren	M. denudata	Yulan magnolia
hō-no-ki	M. obovata	Japanese big-leaved magnolia
taisan-boku	M. grandiflora	Southern magnolia
keyaki	Zelkova serrata	zelkova
muku-no-ki	Aphananthe aspera	
eno-ki	Celtis sinensis v. japonica	Japanese hackberry
aki-nire	Ulmus parvifolia	elm
momiji (kaede) zoku	Genus Acer	maples
iroha kaede (momiji)	A. palmatum	Japanese maple
ō-momiji	A. palmatum v. amoenum	
fuji zoku	Genus Wisteria	wisteria vines
noda fuji	W. floribunda	
yama fuji	W. brachybotrys	
nemu-no-ki	Albizzia julibrissin	silk tree
hari-enju (nise-akashia)	Robinia pseudo-acacia	black locust
hagi	Genus Lespedeza	bushclovers
kuwa	Morus sp.	mulberry tree
kaji-no-ki	Broussonetia papyrifera	paper mulberry
kōzo	Broussonatia kazinoki	
urushi-zoku	Genus Rhus	sumacs
nurude	R. javanicahus	
yama urushi	R. trichocarpa	
tsuta urushi	R. ambigua	sumac vine
urushi	R. verniciflua	
murasaki shikibu	Callicarpa japonica	
kusagi	Clerodendron trichotomum	
gonzui	Euscaphis japonicus	
mayumi	Euonymus sieboldiana	Siebold's wahoo
nishiki-gi	Euonymus alatus	
gamazumi	Viburnum dilatum	viburnum
akebi	Akebia quinata	

JAPANESE NAME	SPECIES NAME	ENGLISH NAME/EQUIVALENT
mitsuba akebi	akebia trifoliata	
karasu-uri	Trichosanthes cucumeroides	
suzume-uri	Melothria japonica	
sarutori-ibara	Smilax china	smilax vine

CONIFERS •Pages 177–81•

matsu zoku	Genus Pinus	pines
kuro matsu	P. thunbergii	Japanese black pine
aka matsu	P. densiflora	Japanese red pine
goyō matsu	P. parviflora	
sugi	Cryptomeria japonica	Japanese cryptomeria (Japanese cedar)
hinoki	Chamaecyparis obtusa	hinoki cypress (false cypress)
sawara	Chamaecyparis pisifera	

STREET AND PARK TREES •Pages 182–95•

suzukake zoku	Genus Platanus	platanus (plane trees)
amerika suzukake	P. occidentalis	American plane
suzukake-no-ki	P. orientalis	Oriental plane
momijiba suzukake	P. acerifolia	London plane
amerika-fū (momijiba-fū)	Liquidamber styraciflua	American sycamore (sweetgum)
yuri-no-ki	Liriodendron tulipifera	tulip tree
fū	Liquidamber formosana	Chinese sycamore
ao-giri	Firmiana platanifolia	phoenix tree
akame-gashiwa	Mallotus japonicus	
ichō	Gingko biloba	ginkgo, maidenhair tree
tō-kaede	Acer buergerianum	Tang maple
Nankin haze	Sapium sebiferum	Chinese tallow tree
shidare yanagi	Salix babylonica	weeping willow
hana mizuki	Cornus florida	flowering dogwood
yama-bōshi	Cornus kousa	
sakura zoku	Genus Prunus	cherry trees
somei yoshino	P. yedoensis	
Edo higan	P. pendula	
Ōshima-zakura	P. lannesiana	
sato-zakura	P. lannesiana cv.	
shidare-zakura	P. spachiana	weeping cherry
tochi-no-ki	Aesculus turbinata	Japanese horse chestnut
maronie	Aesculus hippocastanum	common horse-chestnut
kusu-no-ki	Cinnamomum camphora	camphor tree
yama-momo	Myrica rubra	bayberry (wax myrtle)
mateba-shii	Pasania edulis	tan oak
Himaraya sugi	Cedrus deodara	Himalayan cedar
metasekoia	Metasequoia glyptostroboides	dawn redwood

JAPANESE NAME	SPECIES NAME	ENGLISH NAME/EQUIVALENT
numa sugi (rakūnshō)	Taxodium distichum	swamp cypress
inu-maki	Podocarpus macrophylla	podocarp

SPRING WILDFLOWERS •Pages 196–217•

inu-no-fuguri zoku	Genus Veronica	speedwells
ō-inu-no-fuguri	V. persica	common field speedwell
inu-no-fuguri	V. didyma	native speedwell
odoriko-sō zoku	Genus Lamium	dead-nettles
hotoke-no-za	L. amplexicaule	henbit dead-nettle
hime-odoriko-sou	L. purpureum	purple dead-nettle
odoriko-sō	L. album	native species
nazuna	Capsella bursa-pastoris	shepherd's purse
ko-hakobe	Stellaria media	chickweed
shunran	Cymbidium goeringii	orchid
ebine	Calanthe discolor	orchid
kumagai-sō	Cypripedium japonicum	Japanese lady slipper orchid
amadokoro-zoku	Genus Polygonatum	Solomon's seal lilies
amadokoro	P. odoratum	
naruko-yuri	P. falcatum	
chigo yuri zoku	Genus Disporum	fairy bell lilies
hōchakusō	D. sessile	
chigo yuri	D. smilacinum	
tachi-tsubo sumire	Viola grypoceras	violet
tennanshō-zoku	Genus Arisaema	jack-in-the-pulpits
mamushi-gusa	A. japonica	Japanese jack-in-the-pulpit
Urashima-sō	A. urashima	Urashima jack-in-the-pulpit
tane-tsuke-bana	Cardamine flexuosa	bittercress
sugina (tsukushi)	Equisetum arvense	horsetail
fuki	Petasites japonicus	Japanese butterbar
yomogi	Artemisia princeps	mugwort
warabi	Pteridium aquilinum	fern
zenmai	Osmunda japonica	fern
seiyō aburana	Brassica napus.	rape
seiyō karashina	Brassica juncea	wild mustard
ō-ara-seitō	Orychophragmus violaceus	
tanpopo zoku	Genus Taraxacum	dandelions
seiyō tanpopo	T. officinale	common dandelion
Kantō tanpopo	T. platycarpum	Kanto dandelion
shiro-bana tanpopo	T. albidium	white-flowered dandelion
noboro-giku	Senecio vulgaris	groundsel (butterweed)
no-geshi zoku	Genus Sonchus	sow thistles
no-geshi	S. oleraceus	
oni no-geshi	S. asper	
oni tabirako	Youngia japonica	
jishibari	Ixeris stolonifera	

JAPANESE NAME	SPECIES NAME	ENGLISH NAME/EQUIVALENT
ō-jishibari	Ixeris debilis	
nigana	Ixeris dentata	
hana nigana	Ixeris dentata v. amplifolia	
haru-ji-on (haru jo-on)	Erigeron philadelphicus	fleabane
hime jo-on fleabane	Erigeron annus	
katabami	Oxalis corniculata	wood sorrel
aka katabami	Oxalis corniculata v. rubrifolia	
kinpouge zoku	Genus Ranunculus	buttercups
uma-no-ashigata (kinpōge)	R. japonicus	Japanese buttercup
ta-garashi	R. sceleratus	rice paddy buttercup
kitsune-no-botan	R. quelpaertensis	
ke-kitsue-no-botan	R.cantoniensis	
kiji-mushiro zoku	Genus Potentilla	cinquefoils
mistuba-tsuchiguri	P. freyniana	
ō-hebi-ichigo	P. kleiniani	
kiji-mushiro	P. fragarioides	
hebi-ichigo	Duchesnea chrysantha	
yabu hebi-ichigo	Duchesnea indica	

SUMMER WILDFLOWERS •Pages 218–36•

doku-dami	Houttuynia cordata	houttuynia (lizard's tail)
tsuyu kusa	Commelina communis	day flowers
yabu-garashi	Cayratia japonica	cayratia vine
hirugao zoku	Genus Calystegia	bindweeds
hiru-gao	C. japonica	Japanese bindweed
ko-hiru-gao	C. hederacea	
hekuso-kazura	Paederia scandens	paederia vine
kana-mugura	Humulus japonicus	
kuzu	Pueraria lobata	kudzu vine
ayame zoku	Genus Iris	irises
kaki-tsubata	I. laevigata	
no-hana-shōbu	I. ensata v. spontanea	
ayame	I. sanguinea,	
ki-shōbu	I. pseudoacorus	yellow flag iris
suiren zoku	Genus Nymphaea	water lilies
suiren	N. sp.	
hitsuji-gusa	N. tetragona	
hasu	Nelumbo nucifera	lotus
kōhone	Nuphar sp.	spatterdock
junsai	Brasenia schreberi	water shield
oni-basu	Euryale ferox	
asaza	Nymphoides peltata	
gama zoku	Genus Typhacea	cattails

JAPANESE NAME	SPECIES NAME	ENGLISH NAME/EQUIVALENT
gama	T. latifolia	
ko-gama	T.orientalis	
hime-gama	T. australis	
yama yuri	Lilium auratum	
kanzō zoku	Genus Hemerocallis	day lilies
no-kanzō	H. longituba	
yabu-kanzō	H. fulva	
kitsune-no-kamisori	Lycoris sanguinia	spider lily
machiyoi-gusa	Oenothera sp.	evening primrosess
tsume kusa zoku	Genus Trifolium	clovers
shiro tsume-kusa	T. repens	white clover
aka tsume-kusa	T. pratense	red clover
(murasaki tsume-kusa)		
murasaki katabami	Oxalis sp.	wood sorrel
niwa-zekishō	Sisyrinchium atlanticum	blue-eyed grass
neji-bana	Spiranthes sinensis	lady's tresses orchid
waru-nasubi	Solanum carolinense	Carolina nightshade
kikyō	Platycodum grandiflorum	balloon flower
asagao	Pharbitis nil	morning glory
hōzuki	Physalis alkekengi	Chinese lantern plant

AUTUMN WILDFLOWERS •Pages 237–45•

susuki zoku	Genus Miscanthus	plume grasses
susuki	M. sinensis	
ogi	M. sacchariflorus	
nanban-giseru	Aeginetia indica	broomrape
seitaka-awadachi-sō	Solidago altissima	tall goldenrod
nadeshiko	Dianthus superbus	pink
ominaeshi	Patrinia villosa	
hagi	Lespedeza sp.	bush clovers
fujibakama	Eupatorium fortunei	
azami zoku	Genis Cirsium	thistles
no azami	C. japonicum	Japanese thistle
nohara azami	C. tanakae	
waremokō	Sanguisorba officinalis	
tsurigane ninjin	Adenophora triphylla v. japonica	
Akino-no-geshi	Lactuca indica	
tade zoku	Genus Polygonum	knotweeds
inu-tade	P. longisetum	
mizo-soba	P. thunbergii	
mamako-no-shiri-nugui	P. senticosum	
gen-no-shōko	Geranium thunbergii	Thunberg's geranium
higan-bana	Lycoris radiata	spider lily

LIST OF NATURE SITES

Akatsuka Park（赤塚公園 ✳ Akatsuka Kōen）　　　　　　　　304
Aoyama Cemetery（青山霊園 ✳ Aoyama Reien）　　　　　　　281
Asukayama Park（飛鳥山公園 ✳ Asukayama Kōen）　　　　　291

Benkei Moat（弁慶濠 ✳ Benkeibori）　　　　　　　　　　　260

East Gardens, The（東御苑 ✳ Higashi Gyoen）　　　　　　　257
Edogawa Park（江戸川公園 ✳ Edogawa Kōen）　　　　　　　274

Funabashi Fishing Port　　　　　　　　　　　　　　　　　333
Funabashi Seaside Park（船橋海浜公園 ✳ Funabashi Kaihin Kōen）　332

Gyōtoku Sanctuary（行徳野鳥観察舎 ✳ Gyōtoku Yachō Kansatsusha）　331

Hamarikyū Gardens（浜離宮恩賜庭園 ✳ Hamarikyū Onshi Teien）　317
Hibiya Park（日比谷公園 ✳ Hibiya Kōen）　　　　　　　　　316
Hie Shrine（日枝神社 ✳ Hie Jinja）　　　　　　　　　　　258
Hikawa Shrine（氷川神社 ✳ Hikawa Jinja）　　　　　　　　259

Inner Palace Moats（皇居内濠✳ Kōkyo Uchibori）　　　　　　253
Inokashira Park（井の頭公園 ✳ Inokashira Kōen）　　　　　292
Institute For Nature Study（国立科学博物館付属自然教育園 ✳ Kokuritsu
　　Kagaku-hakubutsukan Fuzoku Shizen-kyōiku-en）　　　　282

Jindai Botanical Park（神代植物公園 ✳ Jindai Shokubutsu Kōen）　298

Kasai Seaside Park（葛西臨海公園 ✳ Kasai Rinkai Kōen）　　330
Kinuta Park（砧公園 ✳ Kinuta Kōen）　　　　　　　　　　300
Kitanomaru Park（北の丸公園 ✳ Kitanomaru Kōen）　　　　256
Kiyosumi Gardens（清澄庭園 ✳ Kiyosumi Teien）　　　　　319
Koganei Park（小金井公園 ✳ Koganei Kōen）　　　　　　　289
Koishikawa Botanical Gardens（小石川植物園 ✳ Koishikawa Shokubutsuen）　271
Koishikawa Kōrakuen Gardens（小石川後楽園 ✳ Koishikawa Kōrakuen）　262
Kyū-Furukawa Gardens（旧古河庭園 ✳ Kyū-Furukawa Teien）　272
Kyū-Shibarikyū Gardens（旧芝離宮恩賜庭園 ✳ Kyū-Shibarikyū Onshi Teien）　318

Makino Memorial Gardens（牧野記念庭園 ✳ Makino Kinen Teien）　305
Meiji Jingū Outer Gardens（明治神宮外苑 ✳ Meiji Jingū Gaien）　280
Meiji Jingū Shrine（明治神宮 ✳ Meiji Jingū）　　　　　　　279
Mizumoto Park（水元公園 ✳ Mizumoto Kōen）　　　　　　　313
Mukōjima Hyakka-en Gardens（向島百花園 ✳ Mukōjima Hyakka-en）　315

National Science Museum（国立科学博物館 ✳ Kokuritsu Kagaku-hakubutsukan） 268
Nezu Shrine（根津神社 ✳ Nezu Jinja） 270
Nogawa Park（野川公園 ✳ Nogawa Kōen） 296

Odaiba Marine Park（お台場海浜公園 ✳ Odaiba Kaihin Kōen） 326
Ogunohara Park（尾久の原公園 ✳ Ogunohara Kōen） 314
Ōi Futō Chūō Seaside Park（大井ふ頭中央海浜公園 ✳ Ōi Futō Chūō Kaihin Kōen） 324
Outer Gardens, The（皇居外苑 ✳ Kōkyo Gaien） 257

Rikugi-en Gardens（六義園 ✳ Rikugi-en） 273
Rinshi no Mori Park（林試の森公園 ✳ Rinshinomori Kōen） 306

Sengenyama Park（浅間山公園 ✳ Sengenyama Kōen） 297
Shakujii Park（石神井公園 ✳ Shakujii Kōen） 290
Shiba Park（芝公園 ✳ Shiba Kōen） 282
Shinjuku Gyoen Gardens（新宿御苑 ✳ Shinjuku Gyoen） 276
Shinobazu Pond（不忍池 ✳ Shinobazu-no-ike） 269
Sotobori Park（外濠公園 ✳ Sotobori Kōen） 260

Tamagawa Aqueduct（玉川上水緑道 ✳ Tamagawa Jōsui Ryokudō） 301
Tamagawadai Park（多摩川台公園 ✳ Tamagawadai Kōen） 303
Tama River Mouth（六郷土手 ✳ Rokugō-dote） 323
Tatsumi Seaside Park（辰巳の森海浜公園 ✳ Tatsuminomori Kaihin Kōen） 328
Todoroki Gorge（等々力渓谷 ✳ Todoroki Keikoku） 302
Tokyo Port Wild Bird Park（東京港野鳥公園 ✳ Tokyo-kō Yachō Kōen） 326
Tokyo Sea Life Park（葛西臨海水族園 ✳ Kasai Rinkai Suizoku-en） 330
Tokyo University（東京大学 ✳ Tōkyō Daigaku） 271
Toyama Park（戸山公園 ✳ Toyama Kōen） 275

Ueno Park（上野公園 ✳ Ueno Kōen） 267
Ueno Zoo（上野動物園 ✳ Ueno Dōbutsuen） 269

Wadabori Park（和田堀公園 ✳ Wadabori Kōen） 295
Wakasu Seaside Park（若洲海浜公園 ✳ Wakasu Kaihin Kōen） 328

Yanaka Cemetery（谷中霊園 ✳ Yanaka Reien） 265
Yatsu Tidelands（谷津干潟 ✳ Yatsu-higata） 334
Yoyogi Park（代々木公園 ✳ Yoyogi Kōen） 280
Yumenoshima Seaside Park（夢の島海浜公園 ✳ Yumenoshima Kaihin Kōen） 328
Yushima Confucian Shrine（湯島聖堂 ✳ Yushima Seidō） 264
Yushima Tenjin Shrine（湯島天神 ✳ Yushima Tenjin） 270

Zenpukijigawa Park（善福寺川緑地 ✳ Zenpukujigawa Ryokuchi） 295
Zenpukuji Park（善福寺公園 ✳ Zenpukuji Kōen） 294

ACKNOWLEDGMENTS

This book is the result of more than a decade of botanical and ecological field-work in the Tokyo area. During that time I received invaluable help and guidance from numerous Japanese scientists, museums, and nature centers. Responsibility for the accuracy of the text and illustrations, however, resides solely with me. Some of the material used in this book first appeared in essays in the *Daily Yomiuri*, the *Japan Times*, *Winds*, and various other newspapers and magazines. I would like to thank the staffs of all these fine periodicals for their kind support. I would also like to thank Barry Lancet and Machiko Moriyasu, my editors at Kodansha International, for miraculously turning an enormous jumble of text, photos, and illustrations into a coherent book.

とうきょう
東京ネイチャー・ウオッチング
NATURE IN TOKYO

2000 年 12 月 8 日　第 1 刷発行

著　者　ケビン・ショート
発行者　野間佐和子
発行所　講談社インターナショナル株式会社
　　　　〒112-8652 東京都文京区音羽 1-17-14
　　　　電話：03-3944-6493

印刷所　株式会社 東京印書館
製本所　株式会社 堅省堂

Printed in Japan
ISBN 4-7700-2535-1

Map of Japan

Japan Sea

Chūgoku

Kinki

Kyot

Shikoku

Kyūshū

Ryūkyū Islands